PET POLITICS

NEW DIRECTIONS IN THE HUMAN-ANIMAL BOND
Series editors Alan M. Beck and Marguerite E. O'Haire

PET POLITICS

The Political and Legal Lives
of Cats, Dogs, and Horses in Canada and the United States

Susan Hunter and Richard A. Brisbin, Jr.
Purdue University Press
West Lafayette, Indiana

Copyright 2016 by Purdue University. All rights reserved.
Printed in the United States of America.

Library of Congress Cataloging-in-Publication Data

Names: Hunter, Susan, 1947 April 13- author. | Brisbin, Richard A., author.
Title: Pet politics: the political and legal lives of cats, dogs, and horses in Canada and the United States / Susan Hunter and Richard A. Brisbin Jr.
Description: West Lafayette, Indiana : Purdue University Press, 2016. | Series: New directions in the human-animal bond | Includes bibliographical references and index.
Identifiers: LCCN 2015045013 (print) | LCCN 2015051468 (ebook) | ISBN 9781557537324 (pbk. : alk. paper) | ISBN 9781612494357 (ePub) | ISBN 9781612494340 (ePDF)
Subjects: LCSH: Pets—Law and legislation. | Pets—Social aspects. | Pets—Law and legislation—United States. | Pets—Social aspects—United States. | Pets—Law and legislation—Canada. | Pets—Social aspects—Canada.
Classification: LCC K564.A55 H86 2016 (print) | LCC K564.A55 (ebook) | DDC
343.7307/660887—dc23
LC record available at http://lccn.loc.gov/2015045013

Contents

PREFACE, *vii*

1 Why Study Pet Politics? *1*

2 The Evolution of Pet Policy, *45*

3 What Is a Pet? Popular Conceptions of Animals and the Pet Policy Agenda, *87*

4 The Formation of a Pet Policy Agenda: Activists and Organized Interests, *123*

5 Making Pet Policy: Anti-cruelty Laws, *175*

6 Making Pet Policy: Kennel Licensing Legislation, *207*

7 Making Pet Policy: The Disposition of Unwanted Horses, *249*

8 Making Pet Policy: Roaming and Feral Cats, *285*

9 Making Pet Policy: Breed-Specific Laws, *313*

10 The Enforcement of Pet Legislation, *351*

11 Conclusion: The Meaning of Pet Politics Policy, *397*

INDEX, *405*

Preface

This book has grown out of the authors' mutual concern about the plight of animals. Despite our concern, we have not engaged in a prescriptive or normative endeavor. Our aim is to disclose how politics affects the lives of animals through the analysis of the everyday political origins, advocacy, formulation, and implementation of law and policy. Additionally, we have decided to concentrate this study of the companion animals and politics or, in the vernacular, the pet laws, policies, and policymaking that affect the lives of cats, dogs, and horses in Canada and the United States. The range of policies affecting animals is vast, but cats, dogs, and horses have perhaps the closest association with humans and have far and away generated the most attention from public policymakers. Other animals considered as pets, including birds, amphibians, reptiles, fish, rabbits, mice, rats, gerbils, hamsters, ferrets, monkeys, and chimpanzees have generated far fewer political controversies and far less attention from policymakers. We will only note in passing how public policies affect these species.

North American policymakers have tended to regard companion animals as humans' possessions. However, by coupling emotional concerns about pets with an ethics of respect for life, during the past forty years political activists have mobilized to seek the enactment of more stringent laws to require people to engage in legal accountability for the welfare of pets. Consequently, we might expect that policymakers would act to protect their constituents' interest in their animal companions, but is this the case? Has the identity of pets evolved from property toward legalized protective rules or rights and personhood for companion animals?

Although legal and historical scholars and sociologists, psychologists, philosophers, and anthrozoologists have published a considerable number of prescriptive, normative, and theoretical studies of companion animal welfare laws and rights, political scientists have ignored comprehensive empirical examination of pet politics and policymaking in Canada and the United States. In many respects the study of public policies about animals reflects the state of political scientists' study of environmental, education, and morality politics during the 1960s. Also, political scientists have centered their study less holistically on stages of or phases of policy development, such as lobbying, elections, legislative committees, presidential staff, or decision making by Supreme Courts. However, as we enter an ignored policy arena such as pet politics, we try to present a comprehensive overview of the complexities of political actions and inaction that shape the lives of cats, dogs, and horses.

Because we recognize distinctive differences between pet politics and policies that affect other animals, this study will not address policies related to controversial commercial animal husbandry practices, such as factory farming, the processing of animals for food, the use of animals in commercial and scientific research, and the employment of animals for entertainment by circuses and zoos. We will not discuss the handling or killing of animals in religious rites. We also will not address policies about animals as wildlife, such as endangered species laws, marine mammal laws, hunting regulations, animal habitat laws and regulations, and legislation requiring the control or elimination of nonnative, invasive, or "exotic" species.[1] Public policies and political action on these topics also deserve much more descriptive and empirical study, but a single book about animals and politics cannot address all of them. Finally, because pet politics is an arena of constantly changing laws and policies, readers should know that we recount events to August 2015.

ACKNOWLEDGMENTS

This is a jointly authored work, and the order of the authors' names does not imply the preeminence of the efforts or ideas of one of the authors. We especially thank the many animal policy activists, pet rescue coordinators, public officials, and the staff of publicly and privately supported animal control and shelter agencies interviewed for this book. To list them separately would consume many pages; however, Cathy Prothro-Short greatly assisted our research trip to Nova Scotia. The authors also thank the Embassy of Canada in the United States, the Office of the Dean, Eberly College of Arts and Sciences, the Department of Political Science, and the Institute for Public Affairs of West Virginia University for their financial support of this study. Early in this study Kyle Christensen and Bret Wilson provided valuable research assistance. Portions of this book were presented as papers at annual meetings of the Law and Society Association in 2007, 2008, 2009, 2011, and 2012 and the Western Political Science Association in 2006, 2007, and 2009. We thank the discussants at those meetings for their comments. Finally, we thank Kelley Kimm of Purdue University Press for her expert copy editing.

NOTE

1. For an overview of policies affecting these animals, see Susan Hunter, "Animal Policy," in *Governing America: Major Policies and Decisions of Federal, State, and Local Government from 1789 to the Present*, ed. Paul Quirk and William E. Cunion (New York: Facts on File, 2011), 1:184–90. Older but more detailed discussion of some of the policies appears in Jordan Curnutt, *Animals and the Law: A Sourcebook* (Santa Barbara, CA: ABC-CLIO, 2001).

1

Why Study Pet Politics?

Whether referred to as pets or companion animals, cats and dogs reside in a majority of homes in North America.[1] Recent survey data indicate that in the United States, dogs live in 56 percent of households, cats live in 30.4 percent of households, and 1.5 percent of residents possess horses—a total of 70.1 million cats, 69.9 million dogs, and 4.9 million horses. In addition, birds, fish, reptiles, and mammals of other species live in approximately 13.7 million U.S. households.[2] And more than 6.4 million dogs and 8.5 million cats live in Canada.[3] These animals often provide people with recreation and affection as well as assistance as guards, herders, aides to the disabled, and vermin killers. Yet, every year governments in these nations spend untold millions of dollars managing, controlling, and disposing of millions of abandoned or unwanted pets. Although survey data find that 84.7 percent of American households would likely obtain a new dog from a *shelter* or *rescue group* (see the appendix to this chapter for definitions),[4] estimates are that most publicly supported shelters in the United States deliberately put to death 40 to 65 percent of the dogs and 60 to 90 percent of the cats that come under their control—from three to four million animals a year.[5] However, the political effect of pets extends far beyond the cost of operating a pound to house or destroy unwanted cats and dogs and the revelation of a message of moral disengagement and casual human disregard for living beings that the abandonment and mass killing implicitly conveys. As the following five vignettes relate, with so many people in contact with so many animals, pets cannot escape a broad range of politics, law, public policies, and actions of political institutions that influence their lives.

The Katrina Pets

Before Hurricane Katrina swamped the city of New Orleans in August 2005, the Louisiana Society for the Prevention of Cruelty to Animals evacuated about 250 animals from its shelter. Two days later the hurricane destroyed the shelter. The Humane Society of the United States (HSUS) estimated that, because they were not evacuated from the city, 50,000 pets died. Because officials and rescue teams would not allow them to take their pets on the buses, boats, and helicopters used in the evacuation, some pets' caretakers refused evacuation and perhaps died. Volunteers rescued about 15,000 pets, including thousands of cats and dogs and a few birds, fish, pot-bellied pigs, one emu, and a tarantula. Some of those volunteers traveled thousands of miles to rescue various animals and transport them for health care or to *foster homes* (see the appendix to this chapter for definition) in other states.[6] Animal-oriented organizations such as Noah's Wish, Best Friends Animal Sanctuary, and HSUS rescued the majority, but many small organizations also participated in the rescue effort. The rescue groups established a large temporary shelter for dogs and cats at the Lamar-Dixon Exposition Center in Gonzales, Louisiana. Volunteers, rescue organization members, veterinary faculty and students from Louisiana State University, and first responders located, captured, and transported abandoned horses to an equine treatment facility at Louisiana State University in Baton Rouge.[7]

Media coverage of the plight of the New Orleans pets and the rescue effort, including pictures of thousands of caged dogs and cats at two temporary shelters, aroused angry reactions from animal lovers across the nation.

Suddenly pets were on the national political agenda. Animal-oriented interest groups began to press for legislation that would impose requirements on government agencies to care for pets after natural disasters. Unlike with the disregard it showed toward many issues on its agenda, Congress rapidly responded. A House version of the Pets Evacuation and Transportation Standards bill passed on May 22, 2006, by a vote of 349–24. On August 3, 2006, the Senate passed its version by unanimous consent, and President George W. Bush signed the bill into law on October 6, 2006. The law required that state and local governments seeking federal disaster assistance adopt provisions to evacuate household pets and service animals in their disaster evacuation plans. Congress also enacted further requirements for pet rescue during disasters in the Post-Katrina Emergency Management Reform Act.[8] Besides devising rules for the implementation of the Act, the Federal Emergency Management Agency (FEMA) now provides training to assist the development of plans for pet rescue during disasters. Additionally, provisions of federal laws allowed state and local governments to seek compensation for emergency care for pet rescue, sheltering, and evacuation support, as well as labor costs that result from disasters.[9] By the summer of 2012, emergency management agencies in some states and localities had revised disaster plans to include pet rescue and care.[10]

Legislators and Rottweilers

In 2003 on the Kingston Peninsula near Saint John, New Brunswick, three Rottweiler dogs mauled four-year-old James Waddell to death. One of the dogs, Thor, had been injured in a car accident several months previous to the attack. Also, James had suffered a dog bite eleven months before the attack, and an emergency room doctor reported the boy's father was drunk when he brought James to the hospital. Police accounts of the death of James and an inquest into the child's death in November 2003 found that the boy, left alone with the dogs by his father and other adults who had been drinking, became entangled with dogs excited into aggression by a female in heat. No evidence indicated that the father had trained the dogs to be aggressive.

To prevent future incidents, in May 2004 New Brunswick Legislative Assembly Member Kelly Lamrock introduced a bill to impose special license, insurance, and liability requirements on the custodians of Rottweilers, Staffordshire Bull Terriers, American Staffordshire Terriers, and Akitas. In the fall a provincial legislative committee held public hearings and received 203 public comments about the bill. Following discussions among the legislators and consultations with a working group of animal interest groups, the committee killed the breed ban bill. It then proceeded to draft a substitute that removed the breed-specific language and adopted a revised law on dog owner responsibility with tougher penalties and animal seizure standards applicable to all dogs judged dangerous, mandatory licensing, and targets for education and enforcement. Justice Minister Brad Green thought this solution was practical and not a gimmick to appease the public. Acting with caution and searching for information, the Legislative Assembly had formulated a law that demanded the possessors of all dogs promote their welfare and train them to interact without aggression toward humans and other dogs. Even Lamrock agreed that the revised bill was better than a ban on the existence of specific breeds of dogs.[11]

Chelsea: Poisoned Pets, the Courts, and Regulators

Chelsea was an AKC Champion Boston Terrier who lived as a companion to a Maryland family with a special needs child. The family put a life preserver on Chelsea and took her sailing on Chesapeake Bay. They dressed her as a princess for Halloween. When she died in November 2007 they posted a touching, sentimental tribute about their affection for her on the Internet.[12] Why did she die? Apparently the cause was dog food tainted with aminopterin (a chemical used as rat poison), melamine (a plastic precursor often used as a fertilizer), and cyanuric acid (which is used to stabilize chlorine in swimming pools). The chemicals had become mixed in wheat gluten imported from China that was used in the production of a Canadian firm's ninety-five brands of American-manufactured dog and cat food. As with hundreds of dogs and cats, the chemicals caused Chelsea's kidneys to fail. Owners of injured or deceased dogs such as Chelsea filed class actions lawsuits against pet food processors. An unusual joint Canadian and U.S. settlement agreement suspended the litigation of more than one hundred class action law suits in Canada and the United States. The settlement agreement created a $24 million settlement fund to compensate the caretakers of the dead and injured pets who filed claims for the euthanasia, cremation, burial, and autopsy costs, costs of new pets, costs of pet screenings, and other expenses. The settlement, however, did not compensate for emotional damages or any future expenses of pet caretakers.[13]

The settlement also did not serve as a warning to pet food processors. Between 2007 and 2013 evidence of hundreds of canine deaths and thousands of canine gastrointestinal, kidney, and urinary illnesses from Chinese-made chicken, duck, and sweet potato jerky dog treats accumulated. An investigation by the U.S. Food and Drug Administration (FDA), including more than 1,000 tests, visits to multiple manufacturers, and requests for assistance from veterinarians, failed to locate the source of the illnesses. Finally, in October 2013, the FDA began the process of drafting regulations to ensure the safety of pet and other animal food.[14] Unfortunately the regulations will come too late for dogs such as Chelsea.

Ambro, Poco, and PJ: The Disposal of Old Horses

Ambro is a former racehorse who is currently living in a rescue center. He ended his racing and stud careers and then was turned out to fend for himself until he was sold to a slaughterhouse. Because he was extremely emaciated, could barely walk, and had no commercial value, the slaughterhouse allowed a rescue volunteer to take him. Ambro was one of the few lucky horses. Because racehorses live up to thirty years but have a short career—five to six years racing with perhaps a few years at stud if they are big winners—most profit-seeking owners want to dispose of them when their career is over. The primary means of disposal has been sale to a slaughterhouse.

Additionally, many other horse owners have found themselves unwilling or unable to incur the continued expense of caring for horses they have used for recreation. Even when they think they have found a safe haven for their pets, this is often untrue. For example, Poco and PJ were owned and loved for about fourteen years until their owner became ill and was unable to care for them. She asked her neighbors if they would take the horses and care for them. They agreed, but almost immediately sent the horses to slaughter. After suing for emotional distress, the former owner succeeded in securing monetary damages.[15] Affected by this and other stories of the treatment of old horses and the effect of horse slaughterhouses on public health, federal lawmakers adopted laws that have effectively induced all U.S. horse slaughterhouses to close. However, animal buyers still can purchase horses at auctions and ship them to Canada and Mexico for slaughter. Congress is currently considering a ban on the export of horses for slaughter, but thousands of U.S. horses, even famous racehorses past their prime and beloved family pets, still are slaughtered every year.[16]

Sammie: Politics and the Pet Business

Volunteers rescued Sammie, a Dachshund, and 926 other dogs from the Whispering Oaks kennel near Parkersburg, West Virginia. Jammed into a cage with other dogs, Sammie had an untreated wound on his leg, his teeth were ground to the gums from chewing on his wire crate, and his feet were splayed from standing on the wire floor of the crate all of his life. He was infested with fleas and intestinal parasites, and he was underweight. Sammie was not rescued because state or local officials filed charges of cruelty or cited Whispering Oaks management for a violation of laws regulating kennels. At the time of these abuses West Virginia had no law that regulated commercial kennels, and the operator of the kennel exploited a loophole in the federal Animal Welfare Act. Instead, after operating for decades without a sewage disposal system a citizen complaint resulted in an environmental inspector with the West Virginia Department of Environmental Protection finding that feces dumped at the site had contaminated a stream. After serving a search warrant, officials discovered hundreds of caged dogs in unsanitary conditions. The prosecuting attorney reached an agreement with the kennel owner that permitted the immediate rescue of the dogs and the transfer of their ownership to Humane Society of Parkersburg in exchange for the diversion of criminal charges against the kennel owner and her agreement not to operate a commercial kennel. A year later the kennel owner complied with an Order for Compliance issued by the Department of Environmental Protection by cleaning the site, but she violated the agreement by continuing to own dogs. Charged with the failure to pay the county dog tax, she pleaded guilty and paid fines and fees. By then the kennel owner had reopened operations nearby in the state of Ohio. Six months later she was charged with violating Ohio's kennel law, but she was not indicted. Meanwhile, Sammie was one of the lucky ones. Volunteers found him a new home. As with Sammie, thousands of dogs and cats live their entire lives in small wire cages with no socialization, no exercise, and no veterinary care so that people can profit from the puppies and kittens they produce.[17]

POLITICS AND PETS

In each of the five stories in the previous section, the animals lived in close association with humans and were considered to be pets. These stories raise three important questions about law and policy: First, What is a pet? Is a pet, as the *Oxford English Dictionary* states, "An animal (typically one which is domestic or tame) kept for pleasure or companionship"? Or, is there more to being a pet? Second, Does the treatment of pets possess any political importance? Finally, What duties do political institutions impose on human relationships with companion animals? In addressing these questions in this section, we will not only explore the governance of human-pet relations but also assess the treatment of pets within the broader dimensions of the modern governance of human behavior.

What Is a Pet?

"The animal is a word, it is an appellation that men have instituted, a name they have given themselves the right and authority to give to the living other," wrote Jacques Derrida.[18] So too "pet" is a socially constructed category that is not rigidly definable but depends instead "upon time, space, and situation."[19] Being a "pet" is a "contingent status" and contradictory situation for an animal.[20] In part the definition of an animal as a pet is associated with whether people perceive an animal as useful in certain ways, more like me or less like me or, perhaps, as cleaner or less clean.[21] In this sense being a pet means that, at least temporarily, humans have singled out an animal for "special attention intended to promote [its] well-being."[22] The attention can include inviting the animal into a residence, sleeping with it, feeding it, naming it, playing with it, dressing it up, displaying it for rewards or as a threat to others, breeding it, protecting its health, and coping with the responsibilities and inconveniences of pet care. As with the Katrina pets, Sammie, Chelsea the Boston Terrier, the horses Ambro, PJ, and Poco, and even the New Brunswick Rottweilers, humans provided for animals and offered them food and often inordinate affection. The named family cat or dog, the dog who resides in the house or a kennel, a cat who occasionally prowls the neighborhood but is regularly fed and cared for by humans, and horses used for recreational riding clearly fit into the category of pet. Because they inhabit special spaces designated by humans and have close, regular association with humans who act as caretakers, these animals exist as companion animals. Some owners also refuse to use the word *pet*. They contend that the animal is their companion or even their "fur baby" and they are its caretaker or guardian and not its "owner."

However, a point exists at which an animal is less an affectionate companion and more a utilitarian object. If cats are left to run free, people can regard them as a noisy, dirty menace to human health and songbirds. People can view dogs as a vicious threat to themselves or their family or as producers of filth. Horses can be a valuable commodity when used for racing, dressage, show, and stud. Yet, free or wild horses can be treated as a threat to the environment or a potential source of food. Because they are usually slaughtered for food when their usefulness to their owners has ended, domesticated horses also possess a contingent status. Everywhere in the United States and Canada, any homeless animal picked up by animal control faces death by guillotine, clubbing, stabbing, gassing, gunshot, or lethal injection. Animals, even those that have been lost from owners, have only a few days to be claimed, adopted, or rescued before they are put to death in ways too inhumane to use on vicious humans who commit murder.

The contingent status of dogs, cats, and horses also appears in their legal definition. However, most North American jurisdictions do not define the word *pet* in statutes and judicial decisions that address animal welfare. Instead, they imply that a pet is a domesticated animal purchased or held as a form of property, or they simply use the word *pet* without fully defining its meaning.[23] In Vermont, a few judges have begun to recognize that "pets do not fit within traditional property principles."[24] As stated by a New York judge, "a pet is not just a thing but occupies a special place somewhere in between a person and a piece of personal property. ... [Property,] while it might be the source of good feelings is merely an inanimate object and is not capable of returning love and affection. ... To say [a dog] is a piece of personal property and no more is a repudiation of our humaneness."[25] To compound matters, in place of the term *pet*, many jurisdictions in Canada and the United States use the term *companion animal*. For example, in Virginia the term *companion animal* is defined as "any domestic or feral dog, domestic or feral cat, nonhuman primate, guinea pig, hamster, rabbit not raised for human food or fiber, exotic or native animal, reptile, exotic or native bird, or any feral animal or any animal under the care, custody, or ownership of a person or any animal that is bought, sold, traded, or bartered by any person."[26]

However, some jurisdictions tautologically define a companion animal as a pet. For example, in Illinois the term *companion animal* means "an animal that is commonly considered to be, or is considered by the owner to be, a pet."[27] In Idaho *companion animal* means "those animals including, but not limited to, domestic dogs, domestic cats, rabbits, companion birds, and other animals commonly kept as pets,"[28] and in British Columbia a companion animal is defined as "an animal kept as a pet or as a guide animal."[29] Regardless of the term used—*pets* or *companion animals*—the law almost always defines or implies that they are a category of personal property.

Nevertheless, an animal can readily slip out of the legal categories of property, pet, and companion animal. For example, a cat that is usually under human care and housed with humans is regarded as owned, and legal liability for the behavior of the cat is attached to its owners. If the cat is allowed to roam free with identification, it usually remains owned. If it roams free without identification but is fed by humans, animal control officers can treat it as a stray. However, if the cat roams free, avoids human contact, and, often, lives in a colony with similar cats, it is feral. Feral cats can have a special legal status, and some jurisdictions have attempted to manage them through the passage of euthanasia or colony caretaker legislation. A few states regard them as protected wildlife that require a license to destroy, such as deer, antelope, or bear, or as unprotected vermin such as rats, mice, and coyotes.[30]

The answer to the question What is a pet? therefore is that the identity of an animal as a pet can best be defined by its location on a continuum of humans' classifications of mammals and other species. However, the identity of an animal as a pet is contingent upon human discretion exercised in political and legal settings and therefore can become the subject of a series of dynamic political–legal struggles about the power to name and control.

Does the Treatment of Pets Possess Any Political Importance?

What makes the study of pets and politics important? The treatment of pets is intertwined with politics. As the vignettes that open this chapter suggest, the identification of an animal as a pet, demands for political action, the practices of political institutions, public policies, and criminal and regulatory law enforcement agencies and courts affect the lives of animals in Canada and the United States. The treatment of cats, dogs, and horses by humans has also generated political conflicts. In the media, legislatures, and courtrooms in both Canada and the United States, heated debates have arisen about policies that affect the treatment of pets. Since the early nineteenth century, animal welfare interest groups and the animal anti-cruelty and rescue movements have demanded legislation about animal welfare. More recently the limited enforcement of these laws has aroused concern because scholarly debate has arisen about whether pet cruelty, especially by adolescents, is a possible predictor of interpersonal violence and related criminal acts against humans.[31] Widely publicized litigation about animal fighting, such as the conviction of star football quarterback Michael Vick for participation in a dogfighting ring,[32] and legislative conflicts about pet policies, such as breed bans, penalties for animal hoarding, kennel licensing, horse slaughter, and feral cat management, attracted more public and interest group attention to the political status of pets. Today a wide range of legislation and judicial decisions about housing, property ownership, estates, family law, and veterinary practice, as well as those related to animal abuse, affect the human–pet relationship.[33] Finally, a few studies associate pet ownership with voters' preferences among candidates and the presence of dogs in news coverage of a range of issues with public attention to an issue.[34]

Additionally, academics have raised important normative questions about the treatment of the natural world and the meaning of rights and of humane behavior and how humans should express compassion, benevolence, or affection, toward pets and other animals. Philosophers, sociologists, and law professors have begun to explore the meaning and ethics of pet possession and treatment. By the end of the first decade of the twenty-first century, a majority of American law schools offered courses in animal law.[35] These courses and related legal scholarship proposed the inclusion of academic formulations of ethical duties toward animals and ideas of animal rights in legislation and in arguments made during adjudications.

Pets also affect the lives of the public. Data show that in addition to residing in a majority of U.S. households and about half of all Canadian households,[36] in the United States pets reside more frequently with home-owning white married families with children. Pet owners' income, education, employment status, and population of community vary little from that of the population in general.[37] With such numbers and demographic characteristics that especially align them with the middle class, pet caretakers are a potential political force.

However, pets have a much broader significance in contemporary society. The humanization of animals by some pet caretakers has encouraged the development of a huge market for pet goods and services. It appears that people who are excessive buyers especially spend when they humanize pets.[38] Such an attachment to a pet also affects spending on the health and veterinary treatment of a companion animal. One study found that "people who consider their pets as cherished others are more willing to keep these animals alive regardless of the costs, whereas those who are moderately attached are more willing to consider the trade-offs in their decisions."[39] The businesses servicing pets' needs have experienced rapid growth in recent decades. With approximately $55 billion spent on pets in the United States per year, pets create the seventh largest segment of retail market. This market generates jobs for pet groomers, veterinary clinics, dog walkers, animal boarding facilities, trainers, pet cemetery and crematoria operators, insurers, pet store owners and salespersons, and the manufacturers of products designed for pets: leashes, clothing, beds, and other accouterments. It is estimated that Americans spend more than $28 billion a year on veterinary services.[40] Pet caretakers spend $20.6 billion on pet food, which has a significant effect on the income of farmers, fishermen, and agricultural product processors, agricultural subsidies, grocery stores, and pharmaceutical firms. Although few Americans carry insurance on their pets (2.6 percent of cats, 5.7 percent of dogs, 9.3 percent of horses), this expenditure is another contribution to the economy.[41] The size of this retail market has encouraged its rationalization and consolidation by North American firms such as Petco and PetSmart.[42] Finally, the presence of cats, dogs, and horses as loved ones, as symbols, or in service to humans in consumer advertisements for non-pet products, such as food and drinks, automobiles, and liability insurance, is an indication of the perceived significance of cats, dogs, and horses in stimulating or manipulating consumer expenditures in a variety of product markets.[43]

Pets can also affect public health and welfare.[44] A plethora of studies have found that pets, especially cats and dogs, encourage physical activity and fitness among humans, reduce stress and blood pressure, and induce the bodily production of hormones associated with pleasure, speed recovery of cardiac patients, and reduce the chance of a child's development of asthma, eczema, and allergies.[45] Pets also can provide psychological benefits. Studies have found that they affect child development, provide companionship and psychological comfort for seniors, shut-ins, and Alzheimer's patients, improve mental health, enhance self-esteem, and combat anxiety, depression, and grief.[46] According to the American Veterinary Medical Association, 63.2 percent of U.S. pet owners treat their pets and family members similarly and 35.8 consider the pet a companion.[47] This emotional bond is deep. In 2012 the Harris poll reported that 51 percent of U.S. pet owners frequently slept with their pets, 62 percent have purchased holiday presents for their pets, and 40 percent have purchased birthday presents for their pets.[48]

On the other hand pets can generate costs to public health and welfare. Defecation by dogs does not only soil streets and parks; a study has found that dog feces are a dominant source of bacteria in the outdoor air in sampled Midwestern metropolitan areas.[49] As when in 1977 New York City modified its health law to require that owners scoop and properly dispose of dog feces deposited in public spaces, pet defecation in public has become a heated political issue.[50] Other costs associated with pets can affect the quality of life in a community, including the noise and odors they can produce, ecological damage such as when cats kill songbirds, roaming rural dogs' harassment of livestock and wildlife, cat, dog, and horse feces that taint water supplies, animal bites, the raiding of garbage and spewing of refuse, and the causation of vehicle accidents.[51] Often the public responds to such issues by political actions such as complaints to local elected officials or various local and provincial or state bureaus.

Therefore the law, the economic importance of pets, their influence on the physical and mental welfare of the public, and, additionally, the public's moral concerns about the treatment of animals intersect to place pets inside the realm of politics. Also, to protect their interest or investment of money, affection, or moral concern in cats, dogs, and horses, animal welfare groups, agribusiness, veterinarians, insurance companies, and pet supply trade associations have organized as interest groups and attempted to mobilize the power of government on behalf of their interest in companion animals. By undertaking these actions people have politicized pets.

What Do Political Institutions Require of Human Relationships with Pets?

If the pet is a political subject of importance, what responsibilities do political institutions impose on humans' relationships with cats, dogs, and horses? As with other political topics, pet politics reveals how people perceive their duties toward others or the natural world and how they have chosen to govern their own behavior. As illustrated in the stories of Sammie and PJ and Ambro, humans can commit unspeakable acts of cruelty toward animals while other persons will devote their time and money to rescue them. However, humans also dispose of innumerable thousands if not millions of unwanted pets each year through extermination or "euthanasia." These pets' lives end in part because of the costs that laws and policies surrounding their care, housing, and ownership assign to persons. Pets, therefore, pose problems of human responsibility toward companion animals and the management of the pet population. Why, when, and how then do political institutions effectively intervene or design policies to protect pets from ill-treatment by humans?

In the remainder of this book we will address this question. As illustrated in the vignettes earlier in this chapter, the persistence of injuries to pets implies that Canada and the United States have yet to develop and provide a uniform policy for the treatment of cats, dogs, and horses. Building on this estimation of the political condition of pets' lives, *the thesis of this book is that several factors have contributed to a complex series of political struggles about the treatment of cats, dogs, and horses.* What are these factors? To focus the analysis of the political struggles or conflicts about pet policy, we set forth a framework that outlines how the identity of animals, normative attitudes about cruelty, and political institutions and the idea of legality have influenced the evolution of policies that define the appropriate human treatment of pets.

EXPLAINING PET POLITICS: A FRAMEWORK FOR ANALYSIS

In the broadest sense pets are a component part of a culture: the explicit and implicit "patterns of representations, actions, and artifacts that are distributed or spread by social interaction."[52] This representation provides special meaning and expectations about animals. However, within the broad confines of any culture people will also vary to some extent in their assignment of a specific meaning to companion animals. Individuals might conflict about perceptions of specific facts and events, differ in interpretations of history or the natural world, or disagree during interactions and communications with others in everyday life in ways that define their preferences for the treatment of pets in dissimilar ways.[53] For example, studies indicate that dissimilarity exists between the personality attributes of "dog people" and "cat people,"[54] and people will disagree about whether an animal is a friend or a nuisance.

To express their various meanings and preferences for the treatment of cats, dogs, and horses, humans have constituted sociopolitical frames. A sociopolitical frame is a collective human vision of existence. It offers a simple and condensed diagnosis of how things are, what they might be, and how the future might be shaped.[55] As with the beams, studs, trusses, and blocks used to frame the interior core of most American and Canadian homes, any sociopolitical frame provides a structure that limits what we can choose to include within and on the surface of the building and what we both imagine and calculate to be the potential uses of the building. A frame therefore offers an "underlying infrastructure that provides coherence and a storyline to a range of facts, says which facts are important and relevant and which are not, and provides an ongoing interpretation that can incorporate new happenings and factual claims."[56] Beyond providing structured interpretations, frames are constitutive. They impose psychological and social constraints on human perceptions and the legitimacy of behavioral norms. Frames configure how people gather information, identify problems, and attribute blame for what they regard as risks to their interests. Frames define certain political strategies and policy alternatives as reasonable, moral, and creditable ways of averting risks. Frames therefore can provide a dominant narrative for the discussion of people, animals, and events.[57]

As within the frame of a house, certain materials—"conceptual structures"—contribute to the construction of the interior elements and the edges or boundaries of a sociopolitical frame.[58] Based on his study of conversations about American politics, William Gamson has observed that frames contain individuals' perceptions and discussions of three important conceptual components: (1) social identity or the definition of the status of the self and others; (2) the authority of social norms, especially about injustice and normative judgments about fairness and responsibility; and (3) agency or perception of the appropriate collective uses of power for altering social conditions or public policies.[59] Although we adjust Gamson's terminology for the analysis of pet politics, these three components help construct a framework for our study of how cats, dogs, and horses are treated. We employ "identity" more narrowly, defining it as the category and status that people assign to cats, dogs, and horses. Our assessments of injustice and the force of social norms are focused on the norms and ethics that people use to define the fair and cruel treatment of pets. Our discussion of agency addresses the power of political institutions and the conception of legality that people use to establish and alter the conditions and practices that affect the lives of cats, dogs, and horses.

The Social Identity of Companion Animals

A crucial component of frames in policymaking about companion animals is the human constitution of a *social identity* for animals. The social identity of a pet is a cultural category that people have constituted based on their comparisons among the distinctive physical, cognitive, and emotional characteristics and the social purposes, status, interests, rights, and responsibilities of the animal. The social identity of pets therefore is a "constructed" category. However, because of the lack of a precise empirical basis for the identity of animals, public perspectives on cats, dogs, and horses are "negotiated" or open to debates among humans about the structure of the categories. As with most debatable human identities such as race or sexuality, the identity of animals has become a subject for political consideration and definition.[60] For example, humans have debated whether cats, dogs, and horses exist as a biological entity, powerful totem, danger, commodity, legal property, legally regulated being, benevolent companion, sentient rights-bearer, or other sort of object.[61] The consequence is variance, ambivalence, or imprecision in the identity of companion animals and the differences between humans and other animals and the potential for political struggles about their treatment.

Norms: Fairness and Cruelty toward Companion Animals

Shaped by organized religion and contact with nature, we assume that perspectives about the moral duties of humans toward animals, including conceptions of cruelty, fairness, and responsibility for animals' welfare and

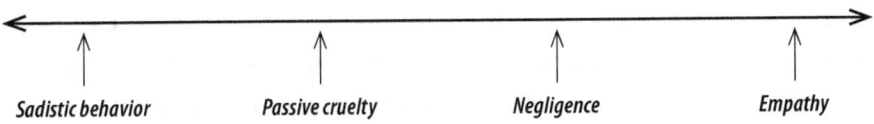

FIGURE 1.1 Continuum of normative treatments of companion animals.

liberty, are a component in the framing of policy choices about the treatment of pets. In particular humans have employed various standards of cruelty to constitute the boundary between the responsible, fair, and just treatment of companion animals and the suffering and pain that humans might inflict upon them.[62] Following Kathleen Taylor, we define cruelty as the infliction of suffering or pain by a perpetrator on an undeserving subject.[63] In animal–human relationships, who are the perpetrators and who are the undeserving subjects? The perpetrator's choice to inflict suffering is voluntary and varies because of intentions in diverse cultures and political jurisdictions. As illustrated in Figure 1.1, intentions can be scaled on a continuum that ranges from voluntary actions designed to cause pain in the animal while delighting his sexual or possessive desires or sadistic behavior, to callousness, thoughtlessness, or what we call "passive cruelty," to neglect or a lack of due care in making voluntary choices that affect animals, to a point of greatest empathy with the plight of pets and the human enrichment of the lives of cats, dogs, and horses.[64]

Sadistic behavior includes intentional murder or genocide generated by racial or ethnic conflict or ideological fantasies.[65] It includes harms perpetrated because of threat or encouragement by authority figures, as with the individuals who willingly administered electric shocks to "victims" in psychological experiments.[66] Additionally it is the pleasurable sense of empowerment that angry, psychologically stressed youth who hang cats or that a dogfighting audience experiences.[67]

Passive cruelty reflects "ignorance, laziness, impulsiveness, an immature sense of empathy"[68] that places boundaries on how people voluntarily define and justify their acts of affection and rationalize the imposition of suffering on non-consenting humans and animals. Often the rationalization stems from an emotional response of disgust with the behavior of the animal or an ambivalence about its value as a being or a commodity.[69] The moral consequence is that persons "unsee" the suffering of an animal.[70] In particular the suffering results from a range of acts such as a lack of social interaction with a pet, ostracism (including the long-term tethering or caging of pets, or shelter workers joking while killing animals), cleansing (including the lawful removal of stray pets from the streets or pets from housing complexes), and expulsion and elimination (including the lawful extermination of unwanted pets because of excessive breeding).[71] Passively cruel actions are not usually defined as criminal or pathological and, as with the euthanasia of animals at shelters, can be legal. Therefore, because of official or legal approval of many of these violent or symbolically violent actions, there is confusion and ambivalence about the meaning of passive cruelty.[72]

Passive cruelty differs from the suffering produced by neglect, negligence, or an involuntary lack of due care, such the failure of a caretaker to have a veterinarian examine an ill horse. Often the lack of due care is not directly aimed at causing the suffering of a specific pet. As with other forms of negligence, remedies for such suffering are often afforded by personal liability or tort law. However, as illustrated by the death of Chelsea the Boston Terrier, tort law can provide monetary relief to the pet's owner or caretaker only when negligence exists.[73]

Regardless of the motives of the perpetrator, we assume that in most instances the companion animal has not intentionally acted to deserve the cruelty. Although Western morality presupposes that some persons should be the subjects of imprisonment or death because of genocidal or criminal acts, normally legal procedures demand that they be proven to have acted with intent to cause suffering. However, it is questionable whether companion animals can intentionally impose unprovoked suffering on a human subject and then be penalized for their actions. Human training and treatment and the pet's instinctual responses to threats trigger much of the suffering that pets cause humans, such as dog and cat bites and throws from horses. It appears that intentional harm by pets upon humans is induced, and in most instances pets are not subjects who deserve cruel punishment.[74]

What then causes various forms of human cruelty toward companion animals? Although no complete explanation exists, initially people must define the companion animal as "other" or different from humans because of their appearance, behavior, and reputed intelligence. In some circumstances people then perceive that the "other" has become a threat to their existence, identity, or ego gratification and should be neutralized. To neutralize the threat people can choose to teach the animal as other a lesson by imposing suffering on it. Cruelty in its various forms thus is a human emotional and cognitive response to perceptions or predictions of unpleasant contacts with companion animals.

These perceptions can result in deliberate sadistic cruelty toward animals. Its specific causes include emotional responses to pets, such as culturally acquired perceptions of disgust, fear or anxiety, threat of physical harm, or displaced sexual urges.[75] Passive cruelty and neglect appear to be caused more by convenience or utility. In constructing the calculus, people assess the threat of a pet to their economic interests, such as damage to property and personal possessions by a pet, the costs of insurance and care, its utility as guard, herder, fighter, or hunter, or its failure to produce products, such as puppies, that can be marketed. In this calculus the companion animal is often reified into a commodity. People also assess the psychological benefits and costs of the pet, including the affection it provides and the extent to which it is disgusting. In this calculus the pet can be stereotyped as friend or a dangerous or diseased "other."

How then do people accommodate the consequences of cruelty for cats, dogs, and horses? Arnold Arluke's ethnographic study of animal control officers, adolescents, animal hoarders, shelter workers, and human societies has illustrated how an individual's identification of animals interacts with emotions, professional standards and practices, willingness to obey authority, personal identity and social role, socially generated ethos, and efforts to validate a personal status to produce "social confusion" about the ethical treatment of companion animals.[76] Other studies have indicated that aspects of childhood socialization, experiences with cruelty toward animals, gender, the need for power among men, an attitude of hostility toward others, and, in some studies, other demographic factors affect the assessment calculus and, consequently, the passive cruelty or neglect and empathy that people direct toward animals.[77] This evidence therefore indicates that cruelty in the treatment of animals is context dependent.[78]

Also, assessments of animal cruelty might be influenced by the visibility of the actions humans direct at animals. Siobhan O'Sullivan has argued that interpretations of cruelty toward different species or the same species in different contexts is normal. Further, she asserts that variations in the visibility of harms directed at animals (direct personal visibility, indirect popular visibility, and indirect visibility mediated by public officials) influence the conception of normative assessments of cruelty and, ultimately, legislation to protect animals.[79]

Finally, to justify their sadistic behavior, passive cruelty, or neglect, persons often exercise moral disengagement. Moral disengagement is behavior designed to avoid censure for injurious conduct. It affords people the opportunity to justify cruelty and aggressiveness or irresponsible behavior as a bystander. Morally disengaged persons utilize euphemisms and distorting language, such as "euthanasia," to mask cruelty and assert the morality of their actions. They minimize the consequences of their choices through advantageous comparisons of their actions to the harmful acts of others. They blame the animal victim for its suffering.[80] The perpetrators and bystanders of cruelty also can compartmentalize feelings of moral duty in these circumstances and either refuse to recognize suffering or rationalize the infliction of cruelty.[81] Although only one study has applied the concept of moral disengagement to animal cruelty, the findings were that individuals "exhibiting mechanisms of moral disengagement in regard to the treatment of animals displayed less concern about violence against animals and were less punitive in their attitudes toward such acts." Also, "moral disengagement ... accounted for a substantial proportion of the variation in attitudes reflecting concern and punitiveness regarding animal cruelty."[82]

Political Institutions and Practices

Frames specify the agents who can fix or alter social conditions and power relationships. Often this component recognizes certain *institutions* and the people who serve them to be decision makers who, for example, can legitimately define or alter the treatment of companion animals. In Canada and the United States, provincial, state, county, municipal, and other local legislative institutions and administrative agencies and local courts—those of magistrates and trial judges—are usually these decision makers.

In particular, contemporary political decision makers construct issues that affect pets with reliance on the core value of "legality."[83] In Canada and the United States, political order, moral conduct, and the control of cruelty toward others is a matter of following the law, respecting the rights of others, and adhering to required legal duties.[84] Legality or the texts of law, the history of their institutional interpretation and enforcement, widespread popular understandings of law and legal practices, and a structure of institutional practices and decision makers govern people's choices and relationships. As a constitutive way of "imaging reality," legality pervades how people treat companion animals, interact with them, and assess the importance of pets. Legality might limit people's preferences. It might predispose people to assume that certain values and actions toward pets are normal, conventional, and rational. It might guide how people interpret situations and behavior. Legality provides the means for the establishment of the political legitimacy "in law" of specific identities of animals and the moral norms that govern humans' treatment of cats, dogs, and horses. Finally, by defining the power of political institutions, legality acts as a boundary—a negative—on the choices made by these decision makers, controls a range of violent acts, and imposes varying degrees of legal accountability upon the humans who interact with animals.[85]

In particular, faith in legality often has stimulated politicians to adopt and then expand a practice of governance identifiable as *legalized accountability*. Our definition of legalized accountability has three parts. First, it is a means of social control that relies on laws and rules developed by governmental institutions that convey rational and nonarbitrary principles of civic order and personal responsibility. Second, it establishes comprehensive administrative and judicial systems to enforce the laws and rules. In support of the practice and morality of law following, legislators and senior administrators develop systems of training, internal agency oversight, service and regulatory practices, and internal and external communication to ensure the public that its administrators accept the legitimacy of law. Third, as insurance that laws and rules are enforced, the public often possesses the capacity to challenge and adjudicate the decisions of administrators through the use of personal injury (tort), civil rights, equitable remedy (injunctions, mandamus), or internal administrative agency adjudications.[86]

In an "ever-deepening quest" to regulate the problems of urban life and complex economic organizations, we contend that legalized accountability became the primary instrument for the implementation and enforcement of companion animal policies in North America. Whether through the American development of the police powers to regulate property and commerce and protective legislation to prevent discrimination and threats to health and safety or the Canadian legislative effort to ensure "peace, order, and good government," laws and regulations adopted by the public's representatives came to define individual, public, and private organizational behavior toward companion animals.[87] Fearing the costs of civil penalties for violations of statutes, regulations, and private personal injury litigation and to protect against legal challenges to their accountability, firms have adopted internal self-regulatory procedures, risk management strategies, and acquired insurance.[88] Finally, legal accountability has become infused in the behavior of organized interests and social movements. It is part of their belief and practice.[89]

Stability, Political Struggles, and Political Change

Given that the social identity of pets, moral responsibilities of humans, and legality are crucial components that frame the political discussions and policy choices about the treatment of pets, why are there political struggles about the identity of pets? The answer we proffer throughout this book is that the different and competing conceptual components of frames have produced continuing political struggles and conflicts about the treatment of pets. As noted, the frames and conceptual structures that people create are multiple and contingent. Additionally, the content of frames can undergo change as a consequence of the emergence of new events, new technologies, cultural practices, intellectual arguments, technology, and institutional operations. By offering counter-frames, political activists can destabilize the dominant, hegemonic, or "master" frames that might limit the consideration of policy options. Such instability can readily evolve into political struggles as activists strive to alter popular preferences and seek the support of government to gain legitimacy for their vision of animals.[90] "Framing contests" or political conflicts thus commonly occur as activists endeavor to mobilize bystanders to support their values and undertake lobbying, protests, litigation, and other political actions designed to make an identity and moral and political meaning of pets dominant.[91] However, old frames and conceptual structures often survive in new political contexts. In chapters 4 through 9 we will describe numerous political struggles about the treatment of pets, contests that remain ongoing.

"Animal Rights" and "Animal Welfare" as Social Movements

Although our thesis is that a series of political struggles about the treatment of cats, dogs, and horses exists, we will also assess a related contention about the struggles that marks pet politics. The public, the media, and many scholars often speak of the individuals and organizations that engage in political and legal activity to protect animals as an "animal rights" social movement. Social movements are large informal groupings of individuals and organizations that appear to be focused on specific political or social issues and make an effort to carry out, resist, or undo social or political change related to that issue.[92]

However, we contend that the idea of an animal rights movement fails to capture the reality of the disaggregated set of ideas and emotions, cultural conflicts, organized interests, and political behavior that contribute to advocacy for the improved or "humane" treatment of cats, dogs, and horses. First, as we discuss in chapters 2 through 4, beliefs, advocacy, and actions in support of the enhancement of the lives of cats, dogs, and horses are not monolithic. Many persons and groups, such as animal rescuers and shelter volunteers, attempt to improve the treatment of companion animals though acts of benevolence and compassion, while others seek laws that require responsible stewardship. These individuals and organizations imply that their collective identity is as a movement for "animal welfare." However, we will show that today a much smaller set of individuals and organizations speak of animal rights. Rather than focusing on the responsible care of pets, supporters of animal rights seek to establish that animals have an autonomous identity and, hence, rights and liberties akin to those of humans. These distinctions, we find, create the existence of at least *two* social movements advocating the improved treatment of pets: "animal welfare" and "animal (legal) rights."

Second, activists and interest group members concerned about the welfare and responsible stewardship of pets often have had their identity with and membership in an animal rights movement foisted on them by opponents of the various norms and policies they support. When it originated during the nineteenth century, rights meant control over an object or thing, and the term *animal rights* described a collective social duty of humans to care for and protect certain dependent species. In the late twentieth century, however, for some groups the term *animal rights* came to mean animal legal rights or an instrument to be employed to impose a negative check on public and private control of animals as well as a degree of legal equality for animals with humans.[93] Yet, "the increasing frequency with which it [the term *animal rights*] was used ... did not correlate with any increase in the clarity of its meaning."[94] Consequently, as the media coverage of public protests of organized animal legal rights interest groups such as People for the Ethical Treatment of Animals (PETA) and the Animal Liberation Front (ALF) expanded in the 1990s, the political efforts of animal welfare groups such as the American Society for the Prevention of Cruelty to Animals (ASPCA), HSUS, and largely nonpolitical animal stewardship and rescue groups to distance themselves from the legal rights groups was lost.

Interest groups opposed to greater legal protection for companion animals and in support of measures that treated them as a commodity in particular perceived the value of labeling any supporters of pro-animal welfare laws and policy as animal rights "extremists."[95] These extremists, they asserted, presented an extravagant or irrational misreading of the nature of legal rights to advance a special interest or right alien to the political culture.[96] Through a "marketing" of the message of animal rights radicalism and the attribution of a threat to meat eating, pharmaceutical research, and the economic uses of animals in general, agribusiness and supporters of the use of animals as a commodity sought to discredit all sorts of pro-animal organized interests.[97] For example, the American Dog Breeders Association has claimed that "*the truth is that animal rights is a mental illness masquerading as philosophy. There are no longer any nationally* known organizations that just want good care for animals; from 1980-on, they were all taken over by animal rights zealots who continue to operate them under the 'animal welfare' banner."[98] Consequently, "animal rights" became a contrivance in a campaign to damage all sorts of campaigns for legal and policy change to improve the treatment of animals by organized interests who identified animals as subjects of human stewardship.[99] Only after 2010 did groups such as the ASPCA mount extensive media campaigns to establish the need for companion animal stewardship. Through the use of language, music, and symbols about the abuse of cats and dogs, these interests sought to give legitimacy to the idea of companion animal stewardship. However, their message was not a direct counter-performance that protested the identification of pets as autonomous, nor did it directly argue against the treatment of pets as a valuable commodity.[100]

Has the political construction of an animal rights movement had an effect on the public policy agenda? Successful social movements mobilize constellations of organized interests and individuals and align their interests with a broader public agenda.[101] They can destabilize social identities and law and policies. But, as we will show, with interests identifying animals quite differently, acting politically in different ways, lacking a shared understanding of rights and the acts that constitute animal cruelty, and disagreeing about a political agenda to address the suffering of animals, it is difficult to pronounce that a *unified* animal rights social movement has an effect on policy. The reality, we argue, is that pet politics is a set of complex and messy struggles among both those who seek to aid animal welfare—animal rights advocates—and the individuals, groups, and interests who identify cats, dogs, and horses as a valuable property or as a commodity.

EXAMINING PET POLITICS

Pet policymaking is in some ways a mixture of politics and policymaking that is not quite like other policymaking arena. Pet policymaking is not just a set of regulatory policies governing animal cruelty, nuisance animals, and threats to public health posed by feral cats and vicious dog breeds. It is not just a struggle to achieve a morality policy that pursues anti-cruelty laws that impose ethical duties on human interactions with cats, dogs, and horses. It is not just about the creation of a post-material policy that emphasizes the treatment of animals as emotional kinship with an autonomous, rights-bearing being.[102] Instead, the pet policymaking illustrates the complexity of conflicting public efforts to cope with pets as objects of affection, economic value, respect, or abuse in a unique policy domain.

To describe and assess the unique political struggles that define the life of American and Canadian pets, we employ a comparative analysis of the ideas and practices of people in Canada and the United States, and we rely on multiple social scientific methods of analysis. Our eclectic approach adopts the application of statistical techniques to both quantitative and qualitative case studies. In our effort to apply these methods we have encountered three limitations. First, there is a lack of comparative quantitative and qualitative data on North American companion animal politics. For example, national survey data on support and opposition to the broad range of pet policy options is nonexistent. Data collection about the activities of animal policy activists and organizations is quite limited and topic specific. Most critically, agencies involved in the implementation of animal policies—shelters, inspectors, law enforcement personnel, prosecutors, and others—either keep no records of animal-related actions or collect data in ways that preclude effective comparative analysis of their activities. Although it compiles data on a wide range of crimes and criminal justice topics, even the U.S. Bureau of Justice Statistics does not record any information on crimes associated with companion animal welfare. Compounding the data and information problem is the failure of public and private organizations to fund the collection of such information. However, in the future this situation might change. In October 2014 the U.S. Federal Bureau of Investigation (FBI) indicated that it would begin to ask law enforcement agencies to report animal-related incidents and arrests for simple or gross neglect, intentional abuse and torture, organized abuse, including dogfighting and cockfighting, and animal sexual abuse.[103] Also, interest groups, especially the Animal Legal Defense Fund, have initiated an effort to adopt a model Animal Abuse Registry Act. It would require the registration of persons convicted of an animal cruelty or neglect misdemeanor or felony. As with sex offenders, information on their conviction would be posted on the Internet and accessible to law enforcement and the public.[104] At present only a few U.S. municipalities and no states have a registry.[105]

Second, with pet policy made by the federal governments, states, provinces, and thousands of regional, county, and municipal governments in the two nations, we can only depict general patterns and include a limited number of jurisdictions through our case studies and examples. With well more than 100,000 legislative, administrative, and judicial institutions participating in or with the authority to participate in pet policymaking, we cannot account for all of the dimensions of political struggles that occur in North America.

Third, because of the complexity of pet politics and the limited situations we examine, we cannot offer a formal policymaking model that rests on universal assumptions and laws of political behavior. Instead we can only offer a framework for the analysis of pet politics. Unlike a theory, the framework we offer organizes inquiry around the idea of competing components of frames and uses partial theories about the influence of ideas and political mechanisms or discrete parts of the policymaking process to describe and evaluate generalizations about aspects of governance.[106] However, since political scholars have largely ignored companion animal policymaking, we believe that we "break the ice" and offer a guide for further inquiry into a topic that affects an enormous number of people in the two nations.

Therefore, to elucidate the identities of pets for their treatment, in chapter 2 we describe historically how the identities, norms, and legal status assigned to pets have been, for the most part, constituted or created and recreated by intellectuals and activists and then brought to public attention by *policy entrepreneurs*—individuals who propose policy measures, pressure politicians, influence elections, use public relations and the media, litigate, arrange public demonstrations, or win allies to support a political goal—or political activists.[107] Turning to contemporary politics, in chapter 3 we describe empirically the contending contemporary social identities of pets that exist among the mass public of the two nations and explore the policy implications of the identities. As recounted in chapter 4, in both countries the existence of multiple and often conflicting identities has stimulated efforts by individual activists and organized interests such as interest groups and corporations to induce public officials to legalize their understanding of the social identity of cats, dogs, and horses. To account for the situational and inconsistent norms of cruelty and empathy possessed by the organized interests and public officials who shape the American and Canadian regulation of pets, we include empirical assessments of the sources of normative standards in chapter 3.

In chapters 5 through 10 we then examine how differing normative conceptions of cruelty influence the public, organized interests, policymakers, and law enforcement officers. In chapter 5 we address the question, Why do legislators adopt or not adopt anti-cruelty pet legislation? Using an extensive quantitative database of U.S. state– and Canadian province–level variables and information on state animal-related laws, we explore whether political and socioeconomic variables affect the adoption of anti-cruelty pet legislation by the states and provinces. To provide a richer explanation of the variations in the legislative and administrative formulation of pet policies, chapters 6 through 9 offer a series of case studies of cat, dog, and horse policymaking to examine the interaction of public social identification of pets, normative standards, and interest groups with legislators and, on occasion, political executives in the formulation and adoption of laws and policies that affect the treatment of cats, dogs, and horses. The case studies illustrate how policymakers have reacted in quite different ways to events, the social identity of animals, normative values, and the demands of organized interests when considering laws and policies that affect cats, dogs, and horses.

Chapter 10 turns to a second question. Are companion animal laws and policies enforced? Studies of the implementation and enforcement of laws by public agencies have frequently detected a gap between the aim of a law and its enforcement by public administrators and the judiciary. With animal law and policy, we argue that the gap is significant. We examine why it has occurred and its consequences for the treatment of cats, dogs, and horses through a series of case studies of the administration and adjudication of several categories of companion animal laws. In conclusion we question whether the result of policy formulation and enforcement is too often laws and policies that express symbolic concern for the well-being of pets but that have little direct effect on the everyday treatment of cats, dogs, and horses.

Now we turn to explore the complexities of the political struggles about the lives of pets.

NOTES

1. We use the terms *pet* and *companion animal* interchangeably. For other views on terminology see Hillary Bok, "Keeping Pets," in *The Oxford Handbook of Animal Ethics*, ed. Tom L. Beauchamp and R. G. Frey (New York: Oxford University Press, 2011), 791, n. 1; Donna J. Haraway, *When Species Meet* (Minneapolis: University of Minnesota Press, 2008), 16–18, 133–35; Hal Herzog, *Some We Love, Some We Hate, Some We Eat* (New York: Harper, 2011), 72–74.
2. "Industry Statistics & Trends, Pet Ownership," American Pet Products Association, accessed August 10, 2012, http://www.americanpetproducts.org/press_industrytrends.asp; American Veterinary Medical Association, *U.S. Pet Ownership and Demographics Sourcebook (2012)* (Schaumburg, IL: American Veterinary Medical Association, 2012), 5–49.
3. Terri Perin, "The Business of Urban Animals Survey: The Facts and Statistics on Companion Animals in Canada," *The Canadian Veterinary Journal* 50 (2009): 48–52; John Sorenson, *About Canada: Animal Rights* (Winnipeg: Fernwood, 2010), 9.
4. American Veterinary Medical Association, *U.S. Pet Ownership and Demographics Sourcebook (2012)*, 19.
5. Contrast Paul C. Bartlett et al., "Rates of Euthanasia and Adoption for Dogs and Cats in Michigan Animal Shelters," *Journal of Applied Animal Welfare Science* 8 (2005): 97–104, with "HSUS Pet Overpopulation Estimates," Nov. 23, 2009, Humane Society of the United States, accessed Apr. 17, 2010, http://www.humanesociety.org/issues/pet_overpopulation/facts/overpopulation_estimates.html. Shelter intake of pets might be in long-term decline: see Kevin N. Morris and David L. Gies, "Trends in Intake and Outcome Data for Animal Shelters in a Large U.S. Metropolitan Area, 1989 to 2010," *Journal of Applied Animal Welfare Science* 17 (2014): 59–72.
6. Cathy Scott, author of *Pawprints of Katrina: Pets Saved and Lessons Learned* (Hoboken, NJ: Wiley, 2008), letter to Susan Hunter, Sept. 3, 2009, provided these estimates on the animal victims of Hurricane Katrina. See also Leslie Irvine, *Filling the Ark: Animal Welfare in Disasters* (Philadelphia: Temple University Press. 2009), 19–26.

7. "Adventures with Hurricane Katrina Animals," Margaret Auld-Louie, accessed July 15, 2009, http://www.optimumchoices.com/adventures.htm; Irvine, *Filling the Ark*, 26–39; Ky Evan Mortensen, *Horses of the Storm: The Incredible Rescue of Katrina's Horses* (Lexington, KY: Eclipse Press, 2008).
8. 42 *United States Code* § 5196–5196b; Hillary A. Leonard and Deborah L. Scammon, "No Pet Left Behind: Accommodating Pets in Emergency Planning," *Journal of Public Policy and Marketing* 26 (2007): 49–53; Marita Mike, Rebecca Mike, and Clark J. Lee, "Katrina's Animal Legacy: The Pets Act," *Journal of Animal Law and Ethics* 4 (2011): 133–60.
9. U.S. Congress, Sections 403 and 502 of the Robert T. Stafford Disaster Relief and Emergency Assistance Act (Stafford Act), 42 *United States Code* §§ 5170b, 42 *United States Code* § 5192; the Pets Evacuation and Transportation Standards Act (PETS Act) of 2006, Public Law. No. 109–308, § 4, 120 *United States Code* § 1725 (2006); 44 *Code of Federal Regulations* §§ 206.223(a), 206.225(a); Federal Emergency Management Agency, Disaster Assistance Policy (DAP) 9523.19, Eligible Costs Related to Pet Evacuations and Sheltering (Oct. 24, 2007), accessed Oct. 7, 2014, http://www.fema.gov/pdf/government/grant/pa/9523_19.pdf.
10. Shauna M. Decker et al., "Emergency and Disaster Planning at Ohio Animal Shelters," *Journal of Applied Animal Welfare Science* 13 (2010): 66–76. See also Carin Wittich and Michael Belanger, "How Is Animal Welfare Addressed in Canada's Emergency Response Plans?," *Journal of Applied Animal Welfare Science* 11 (2008): 125–32.
11. Confidential Interview by Susan Hunter, Sept., 2006. See also "Waddell Inquest," Dog Legislation Council of Canada, accessed Sept. 16, 2009, http://www.dlcc.ca/public/about-the-dlcc/james-waddell/; "New Dog Law Will Have Bite," accessed May 26, 2006, http://canadaeast.com; "N.B. Inquest to Probe Deadly Rottweiler Attack," CTV, accessed May 26, 2006, http://lists.envirolink.org/pipermail/ar-news/Week-of-Mon-20031027/009199.html; New Brunswick, *Acts*, Chapter S-12; New Brunswick, Regulation 84-85.
12. "Champion Libertree's Chelsea's Legacy-Chelsea," accessed Sept. 16, 2009, http://www.bthaven.org.
13. *In re* Pet Food Products Liability Litigation, Dist. Ct. N.J., 2008 U.S. Dist. LEXIS 4603; Des Côteaux c. Menu Foods Genpar Ltd., 2008 QCCS 6561; Pet Food Products Liability Settlement, accessed July 5, 2011, http://www.petfoodsettlement.com; Kate Paulson, "See Spot Eat, See Spot Die, The Pet Food Recall of 2007," *Animal Law* 15 (2008): 113–39; Marion Nestle, *Pet Food Politics: The Chihuahua in the Coal Mine* (Berkeley: University of California Press, 2008); "Pet Food," U.S. Food and Drug Administration, accessed Oct. 7, 2014, http://www.fda.gov/AnimalVeterinary/Products/AnimalFoodFeeds/PetFood/default.htm.

14. "FSMA Public Meeting: Proposed Rule to Establish Current Good Manufacturing Practice and Hazard Analysis and Risk-Based Preventive Controls for Food for Animals—College Park, MD," U.S. Food and Drug Administration, accessed July 8, 2015, http://www.fda.gov/Food/GuidanceRegulation/FSMA/ucm368989.htm; "Current Good Manufacturing Practice and Hazard Analysis and Risk-Based Preventive Controls for Food for Animals," U.S. Food and Drug Administration, accessed July 8, 2015, http://www.regulations.gov/#!documentDetail;D=FDA-2011-N-0922-0002.
15. See Burgess v. Taylor, 44 S.W.3d 806 (Ct. App. Ky. 2001).
16. See James M. Lewis, "Big Battle Shaping over Horse Slaughter," *DVM Newsmagazine* (Apr. 2009): 1, 69.
17. Sammie's story was recounted to Susan Hunter by a rescue volunteer, Sept., 2008. See also John A. Gill, "Environmental Impacts of One Puppy Mill among Many: A Case History," accessed Aug. 15, 2013, http://animalstudiesrepository.org/acwp_cdbpm/1/.
18. Jacques Derrida, *The Animal That Therefore I Am*, ed. Marie-Louise Mallet, trans. David Will (New York: Fordham University Press, 2008), 23, see also at 32.
19. Jennifer Wolch, Alec Brownlow, and Unna Lassiter, "Constructing the Animal Worlds of Inner City Los Angeles," in *Animal Spaces: Beastly Places: New Geographies of Human-Animal Relations*, ed. Chris Philo and Chris Wilbert (London: Routledge 2000), 93.
20. Katherine C. Grier, *Pets in America: A History* (Orlando: Harcourt, Inc., 2006), 8–11.
21. See Edmund Leach, "Anthropological Aspects of Language: Animal Categories and Verbal Abuse," in *New Directions in the Study of Language*, ed. Eric H. Lenneberg (Cambridge, MA: MIT Press, 1964), 23–63.
22. Grier, *Pets in America*, 11.
23. See City of Rolling Meadows v. Kyle, 484 N.E.2d 766 (Ill. 1986); Gallick v. Barto, 828 F. Supp. 1168 (M.D. Pa. 1993); Combined Health District v. Rittenhouse, 689 N.E.2d 1036, 1039 (Ohio Ct. App.1997); Turudic v. Stephens, 31 P.3d 471 (Ore. Ct. App. 2001); Morabito v. Savoie, [1981] O.J. No. 67 (Ont. Sup. Ct.). Alberta and Nevada are examples of jurisdictions whose statutes and regulations use the word *pet* without supplying a definition. For a general discussion of the legal meaning of pets, see David Favre and Peter L. Borchelt, *Animal Law and Dog Behavior* (Tucson: Lawyers and Judges Publishing Co., 1999), 10–13.
24. Morgan v. Kroupa, 702 A.2d 630, 633 (Vt. 1997).
25. Corso v. Crawford Dog and Cat Hospital, Inc., 415 N.Y.S.2d 182, 183 (N.Y. City Civ.Ct. 1979).
26. *Virginia Code Annotated* § 3.2-6500 (2009).
27. *Illinois Compiled Statutes Annotated* §510 ILCS 70/2.01a (2009).

28. *Idaho Code* § 25-3502 (2009).
29. *Revised Statutes of British Columbia*, 1996, c. 323, s. 707.1.
30. Verne R. Smith, "The Law and Feral Cats," *Journal of Animal Law and Ethics* 3 (2009): 7–27. Compare Commonwealth v. Massini, 188 A.2d 816 (Pa. 1963), with Commonwealth v. Comella, 735 A.2d 738 (Pa. 1999), and Thurston v. Carter, 92 A. 295 (Me. 1914).
31. As an introduction to studies of this topic, see Sharon L. Nelson, "The Connection between Animal Abuse and Family Violence: A Selected Annotated Bibliography," *Animal Law* 17 (2010–2011): 369–414. Among the many psychological studies of the linkage of animal cruelty to human-on-human abuse and violence, see Frank R. Ascione and Phil Arkow, eds., *Child Abuse, Domestic Violence, and Animal Abuse: Linking The Circles of Compassion for Prevention and Intervention* (West Lafayette, IN: Purdue University Press, 1999); Frank R. Ascione and Kenneth Shapiro, "People and Animals, Kindness and Cruelty: Research Directions and Policy Implications," *Journal of Social Issues* 65 (2009): 569–87; Herzog, *Some We Love, Some We Hate, Some We Eat*, 29–35; Randall R. Lockwood and Frank R. Ascione, eds., *Cruelty to Animals and Interpersonal Violence: Readings in Research and Application* (West Lafayette, IN: Purdue University Press, 1998); Marti T. Loring, Robert Geffner, and Janessa Marsh, eds., *Animal Abuse and Family Violence: Linkages, Research, and Implications for Professional Practice* (Binghamton, NY: Haworth Maltreatment and Trauma Press, 2007); Linda Merz-Perez and Kathleen M. Heide, *Animal Cruelty: Pathway to Violence Against People* (Walnut Creek, CA: AltaMira Press, 2004); Samara McPhedran, "Animal Abuse, Family Violence, and Child Wellbeing: A Review," *Journal of Family Violence* 24 (2000): 41–52. For criticism of these studies, see Emily G. Patterson-Kane and Heather Piper, "Animal Abuse as a Sentinel for Human Violence: A Critique," *Journal of Social Issues* 65 (2009): 589–614.
32. Rebecca J. Huss, "Lessons Learned: Acting as Guardian/Special Master in the Bad Newz Kennels Case," *Animal Law* 15 (2008): 69–85; Jim Gorant, *The Lost Dogs: Michael Vick's Dogs and Their Tale of Rescue and Redemption* (New York: Gotham, 2011); Kathy Strouse, *Badd Newz: The Untold Story of the Michael Vick Dog Fighting Case* (Charleston, SC: BookSurge Publishing, 2009).
33. Rebecca J. Huss, "The Pervasive Nature of Animal Law: How the Law Impacts the Lives of People and Their Animal Companions," *Valparaiso Law Review* 43 (2009): 1137–53.
34. Diana Mutz, "The Dog that Didn't Bark: The Role of Canines in the 2008 Campaign," *P.S.: Political Science and Politics* 43 (2010): 707–12; Forrest Maltzman et al., "Unleashing Presidential Power: The Politics of Pets in the White House," *P.S.: Political Science and Politics* 45 (2012): 395–400; Matthew

L. Jacobsmeier and Daniel C. Lewis, "Barking Up the Wrong Tree: Why Bo Didn't Fetch Many Votes for Barack Obama in 2012," *P.S.: Political Science and Politics* 46 (2013): 49–59; Matthew D. Atkinson, Maria Deam, and Joseph E. Uschinski, "What's a Dog Story Worth?," *P.S.: Political Science and Politics* 45 (2014): 819–23.

35. "Animal Law Courses," Animal Legal Defense Fund, accessed Sept. 30, 2014, http://aldf.org/animal-law-courses/.
36. American Veterinary Medical Association, *U.S. Pet Ownership and Demographics Sourcebook (2012)*, 1; Perin, "Business of Urban Animals Survey," Table 1.
37. American Veterinary Medical Association, *U.S. Pet Ownership and Demographics Sourcebook (2012)*, 117–37, 144–77.
38. Nancy M. Ridgway et al., "Does Excessive Buying for Self Relate to Spending on Pets?," *Journal of Business Research* 61 (2008): 392–96.
39. Beverly K. Brockman, Valerie A. Taylor, and Christopher M. Brockman, "The Price of Unconditional Love: Consumer Decision Making for High-Dollar Veterinary Care," *Journal of Business Research* 61 (2008): 404.
40. American Veterinary Medical Association, *U.S. Pet Ownership and Demographics Sourcebook (2012)*, 57.
41. Ibid., 71, 84, 97, 108.
42. American Pet Products Association, *2009/2010 APP Daniel C. Lewis, MA National Pet Owners Survey* (Greenwich, CT: American Pet Products Association, 2009); "U.S. Pet Industry Spending Figures & Future Outlook," American Pet Products Association, accessed Mar. 28, 2013, http://www.americanpetproducts.org/press_industrytrends.asp; Grier, *Pets in America*, 354–409.
43. Karen M. Lancendorfer, JoAnn L. Atkin, and Bonnie B. Reece, "Animals in Advertising: Love Dogs? Love the Ad," *Journal of Business Research* 61 (2008): 384–91; Jennifer E. Lerner and Linda Kalof, "The Animal Text: Message and Meaning in Television Advertisements," *The Sociological Quarterly* 40 (1999): 565–86.
44. For broad reviews of these benefits, see James Serpell, *In the Company of Animals: A Study of Human-Animal Relationships,* Canto edition (Cambridge: Cambridge University Press, 1996), 89–143; Sarah Knight and Harold Herzog, "All Creatures Great and Small: New Perspectives on Psychology and Human-Animal Interactions," *Journal of Social Issues* 65 (2009): 451–61. See also Marc Bekoff, ed., *Encyclopedia of Human-Animal Relationships: A Global Exploration of Our Connections with Animals*, 4 vol. (Westport, CT: Greenwood Press, 2007).
45. Among the many studies of the association of pet companionship with physical health, see Hayley Cutt et al., "Dog Ownership, Health and Physical Activity: A Critical Review of the Literature," *Health and Place* 13 (2007) 261–72; Erika Friedmann, Sue A. Thomas, and Timothy J. Eddy, "Companion Animals and

Human Health: Physical and Cardiovascular Influences," in *Companion Animals and Us*, ed. Anthony L. Podberscek, Elizabeth S. Paul, and James A. Serpell (Cambridge: Cambridge University Press, 2000), 125–42; Rebecca Johnson, Alan Beck, and Sandra McCune, eds., *The Health Benefits of Dog Walking for People and Pets: Evidence and Case Studies* (West Lafayette, IN: Purdue University Press, 2011); Peggy D. McCardle et al., eds., *How Animals Affect Us: Examining the Influence of Human-Animal Interaction on Child Development and Human Health* (Washington, DC: American Psychological Association, 2011); Deborah L. Wells, "The Effects of Animals on Human Health and Well-Being," *Journal of Social Issues* 65 (2009): 523–43; Cindy C. Wilson and Dennis C. Turner, eds., *Companion Animals in Human Health* (Thousand Oaks, CA: Sage 1998), and the studies cited in these works.

46. Among the many studies that assess the psychological benefits of interaction with pets are P. Elizabeth Anderson, *The Powerful Bond between People and Pets: Our Boundless Connections to Companion Animals* (Westport, CT: Praeger, 2008), 82–108, 142–53, 181–85; Allan Beck and Aaron Katcher, *Between Pets and People: The Importance of Animal Companionship*, rev. ed. (West Lafayette, IN: Purdue University Press, 1996): Shelia Bonas, June McNicholas, and Gwyn M. Collis, "Pets in the Network of Family Relationships: An Empirical Study," in *Companion Animals and Us*, 209–36; Andrew Gilbey, June McNicholas, and Glyn M. Collist, "A Longitudinal Test of the Belief that Companion Animal Ownership Can Help Reduce Loneliness," *Anthrozoös* 20 (2007): 345–53; Andrew Gilbey and Kawtar Tani, "Companion Animals and Loneliness: A Systematic Review of Quantitative Studies," *Anthrozoos* 28 (2015): 181–97; Lynette Hart, "Dogs as Human Companions: A Review of the Relationship," in *The Domestic Dog, Its Evolution, Behaviour, and Interactions with People*, ed. James Serpell (New York: Cambridge University Press, 1995), 161–78; Lynette A. Hart, "Psychosocial Benefits of Animal Companionship," in *Handbook of Animal-Assisted Therapy*, ed. A. Fine (London: Academic Press), 59–78; Henri Julius et al., *Attachment to Pets: An Integrative View of Human-Animal Relationships with Implications for Therapeutic Practice* (Cambridge, MA: Hogrefe Publishing, 2012); Susan M. Keaveney, "Equines and Their Human Companions," *Journal of Business Research* 61 (2008): 444–54; Peggy McCardle et al., eds., *Animals in Our Lives: Human-Animal Interaction in Family, Community, and Therapeutic Settings* (Baltimore: Paul H. Brookes Publ., 2011); Johannes Odenall, *Pets and Our Mental Health: The Why, the What, and the How* (New York: Vantage Press, 2002). For bibliographies and criticism of the methodology of psychological studies of the animal-human bond, see David C. Anderson, *Assessing the Human-Animal Bond: A Compendium of Actual Measures* (West Lafayette, IN: Purdue University Press, 2007).

47. American Veterinary Medical Association, *U.S. Pet Ownership and Demographics Sourcebook (2012)*, 5.
48. "Pets Aren't Just Animals; They are Members of the Family," The Harris Poll, accessed Oct. 22, 2013, http://www.harrisinteractive.com/vault/Harris%20Poll%2054%20-%20Pet%20Ownership_9%2013%2012.pdf.
49. Robert M. Bowers et al., "Sources of Bacteria in Outdoor Air across Cities in the Midwestern United States," *Applied and Environmental Microbiology* 77 (2011): 6350–56.
50. Michael Brandow, *New York's Poop Scoop Law: Dogs, the Dirt, and Due Process* (West Lafayette, IN: Purdue University Press, 2008).
51. For a summary of these costs, see B. M. Feldman and T. H. Carding, "Free-Roaming Urban Pets," *Health Services Report* 88 (1973): 956–62.
52. Hazel Rose Markus and MarYan G. Hamedani, "Sociocultural Psychology: The Dynamic Interdependence among Self Systems and Social Systems," in *Handbook of Cultural Psychology*, ed. Shinobu Kitayama and Dov Cohen (New York: Guilford Press, 2007), 11–12.
53. On preference formation, see James N. Druckman and Arthur Lupia, "Preference Formation," *Annual Review of Political Science* 3 (2000): 1–24.
54. Samuel D. Gosling, Carson J. Sandy, and Jeff Potter, "Personalities of Self-Identified 'Dog People' and 'Cat People,'" *Anthrozoös* 23 (2010): 213–22. See also Herzog, *Some We Love, Some We Hate, Some We Eat* (New York: Harper, 2011), 26–28.
55. Francesca Polletta and M. Kai Ho, "Frames and their Consequences," in *The Oxford Handbook of Contextual Political Analysis,* ed. Robert E. Goodin and Charles Tilly (New York: Oxford University Press, 2006), 189–97; Robert D. Benford and David A. Snow, "Framing Processes and Social Movements: An Overview and Assessment," *Annual Review of Sociology* 26 (2000): 611–39; James N. Druckman, "Political Preference Formation: Competition, Deliberation, and the (Ir)relevance of Framing Effects," *American Political Science Review* 98 (2004): 671–86; Erving Goffman, *Frame Analysis: An Essay on the Organization of Experience* (Cambridge, MA: Harvard University Press, 1974), 21–26.
56. William A. Gamson, "Beyond the Science-versus-Advocacy Distinction," *Contemporary Sociology* 28 (1999): 24.
57. Benford and Snow, "Framing Processes," 618–22; Donald R. Kinder and Thomas E. Nelson, "Democratic Debate and Real Opinion," in *Framing American Politics*, ed. Karen Callaghan and Frauke Schnell (Pittsburgh: University of Pittsburgh Press, 2005), 104; Donald Schön and Martin Rein, "Frame-Critical Policy Analysis and Frame-Reflective Policy Practice," *Knowledge and Policy* 9 (1996): 85–105. On the importance of frames in the construction of American public policies, see Frank R. Baumgartner et al., *Lobbying and Policy Change: Who Wins,*

Who Loses, and Why (Chicago: University of Chicago Press, 2009), 166–89; James N. Druckman and Kjersten R. Nelson, "Framing and Deliberation: How Citizens' Conversations Limit Elite Influence," *American Journal of Political Science* 47 (2003): 729–45; Daniel Kahneman and Amos Tversky, "Choices, Values, and Frames," *American Psychologist* 39 (1983): 341–50.

58. Clifford Geertz, "Thick Description: Toward an Interpretive Theory of Culture," in *The Interpretation of Cultures* (New York: Basic Books, 1973), 27–28.

59. William A. Gamson, *Talking Politics* (Cambridge: Cambridge University Press, 1992), 7–8, 31–114.

60. Rawi Abdelal et al., "Identity as a Variable," in *Measuring Identity: A Guide for Social Scientists*, ed. Rawi Abdelal et al. (Cambridge: Cambridge University Press, 2009), 17–32; Marilynn B. Brewer, "The Many Faces of Social Identity: Implications for Political Psychology," *Political Psychology* 22 (2001): 115; Karen A. Cerulo, "Identity Construction: New Issues, New Directions," *Annual Review of Sociology* 23 (1997): 385; Leonie Huddy, "From Social to Political Identity: A Critical Examination of Social Identity Theory," *Political Psychology* 22 (2001): 127.

61. On the social construction of the identity of animals, see Adrian Franklin, *Animals and Modern Cultures: A Sociology of Human-Animal Relations* (London: Sage Publications 1999), 9–61. For discussion of the identity of animals from a variety of vantage points, see Tim Ingold, ed., *What Is an Animal?* (Boston: Unwin Hyman, 1988); for the identities assigned to dogs, see James Serpell, "From Paragon to Pariah: Some Reflections on Human Attitudes to Dogs," in *The Domestic Dog: Its Evolution, Behaviour, and Interactions with People*, ed. James Serpell (New York: Cambridge University Press, 1995), 245–56; for the identities assigned to cats, see Katherine M. Rogers, *The Cat and the Human Imagination: Feline Images from Bast to Garfield* (Ann Arbor: University of Michigan Press, 1998); for the identities assigned to horses, see Elizabeth Atwood Lawrence, *Hoofbeats and Society: Studies of Human-Horse Interactions* (Bloomington: Indiana University Press, 1985).

62. In Tom L. Beauchamp and R. G. Frey, eds., *The Oxford Handbook of Animal Ethics* (New York: Oxford University Press, 2011), chapters 3–19, the contributors discuss a range of moral and ethical approaches to the treatment of animals.

63. Kathleen Taylor, *Cruelty: Human Evil and the Human Brain* (New York: Oxford University Press, 2009), 20–22.

64. Ibid., 7, sets forth the idea of the continuum, and its key categories are developed at 30–31. On the voluntariness of cruelty, see at 24–25. On sadistic behavior, see at 61, 203–32.

65. See Daniel Jonah Goldhagen, *Hitler's Willing Executioners: Ordinary Germans and the Holocaust* (New York: Alfred A. Knopf, 1996.), 375–415, esp. at 414; Jan

T. Gross, *Neighbors: The Destruction of the Jewish Community in Jedwabne, Poland* (Princeton: Princeton University Press, 2001).
66. See Stanley Milgram, *Obedience to Authority: An Experimental View* (New York: Harper and Row, 1974).
67. See Christopher Hensley and Suzanne E. Tallichet, "Animal Cruelty Motivations: Assessing Demographic and Situational Influences," *Journal of Interpersonal Violence* 20 (2005): 1429–43.
68. Taylor, *Cruelty*, 31.
69. Heather Looy, "Embodied and Imbedded Morality: Divinity, Identity, and Disgust," *Zygon* 39 (2004): 219–35.
70. The notion that people learn to "unsee" cruelty is drawn from a novel, China Miéville, *The City and the City* (New York: Del Rey Ballantine Books, 2009).
71. Taylor, *Cruelty*, 170–71. It is our intention with these examples to categorize behavior. The examples are not designed to indicate any equivalent degree of immorality.
72. Arnold Arluke, *Just a Dog: Understanding Animal Cruelty and Ourselves* (Philadelphia: Temple University Press, 2006), 1–11, 183–303. See also the discussion of legalized physical violence, symbolic violence, repression, and subjection in Richard A. Brisbin, Jr., "Antonin Scalia, William Brennan, and the Politics of Expression: A Study of Legal Violence and Repression," *American Political Science Review* 87 (1993): 912–27.
73. See Lynn A. Epstein, "Resolving Confusion in Pet Owner Tort Cases: Recognizing Pets' Anthropomorphic Qualities under a Property Classification," *Southern Illinois University Law Journal* 26 (2001): 31–51.
74. See Franklin D. McMillan, Deborah L. Duffy, Stephen L. Zawistowski, and James A. Serpell, "Behavioral and Psychological Characteristics of Canine Victims of Abuse" *Journal of Applied Animal Welfare Science* 18 (2015): 92–111.
75. Taylor, *Cruelty*, 71–89. See also Frank R. Ascione and Kenneth Shapiro, "People and Animals, Kindness and Cruelty: Research Directions and Policy Implications," *Journal of Social Issues* 65 (2009): 569–87; Clifton P. Flynn, "Acknowledging the 'Zoological Connection': A Sociological Analysis of Animal Cruelty," *Society and Animals* 9 (2001): 71–87; Jamie L. Goldenberg et al., "I Am *Not* an Animal: Mortality Salience, Disgust, and the Denial of Human Creatureliness," *Journal of Experimental Psychology: General* 130 (2001): 427–35; Bill C. Henry, "Empathy, Home Environment, and Attitudes toward Animals in Relation to Animal Abuse," *Anthrozoös* 20 (2006): 17–34; Judith C. Oleson and Bill C. Henry, "Relations among Need for Power, Affect and Attitudes toward Animal Cruelty," *Anthrozoös* 22 (2009): 255–65; Camilla Pagani, Francesco Robustelli, and Frank R. Ascione, "Investigating Animal Abuse: Some Theoretical and Methodological Issues, *Anthrozoös*. 23 (2010): 259–76;

Maria Vaca-Guzman and Arnold Arluke, "Normalizing Passive Cruelty: The Excuse and Justifications of Animal Hoarders," *Anthrozoös* 18 (2005): 338–57.
76. Arluke, *Just a Dog*, 53 and passim.
77. Bill C. Henry, "Exposure to Animal Abuse and Group Context: Two Factors Affecting Participation in Animal Abuse," *Anthrozoös* 17 (2004): 290–305; Bill C. Henry, "The Relation between Animal Cruelty, Delinquency, and Attitudes toward the Treatment of Animals," *Society and Animals* 12 (2004): 185–207; Henry, "Empathy, Home Environment, and Attitudes toward Animals," 17–34; Oleson and Henry, "Relations among Need for Power, Affect and Attitudes toward Animal Cruelty," 255–65; Tania D. Signal and Nicola Taylor, "Attitudes to Animals: Demographics within a Community Sample," *Society and Animals* 14 (2006): 147–57; Nicola Taylor and Tania D. Signal, "Empathy and Attitudes toward Animals," *Anthrozoös* 18 (2005): 18–27.
78. Joshua D. Greene et al., "An fMRI Investigation of Emotional Engagement in Moral Judgment," *Science* 293 (2001): 2105–8; Joshua D. Greene et al., "The Neural Bases of Cognitive Conflict and Control in Moral Judgment," *Neuron* 44 (2004): 389–400; Piercarlo Valdesolo and David DeSteno, "Manipulations of Emotional Context Shape Moral Judgment," *Psychological Science* 17 (2006): 476–77.
79. Siobhan O'Sullivan, *Animals, Equality, and Democracy* (Houndsmills, UK: Palgrave Macmillan, 2011), 60–158.
80. Albert Bandura et al., "Mechanisms of Moral Disengagement in Exercise of Moral Agency," *Journal of Personality & Social Psychology* 71 (1996): 364–74; Albert Bandura, "Moral Disengagement in the Perpetration of Inhumanities," *Personality and Social Psychology Review* 3 (1999): 193–209; Albert Bandura, "Selective Moral Disengagement in the Exercise of Moral Agency," *Journal of Moral Education* 31 (2002): 101–19; Albert Bandura et al., "Sociocognitive Self-Regulatory Mechanisms Governing Transgressive Behavior," *Journal of Personality and Social Psychology* 80 (2001): 125–35; Alfred L. McLister, Albert Bandura, and Steven V. Owen, "Mechanisms of Moral Disengagement in Support of Military Force: The Impact of Sept. 11," *Journal of Social and Clinical Psychology* 25 (2006): 141–65; Marinella Paciello et al., "Stability and Change of Moral Disengagement and Its Impact on Aggression and Violence in Late Adolescence," *Child Development* 79 (2008): 1288–1309.
81. These arguments modify the argument in Ervin Staub, *The Psychology of Good and Evil: Why Children, Adults, and Groups Help and Harm Others* (Cambridge: Cambridge University Press, 2003), 291–315.
82. Scott Vollum, Jacqueline Buffington-Vollum, and Dennis R. Longmire, "Moral Disengagement and Attitudes about Violence toward Animals," *Society and Animals* 12 (2004): 227.

83. For an overview of laws that affect all animals, see Joan E. Schaffner, *An Introduction to Animals and the Law* (New York: Palgrave Macmillan, 2011).
84. Judith Shklar, *Legalism: An Essay on Law, Morals, and Politics* (Cambridge, MA: Harvard University Press, 1964), 1.
85. Patricia Ewick and Susan S. Silbey, *The Common Place of the Law: Stories from Everyday Life* (Chicago: University of Chicago Press, 1998), 22; Clifford Geertz, "Local Knowledge: Fact and Law in Comparative Perspective," in *Local Knowledge: Further Studies in Interpretive Anthropology* (New York: Basic Books, 1983), 170–75, 230; Michael McCann, "Causal versus Constitutive Explanations (or, On the Difficulty of Being so Positive …)," *Law and Social Inquiry* 21 (1996): 457–82; Austin Sarat and Thomas R. Kearns, "Beyond the Great Divide: Forms of Legal Scholarship and Everyday Life," in *Law in Everyday Life*, ed. Austin Sarat and Thomas R. Kearns (Ann Arbor: University of Michigan Press, 1993), 27–32; Helena Silverstein, *Unleashing Rights: Law, Meaning, and the Animal Rights Movement* (Ann Arbor: University of Michigan Press, 1996), 2–16.
86. The description of legalized accountability extends its construction as presented in Charles R. Epp, *Making Rights Real: Activists, Bureaucrats, and the Creation of the Legalistic State* (Chicago: University of Chicago Press, 2009), 24–27; Philip Selznick, *Law, Society, and Industrial Justice* (New York: Russell Sage Foundation, 1969), 4–18. The discussion here was also influenced by the comments of Malcolm Feeley, Robert Kagan, Michael McCann, and R. Shep Melnick at "Book Roundtable on Charles R. Epp's *Making Rights Real: Activists, Bureaucrats, and the Creation of the Legalistic State*," American Political Science Association Meeting, Washington, D.C., Sept. 3, 2010.
87. On the United States, see Lawrence Friedman, *Total Justice* (New York: Russell Sage Foundation, 1985); Samuel P. Hays, "Political Choice in Regulatory Administration," in *Regulation in Perspective: Historical Essays*, ed. Thomas K. McGraw (Cambridge, MA: Harvard University Press, 1981), 124–54; Robert A. Kagan, *Adversarial Legalism: The American Way of Law* (New Haven, Yale University Press, 2001), 34–58. Legalized accountability in Canada appears to depend more on legislative action in contrast to the judicial action associated with legalized politics in the United States. See for examples M. Paul Brown, "Organizational Design as Policy Instrument: Environment Canada in the Canadian Bureaucracy," in *Canadian Environmental Policy: Ecosystems, Politics, and Process*, ed. Robert Boardman (Toronto: Oxford University Press, 1992), 24–42; Michael Howlett, "The Judicialization of Canadian Environmental Policy 1980–1990: A Test of the Canada–United States Convergence Thesis," *Canadian Journal of Political Science* 27 (1994): 99–127; Carolyn Strange and Tina Merrill Loo, *Making Good: Law and Moral Regulation in Canada, 1867–1939* (Toronto: University of Toronto Press, 1997).

88. For examples of the measures undertaken by private organizations, see Lauren B. Edelman, "Legal Environments and Organizational Governance: The Expansion of Due Process in the American Workplace," *American Journal of Sociology* 95 (1990): 1401–40; Lauren B. Edelman and Mark C. Suchman, "The Legal Environments of Organizations," *Annual Review of Sociology* 23 (1997), 479–515; Selznick, *Law, Society, and Industrial Justice*, 75–240.
89. John Brigham, "Right, Rage, and Remedy: Forms of Law in Political Discourse," *Studies in American Political Development* 2 (1987): 303–16.
90. Robert D. Benford, "An Insider's Critique of the Social Movement Framing Perspective," *Sociological Inquiry* 67 (1997): 415–18; Benford and Snow, "Framing Processes," 624–30; Polletta and Ho, "Frames and their Consequences," 190.
91. Dennis Chong and James N. Druckman, "Counterframing Effects," *Journal of Politics* 75 (2013): 1–16; William A. Gamson, "Bystanders, Public Opinion, and the Media," in *The Blackwell Companion to Social Movements*, ed. David A. Snow, Sarah A. Soule, and Hanspeter Kriesi (Malden, MA: Blackwell Pub., 2004), 242–61.
92. David A. Snow, Sarah A. Soule, and Hanspeter Kriesi, "Mapping the Terrain," in *The Blackwell Companion to Social Movements*, 6–11.
93. Susan J. Pearson, *The Rights of the Defenseless: Protecting Animals and Children in Gilded Age America* (Chicago: University of Chicago Press, 2011), 109–10, 133–36; Susan J. Pearson and Kimberly K. Smith, "Developing Animal Welfare Law," in *Statebuilding from the Margins: Between Reconstruction and the New Deal*, ed. Carol Nackenhoff and Julie Novkov (Philadelphia: University of Pennsylvania Press, 2014), 123–24. On the change in the meaning of rights in general, see William J. Novak, "The Legal Origins of the Modern American State," in *Looking Back at Law's Century*, ed. Austin Sarat, Bryant Garth, and Robert A. Kagan (Ithaca, NY: Cornell University Press, 2002), 265; and especially Pierre Schrag, "Right in the Postmodern Condition," in *Legal Rights*, ed. Austin Sarat and Thomas R. Kearns (Ann Arbor: University of Michigan Press, 1996), 263–304.
94. Elizabeth L. DeCoux, "Speaking for the Modern Prometheus: The Significance of Animal Suffering to the Abolition Movement," *Animal Law* 16 (2009–2010): 28.
95. Studies of events to the early 1990s depict the origins of this tendency: see James M. Jasper and Dorothy Nelkin, *The Animal Rights Crusade: The Growth of a Moral Protest* (New York: The Free Press, 1992), 68–70; Helena Silverstein, *Unleashing Rights: Law, Meaning, and the Animal Rights Movement* (Ann Arbor: University of Michigan Press, 1996), 32–34, 55–79.
96. See Jonathan Goldberg-Hiller and Neal Milner, "Rights as Excess: Understanding the Politics of Special Rights," *Law and Social Inquiry* 28 (2003): 1075–1118.

97. The early stages of the backlash against animal legal rights interests are recounted in James M. Jasper and Jane Poulsen, "Fighting Back: Vulnerabilities, Blunders, and Countermobilization by the Targets in Three Animal Rights Campaigns," *Sociological Forum* 8 (1993): 639–57. On the media and counter-framing tactics, see Dennis Chong and James N. Druckman, "Counterframing Effects," *Journal of Politics* 75 (2013): 1–16.

98. "What are Animal Rights … And Why You Should Care," American Dog Breeders Association, accessed July 24, 2012, http://www.adbadog.com/p_pdetails.asp?fpid=779.

99. DeCoux, "Speaking for the Modern Prometheus," 28–30, 35–39.

100. See William A. Gamson, "Bystanders, Public Opinion, and the Media," in *The Blackwell Companion to Social Movements*, 242–61.

101. Jackie Smith and Tina Fetner, "Structural Approaches in the Sociology of Social Movements," in *Handbook of Social Movements across Disciplines*, ed. Bert Klandermans and Conny Roggeband (New York: Springer, 2010), 29.

102. For typologies of policies, see Theodore J. Lowi, "Four Systems of Policy, Politics, and Choice," *Public Administration Review* 32 (1972): 298–310; Christopher Z. Mooney, "The Public Clash of Private Values," in *The Public Clash of Private Values*, ed. Christopher Z. Mooney (Chatham, NJ: Chatham House, 2001), 3–18. On the linkage of postmaterial values to animal policies, see Adrian Franklin, Bruce Tanter, and Robert White, "Explaining Support for Animal Rights: A Comparison of Two Recent Approaches to Humans, Nonhumans, and Postmodernity," *Society and Animals* 9 (2001): 127–44.

103. Sue Manning, "FBI Turns Animal Cruelty into Top-Tier Felony, Allowing Easier Tracking of Crimes against Pets," *U.S. News and World Report*, Oct. 1, 2014, accessed Oct. 7, 2014, http://www.usnews.com/news/us/articles/2014/10/01/fbi-turns-animal-cruelty-into-top-tier-felony.

104. "Model Laws: Animal Abuser Registry Act," Animal Law Resource Center, accessed Oct. 7, 2014, http://www.animallaw.com/Model-Law-Animal-Abuse-Registry.cfm.

105. "Albany County, NY Passes Nation's Third Animal Abuser Registry Law," Animal Legal Defense Fund, accessed Oct. 7, 2014, http://aldf.org/blog/albany-county-ny-passes-nations-third-animal-abuser-registry-law/; "Animal Abuser Registry Website," Suffolk County (N.Y.) S.P.C.A., accessed Oct. 7, 2014, https://suffolkspca.org/Abuser%20Registry.html; National Ant-Vivisection Society, "New State Animal Abuser Registries Proposed in 2015," accessed June 27, 2015, http://www.navs.org/news/new-state-animal-abuser-registries-proposed-in-2015.

106. Fritz. W. Scharpf, *Games Real Actors Play: Actor-Centered Institutionalism in Policy Research* (Boulder, CO: Westview Press, 1997), 30–34, 37.

107. John Kingdon, *Agendas, Alternatives, and Public Policies*, 2nd ed. (New York: HarperCollins, 1995), 122–31, 179–83, 204–6; Michael Mintrom, "Policy

Entrepreneurs and the Diffusion of Innovation," *American Journal of Political Science* 41 (1997): 738–70; Mark Schneider and Paul Teske, with Michael Mintrom, *Public Entrepreneurs: Agents for Change in American Government* (Princeton: Princeton University Press, 1995).

APPENDIX
Definitions of Terms

Foster home: A type of shelter consisting of the premises of an individual volunteer who provides temporary care for one or more animals owned or in the control of a government, private shelter, or rescue organization. These homes must satisfy certain legal requirements such as registration, permits, licenses, and standards for care in Connecticut, Georgia, Kansas, Massachusetts, Missouri, Pennsylvania, and Virginia, but most states have no regulations governing animal foster homes. In most states anyone can foster animals with no oversight.

Rescue group: Rescue groups are organizations, commonly with Canadian or U.S. tax registration as nonprofit corporations, which acquire unwanted animals from shelters or owner surrenders. Their goal is to find permanent caregivers for the animal. Rescue groups can be species or breed specific. All American Kennel Club (AKC) breed clubs have a rescue coordinator and most affiliate clubs also rescue their breed. Rescue groups are normally managed by volunteers and funded through donations and low-cost placement fees. Prior to placement the animal may be held at a cooperating shelter, shelter operated by the rescue group, or foster home. State, province, county, or municipal laws may but usually do not apply to these groups. Rescue groups can be subject to licensing requirements, record-keeping requirements, sterilization and vaccination requirements, laws on importing animals from across state lines, laws that limit the number of pets permitted on private property, zoning and nuisance laws, tethering restrictions, breed-specific legislation, and tort liability. In jurisdictions without licensing or registration laws, it is possible for anyone to call themselves a rescue organization and to accept animals from owners or shelters. Many animal hoarders call themselves animal rescuers. There are virtually no standards governing the placement of animals for adoption, the number of animals held by a rescue organization, or the standard of care provided to rescued animals. In addition, commercial, for-profit firms can call themselves a rescue organization in order to sell animals bred by commercial breeders rather than unwanted animals. Such organizations may accept animals from shelters and then breed them to produce puppies or kittens to sell.

Shelter: A facility operated by a government or a nonprofit private organization for the temporary housing of abandoned, lost, stray, or unwanted animals. In some instances they are referred to as a "pound." Anyone can claim to operate a shelter in states without licensing or kennel regulations. Many hoarders refer to their home as a shelter.

Kill shelter means that, unless animals are adopted or reclaimed by the owner, they are euthanized after the passage of a specific time period. For government-operated shelters, a state, province, or local law can specify the length of the time period. Kill shelters must accept all strays and owner surrenders of any accepted species.

No-kill shelter means that the only animals that are euthanized are those that are irremediably suffering or truly vicious and a danger to the public. No-kill shelters generally refuse to accept sick, elderly, or vicious animals and can refuse to accept animals when they have reached capacity.[1]

Note

1. See Kristen Pariser, "Detailed Discussion of the Laws Regulating Rescue and Foster Care Programs for Companion Animals," Animal Legal and Historical Center, Michigan State University, accessed Oct. 4, 2014, https://www.animallaw.info/article/detailed-discussion-laws-regulating-rescue-and-foster-care-programs-companion-animals.

2

The Evolution of Pet Policy

Pets cannot vocalize a self-identification or articulate their suffering at the hands of humans. Instead, humans have framed the social identity, normative value, and political and legal status of companion animals in a variety of ways. The historical evolution of the construction of competing identities, norms, and laws about cats, dogs, and horses are the roots and sources of contemporary political struggles about pet law and policy. These frames limit how people identify companion animals, constitute the acceptable treatment of pets, and "bound the rationality" of the legal and policy options they consider to be rational and legitimate. In this chapter we recount the historical context of pet policymaking with special attention to the evolution of the identities of cats, dogs, and horses, norms of cruelty, and the legal status of pets. Especially we address the question, "What ideas and laws have contributed to the attitudes and practices of contemporary pet politics decision making?"

For much of recorded history the Western perception of animals has been anthropocentric. It has conveyed the idea that humans are exceptional and the primary and central species in the world. As stated by Jacques

Derrida, people have assumed that, "man installs or claims in a single stroke his *property* ... and his superiority over what is called animal life. This latter superiority, infinite and par excellence, has as its property the fact of being at one and the same time *unconditional* and *sacrificial*."[1] Only during recent decades have academics and animal caretakers initiated a holistic conception of the relationships among species that questions the anthropocentric perspective and the cultural beliefs and laws and policies that separate humans from other animals.[2] Therefore in this chapter we will depict the evolution of several social identities, moral statuses, and legal standards for horses, dogs, and cats. The mere existence of multiple identities, norms, and laws for cats, dogs, and horses indicates that the public has long debated the meaning of animals and has sometimes expressed multiple or contradictory identities of them.[3] This debate has contributed to struggles and inconsistency in the social and political status of these animals.

THE GREAT CHAIN OF BEING AND HUMAN DOMINION

The assumption of human dominion has long framed the identification and the normative and political treatment of cats, dogs, and horses in the West. Initially the vision of human dominion found intellectual expression as an element of the Great Chain of Being. Rooted in ideas of natural law and religious beliefs, the Great Chain of Being was a central motif in the ancient Greek and medieval Christian understanding of existence.[4] Adopting this motif, philosophers and clergy envisioned the world as degrees of imperfection among creatures. In this cosmological vision, under God fell humankind. Following the biblical injunction, humankind was to have "dominion over the fish of the sea, and over the birds of the air, and over cattle, and over all the wild animals of the earth, and over every creeping thing that creeps upon the earth."[5]

Although clerics and intellectuals communicated the subordinate social identity of animals and their lack of moral agency, popular culture still recognized the economic or totemic importance of certain animals.[6] Therefore, some animals ranked higher on the chain of being, and they required better treatment from humans. For example, in 1683 a British author wrote that "among all irrational creatures, Dogs may deservedly claim a most particular Preference, both for their love and service to Man; using Humiliation and Prostration as the onely [sic] means to pacific his angry Master who beats him, and turns his Revenge, after beating, into a more fervent Love."[7] Also, animals that provided material benefits such as food and power—cattle, horses, and sheep—ranked higher in the chain of being than other species.[8] However, despite service as companions and use as herders, guards, or vermin chasers, cats and dogs often served as scapegoats for displaced human fears of evil, anger, and emotional anxiety.[9]

The assumptions of the Great Chain of Being reinforced the legitimacy of laws that allowed humankind to direct violence toward or subject animals to disciplinary practices.[10] During its formative stage in medieval and early modern England, the law iterated the popular assumption that cats, dogs, and horses had no soul and no feelings.[11] Additionally, in Britain laws created a scale of social privileges and obligations in the use of animals of benefit to the aristocracy and detriment to tenants.[12] Control of domestic animals *(domitæ* or *mansuetæ naturae)*, encumbered by customary, feudal, and tenancy duties into the 1700s, meant that commoners did not speak of personal property rights or ownership of animals in the modern sense as objects with value for sale or exchange.[13]

In the premodern era, legal definitions of the status of animals by legislators and judges were few in number and largely governed toward horse, cattle, and sheep sales, theft of economically valuable animals, poaching, and trespass or injuries caused by bolting horses, dog bites, and stray cattle.[14] Criminal animal cruelty was not a specifically recognized offense.[15] Written title to property in cats and dogs was absent. Statutes governing horse sales gradually appeared, but no legislation governed other animals that became companions. The leading manual for justices of the peace in seventeenth- and early eighteenth-century England recognized only horses, cattle, and sheep as personal property that could be bought and sold. It discussed dogs when they were used to violate game laws and indicated that the theft of dogs was not a larceny or felony but either a breach of peace or a civil wrong to be treated as a trespass. It did not mention cats.[16] By the later eighteenth century, Parliament had changed the law to allow fines, whipping, and limited jail time for the theft of dogs.[17] Nonetheless the law regarded the dog as a personal "thing of value" whose existence depended on the interests of the possessor in the prestige of its possession. Possessors could acquire, sell, breed, feed, pet, beat, train, work, confine, or kill the dog at will. For the upper classes this meant that dogs could be bred and kept for the hunt.[18] As lower-class entertainment dogs could be bred to fight to the death or bait bears and badgers or course deer and hares.[19] Into early modern times if a dog misbehaved or became bewitched it could be tried and executed by the state as a devil or an outlaw. In times of plague and other epidemics, English and Scottish local officials employed dog killers, urban churches employed dog whippers to keep them out of services, and people often killed dogs that wandered the streets.[20] In part because they were regarded as vermin or were associated with witchcraft, the occult, and predatory sexuality, cats possessed no legal status or protection. During the drunkenness of carnivals and workers' protests against the bourgeoisie they were often rounded up and massacred.[21]

As a "domestic" animal with greater economic value, the law made human control of horses different from that of cats and dogs.[22] By 1555 the value of horses as property was legally recognized when the English parliament adopted legislation to regulate horse markets to curtail horse theft.[23] Horses were especially valued for use as "a servant of the elite." Their possessor had to have the money to purchase them, outfit them with harnesses, saddle, and other tack, and buy grain as feed. Because of their association with land ownership, hunting, racing, and the military, horses symbolized power and status. Other uses of horses, such as pulling coaches, also symbolized the dominion of the upper classes.[24] To protect the symbolic linkage of horses with the upper classes, in 1740 Parliament regulated the prizes at horse races to eliminate races with entry fees affordable by lower-class contestants.[25] For agricultural workers, horses, often owned by landlords, served as draft animals.[26] Only in the eighteenth century did the middle classes begin to own horses for travel and recreation.

Regardless of their use, horses were not protected against abuse. Coercion was common in the training of horses. Horses could be beaten or overworked in many ways without legal consequence. People simply disposed of the aged or injured horse. The hide could then be stripped for sale and the meat given to dogs.[27] Because of the assumption of human dominion, most of these actions did not face even social reprobation.[28]

Validated by religion and the laws of nature, the premodern assertion of human dominion justified acts of cruelty or indifference to the suffering of cats, dogs, and horses as morally acceptable. However, moral disengagement from the abuse of animals and the acceptance of human dominion continues to find justification in some contemporary circumstances. For example, continuing patterns of abandonment, starvation, or hoarding of cats, dogs, and horses, the tethering of unattended dogs, the endurance of dogfighting despite legislation, and an Akron, Ohio, program of trapping and killing more than 3,000 free roaming cats provide evidence that a segment of the North American population thinks it can dominate or destroy companion animals at will.[29] Finally, the continuing publication of "fantasies of cruelty" such as *The Official I Hate Cats Book, 101 Uses for a Dead Cat, 101 More Uses for a Dead Cat,* and *How to Kill Your Girlfriend's Cat* testify to the endurance of the sentiment that pets are a subordinate subject of human power and can be subjected to sadistic cruelty.[30] Under human dominion thus remains an identity of animals that people seeking more protective laws must continue to confront in ongoing political struggles about pet policies.

BENEVOLENT COMPANION AND PROPERTY: THE EMERGENCE OF NEW IDENTITIES AND NORMS

Just before her secret marriage to Robert Browning in 1846, the English poet Elizabeth Barrett had her cocker spaniel, Flush, seized by a dog-stealing ring. After Barrett journeyed to the criminal underworld of Whitechapel and paid a ransom of six guineas, Flush was returned.[31] Flush's tale illustrates the emergence of two conceptions of animals in the nineteenth century. By purloining Flush, the dog stealers recognized that he was an object of monetary value. Indeed, in 1845 Parliament made the stealing of a dog a crime, a larceny of personal property.[32] Yet, Barrett's response indicates that she identified Flush sentimentally as a subject of her benevolence. Flush brought her joy and pleasure. Flush was akin to a child or a faithful friend toward whom a superior person acts with kindness and generosity. Barrett's response to the kidnapping of Flush suggests that something important had happened: during the nineteenth century people reframed the identity of some animals from objects of human dominion into property and objects of benevolent action.[33]

Pets and Benevolence

Although of little immediate consequence, in the late seventeenth century commentary on the moral obligation of humans toward animals appeared in print.[34] By the late eighteenth century, drawing upon a variety of themes in this literature, radical authors such as Thomas Taylor would argue that in an enlightened age, "brutes are equal to men."[35] In Britain, Quakers and evangelical religious figures such as John Wesley, a founder of Methodism, began teaching a philosophy of benevolence, compassion, and love toward the poor and dispossessed, including animals.[36] The efforts of other pamphleteers and poets spread the message of the immorality of animal cruelty. When merged with new scientific knowledge about the capabilities of animals, philosopher Jeremy Bentham's expression of horror at the infliction of pain, evangelical Christian perfectionism, and the idealization of nature expressed by Romantic authors, a new identification of animals evolved.[37] Treating them as helpless objects of sentimental value, people began to ascribe an identity as defenseless beings to cats, dogs and horses. Benevolent acts to care for these animals provided a moral lesson about the evil of violence toward the helpless and especially taught children kindness and self-control.[38]

Benevolent actions toward pets as family member or friend and sympathy for the suffering of animals therefore became a distinguishing symbol of membership in the cultivated and more intellectually sophisticated class of English-speaking regimes and the French bourgeoisie. As one component of a mix of sentiments, in Britain, France, and North America an emerging middle class began to express greater recognition of the sentient qualities of animals. Aping the aristocracy, the urban middle class also undertook benevolent pet keeping. Contact with dogs and cats influenced more and more people to recognize the physical and emotional needs of animals and to provide better living conditions, food, exercise, cleanliness, and health care to them. They named pets, associated them with moral virtues such as fidelity, and connected them to domesticity, culture, and home.[39] For example, Abraham Lincoln named his dog Fido from the Latin *fidelis* or faithful, let him wander unchained, allowed him to roam the house, and fed him from the table.[40] A cultural appreciation of normative ideas of sympathy, sentimentality, and kindness toward companion animals thus spread among the educated classes.[41]

Benevolence required a duty to care and be merciful to animals.[42] The stories of the moral duties of people toward animals framed an understanding of animals that resembled the plots that frequently appeared in the romantic literature of the nineteenth century. Romantic stories, such as Anna Sewell's *Black Beauty*, the Canadian novel *Beautiful Joe*, and a host of American books, identified animals as named beings deserving human protection and as companions with whom humans could have an emotional bond. In an effort to use animals to teach social values to children, some other writers portrayed dogs and horses as moral exemplars. They also taught the value of affective discipline or training through love and benevolence rather than force.[43]

Nonetheless, the identification of the pet as an object of benevolence still treated it as a useful possession subject to human control. Human enterprise—selective breeding and training—and human cultural desires began to construct the identity of companion animals. Often people used pets as a "cosmeticized creature whose main virtue was complete docility" and assigned them the role of surrogate infant or dependent.[44] A pet's value was in its use when bred, trained, and pacified to offer nonverbal expressions of affection that serve the ego of humans. (Indeed, empirical studies that find dogs resemble their owners suggest that a pet can support the ego-ideal of its caretaker[45]). Humans then might enjoy the companionship and sentimental, emotional, spiritual, recreational, or aesthetic pleasure afforded by their pet. They also could suffer grief with the loss or death of the faithful pet.[46] Finally, a pet could express some humans' quest for an object of empathy and benevolence that added to or replaced bonds with other humans.[47]

The Pet as Property

Although the nineteenth century witnessed the emergence of benevolent actions toward horses, dogs, and cats, it also saw the emergence of representative governments that rested on the idea of the rule of law. The privileged authority of law provided the political instrument for policy change that allowed individuals and groups to secure the benevolent treatment of cats, dogs, and horses as well as to suppress drunkenness and other forms of vice.[48] To promote regulatory laws to suppress these amusements and protect animals from cruelty, throughout the nineteenth century animal-oriented interest groups formed to publish pamphlets and news stories that called for legislation to criminalize sadistic acts of animal cruelty. Often led by well-to-do urban political activists, these groups served as a crucial part of a "support structure" that pursued the reduction of the pain experienced by animals through the enactment of regulatory laws and institutions for their enforcement.[49] Their appeal for popular support relied on stories, of which *Black Beauty* is one example, that condensed the harms inflicted on animals and attempted to administer a "moral shock" upon readers.[50] They lobbied for laws that remain a critical component for the protection of cats, dogs, and horses today. As a result of the efforts to end bull baiting, Parliament adopted the first British anti-cruelty law in 1822.[51] The failure of Parliament to adopt other anti-cruelty laws encouraged animal advocates to organize a Society for the Prevention of Cruelty to Animals (SPCA) in 1824. Gradually the SPCA succeeded in having Parliament extend the protection of animals at risk for cruel treatment.[52] The SPCA also became concerned with the enforcement of legislation.[53] In an era in which the administration of the law was not fully institutionalized in police departments and private criminal prosecution existed, it hired constables and inspectors as a private police with power to detect and prosecute incidents of animal cruelty. It also encouraged magistrates to penalize abusers.[54] However, with a membership drawn from the "leisured classes" and aristocracy and with SPCA given royal patronage, the enforcement actions of the Royal SPCA avoided censuring the cruelty associated with foxhunting and bird shooting.[55] Instead, the effort to secure the humane treatment of animals was focused on the suppression of lower-class behavior such as gambling on dogfighting and the sadistic beating and killing of horses.[56]

The stimulus for anti-cruelty policies and legislation in the United States came from activists who had reached political maturity in the milieu of the crusades for temperance and the abolition of slavery.[57] Henry Bergh was the most renowned of these activists.[58] Bergh had acquired familiarity with the efforts of the Royal SPCA. With the support of New York social reformers, in 1866 he founded the American Society for the Prevention of Cruelty to Animals (ASPCA). In 1867 Bergh and the ASPCA persuaded New York to pass a law that criminalized as a misdemeanor neglect, malicious killing, maiming, starvation, use in fighting or baiting, or overwork of any animal.[59] Until his death in 1888, Bergh engaged in publicity stunts, litigation, and lobbying tactics to address the abuse of animals by commercial interests, to alert people to recognize animal cruelty, and to characterize its immorality. He also founded the American Humane Education Society to disseminate literature and to support the activities of a group of largely female activists who educated children through various "Be Kind to Animals" programs.[60]

Thanks to the efforts of figures such as Bergh and other activists, other animal welfare groups, often with specific local legislative agendas and loose alliances with other groups, sprang up across the northern, midwestern, and western cities of the United States. By the end of the century these groups secured anti-cruelty laws to protect domestic and draft animals in almost all states and territories.[61] Almost all of the anti-cruelty groups sought criminal penalties for the abuse of animals. Many followed the British model of law enforcement, and either individual humane society members or private humane agents employed by the group prosecuted the criminal charges. Effectively recognizing humane societies as subordinate public agencies, the judiciary permitted legislators to deputize them so they could operate as a quasi-public police force.[62] However, fewer than one in ten prosecutions brought convictions, and state appellate courts defined cruelty only as acts that visit "unjustified" physical pain on an animal. Judges and the law exempted many painful practices used in training dogs and horses and conducting medical experiments (a policy which continues to the present day in many jurisdictions).[63]

Anti-cruelty groups also supported efforts to "protect" animals subjected to mistreatment through the development of institutions such as rest homes for old draft horses and shelters for stray dogs and cats. Modeled on the asylums for the mentally ill, poor, juveniles, and unwed mothers that proliferated in nineteenth-century America, the shelters provided an institutional means for the control of abandoned and abused animals. Although a group in New York City established a no-kill shelter in 1903, almost all shelters "released" cats and dogs from "suffering" by "humane" destruction.[64]

Canadian events paralleled activity south of the border. Prior to confederation, most of the provinces enacted few statutes to protect horses and dogs. Following confederation, in 1869 the Canadian Parliament adopted an anti-cruelty law to protect horses, cattle, other domestic animals, and birds. The next year it banned the baiting of any animal. The 1869 formation of the Canadian Society for the Protection of Animals (CSPCA) by English-speaking, politically influential Montreal professional men abetted the legislative effort. Besides supporting legislation on a range of animal protection measures, the Society followed British and American practice by providing an educational program and initiating "inspections" and prosecutions of offenders. The Society directed much of its effort toward the enactment of laws to improve conditions for draft horses and ensuring water and safe conditions for horses on city streets. However, the CSPCA remained largely a Montreal-based organization. Separate societies with similar objections and operations formed in Toronto (the Toronto Humane Society), Halifax, Quebec City, several Ontario cities, and, later, in the western provinces. Only in 1957 did these local units unite as a Canadian Federation of Humane Societies.[65]

Anti-cruelty Laws

What was the character of the legislation affecting cats, horses, and dogs pressed forward by the animal-oriented groups? The effort to control the human abuse of pets had two instrumental consequences for animals: (1) the legal categorization and regulation of the proprietary interests of man in animals, and (2) the regulation, often through the criminal law, of the cruel use of animals or the dangerous passions man might express toward animals.

Property Interests in Pets

Casting aside older notions, by the 1830s American and Canadian lawyers assumed that domestic animals were a category of personal property. As with most forms of property, any adult person might own, acquire, trade, sell, or dispose of animals.[66] Persons also could be civilly or criminally liable for injury to property in pets.[67] However, legislatures adopted few laws that explicitly defined pets as property.[68] Instead judicial interpretations of the law implicitly treated companion animal as property and subjected humans who injured or stole pets to criminal or civil action.[69] Nuisance law implied that pets could be property, the use and behavior of which was under human control. Nonetheless, judges often treated cats, dogs, and horses as a special and less valuable category of property.[70] At the end of the nineteenth century, the Supreme Court of the United States repeated the doctrine that dogs could not be considered "as being upon the same plane with horses, cattle, sheep, and other domesticated animals" but instead existed in a different category of animal with a legal status determined by specific statutes or by courts.[71]

Canadian courts also treated companion animals as property. For example, a Prince Edward Island court ruled that "tame animals" are "a subject of absolute property."[72] Statutes also express the idea that pets are property. Since 1892 Canadian federal animal cruelty law has implied that pets are owned as property,[73] and the Animal Protection Act of Saskatchewan recognizes that pets can be owned or in a person's custody.[74] The very title of the current Ontario anti-cruelty law, The Dog Owner's Liability Act, conveys the notion that pets are property.[75] In a 2002 case about the issuance of a patent for "transgenic" mice created in a laboratory, the dissenting justices of Canada's Supreme Court noted in passing that "pets are property."[76]

The Regulation of Pets as Property

During the nineteenth century, the judicial development of the common law stated that owners had obligations to protect their property in animals from causing injury or posing a nuisance to the person or property of others.

The judiciary could use its remedial powers to penalize owners when there was evidence that unreasonable actions by owners resulted in their animals posing a threat or causing an injury. Also, cats, dogs, and horses without a recognized owner could be dispatched by government under the *common law of nuisance,* a body of law that permits governments to regulate or eliminate an activity or condition deemed harmful or annoying to others. As stated by a Vermont judge, "Nuisances may be abated in the most summary manner; dogs found chasing sheep may be shot down; ... and race horses may be declared forfeited."[77] Additionally, owners can be held liable under the common law of personal injury or torts for bites, other injuries to persons, and property damage by pets.[78]

Also, nineteenth-century law treated rights as a possession that bestowed control over things, such as animals.[79] Critically, however, animal protection advocates such as Bergh assumed that law protected property rights only to the extent that they conformed to uses supporting the public interest in a "well-ordered society."[80] This conception of the nature of property, a cornerstone of nineteenth-century Anglo-American legal and political thought, permitted legislatures to extend their authority and impose duties and discipline on owners' rights because of the potential harms, insecurity, or disorder their animals might cause the populace.[81] Based on this assumption, preventive legislation action to control animals developed as an element of the U.S. state's police powers and similar Canadian regulatory laws designed to ensure "peace, order, and good government."[82]

A U.S. state's exercise of police power ensured quiet enjoyment of liberty and property but penalized its intemperate or unreasonable use in ways that potentially threatened the health, safety, or morals of the public. Therefore, U.S. state police powers legislation created a duty for property owners to "reasonably" care for their animal property. Legislation criminalized acts that used, injured, or despoiled property in animals in an intentional, willful, wanton, diabolical, or evil manner (malum in se).[83] To control diseases such as rabies, communities also adopted licensing and vaccination policies. They adopted zoning laws to control the locations where companion animals could be kept. They hired officers to "control" roaming pets that might spread disease.[84] Other laws regulated the animal marketplace to protect consumers against diseased animals or to protect animal owners against the abuse of their property by others.[85] Additionally, property that potentially threatened the public welfare became subject to summary destruction by government administrators without compensation of its owner. Such nuisance property included not only buildings that were fire hazards, unsanitary houses, infectious materials, pornography, gambling devices, and alcoholic beverages, but also farm animals and horses that harbored diseases and rabid dogs and cats.[86]

Because the Canadian federal government and courts administer the criminal law, since 1892 animal cruelty, including cockfighting and baiting, has been a federal crime.[87] To further secure public peace and order, the provinces adopted additional laws to protect cats, dogs, and horses, empower private anti-cruelty associations with law enforcement powers, define duties of care toward companion animals, and impose liability for injuries to pets or cats and dogs.[88] They also adopted laws to control and dispose of dangerous dogs and to impose liability for injuries caused by dogs.

As dogs became identified as regulated property, governments enacted dog taxes or license requirements. Developed in France, payment of a dog tax (Germany, Switzerland, and West Virginia) or a dog license (Britain, Canadian, and U.S. local governments) indicated dog ownership. Possession of a license protected the property rights of a dog owner and made the dog into an object with value. Government officials could exterminate unlicensed dogs as a nuisance and not have to compensate owners. The justification for such treatment of dogs was the power of state, provinces, and municipalities to enforce "reasonable" use of dogs as property.[89] The license fee also came to contribute to the operation of pounds or shelters that held animals until rescue or, more commonly, extermination.

Finally, in their interpretations of police regulations, judges ruled that not all suffering by animals was cruelty.[90] Animal owners could justify the killing or infliction of pain on domestic animals for food or to prevent disease in humans or injury to themselves or others.

Private Legislation and Litigation

In addition to governmental action, during the later nineteenth century groups formed to devise private legislation to regulate pets. Groups such as the American Kennel Club, Canadian Kennel Club, American Cat

Fanciers, and specialized dog, cat, and horse owners and breeders associations developed breed standards and rules about breeding to protect or improve the value of the animals they owned. To protect the prestige of purebred or thoroughbred animals, they developed a system of private rules and penalties designed to protect the status of purebred pet ownership. Designation as a purebred additionally raised the economic value of cats and dogs. People began to purchase and show purebred pets not just as an object of prestige but to raise the market value of the animal and its offspring. Pet grooming, pet supply businesses, veterinary medical services, and puppy mills expanded to service the growing trade in the pet as valuable property.[91] As property, a pet could satisfy a person's egotistical desire for prestige, such as winning a blue ribbon at a cat, dog, or horse show.[92] Owning prize-winning thoroughbred horses or powerful and reputedly vicious dog breeds became a symbol or ornament of some people's desire for status, power, or potency.[93]

Also, cats, dogs, and horses became a subject of private legal agreements recognized by the state. Private parties can call upon the judiciary to enforce the provisions of private contracts developed to define title or ownership of companion animals and lawful transfers of pets by lease (horse rental), gift, or adoption.[94] Adjudication can be used to control the disposition of pets upon the death of the owner by the application of the law of wills, estates, and trusts. Many aspects of the treatment of pets after the death of the owner remain the subject of varying state laws, and the Canadian law on pet trusts is unsettled.[95] Judges have had to sort out the meaning of statutes and administrative rules governing the treatment of pets that function as service animals.[96] The restrictive covenants of private homeowner associations that bar pets or certain breeds or species of pets from gated communities, bans on pets in leased private or public housing, and landlord restrictions on the possession of pets in rental property have required judicial interpretation.[97]

By treating pets as property, American and Canadian common law has compensated only the economic loss to human owners when a pet was injured or killed by the wrongful action of another.[98] Only six states and the District of Columbia have expressed a willingness to accept private suits requesting damages to compensate for the emotional distress of the owner.[99] The liability for damages issue is further complicated when the owner insures the pet, and when the pet is temporarily boarded in a kennel, in a stable, or by another person such as a groomer.[100] Rescue and humane organizations also can be liable for negligence for the placement of animals that injure persons, for placement of animals without proper appraisal of ownership, and for defamation of prior owners.[101] State legislatures have, however, adopted laws to limit liability for injuries suffered by horses during equestrian events and "livestock activity."[102] Regulations governing veterinary practice have limited veterinary malpractice cases in the United States, but the issue of compensation for injured cats, dogs, and horses remains unsettled.[103] Canadian provincial colleges of veterinarians and U.S. state veterinary boards can suspend licenses, reprimand, or fine veterinarians for malpractice, but, as with other types of quasi-public professional regulatory organizations, they cannot award damages to injured parties.[104]

The Implications of Benevolence and Property

Composed of well-to-do activists, the nineteenth-century anti-cruelty movement reframed the identity, moral duties, and law and policies that affected pets in ways that resonate today. Their actions resulted in the identification of cats, dogs, and horses as a specific category of regulated property. Legislators and judges therefore affirmed that pets were property: an "interest," "thing," or "artifact" with a socially relevant use *and* a commodity value.

The value could be in the pets use as a benevolent companion. Thus pets remained useful as long as the animal reacted to human desires. Of course, when human sentiments were not reciprocated and the animal became a nuisance, moral disengagement could set in and the pet could be left—legally—to sale, abandonment, or death.[105] As a common nuisance or nuisance property, its use value as companion subject to benevolent acts thus evaporated.

Also during the nineteenth and early twentieth century, pets, especially purebred cats and dogs, gradually became a *commodity* with value in exchanges. However, the commodification of cats, dogs, and horses in quantitative or monetary terms remained incomplete.[106] Prior to the twentieth century it was rare to find economic exchanges of cats and dogs that produced any denomination of their monetary value as a commodity. Only horses possessed value as a commodity bred for exchange. However, the moral disengagement encouraged by commodification of horses at least taught that all animals potentially could be bought and sold and treated with care or disregard as with any chattels.[107]

ANIMAL WELFARE: HUMAN STEWARDSHIP AND LEGALIZED ACCOUNTABILITY

During the first decades of the twentieth century, the passage of anti-cruelty legislation in Canada and the United States left the leading animal-oriented interest groups without a political cause. Many groups focused efforts on the provision of shelters for cats and dogs, animal health programs, and childhood humane education.[108] The only exception to these efforts was the emergence of anti-vivisection organizations in Britain and the United States. Their members' disgust with the immorality of the infliction of pain by medical professionals and scientists who used dissection in the study of physiology led them to seek laws to end vivisection.[109] Yet, they failed to expand the debate about the meaning of animal cruelty to cover medical research that injured or killed companion animals.

By mid-century, however, some individuals and interest groups began to reframe the human–companion animal relationship in terms of stewardship. The political agenda of animal welfare proponents rested on mid-twentieth-century suppositions about the role of the state that encouraged more extensive governmental intervention to affect the lives of cats, dogs, and horses. These suppositions altered nineteenth-century assumptions about (1) the meaning of the public good of animal protection activity, (2) the location and desirability of governmental administrative power, and (3) the role of law and regulation as a means of social control.[110]

First, instead of focusing on the penalization of the sadistic treatment of animals as a moral evil or affront to sentimental values, animal welfare proponents aimed at the elimination of passive cruelty and the establishment of the welfare of animals as a social good. As articulated by Kimberly Smith, the underlying aim of animal welfare proponents became the protection of "individual animals by protecting good human/animal relationships. The best protection for animal welfare is to promote those relationships by supporting good practices of animal husbandry and stewardship." This requires that people begin to "speak to and for them" and that humans align their interests with those of animals.[111]

Consequently a "duty to care" has become a central part of the mission of *private* associations that seek to prevent the destruction or suffering of cats, dogs, and horses. For example, acting as caretakers, some local groups have established new no-kill shelters. Rescue groups, often specializing in the adoption of horses or specific breeds of dogs or cats, have attracted supporters and created informal national networks. Unlike the policymakers and interest groups who regarded the destruction of unwanted pets as a humane means for the management of a problem created by undisciplined pet keeping, the proponents of no-kill shelters and rescue have regarded themselves as stewards who protect and fight for the lives of abandoned pets. They consider all pets as adoptable and work to find perfect adopters.[112] The welfare groups thus created dispersed forms of private governance of pets, and a variety of practices emerged to govern pet welfare in different sites in relation to different objectives.[113]

Second, for the activists and interest groups concerned about animal welfare, law and the administrative power of the state still was viewed as a powerful tool to support the ethic and techniques of responsible stewardship. During the 1950s the development of national interest groups concerned about responsible stewardship, such as the Humane Society of the United States and Canadian Federation of Humane Societies, provided a means for greater nationwide education about cruelty and political pressure for national political action to protect cats, dogs, and horses. For example, national groups used stories of the abuse of cats, dogs, and other animals in laboratories to lobby for the adoption of U.S. federal legislation to manage the care of animals used in scientific experiments: the Animal Welfare Act of 1966.[114] National groups also pressed state, provincial, and local governments for regulatory actions to protect cats, dogs, and horses. Such regulation required the creation or expansion of the power of administrative agencies, a change that welfare interest groups usually viewed as necessary for animal welfare.

Third, welfare activists and groups pursued the enactment of a broad range of laws and regulations to protect the physical and emotional needs of animals, to legally defend them from exploitation and varieties of cruelty, and to secure respect and compassion for them. For the advocates of the stewardship of animal welfare, legality could extend the range of prohibitions on the passive as well as sadistic abuse of pets. Advocates also believed that law could serve as an educational instrument and convey affirmative ideals about the responsible treatment of animals. Therefore welfare and responsible stewardship groups have concentrated in particular on change in what they have regarded as a nineteenth-century legacy of weak state, provincial, and local anti-cruelty laws and law enforcement efforts.

At the federal, state, and provincial levels, individual activists and professionally managed interest groups alerted officials to the weaknesses of anti-cruelty laws and mobilized animal lovers to lobby for tougher protection laws and to pressure officials to employ administrators to enforce these laws. Testimony at legislative hearings and the encouragement of media reportage of incidents of extreme cruelty and pet hoarding has abetted the lobbying.[115] Using these political tactics, animal stewardship proponents have sought animal anti-cruelty laws with specific penalties for denial of adequate food, water, shelter, exercise space, light, and sanitary living conditions; tougher penalties for abandonment, mutilation, poisoning, and inhumane transport of animals; increased length of criminal sentences or felony status for various acts of cruelty; compensation for the costs of animal care or forfeiture of the animal attached to a sentence upon conviction for animal cruelty; required psychological counseling or treatment upon conviction for animal cruelty; and expansion of requirements for veterinarians to report and prevent cruelty. They have pressed for laws that assign arrest powers to humane officers, agencies to regulate puppy mills, animal breeders, and sales of companion animals, and laws to prevent the slaughter of horses. Their efforts also have included lobbying for spay/neuter legislation to prevent the public health and safety problems and the destruction of abandoned pets they associated with uncontrolled or inhumane breeding. They have sought policies to permit trap, neuter, and return (TNR) of feral cats to the wild and pursued policies and funding to support public no-kill shelters. They have often supported more aggressive enforcement of dog licensing and the creation of cat licensing to generate funding for shelters, as a check on pet hoarding, and as a way to identify people who do not exercise a duty of care toward pets. They have provided relief for pets during disasters. And some welfare groups have campaigned against local, state, and provincial efforts to ban and eventually eliminate specific breeds of dogs such as pit bulls.[116]

Although stewardship encouraged moral engagement with sadistic and passive cruelty, greater legalized accountability for the treatment of pets, and the development of governmental agencies to enforce the law, its proponents often have neglected to address the passive cruelty of the destruction of unwanted pets. Stewardship proponents have also implied that pets remained property, albeit a much more broadly governmentally regulated and protected property. Yet, greater concern about pets did not supplant a pragmatic normative stance toward animals. On one hand, many humans objected to the suffering and exploitation of animals as immoral; however, they continued to rely on cultural norms that assumed humans could use animals for social prestige and could destroy nuisance animals that threatened public health.[117] The identification of pets as objects of human stewardship therefore has selectively protected pets from abuses.[118]

ANIMALS' LEGAL RIGHTS

During the 1970s a distinctively different perspective on the status of animals emerged, one that originated in avant-garde legal and environmental intellectual circles. Drawing on the use of rights discourse by racial minorities and women in their struggle for equality and arguments for environmental rights, in April 1973 philosopher Peter Singer published an essay in the *New York Review of Books* that called for "animal liberation."[119] Singer's call for animal liberation rested upon conceptual paradigms, categories, and language developed with his Oxford University colleagues. They consciously sought to create a new "meaning" for animals.[120] Soon expanded into a book, Singer's essay set forth a call for humans to exercise a moral duty to avoid inflicting pain and dependency upon animals. He furnished an ideational "trigger" for new political demands for animal protection and an attack on anthropocentrism.[121] Exploding in thousands of books, articles, and websites during the decades after the publication of Singer's article, the idea of "animal rights" or the legal autonomy of animals matured as an argument against anthropocentrism.[122] Additionally it resulted in the development of the Universal Declaration of Animal Rights proclaimed at UNESCO headquarters in Paris in 1978.[123]

The emergence of the idea of animal legal rights has attracted a devoted cadre of activists and supporters. Movement members often have adopted a rigid moral orientation on issues and behaviors affecting animals.[124] Their objective is an end to animal subjectivity and the recognition that at least companion animals "are not about oneself. ... They are not a projection or a realization of an intention, nor the telos of anything."[125] Animal legal rights therefore require the end of an "asymmetrical relationship" of humans and pets and the assumption that pets are dependent on humans. Instead the relationship is to either be one of mutuality in which the pet and human each satisfy the other's needs or, for some activists, simply not exist.[126]

However, as the movement for legal rights has matured, intellectual fissures have occurred.[127] Although legal rights proponents recognize that animals are sentient beings and deserve the same respect as humans, animal legal rights activists have divided on the detailed meaning of these assertions. The divisions can be arrayed along a continuum between poles of "utilitarianism" and "absolutism" or "abolitionism." The utilitarians do not treat all animals as rights-bearing subjects in all contexts. For utilitarians "reasonableness" or a "compelling interest" for restrictions on animal legal rights to protect human health and safety could limit the protection afforded by the rights. The absolutists have treated the legal rights of animals as an absolute moral requirement. For some absolutists, even the keeping of pets violates the legal rights of animals. However, as with many utilitarians, the absolutist version of animal legal rights demands that courts and legislatures prevent varieties of human exploitation of animals.[128]

Although it is difficult to sort out shared values amidst such a large outpouring of prescriptive ideas and policy proposals, there are a few key points of commonality among the diverse groups of animal legal rights theorists and proponents. In particular the animal legal rights movement seeks a significant extension of the role of law and legal institutions to govern the lives of animals.[129] Therefore, most animal legal rights activists thus have come to accept several political and legal principles:

Egalitarianism. Animals have an independent, autonomous identity and, hence, rights and liberties, equal to but separate from those of humans.[130] Proof of this identity is revealed in scientific studies of animal individuality, cognition, self-awareness, and emotions.[131] Laws should be enacted to protect the moral dignity or cognitive and emotional independence of companion animals from anthropocentric human behavior and arbitrary threats to their lives and to defend the liberty of animals to live in as natural conditions as possible. To enable the courts to protect the equality of companion animals with humans, animal legal rights advocates argue that companion animals have "natural rights" to a form of "personhood" that political institutions must respect. These rights can be secured through the passage of "animal bills of rights" or other legislation that defines the legal equality and rights of pets.

Guardianship. Humans have a moral duty to respect the autonomous identity of animals.[132] Animals should be freed from human domination, exploitation, cruelty, or discrimination (an attack on "speciesism"[133]). Therefore, humans can no longer serve as owners of animals as property. Instead, they are the legal guardians of animals, including "adopted" companion animals. Laws thus are to be adapted to provide legal requirements—often stated in written documents with accompanying duties or "legal detriments"—on guardianship and pet adoption. Companion animals also are no longer property that is part of a person's estate but beings whose welfare, as with a child, is held in trust.[134] Therefore, the liberty of animals can only be restricted by legislation adopted by representatives of the community, not the choices of "owners" of animals.

Legal standing. To defend their autonomous identity, animals have the capacity to demand legal protection from harms caused by governments or private persons.[135] The ability to legally assert rights in court especially can immunize animals against many or all acts of human domination. Consequently, as first articulated in an article by Christopher Stone and publicized through U.S. Supreme Court Justice William O. Douglas's dissenting opinion in *Sierra Club v. Morton*, the legal leadership of the animal legal rights movement has argued for the conferral of legal standing upon environmental objects so that they might litigate for their preservation as a species or entity.[136]

Assistance in the exercise of legal rights. Animals should be expected to exercise rights as relatively independent legal subjects.[137] This principle assumes that rights are an instrument of political power that can negate governmental actions or transform social relations.[138] To effectuate the power of animal rights, some humans should act *parens patriae* to defend the cognitive and emotional interests of rights-bearing animals from harm. A human, often an attorney, would represent the interests of a nonhuman entity before the law. As guardian *ad litem*, much as the guardian of a minor child or ward, the attorney might claim a companion animal deserves rights protections. This might include the rights to "life, liberty, and property" of humans protected against state action by the Fourteenth Amendment of the U.S. Constitution or Section 15 of the Canadian Charter of Rights and Freedoms, to challenge laws and seek civil damages for state actions that affronted these rights, to seek civil damages for other injuries to body or mind through personal injury, tort litigation, and to seek injunctions and other equitable relief for potential or completed injuries to pets.[139]

Proponents of animal legal rights initially concentrated their efforts on securing the rights of animals that do not have much direct contact with humans: laboratory animals, wildlife and marine species, animals used in circuses and entertainment, and agricultural animals.[140] However, beginning in the 1970s a host of new organized interests organized to make the principles of animal legal rights an element in a campaign to reorient companion animal law.[141] Some of the animal legal rights activists and groups have employed an "inside" strategy and used legislative lobbying and litigation to change the legal identity of animals from property to independent being. The policy proposals of these groups that affect companion animals often include calls for animal bills of rights, bans on the use of companion animals for scientific or commercial animal experimentation and laboratory use, bans on the killing of companion animals in religious rituals, the establishment of no-kill shelters for abandoned pets, and requirements to teach animal legal rights in the public schools.[142]

Some groups devoted to animal legal rights have developed an "outside" strategy in which members engage in peaceful civil disobedience in an attempt to influence public opinion. Other groups resist and violate the law by engaging in acts of violence toward property and people.[143] Consequently, to deter violence against animals regarded as victims, these activists engage in acts of "redemptive" violence against humans they identify as the perpetrators of harms against animals. For example, activists have assaulted individuals wearing fur in efforts to mobilize political action against the legal trapping of wildlife. Although penalized for such actions, the activists accept the penalty as a form of martyrdom in a quest for a legalized social identity, normative status, and legal standing for pets.

To date the activists and groups supporting the animal legal rights identity have delivered shocking evidence about the treatment of animals for commercial purposes. They have placed issues of animal abuse on the political agenda. Group strategies such as protests and civil disobedience have provided forums for the promotion of the idea of animal legal rights. Overall, the movement has expanded the struggle over the human treatment of animals and intensified policy debates. However, as we will detail later in this book, the animal legal rights groups have not effectively participated in the lobbying, legislative testimony, support for candidates, and publicity campaigns that might influence the municipal, state, or provincial policymakers who write much animal-related legislation. During their protests they have often derided more modest efforts to regulate animal owners and questioned the need for pets.[144]

PETS AS COMMODITY

Despite the efforts of supporters of companion animal stewardship and animal legal rights, the anthropocentric message of human dominion and the disengagement of humans from the suffering of companion animals remains deeply rooted in contemporary social practice.[145] Today the identification of pets as subjects of human discretion largely lacks the religious, philosophical, and social class foundations of the early modern identity of human dominion.[146] Instead, the contemporary identity rests more on a far-reaching vision of human freedom to acquire, use, and exchange commodities that is accompanied by a truncated sense of civic responsibilities, moral engagement, and legalized accountability for one's actions toward companion animals. This identity privileges human self-interest, and it identifies animals as a commodity that exists for the benefit of humans. As expressed by Victor Bakke, the attorney for a commercial dog breeding facility manager, dogs are nothing more than "breeding machines." "They're filthy but these are not household animals. They are equivalent to farm animals. They're being housed, fed and bred, and that's basically all that's required."[147]

Consequently, today some persons employ an economic calculus to define human duties toward animals. The calculus assumes that individual or social benefits, defined as efficiently selling or renting pets, eating animals, or exterminating unwanted or threatening animals, can outweigh the costs of the protection of pets from abuse or death.[148] The commodity identification of animals holds that legislative efforts to protect pets must have an economic justification and not impinge on private decisions about the use or exchange of animals. However, negligence or passive cruelty without social benefits, such as the hoarding or torture of animals, can be restricted as crime. Also, property that creates social costs, such as vicious dogs, can be seized from owners and destroyed (much as with child pornography or cocaine). Otherwise, animal regulatory laws are irrational or "extreme" affronts to use "big government" to encroach upon individual freedom.

The contemporary commodity identity of companion animals finds expression in the animal use policy positions held by a wide range of agricultural, hunting, and recreational organized interests, their legislative allies, and governmental law enforcement and agricultural agencies. These interests have pursued policies to protect their economic interest in the unregulated use of animals for commercial purposes by agribusinesses and pet breeders and the research use of companion animals by the pharmaceutical and cosmetics industries.

For example, commercial agricultural and pharmaceutical corporations induced the U.S. Congress to adopt the Animal Enterprise Protection Act (AEPA) of 1992 that established criminal penalties for interstate travel or use of the mails to cause a physical disruption in the operations of an animal enterprise.[149] To achieve even more protection of their business, commercial animal interests continued to press for stronger legal protection of their interests. They secured the passage of the U.S. federal Animal Enterprise Terrorism Act (AETA) of 2006 to criminalize intentional damages or loss of any real or personal property such as animals or records used by an animal enterprise or connected to or in a relationship with an animal enterprise. The AETA also criminalized any intentional action or conspiracy that endangers persons or threatens acts of vandalism, property damage, criminal trespass, and intimidation at such enterprises.[150]

A majority of U.S. states have adopted other laws that protect the treatment of animals as a commodity. These laws make it a criminal offense for persons to enter or conceal themselves without permission in an animal facility closed to the public, such as a kennel or racetrack, with the intent to disrupt operations or do physical damage to the property, animals, records, and equipment, to record electronically activity at the facility, or to free animals from confinement.[151] Additionally, groups with an economic interest in animals have pressured state legislatures to adopt so-called ag-gag laws. These laws criminalize efforts by anonymous groups or individuals to disseminate recorded activity or allegedly false statements about the operation of an animal facility, including a dog breeding kennel and horse stables and riding academies.[152] These laws are evidence of the influence of the commodity identification on the meaning of contemporary pet politics.

CONCLUSION

What ideas and laws have contributed to the attitudes and practices of contemporary pet politics decision making? The answer provided in this chapter is that over centuries the public, intellectuals, and political activists have framed multiple identities, conceptions of cruelty, and policies and laws to define the appropriate treatment of dogs, cats, and horses. Although the identities of pets, norms, and laws and policies emerged through a historical sequence of intellectual theorizing and legislation, each has persisted. Humans have "not yet reached an agreement on the ontological status" or single frame through which they perceive animals. Political elites and the public have yet to agree on the core principles which should constitute the policies and laws about the status of cats, dogs, and horses in North America. Unlike public policies that change incrementally or undergo substantial alteration or conversion into new policies at specific "punctuation points,"[153] the contingent identities and norms about animals and the persistence of older moral and legal perspectives about animals have created complex discontinuities and variability in contemporary policy. For example, in some contexts a dog is treated as a benevolent companion; however, should the same dog become a nuisance or a costly commodity, it can be cast aside as unnecessary. It also can be sold or rescued. This mutability of identities and norms affecting cats, dogs, and horses thus reinforces the contingent status of pets and provides a context for political struggles about their rational and just treatment by humans.

NOTES

1. Jacques Derrida, *The Animal That Therefore I Am*, ed. Marie-Louise Mallet, trans. David Will (New York: Fordham University Press, 2008), 20.
2. Jim Mason, "Animals: From Souls and the Sacred in Prehistoric Times to Symbols and Slaves in Antiquity," in *A Cultural History of Animals in Antiquity*, ed. Linda Kalof (Oxford: Berg, 2007), 31–45; Gary Steiner, *Anthropocentrism and its Discontents: The Moral Status of Animals in the History of Western Philosophy* (Pittsburgh: University of Pittsburgh Press, 2005); Matthew Calarco, *Zoographies: The Question of the Animal from Heidegger to Derrida* (New York: Columbia University Press, 2008); Kelly Oliver, *Animal Lessons: How They Teach Us to Be Human* (New York: Columbia University Press, 2009).
3. For an overview of the study of the historical context of cultural frames of animals, see Molly Mullin, "Mirrors and Windows: Sociocultural Studies of Human-Animal Relationships," *Annual Review of Anthropology* 28 (1999): 201–24. On the evolution of human classifications of animals, see Keith Tester, *Animals and Society: The Humanity of Animal Rights* (New York: Routledge, 1991),

72–146; Rod Preece, *Brute Souls, Happy Beasts, and Evolution: The Historical Status of Animals* (Vancouver: UBC Press, 2005).
4. Arthur O. Lovejoy, *The Great Chain of Being: A Study of the History of an Idea* (Cambridge, MA: Harvard University Press, 1936). For the origins of its views on animals, see Stephen T. Newmayer, "Animals in Ancient Philosophy: Conceptions and Misconceptions," in *A Cultural History of Animals in Antiquity*, 130–74.
5. Genesis 1:26 (New Revised Standard Version); see also Genesis 9:2–3 (New Revised Standard Version); Steiner, *Anthropocentrism and its Discontents*, 38–92, 112–52. For materials that indicate the persistence of an alternative frame of respect for the social identity and moral status of animals, see Rod Preece, *Awe for the Tiger: A Chronicle of Sensibility to Animals* (Vancouver: UBC Press, 2002), 3–90.
6. Gerald Carson, *Men, Beasts, and Gods: A History of Cruelty and Kindness to Animals* (New York: Charles Scribner's Sons, 1972), 3–24; Leviticus 1:1–16; 11:1–46 (New Revised Standard Version); Laura Hobgood-Oster, *Holy Dogs and Asses: Animals in Christian Tradition* (Urbana: University of Illinois Press, 2008), 21–80; Rod Preece and David Fraser, "The Status of Animals in Biblical and Christian Thought: A Study in Colliding Values," *Society and Animals* 8: 245–63; Esther Pascua, "From Forest to Farm: Domestic Animals from ca. 1000 to ca. 1450," in *A Cultural History of Animals in the Medieval Age*, ed. Brigette Resl (Oxford: Berg, 2007), 81–102.
7. Anonymous, *A Treatise of Oxen, Sheep, Hogs, and Dogs; with Their Natures, Qualities, and Uses* (London: Obadiah Blagrave, 1683), 43.
8. On the status of animals espoused by the literate classes, see Stephen R. L. Clark, "Animals in Classical and Late Antique Philosophy," in *The Oxford Handbook of Animal Ethics*, ed. Tom L. Beauchamp and R. G. Frey (New York: Oxford University Press, 2011), 35–60.
9. Hobgood-Oster, *Holy Dogs and Asses*, 81–106; Sophie Page, "Good Creation and Demonic Illusions," in *Cultural History of Animals in the Medieval Age*, 27–57.
10. Thomas G. Kelch, "A Short History of (Mostly) Western Animal Law Part I," *Animal Law* 19 (2012–2013): 23–62.
11. On this assumption, see E. S. Turner, *All Heaven in a Rage* (London: Michael Joseph, 1964), 28–118.
12. Arthur Macgregor, *Animal Encounters: Human and Animal Interaction in Britain from the Norman Conquest to World War One* (London: Reaktion Books, 2012), 14–15; see also the discussion of class and hunting law, 101–95.
13. William Blackstone, *Commentaries on the Laws of England,* 4 vols. (1765–1769; repr., Chicago: University of Chicago Press, 1979), 3: 14, 153, 211, 235; 4: 174–75, 243, 408–9; Erica Fudge, *Perceiving Animals: Humans and Beasts in Early*

Modern English Culture (Urbana: University of Illinois Press, 2002), 115–42; Jerrold Tannenbaum, "Animals and the Law: Property, Cruelty, Rights," in *Humans and Other Animals*, ed. Arien Mack (Columbus: Ohio State University Press, 1999), 145.

14. S. F. C. Milsom, *Historical Foundations of the Common Law* (London: Butterworths, 1981), 271–72, 295, 297–99, 310–12, 396.
15. Piers Bierne, *Confronting Animal Abuse: Law, Criminology, and Human-Animal Relationships* (Lanham, MD: Rowman and Littlefield, 2009), 21–40; David Favre and Vivien Tsang, "The Development of Anti-cruelty Laws during the 1800's," *Detroit College of Law Review* (1993): 5.
16. See Michael Dalton, *The Country Justice: Containing the Practice, Duty and Power of the Justices of the Peace, as well in as out of Their Sessions* (London: Henry Lintot, 1746). Editions of this work first appeared in 1618.
17. Dog Stealing Act, 1770, 10 George III. c. 18.
18. Macgregor, *Animal Encounters*, 116–21, 167–72.
19. Ibid., 198–209.
20. Carson, *Men, Beasts, and Gods*, 25–35; Esther Cohen, "Law, Folklore, and Animal Lore," *Past and Present* 110 (1986): 6–37; E. P. Evans, *The Criminal Prosecution and Capital Punishment of Animals* (London: Faber, 1906); Walker Woodburn Hyde, "The Prosecution and Punishment of Animals and Lifeless Things in the Middle Ages and Modern Times," *University of Pennsylvania Law Review* 64 (1916): 696; Mark S. R. Jenner, "The Great Dog Massacre," in *Fear in Early Modern Society*, ed. William G. Naphy and Penny Roberts (Manchester: Manchester University Press, 1997), 44–61.
21. Robert Darnton, *The Great Cat Massacre and Other Episodes in French Cultural History* (New York: Vintage Books, 1985), 75–104; Katharine M. Rogers, *The Cat and the Human Imagination: Feline Images from Bast to Garfield* (Ann Arbor: University of Michigan Press, 2001), 45–82, 173–85. See also James Serpell, "Domestication and the History of the Cat," in *The Domestic Cat: The Biology of Its Behaviour*, 2nd ed., ed. Dennis C. Turner and Patrick Bateson (Cambridge: Cambridge University Press, 2000), 186–90.
22. See Peter Edwards, *Horse and Man in Early Modern England* (London: Hambledon Continuum, 2007), 17–34; Peter Edwards, "Domesticated Animals in Renaissance Europe," in *A Cultural History of Animals in the Renaissance*, ed. Bruce Boehrer (Oxford: Berg, 2007), 78–84.
23. Sale of Horses Act, 1555, 2 & 3 Philip & Mary c. 7.
24. Edwards, *Horse and Man*, 69–88, 211–33; see also Macgregor, *Animal Encounters*, 75–92, 101–95; Karen Raber and Treva J. Tucker, "Introduction," in *The Culture of the Horse: Status, Discipline, and Identity in the Early Modern World* (New York: Palgrave Macmillan, 2005), 1–34.
25. Gaming Act, 1739, 13 George II, c. 19; Edwards, *Horse and Man*, 89–117.

26. Edwards, *Horse and Man*, 183–209.
27. Ibid., 35–67.
28. Peter Edwards, "Nature Bridled: The Treatment and Training of Horses in Early Modern England," in *Beastly Natures: Animals, Humans, and the Study of History*, ed. Dorothee Brantz (Charlottesville: University of Virginia Press, 2010), 155–75.
29. Akron ex rel. Christman-Resch v. Akron, 825 N.E.2d 189 (Ohio App. 2005); Verne R. Smith, "The Law and Feral Cats," *Journal of Animal Law and Ethics* 3 (2009): 17–18.
30. Simon Bond, *101 Uses for a Dead Cat* (New York: Clarkson N. Potter, 1981); Simon Bond, *101 More Uses for a Dead Cat* (New York: Clarkson N. Potter, 1982); Robert Daphne, *How to Kill Your Girlfriend's Cat* (New York: Doubleday, 1988); Skip Morrow, *The Official I Hate Cats Book* (New York: Holt, Rinehart, and Winston, 1980); Rogers, *The Cat and the Human Imagination*, 163–64.
31. Philip Howell, "Flush and the *Banditti:* Dog-Stealing in Victorian London," in *Animal Spaces: Beastly Places: New Geographies of Human-Animal Relations*, ed. Chris Philo and Chris Wilbert (London: Routledge 2000), 34–55.
32. Dog Stealing Act, 1845, 8 & 9 Victoria, c. 47.
33. Harriet Ritvo, "Animals in Nineteenth-Century Britain: Complicated Attitudes and Competing Categories," in *Animals and Human Society*, 106–26; Thomas G. Kelch, "A Short History of (Mostly) Western Animal Law Part II," *Animal Law* 19 (2012–2013): 348–59.
34. Aaron Garrett, "Animals and Ethics in the History of Modern Philosophy," in *The Oxford Handbook of Animal Ethics*, 61–87; Andreas-Holger Maehle, "Cruelty and Kindness to the 'Brute Creation': Stability and Change in the Ethics of the Man-Animal Relationship, 1600–1850," in *Animals and Human Society*, 81–105; Karen Raber, "From Sheep to Meat, From Pets to People," in *A Cultural History of Animals in the Age of Enlightenment*, ed. Matthew Senior (Oxford: Berg, 2009), 73–99; Kathryn Shevelow, *For the Love of Animals: The Rise of the Animal Protection Movement* (New York: Henry Holt and Co., 2008), 17–38, 106–81.
35. Thomas Taylor, *A Vindication of the Rights of Brutes* (London: Edward Jeffery, 1792), 9, 103. See also Bierne, *Confronting Animal Abuse*, 43–56, 69–88; Fudge, *Perceiving Animals*; Keith Thomas, *Man and the Natural World: Changing Attitudes in England 1500–1800* (New York: Oxford University Press, 1983), 17–191; Erica Fudge, *Brutal Reasoning: Animals, Rationality, and Humanity in Early Modern England* (Ithaca, NY: Cornell University Press, 2006); Preece, *Awe for the Tiger*, 123–76.
36. "The General Deliverance (Sermon 60), in *The Sermons of John Wesley*, ed. Thomas Jackson, accessed Oct. 15, 2009, http://wesley.nnu.edu/john_wesley/sermons/060.htm.
37. Jeremy Bentham, *Introduction to the Principles of Morals and Legislation*

(London: T. Payne and Son, 1789), 308–9; Moira Ferguson, *Animal Advocacy and Englishwomen, 1780–1900: Patriots, Nation, and Empire* (Ann Arbor: University of Michigan Press, 1997), 7–73; Christine Kenyon-Jones, *Kindred Brutes: Animals in Romantic-Period writing* (Burlington, VT: Ashgate, 2001); Kathleen Kete, "Animals and Human Empire," in *A Cultural History of Animals in the Age of Empire*, ed. Kathleen Kete (Oxford: Berg, 2007), 1–24; David Perkins, *Romanticism and Animal Rights* (Cambridge: Cambridge University Press, 2003); Preece, *Awe for the Tiger*, 177–264.

38. Susan J. Pearson, *The Rights of the Defenseless: Protecting Animals and Children in Gilded Age America* (Chicago: University of Chicago Press, 2011), 21–76.

39. M. J. D. Roberts, *Making English Morals: Voluntary Association and Moral Reform in England, 1787–1886* (Cambridge: Cambridge University Press, 2004); Kathleen Kete, *The Beast in the Boudoir: Petkeeping in Nineteenth-Century Paris* (Berkeley: University of California Press, 1994), 22–38; Thomas, *Man and the Natural World*, 100–20.

40. "Abraham Lincoln's Dog-Fido," Abraham Lincoln Research Site, accessed Aug. 24, 2012, http://americacomesalive.com/2013/07/17/abraham-lincolns-dog-fido/.

41. Dorothee Brantz, "The Domestication of Empire: Human-Animal Relations at the Intersection of Civilization, Evolution, and Acclimatization in the Nineteenth Century," in *Cultural History of Animals in the Age of Empire*, 73–93; Hilda Kean, The Moment of Greyfriars Bobby: The Changing Cultural Position of Animals, 1800–1920," in *Cultural History of Animals in the Age of Empire*, 25–46; Ritvo, "Animals in Nineteenth-Century Britain," 125–30.

42. Brian Harrison, "Religion and Recreation in Nineteenth-Century England," *Past and Present* 38 (1967): 98–125; Chien-hui Li, "A Union of Christianity, Humanity, and Philanthropy: The Christian Tradition and the Prevention of Cruelty to Animals in Nineteenth-Century England," *Society and Animals* 8 (2000): 265–85.

43. Anna Sewell, *Black Beauty: The Autobiography of a Horse* (New York: T. Y. Crowell & Co., 1877, 1895); Margaret Marshall Saunders, *Beautiful Joe: An Autobiography* (Philadelphia: The Griffith and Rowland Press, 1893). Pearson, *The Rights of the Defenseless*, 36–56, examines this literature and affective discipline more extensively.

44. Elizabeth Hirschman, "Consumers and Their Animal Companions," *Journal of Consumer Research* 20 (1994): 618, 621–22; Charles Phineas, "Household Pets and Urban Alienation," *Journal of Social History* 7 (1974): 342.

45. Stanley Coren, "Do People Look Like Their Dogs?," *Anthrozoös* 12 (1999): 111–14; Sadahiko Nakajima, Mariko Yamamoto, and Natsumi Yoshimoto, "Dogs Look Like Their Owners: Replications with Racially Homogenous Owner Portraits," *Anthrozoös* 22 (2009): 173–81; Christina Payne and Klaus

Jaffe, "Self Seeks Like: Many Humans Choose Their Dog Pets Following Rules Used for Assortative Mating," *Journal of Ethology* 23 (2005): 15–18; Michael M. Roy and Nicolas J. S. Christenfeld, "Do Dogs Resemble Their Owners?," *Psychological Science* 15 (2004): 361–63.

46. P. Elizabeth Anderson, *The Powerful Bond between People and Pets: Our Boundless Connections to Companion Animals* (Westport, CT: Praeger, 2008), 162–80.

47. See the discussion in James Serpell, *In the Company of Animals: A Study of Human-Animal Relationships,* Canto edition (Cambridge: Cambridge University Press, 1996), 23–42; and the anecdotes and analysis in Kathleen Szasz, *Petishism? Pets and Their People in the Western World* (New York: Holt, Rinehart and Winston, 1968), 97–144.

48. Morton J. Horwitz, *The Transformation of American Law, 1780–1860* (Cambridge: Harvard University Press, 1977); Christopher L. Tomlins., *Law, Labor, and Ideology in the Early American Republic* (New York: Cambridge University Press, 1993), 21–34.

49. The idea of a support structure as a component of legal change appears in Charles R. Epp, *The Rights Revolution: Lawyers, Activists, and Supreme Courts in Comparative Perspective* (Chicago: University of Chicago Press, 1998). Epp depicts support structures that rely on litigation to achieve legal change, a tactic uncommon among animal welfare proponents of the nineteenth century. Those activists-supporters preferred the use of publicity and lobbying to achieve legislative change.

50. James M. Jasper, *The Art of Moral Protest: Culture, Biography, and Creativity in Social Movements* (Chicago: University of Chicago Press, 1997), 159–80, describes the use of moral shock to reconfigure human's' perspectives on the social identity and moral status of animals.

51. Arthur W. Moss, *Valiant Crusade: The History of the R.S.P.C.A.* (London: Cassell, 1961), 11–19; and especially Shevelow, *For the Love of Animals,* 182–279, offer detailed accounts of these efforts with special attention to the efforts of Richard Martin, a policy entrepreneur engaged in the "sale" of animal protection proposals to Parliament. The text of the 1822 law is reprinted in Shevelow, *For the Love of Animals,* 285–88. See also Richard D. Ryder, *Animal Revolution: Changing Attitudes Towards Speciesism* (London: Bloomsbury Academic, 2000), 79–84; James Turner, *Reckoning with the Beast: Animals, Pain, and Humanity in the Victorian Mind* (Baltimore: The Johns Hopkins University Press, 1980), 39–45.

52. Brian Harrison, "Animals and the State in Nineteenth-Century England," *English Historical Review* 88 (1973): 787–92; Moss, *Valiant Crusade,* 20–32.

53. On the treatment of horses in the nineteenth century, see Clay McShane and Joel A. Tarr, "The Horse in the Nineteenth Century American City," in *Beastly Natures,* 227–45.

54. Harrison, "Animals and the State," 793–804, 810–20; Moss, *Valiant Crusade*, 48–116; Harriet Ritvo, *The Animal Estate: The English and Other Creatures in the Victorian Age* (Cambridge, MA: Harvard University Press, 1987), 130–57.
55. Harrison, "Religion and Recreation in Nineteenth-Century England," 102–3, 108, 116–19.
56. Tester, *Animals and Society*, 94–120.
57. Diane L. Beers, *For the Prevention of Cruelty: The History and Legacy of Animal Rights Activism in the United States* (Athens: Swallow Press/Ohio University Press, 2006), 24–35; Turner, *Reckoning with the Beast*, 45–46.
58. The importance of the role of policy entrepreneurs whose leadership in the definition, creation, organization and maintenance of animal welfare and legal rights groups is set forth in Robert Garner, *Political Animals: Animal Protection Politics in Britain and the United States* (New York: St. Martin's Press, 1998), 73–75.
59. Favre and Tsang, "The Development of Anti-cruelty Laws," 14–18; *New York Revised Statutes* §§ 375.1 et seq. (1867).
60. Beers, *For the Prevention of Cruelty*, 40–45; Carson, *Men, Beasts, and Gods*, 87–106; Sydney H. Coleman, *Humane Society Leaders in America, with a Sketch of the Early History of the Humane Movement in England* (Albany, NY: The American Humane Association, 1924), 33–64; Tannenbaum, "Animals and the Law," 152–53; Turner, *Reckoning with the Beast*, 46–48.
61. Favre and Tsang, "The Development of Anti-cruelty Laws," 20–22.
62. Davis v. American Society for the Prevention of Cruelty to Animals, 75 N.Y. 362 (1873); Favre and Tsang, "The Development of Anti-cruelty Laws," 18–20; Pearson, *The Rights of the Defenseless*, 151–84; Susan J. Pearson and Kimberly K. Smith, "Developing Animal Welfare Law," in *Statebuilding from the Margins: Between Reconstruction and the New Deal*, ed. Carol Nackenhoff and Julie Novkov (Philadelphia: University of Pennsylvania Press, 2014), 130–35.
63. Favre and Tsang, "The Development of Anti-cruelty Laws," 22–30.
64. Beers, *For the Prevention of Cruelty*, 60–66, 72–75; Turner, *Reckoning with the Beast*, 122.
65. Beatrice Johnston, *For Those Who Cannot Speak: A History of the Canadian Society for the Prevention of Cruelty to Animals* (Laval, PQ: Dev-sco Publications, 1970). See also Elaine L. Hughes and Christiane Meyer, "Animal Welfare Law in Canada and Europe," *Animal Law* 6 (2000): 25–29.
66. American courts have recognized the property status of domestic animals since at least Pierson v. Post, 3 Caines 175 (N.Y. Sup. Ct. 1805).
67. For an example of current state laws on this point, see *Connecticut General Statutes Annotated* § 22-350–§ 22-351; *Virginia Code Annotated* § 3.2-6585. The U.S. Animal Welfare Act assumes pets are an item of commerce, 7 U.S.C. §§ 2131–2159. On Canada, see Jacqueline Shaw, "Dangerous Dogs in

Canadian Law," Animal Legal and Historical Center, Michigan State University College of Law, accessed Nov. 9, 2009, https://www.animallaw.info/article/dangerous-dogs-canadian-law.
68. But see *West Virginia Code* §19-20-1, "Any dog shall be and is hereby declared to be personal property within the meaning and construction of the laws of this State, and any dog above the age of six months shall be subject to taxation" (enacted in 1925).
69. See for example Norton v. Ladd, 5 N.H. 203 (1830); Haywood v. Arkansas, 41 Ark. 479 (1883); Thurston v. Carter, 112 Me. 361 (1914).
70. Blair vs. Forehand, 100 Mass. 136, 140–41 (1868). See also State v. Bruner, 12 N.E. 103 (Ind. 1887).
71. Sentell v. New Orleans and Carrollton Railroad, 166 U.S. 698, 701 (1897).
72. Ebers v. MacEachern, 3 D.L.R. 415 (1932).
73. Criminal Code, *Revised Statutes of Canada*, 1985, c. C-46, s. 445.1, 446, 447.1. See also s. 264.1 (1) c.
74. Animal Protection Act, 1999, *The Statutes of Saskatchewan*, Chap. A-21.1 2 (4).
75. *Revised Statutes of Ontario*, 1990, c. D.16.
76. *Harvard College v. Canada (Commissioner of Patents)*, [2002] S.C.J. No. 77, at 100 (Sup. Ct. of Canada) (Binnie, J., dissenting).
77. Lincoln v. Smith, 27 Vt. 328, 343 (1855). For a recent application of this construction, see Altman v. City of High Point, 330 F.3d 194 (4th Cir. 2003).
78. David Favre and Peter L. Borchelt, *Animal Law and Dog Behavior* (Tucson: Lawyers and Judges Publishing Co., 1999), 119–46, 154–56.
79. Pierre Schrag, "Rights in the Postmodern Condition," in *Legal Rights*, ed. Austin Sarat and Thomas R. Kearns (Ann Arbor: University of Michigan Press, 1996), 270–84.
80. William J. Novak, *The People's Welfare: Law and Regulation in Nineteenth-Century America* (Chapel Hill: University of North Carolina Press, 1996), 11. See also Markus Dirk Dubber, *The Police Power: Patriarchy and the Foundations of American Government* (New York: Columbia University Press, 2005), 81–119; Pearson, *The Rights of the Defenseless*, 76–97; Pearson and Smith, "Developing Animal Welfare Law," 125–28; Tomlins, *Law, Labor, and Ideology in the Early American Republic*, 47–98.
81. Dubber, *Police Power*, 113–15.
82. On the United States, see Dubber, *Police Power*, 104–19; On Canada, see British North America Act, sec. 91, (U.K.), 30 & 31 Victoria, c. 3; and Marianna Valverde, "'Peace, Order, and Good Government': Policelike Powers in Postcolonial Perspective," in *The New Police Science: The Police Power in Domestic and International Governance*, ed. Markus D. Dubber and Marianna Valverde (Stanford: Stanford University Press, 2006), 73–106.

83. See Pearson, *The Rights of the Defenseless,* 80–82; Cinadr v. Texas, 300 S.W. 64 (1927). For further discussion of this for the United States, see Sonia S. Waisman, Pamela D. Frasch, and Bruce A. Wagman, *Animal Law: Cases and Materials,* 3rd ed. (Durham: Carolina Academic Press, 2006), 161–81.
84. On the origins of the policing of rabies and animal-borne disease in Britain, see Ritvo, *Animal Estate,* 167–202; John K. Walton, "Mad Dogs and Englishmen: The Conflict over Rabies in Late Victorian England," *Journal of Social History* 13 (1979): 219–29.
85. Favre and Borchelt, *Animal Law and Dog Behavior,* 195–221; Tannenbaum, "Animals and the Law," 157–68.
86. Novak, *The People's Welfare,* 57–59, 65, 68–69, 72–79, 123–24, 137–39, 145, 177, 180, 212–15.
87. *Revised Statutes of Canada,* 1985, c. C-46, s. 445.1, 446, 447, 447.1, Part XI: Wilful and Forbidden Acts in Respect of Certain Property (amended 2008).
88. See Animal Protection Act, *Revised Statutes of Alberta,* 2000, c. A-41; Prevention of Cruelty to Animals Act, *Revised Statutes of British Columbia,* 1996, Chap. 372; Ontario Society for the Prevention of Cruelty to Animals Act, *Revised Statutes of Ontario,* 1990, c. O.36.
89. See Fagin v. Ohio Humane Society, 9 Ohio 341 (1898); Kete, *The Beast in the Boudoir,* 39–55, 97–114; Pearson and Smith, "Developing Animal Welfare Law," 128–29.
90. Missouri v. A. H. Bogardus, 4 Mo. App. 215 (Mo. Ct. App. 1877), a position confirmed nearly a century later, In the Matter of Chernik v. Dept. of Health of the City of New York, 330 N.Y.S.2d 910 (1972).
91. See Anderson, *The Powerful Bond between People and Pets,* 82–108, 142–53, 181–85; Katherine C. Grier, *Pets in America: A History* (Orlando: Harcourt, Inc., 2006), 231–40, 261–77, 281–95, 304–14; Jessica Greenebaum, "It's a Dog's Life: Elevating Status from Pet to 'Fur Baby' at Yappy Hour," *Society and Animals* 12 (2004): 117–35; Kete, *The Beast in the Boudoir,* 64–96.
92. Mark Derr, *Dog's Best Friend: Annals of the Dog-Human Bond* (Chicago: University of Chicago Press, 2004), 186–99, 215–28; Hirschman, "Consumers and Their Animal Companions," 617–18; Szasz, *Petishism?,* 145–87.
93. Hirschman, "Consumers and Their Animal Companions," 617, 620–21; Serpell, *In the Company of Animals,* 43–59.
94. Favre and Borchelt, *Animal Law and Dog Behavior,* 28–33.
95. For the United States, see *Uniform Probate Code* (1969) (Last Amended or Revised in 2010), Section 2-907, accessed July 30, 2012, http://www.uniformlaws.org/shared/docs/probate%20code/upc%202010.pdf; Shidon Aflatooni, "The Statutory Pet Trust: Recommendations for a New Uniform Law Based on the Past Twenty-One Years," *Animal Law* 18 (2011): 1–56; Paige Dowdakin,

"Revisiting Roxy Russell: How Current Companion Animal Trust and Custody Laws Affect Elderly Pet 'Guardians' in the Event of Death or Incapacity," *Elder Law Journal* 20 (2013): 411–47; Rachel Hirschfeld, *Petriarch: The Complete Guide to Financial and Legal Planning for a Pet's Continued Care* (New York: American Institute of Certified Public Accountants, 2010). For Canada, see Lesli Bisgould, *Animals and the Law* (Toronto: Irwin Law, 2011), 157–60. Some judges are beginning to treat pets more like children and consider the best interest of the pet in determining who gains custody of it. Judges have also awarded shared custody, visitation, and alimony payments to the owners: see Rebecca J. Huss, "Separation, Custody, and Estate Planning Issues Relating to Companion Animals," *University of Colorado Law Review* 74 (2003): 181–240; Stacy L. Kelly, "Ownership, Custody, and Keeping of Animals," in *Litigating Animal Law Disputes: A Complete Guide for Lawyers*, ed. Joan Schaffner and Julie Fershtman (Chicago: American Bar Association, 2009), 84–86; Arrington v. Arrington, 613 S.W.2d 565, 569 (Tex. Civ. App. 1981); Dickson v. Dickson, No. 94-1072 slip. op. at 2 (Ark. Garland Co. Ch. Ct. Oct. 14, 1994); Juelfs v. Gough, 41 P.3d 593 (Alaska 2002); Vargas v. Vargas, 1999 Conn. Super. LEXIS 3326 (Conn. Super. Ct. Nov. 30, 1999). For Canada, see Bisgould, *Animals and the Law*, 154–57.

96. Rebecca J. Huss, "Why Context Matters: Defining Service Animals Under Federal Law," *Pepperdine Law Review* 37 (2010): 1163–1215; Gary C. Norman, "The Disabled, Service Animals, and the Law," in *Litigating Animal Law Disputes*, 267–339.

97. For the United States, see Rebecca J. Huss, "The Pervasive Nature of Animal Law: How the Law Impacts the Lives of People and Their Animal Companions," *Valparaiso University Law Review* 43 (2009): 1137–45; Rebecca J. Huss, "No Pets Allowed: Housing Issues and Companion Animals," *Animal Law* 11 (2005): 69–127; David A. Furlow, "Hounded by Homeowner Associations and Dogged by Zoning Boards: Litigating Breed-Specific Restrictions," in *A Lawyer's Guide to Dangerous Dog Issues*, ed. Joan Schaffner (Chicago: American Bar Association, 2009), 75–86; and the older Favre and Borchelt, *Animal Law and Dog Behavior*, 81–86. For Canada, see Bisgould, *Animals and the Law*, 148–54.

98. See for examples Rabideau v. City of Racine, 627 N.W. 795 (Wisc. 2001); Medlen v. Strickland, 353 S.W. 576 (Tex. 2011).

99. See *Richardson v. Fairbanks North Star Borough*, 705 P.2d 454 (Alaska, 1985) (dog); *LaPorte v. Associated Independents, Inc.*, 163 So.2d 267 (Fla. 1964) (dog); *Campbell v. Animal Quarantine Station*, 632 P.2d 1066 (Hawaii, 1981) (dog); *Gill v. Brown*, 695 P.2d 1276 (Ida. App., 1985) (donkey); *Burgess v. Taylor*, 44 S.W.3d 806 (Ky. 2001) (horse); *Corso v. Crawford Dog and Cat Hospital, Inc.*, 415 N.Y.S.2d (182 N.Y. City Civ. Ct., 1979) (dog); *Hyland v. Borras*, 719 A.2d 662 (N.J. Super. A.D., 1998); *Amons v. District of Columbia*, 231 F. Supp 2d. 109 (D.D.C. 2002);

Favre and Borchelt, *Animal Law and Dog Behavior*, 52–64; Sabrina Defabritiis, "Barking Up The Wrong Tree: Companion Animals, Emotional Damages and the Judiciary's Failure to Keep Pace," *Northern Illinois University Law Review* 32 (2012): 237–66; Ronald B. Lansing, "The Animal Companion Puzzle: A Worth Unknown Though Height Taken," *Animal Law* 18 (2011): 105–30; Marcella S. Roukas, "Determining the Value of Companion Animals in Wrongful Harm or Death Claims: A Survey of U.S. Decisions and Legislative Proposal in Florida to Authorize Recovery for Loss of Companionship," *Journal of Animal Law* 3 (2007): 45–58; Sonia S. Waisman, "Non-Economic Damages: Where Does It Get Us and How Do We Get There," *Journal of Animal Law* 1 (2005): 7–21; Lauren M. Sirois, "Recovering for the Loss of a Beloved Pet: Rethinking the Legal Classification of Companion Animals and the Requirements for Loss of Companionship Tort Damages," *University of Pennsylvania Law Review* 164 (2015): 1199–1239. For an argument against the creation of an emotional value for pets, see Phil Goldberg, "Courts and Legislatures Have Kept the Proper Leash on Pet Injury Lawsuits: Why Rejecting Emotion-Based Damages Promotes the Rule of Law, Modern Values, and Animal Welfare," *Stanford Journal of Animal Law and Policy* 6 (2013): 30–80.

100. Favre and Borchelt, *Animal Law and Dog Behavior*, 64–81; Julie I. Fershtman, "Animal Insurance Litigation," in *Litigating Animal Law Disputes*, 341–53; Mark Sadler, "Can the Injured Pet Owner Look to Liability Insurance for Satisfaction of a Judgment? The Coverage Implications of Damages for the Injury or Death of a Companion Animal," *Animal Law* 11 (2005): 283–310; Kelly, "Ownership, Custody, and Keeping of Animals," 103–6.

101. Zandra Anderson, "Legal Issues Involving Animal Associations and People Helping Animals," in *Litigating Animal Law Disputes*, 355–436.

102. See Julie I. Fershtman, "Negligence and Tort Law," in *Litigating Animal Law Disputes*, 18–19; Heidi Walson, "Detailed Discussion of the Equine Activity Liability Act," Animal Legal and Historical Center, Michigan State University College of Law, 2003, accessed July 31, 2012, http://www.animallaw.info/articles/dduseala.htm.

103. For the United States, see Goodby v. Vermont, 974 A. 2d 1269 (2009); Steve Barghusen, "Noneconomic Damage Awards in Veterinary Malpractice: Using the Human Medical Experience as a Model to Predict the Effect of Noneconomic Damage Awards on the Practice of Companion Animal Veterinary Medicine," *Animal Law* 17 (2011): 13–57; Favre and Borchelt, *Animal Law and Dog Behavior*, 233–45; Gregory M. Dennis, "Veterinary Malpractice" in *Litigating Animal Law Disputes*, 127–97; Rebecca J. Huss, "Valuation in Veterinary Malpractice," *Loyola University Chicago Law Review* 35 (2004): 479–553; David S. Favre, "Detailed Discussion of Veterinarian Malpractice," Animal Legal & Historical Center,

Michigan State University College of Law, 2002, accessed July 31, 2012, https://www.animallaw.info/article/detailed-discussion-veterinarian-malpractice. For Canada, see "Animal Care Malpractice and Negligence," Animal Justice Canada, May 28, 2013, accessed May 7, 2015, http://www.animaljustice.ca/wp-content/uploads/2013/06/Animal-Justice-Guide-001-Animal-Care-and-Negligence-13.05.28.pdf

104. For examples, see *Florida Administrative Weekly and Florida Administrative Code*, Board of Veterinary Medicine, 61G18-30.001 Disciplinary Guidelines; Ontario, Veterinarians Act, R.S.O. 1990, Chap. V.3, 23–35; *Oregon Revised Statutes Annotated*, Title 52, Occupations and Professions, Chapter 686.150; *Statutes of Saskatchewan*, 1986-87-88, Chapter V-5.1, 19–33, as amended; The Veterinarians Act, *Texas Statutes and Codes Annotated*. Occupations Code. Title 4. Professions Related to Animal Health. Chapter 801. Veterinarians, Subchapter I.

105. Donna Haraway, *The Companion Animal Manifesto* (Chicago: Prickly Paradigm Press, 2003), 33–39.

106. See Arjun Appadurai, "Introduction: Commodities and the Politics of Value," in *The Social Life of Things: Commodities in Cultural Perspective*, ed. Arjun Appadurai (New York: Cambridge University Press, 1986), 3–58; Karl Marx, *Capital: A Critique of Political Economy*, ed. Frederick Engels, trans. Samuel Moore and Edward Aveling (New York: International Publishers, 1886, 1954), 1: 76–87; Slavoj Žižek, *The Sublime Object of Ideology* (London: Verso, 1989), 16–29. The distinction of use value and exchange value in this segment is derived from Marx, *Capital*, Chap. 1, sec. 1–3.

107. See Wendy A. Adams, "Human Subjects and Animal Objects: Animals as 'Other' in Law," *Journal of Animal Law and Ethics* 3 (2009): 29–51.

108. Beers, *For the Prevention of Cruelty*, 90–109; Turner, *Reckoning with the Beast*, 56–59.

109. Hayley Rose Glaholt, "Vivisection as War: The 'Moral Diseases' of Animal Experimentation and Slavery in British Victorian Quaker Pacifist Ethics," *Society & Animals* 20 (2012): 154–72; Stewart Richards, "Vicarious Suffering, Necessary Pain: Physiological Method in Late Nineteenth-Century Britain," in *Vivisection in Historical Perspective*, ed. Nicolaas A. Rupke (London: Croom Helm, 1987), 125–48; Turner, *Reckoning with the Beast*, 76–121.

110. The identification of these political changes relies in part on William J. Novak, "The Legal Origins of the Modern American State," *In Looking Back at Law's Century*, ed. Austin Sarat, Bryant Garth, and Robert A. Kagan (Ithaca, NY: Cornell University Press, 2002), 247–83; William J. Novak, "Police Power and the Hidden Transformation of the American State," in *Police and the Liberal State*, ed. Markus D. Dubber and Mariana Valverde (Stanford: Stanford Law Books, 2008), 54.

111. Kimberly K. Smith, *Governing Animals: Animal Welfare and the Liberal State* (New York: Oxford University Press, 2012), 69–125, 161.
112. Arnold Arluke, *Just a Dog: Understanding Animal Cruelty and Ourselves* (Philadelphia: Temple University Press, 2006), 115–46.
113. The governance of pets as practiced by animal welfare groups in conjunction with governments resembles the mentality and local and multiple ensemble of practices of "governmentality" first described by Michel Foucault. See Michel Foucault, "Governmentality," *Ideology and Consciousness* 6 (1979): 5–21.
114. Beers, *For the Prevention of Cruelty*, 167–80; Lawrence Finsen and Susan Finsen, *The Animal Rights Movement in America: From Compassion to Respect* (New York: Twayne Publishers, 1994), 56–57. The Animal Welfare Act of 1966 was amended in 1970, 1976, 1985, and 2002, 7 *United States Code* §§ 2131 et seq.
115. Arluke, *Just a Dog*, 147–81.
116. The discussion of the welfare-oriented groups is derived from "ASPCA Policy and Position Statements," American Society for the Prevention of Cruelty to Animals, accessed Nov. 9, 2009, http://www.aspca.org/about-us/policy-positions/; "History and Victories," Animal Alliance of Canada, accessed Nov. 9, 2009, http://www.animalalliance.ca/; "ARI Projects and Issues," Animal Rights International, accessed Nov. 9, 2009, http://ari-online.org/; "Who We Are," Animal Welfare Institute, accessed Nov. 9, 2009, https://awionline.org/content/who-we-are; Canadian Federation of Humane Societies, "Position Statements," accessed Nov. 9, 2009, http://cfhs.ca/info/position_statements/; "Defenders of Animals," accessed Nov. 9, 2009, http://www.defendersofanimals.org/index.htm; "About the DLCC," Dog Legislation Council of Canada, accessed Nov. 9, 2009, http://www.dlcc.ca/public/about-the-dlcc/; "Friends of Animals Programs," Friends of Animals, accessed Nov. 9, 2009, http://www.friendsofanimals.org/programs/index.html; "Issues," Humane Society of the United States, accessed Oct. 5, 2015, http://www.hsus.org/issues/?credit=web_id93480558; "12 Guiding Principles," National Humane Education Society, accessed Nov. 9, 2009, http://www.nhes.org/sections/view/82.
117. See James B. Armstrong and Melissa E. Hutchins, "A Comparison of Attitudes Held by Wildlife Managers and Animal Rights Activists," in *Twelfth Great Plains Wildlife Damage Control Workshop Proceedings*, ed. R. E. Masters and J. G. Huggins (Ardmore, OK: Noble Foundation), 13–20; Monica Pivetti, "Animal Rights Activists' Representations of Animals and Animal Rights: An Exploratory Study," *Anthrozoös* 18 (2005): 140–59; Stephen A. Plass, "Exploring Animal Rights as an Imperative for Animal Welfare," *West Virginia Law Review* 112 (2010): 403–30.
118. For a defense of this position, see Robert Garner, "A Defense of a Broad Animal Protectionism," in *Animal Rights Debate: Abolition or Regulation?*, ed. Gary L. Francione and Robert Garner (New York: Columbia University Press, 2010).

119. The article was expanded into a book: Peter Singer, *Animal Liberation: A New Ethic for Our Treatment of Animals* (New York: Random House, 1975).
120. See Stanley Godlovitch, Roslind Godlovitch, and John Harris, eds., *Animals, Men, and Morals: An Inquiry into the Treatment of Non-Humans* (London: Victor Gollancz, 1971).
121. On political triggers for rights claims, see David Erdos, "Postmaterialist Social Constituencies and Political Triggers: Explaining Bill of Rights Genesis in Internally Stable, Advanced Democracies," *Political Research Quarterly* 62 (2009): 803–7.
122. See John M. Kistler, *Animal Rights: A Subject Guide, Bibliography, and Internet Companion* (Westport, CT: Greenwood Press, 2000); John M. Kistler, *Animals Are the Issue: Library Resources on Animal Issues* (New York: Haworth Information Press, 2004).
123. United Nations, *Universal Declaration of Animal Rights,* accessed Oct. 8. 2014, http://jose.kersten.free.fr/aap/pages/uk/UDAR_uk.html.
124. Shelley L. Galvin and Harold A. Herzog, Jr., "Ethical Ideology, Animal Rights Activism, and Attitudes toward the Treatment of Animals," *Ethics and Behavior* 2 (1992): 141–49; Harold A. Herzog, Jr., "'The Movement Is My Life': The Psychology of Animal Rights Activism," *Journal of Social Issues* 49 (1993): 103–19; James M. Jasper and Dorothy Nelkin, *The Animal Rights Crusade: The Growth of a Moral Protest* (New York: The Free Press, 1992), 42–55; Charles W. Peek, Nancy J. Bell, and Charlotte C. Dunham, "Gender, Gender Ideology, and Animal Rights Advocacy," *Gender and Society* 10 (1996): 464–76; S. Plous, "An Attitude Survey of Animal Rights Activists," *Psychological Science* 2 (1991): 194–96.
125. Donna Haraway, *The Companion Animal Manifesto: Dogs, People, and Significant Others* (Chicago: Prickly Pear Press, 2003) 11–12.
126. Hilary Bok, "Keeping Pets," in *The Oxford Handbook of Animal Ethics,* 769–95.
127. Steiner, *Anthropocentrism and Its Discontents,* 4–36.
128. For introductions to the extensive literature about these two normative approaches, see R. G. Frey, "Utilitarianism and Animals," in *The Oxford Handbook of Animal Ethics,* 172–97; Tom L. Beauchamp, "Rights Theory and Animal Rights," in *The Oxford Handbook of Animal Ethics,* 198–227; Martha Nussbaum, "The Capabilities Approach and Animal Entitlements," in *The Oxford Handbook of Animal Ethics,* 228–51.
129. For discussion of this principle, see Kelly Oliver, *Animal Lessons: How They Teach Us to Be Human* (New York: Columbia University Press, 2009), 34–36.
130. *Universal Declaration of Animal Rights,* Preamble.
131. Studies that assess animal cognition include Marc Bekoff, Colin Allen, and Gordon M. Burghardt, eds., *The Cognitive Animal: Empirical and Theoretical Perspectives on Animal Cognition* (Cambridge, MA: MIT Press, 2002); Marc

Bekoff, *Animal Passions and Beastly Virtues: Reflections on Redecorating Nature* (Philadelphia: Temple University Press, 2006); Marc Bekoff and Jessica Pierce, *Wild Justice: The Moral Lives of Animals* (Chicago: University of Chicago Press, 2009); Nick Lund, *Animal Cognition* (New York: Routledge, 2002); Robert W. Lurz, ed., *The Philosophy of Animal Minds* (Cambridge: Cambridge University Press, 2009); Edward A. Wasserman and Thomas R. Zentall, eds., *Comparative Cognition: Experimental Explorations of Animal Intelligence* (New York: Oxford University Press, 2006); Clive D. L. Wynne, *Animal Cognition: The Mental Lives of Animals* (New York: Palgrave, 2001). For criticism of the idea of animal consciousness, see Stephen Budiansky, *If a Lion Could Talk: Animal Intelligence and the Evolution of Consciousness* (New York: Free Press, 1998); John S. Kennedy, *The New Anthropomorphism* (Cambridge: Cambridge University Press, 1992).

132. *Universal Declaration of Animal Rights*, Articles 2–3.
133. For a discussion of this term see Ryder, *Animal Revolution*, 223–50.
134. See Favre, "New Property Status," 237–39; Francione, *Introduction to Animal Rights*; Francione, "Animals–Property or Person?," 120–34.
135. *Universal Declaration of Animal Rights*, Article 9.
136. Christopher Stone, "Should Trees Have Standing? Toward Legal Rights for Natural Objects," *Southern California Law Review* 45 (1972): 450; Sierra Club v. Morton, 405 U.S. 727, 742–43 (1972); Cass R. Sunstein, "Can Animals Sue?," in *Animal Rights: Current Debates and New Directions*, 251–62; Emma A. Maddux, "Comment: Time to Stand: Exploring the Past, Present, and Future of Nonhuman Animal Standing," *Wake Forest Law Review* 47 (2012): 1243–67.
137. *Universal Declaration of Animal Rights*, Articles 4–8. For a summary of these themes, see Thomas G. Kelch, "Toward a Non-property Status for Animals," *New York University Environmental Law Journal* 6 (1998): 531–85. For criticism of this assumption, see Geordie Drucker, "Two Major Flaws of the Animal Rights Movement," *Animal Law* 14 (2008): 184–99.
138. Schrag, "Rights in the Postmodern Condition," 284–300; Stuart A. Scheingold, *The Politics of Rights: Lawyers, Public Policy, and Political Change*, 2nd ed. (Ann Arbor: University of Michigan Press, 2004).
139. See David Favre, "A New Property Status for Animals: Equitable Self-Ownership," in *Animal Rights: Current Debates and New Directions*, 234–50; Kelch, "Toward a Non-property Status," 531; Enger McCartney-Smith, "Can Nonhuman Animals Find Tort Protection in a Human-Centered Common Law?," *Animal Law* 4 (1998): 173; William C. Root, "Man's Best Friend": Property or Family Member? An Examination of the Legal Classification of Companion Animals and Its Impact on Damage Recovery for Their Wrongful Death or Injury," *Villanova Law Review* 47 (2002): 423–48.
140. Jasper and Nelkin, *Animal Rights Crusade*, 103–66.

141. For the United States, see Finsen and Finsen, *Animal Rights Movement*, 72–107. For a partial list for Canada, see "Animal Rights Groups," iVegan.ca, accessed Oct. 5, 2015, http://ivegan.ca/resources/animal-rights-groups/.
142. On these proposals, see Harold D. Guither, *Animal Rights: History and Scope of a Radical Movement* (Carbondale: Southern Illinois University Press, 1998), 73–131, 163–76; "Animal Bill of Rights," Animal Legal Defense Fund, accessed Apr. 11, 2010, http://animalbillofrights.aldf.org/. "Bill of Rights for Animals," Animal Liberation Front, accessed Apr. 11, 2010, http://www.animalliberationfront.com/Philosophy/BillofRights.htm; "About Us," Animal Legal Defense Fund, accessed Nov. 9, 2009, http://www.aldf.org/section.php?id=3; "ALF Actions Around the World," Animal Liberation Front, accessed Nov. 9, 2009, http://www.animalliberationfront.com/ALFront/Actions-index.htm; "Animal Charter of Rights and Freedoms," Animal Justice Canada, accessed Oct. 5, 2015, http://www.animaljustice.ca/; "Mission Statement," Animal Rights: The Abolitionist Approach, accessed Nov. 9, 2009, http://www.abolitionistapproach.com/about/; "Why Animal Rights?," People for the Ethical Treatment of Animals, accessed Nov. 9, 2009, http://www.peta.org/about-peta/why-peta/why-animal-rights/.
143. For examples of such actions, see Emily Gaarder, *Women and the Animal Rights Movement* (New Brunswick: Rutgers University Press, 2011), 117–47; Robert Garner, *Animals, Politics, and Morality*, 2nd ed. (Manchester: Manchester University Press, 2004), 231–47.
144. Jasper and Nelkin, *Animal Rights Crusade*, 26–70, 167–76. For commentary on the tactics of contemporary animal-oriented welfare and legal rights groups, see Lee Hall, *Capers in the Churchyard: Animal Rights Advocacy in the Age of Terror* (Darien, CT: Nectar Bat Press, 2006), 87–138; Jonathan R. Lovvorn, "Animal Law in Action: The Law, Public Perception, and the Limits of Animal Rights Theory as a Basis for Legal Reform," *Animal Law* 6 (2006): 133–49.
145. Arran Stibbe, "Language, Power, and the Social Construction of Animals," *Society and Animals* 9 (2001): 145–61.
146. See, however, Richard L. Cupp, Jr., "Moving beyond Animal Rights: A Legal/Contractualist Critique," *San Diego Law Review* 46 (2009): 27–83.
147. "Editorial: Clear, Humane Rules Needed for Puppy Mills," *The Honolulu Star-Advertiser*, Mar. 5, 2011.
148. For example, the Court of Appeals of Iowa set aside the conviction of the owner of a Boston Terrier who beat the misbehaving dog to death with a baseball bat because there was no evidence the owner acted with "depraved intent"; See Iowa v. Meerdink, 2013 Iowa App. LEXIS 772.
149. Animal Enterprise Protection Act of 1992, 18 *United States Code* § 43 (1992, amended 1996, 2002).
150. Animal Enterprise Terrorism Act, 2006, 18 *United States Code* § 43. See also

Steven C. Tauber, *Navigating the Jungle: Law, Politics, and the Animal Advocacy Movement* (New York: Routledge, 2016), 98–101, for a discussion of litigation about the Act.

151. For a summary of these laws, see Cynthia Hodges, "Detailed Discussion of State Animal 'Terrorism'/Animal Enterprise Interference Laws," Animal Legal and Historical Center, Michigan State University, accessed Jan. 24, 2014, http://www.animallaw.info/articles/ddusstateecoterrorism.htm.

152. See "Ag-Gag Bills at the State Level," ASPCA, accessed Jan. 24, 2014, https://www.aspca.org/fight-cruelty/advocacy-center/ag-gag-whistleblower-suppression-legislation/ag-gag-bills-state-level. See also Tauber, *Navigating the Jungle*, 97–98. These laws are currently the subject of litigation by groups that claim they violate the freedom of speech: see Animal Legal Defense Fund v. Otter, 2015 LEXIS 102640 (U.S. Dist. Ct., Ida. 2015); "Judge Strikes Down Idaho 'Ag-Gag' Law, Raising Questions for Other States," National Public Radio, accessed Aug. 4, 2015, http://npr.org/sections/thesalt/2015/08/04/4.

153. Bryan D. Jones, Frank R. Baumgartner, and James L. True, "Policy Punctuations: U.S. Budget Authority 1947–95," *Journal of Politics* 60 (1999): 1–30.

3

What Is a Pet? Popular Conceptions of Animals and the Pet Policy Agenda

Although the historical context depicts a long-standing conflict about the social identity, moral status, and legal position of cats, dogs, and horses, this chapter examines the current political status of pets in Canada and the United States. Adults' attitudes toward animals have been the subject of varying forms of scholarly study. However, most studies have not addressed how people identify companion animals and the connection of the identity of pets to normative values and conflicts about public policies.[1]

In representative regimes such as Canada and the United States, public opinion cannot be ignored by public officials. Elected officials who desire reelection must work to satisfy popular beliefs, norms, policy concerns, and demands for policy change. Public opinion therefore contributes to the construction of the policy agenda, including the pet policy agenda. By *pet policy agenda* we mean the set of alternative laws and policies seriously considered for governmental action about the treatment of cats, dogs, and horses.[2] So that we may examine the sources of an agenda of alternative laws and policies, in this chapter we first describe the distribution of popular opinion about the identity, norms, and public policies that influence the treatment of cats, dogs, and horses. Then, to offer a thicker description of public opinion, we analyze the association of the identity of animals and cruelty norms with popular discourse about the proposed adoption of a ban on the ownership of pit bulls and other breeds of dogs in Ontario.

SOURCES OF SOCIAL IDENTITY AND NORMS ABOUT COMPANION ANIMALS

Political scientists have long recognized that core political and legal values develop in childhood.[3] Parallel to political learning, does the assignment of an identity to companion animals and normative values about their treatment originate in childhood? Edward O. Wilson hypothesized that humans have a natural predisposition to an attunement with animals that stems from a genetic source.[4] Other scholars have argued that affinity with pets is a surrogate for relationships people should have with other persons, that pet keeping is an expression of economic affluence, or that ownership of a pet exhibits human domination over nature.[5] Critical of these views, Leslie Irvine has claimed that the significance of pets varies by human experiences of time, place, and culture and their personality and desire for relationships.[6]

What then is known about how people learn about the identity and norms they express toward pets? In one of the first studies of the development of attitudes toward animals, Stephen Kellert and Miriam Westervelt found that children developed emotional and cognitive attitudes for understanding animals over time. Children's attitudes toward animals became less egotistical during their early elementary school years. They became aware of the meaning of affection and animal suffering. They acquired more cognitive knowledge of specific animals and animal–human relationships as they aged.[7] Gail Melson discovered that before they are school age, children often develop intimate dialogues with pets, and at a later age they can learn how to care for and nurture the pet through feeding and play. In her book *Why the Wild Things Are: Animals in the Lives of Children,* she notes that pets provide emotional reassurance to children and that children develop empathy through experiences with pets and learn lessons about grief when a pet dies.[8] Another series of studies noted that parental attitudes about pets and gender affected empathy and interest toward pets.[9] In a comprehensive review of his own and other scholars' research, Frank Ascione found that patterns of empathy or abuse of companion animals "are complex and may vary from individual to individual." He reported that the quality of parental care and attachment with children, physical and emotional child abuse and neglect, domestic violence, and sexual abuse affect the development of either empathy or cruelty toward pets.[10] The research therefore indicates that childhood experiences produce differences in social identification and empathy toward animals. Childhood learning therefore tends to perpetuate the existence of multiple identities and norms about the treatment of cats, dogs, and horses. When coupled with the learning of varying political values, it creates a basis for disputes about pet policies among adults.

COMPANION ANIMAL IDENTITY AND ADULT SOCIAL CHARACTERISTICS

What are the dimensions of contemporary adults' social identification of companion animals in Canada and the United States? This question, a question about a potential source of political conflict, has been neglected. Relying on survey data collected in 1975, Stephen Kellert and Joyce Berry collected information on the meaning of animals in general that still offers valuable evidence of the existence of distinctive public social identifications of animals.[11] The authors' analysis produced evidence of eight independent attitudinal clusters used to identify animals.[12]

In their study, Kellert and Berry identified the "naturalistic" and "ecologistic" clusters of responses and associated them with experiences with interest or concern for wildlife and nature (17 percent of respondents). The "scientistic" attitude cluster indicated "primary interest in the physical attributes and biological functioning of animals" but comprised only 1 percent of respondents.[13] The five other clusters of respondents identified in the study expressed views related in part to their attitudes about companion animals. Although somewhat different in their detailed definition, persons in the "dominionistic" (3 percent of respondents) cluster regarded animals to be an object of human mastery and control.[14] "Negativists" were people who displayed aversion, fear, and dislike of animals (37 percent of respondents).[15] (In a later study Kellert linked negativism with human dominion, abuse of animals, and the destruction of species.[16]) Persons with a utilitarian perspective (20 percent of respondents) perceived animals to be a source of material benefits or of personal pleasure and the psychological feelings of endurance and mastery. The majority of utilitarians implicitly identified animals in accord with the historical social identification of animals as a commodity. A "humanistic" cluster (35 percent of respondents) exhibited "primary interest and strong affection for individual animals, principally pets" akin to identification of animals as objects of benevolence. The "moralistic" cluster (20 percent of respondents) exhibited "primary concern for the right and wrong treatment of animals, with strong opposition to exploitation or cruelty toward animals." Marked by a concern for the ethical treatment of animals, they exhibited values like those associated with the identification of animals as objects of human stewardship.[17]

Other studies have found that personality type, measures of empathy and personal morality, lifestyle, contact with pets and other animals, and economic and demographic characteristics such as gender and occupation contribute to humans' social identification of pets.[18] Studies that address normative attitudes toward animals have associated various perceptions of animals with both justifications for animal abuse and support for various policies that punish animal cruelty.[19] Finally, data from a 2011 survey of pet caregivers indicates that these individuals have a distinctive perspective on their companions. Pet caregivers in general identified their pets as a family member (63.2 percent) or companion (35.8 percent) and not as property (1.0 percent). In particular dogs were regarded as family members (66.7 percent) and companions (32.6 percent) rather than property (0.7 percent). Compared to dogs, cats (56.1 percent) and horses (41.0 percent) were less likely to be identified as family members and more frequently as companions (cats: 41.5 percent; horses: 53.2 percent). Cats (2.4 percent) and horses (5.7 percent) were more likely than dogs (0.7 percent) to be defined as property by pet caregivers.[20]

How Does the Public Identify Animals?

To generate fresh data about the variety of social identities of pets, normative attitudes about animals, and the public's pet policy preferences, we devised an Internet survey that was administered to a four-nation general population sample by Survey Sampling International (SSI). Although Internet surveys eliminate respondents without e-mail or Internet access, they can produce a very large number of respondents, provide automatic entry of responses into a database, and can include interactive components.[21] Our sampling frame consisted of a panel of respondents in four nations compiled by SSI. In this book we report the data from Canada (1,094 responses) and the United States (1,030 responses). The survey asked respondents where they live, whether they own animals, what words they would use to identify animals, and their normative attitudes toward animals. It then asked respondents their level of support—ranging from strong to none—for ten different animal policies. The final section asked demographic questions.[22]

Some of the survey questions, including those regarding the social identity of and normative attitudes about animals, addressed animals in general and not pets specifically. However, approximately half of the respondents cared for a pet. Of the survey respondents, 54.9 percent of Canadians reported having dogs compared to 45.1 percent of U.S. respondents and 49.8 percent of Canadians reported having cats compared to 52.2 percent of U.S. respondents. Of Canadian respondents, 49.2 percent had both a cat and a dog compared to 50.8 of U.S. respondents. Canadian respondents were much more likely to care for another pet species: 62.4 percent compared to 37.6 percent of U.S. respondents.

The data collected by our Internet survey was largely nominal in nature and not in a form for sophisticated data analysis techniques. However, since we aim at understanding the dimensions of support for social identities of animals and support for laws and policies that affect pets, we find no need to employ statistical techniques that predict causality. Therefore, rather than engaging in testing causal hypotheses, the analysis addresses a series of questions about associations among identities of animals,

TABLE 3.1 *Words Used to Describe Animals*

Word(s) Used	Canada (%, N = 968)	U.S. (%, N = 910)	Total (N = 1,878)
Family	41.0	41.4	774
Friend	44.2	41.3	804
Generally "nice" or positive words	58.1	56.3	1,074
Guard/protector	10.6	11.0	203
Property	4.0	4.9	94
Negative words	7.7	7.1	140

animal legislation and policy, and socioeconomic variables for Canada and the United States.

We first asked an open-ended question: Please list up to five words you often use to describe your feelings about animals (words such as *family, property, friend, guard*—what the animals mean to you). A categorization of the range of words chosen is reported in Table 3.1. The data reported in the table reveal that Canadians and Americans are much more likely to use words that reflect a favorable rather than a negative perception of animals. Also, respondents in both countries expressed their general views on animals in a very similar manner.

To address specifically the question about the identity of animals in general, we asked respondents to indicate their level of agreement with each in a series of statements that reflect various attitudes toward animals. There were statistically significant differences in responses to these questions from Canadians and Americans, with the Americans giving more support to the human dominion identity. As indicated in Table 3.2, Canadian and U.S. respondents differed to a statistically significant degree with statements that evidence the identification of animals as objects of stewardship and protection from cruelty, which include "Humans exist as part of a natural community in which all members, including animals, must be treated with respect" (88.3 percent of the total sample: Canada, 90.9 percent; United States, 85.6 percent) and "Because animals feel pain and suffer, government has a duty to protect their welfare" (82.6 percent of the sample: Canada, 87.5 percent; United States, 77.4 percent).

TABLE 3.2 *Social Identities of Animals*

Identification Statement	Respondents Who Agree (%)		
	Canada	U.S.	Total
Legal rights: God created all creatures and gave them all rights that people must respect	77.9 (N = 839)	77.2 (N = 780)	77.5 (N = 1,619)
Stewardship: Humans exist as part of a natural community in which all members, including animals, must be treated with respect	90.9 (N = 979)	85.6 (N = 863)	88.3[a] (N = 1,842)
Stewardship: Because animals feel pain and suffer, government has a duty to protect their welfare	87.5 (N = 943)	77.4 (N = 785)	82.6[a] (N = 1,728)
Commodity: Human progress requires the use of other species as we see fit	31.0 (N = 329)	32.4 (N = 324)	31.7 (N = 653)
Commodity: Animal welfare laws violate and limit my property rights to animals	16.3 (N = 172)	17.9 (N = 177)	17.0 (N = 349)
Human dominion (traditional): God gave humans dominion over animals to use as they see fit	16.4 (N = 174)	25.6 (N = 256)	20.9[a] (N = 430)
Human dominion: Only humans can have rights	10.6 (N = 114)	13.0 (N = 130)	11.8[a] (N = 244)

[a]Chi square significant at 0.000 level.

Both Canadians and Americans responded with considerably less support for the traditional identification of animals as objects of human dominion: "God gave humans dominion over animals to use as they see fit" (20.9 percent); the identification of animals as a commodity: "Animal welfare laws violate and limit my property rights to animals" (17.0 percent); and the shared human dominion and commodity identity view that "only humans can have rights" (11.8 percent).

In both nations the identification of animals as beings with independent worth also received considerable support: "God created all creatures and gave them all rights that people must respect" (77.5 percent of the total sample). The support for these statements suggests most persons accept the idea that animals possess both natural rights and that people and

TABLE 3.3 *Perceptions of Animal Welfare and Rights*

"What rights, if any, do you think animals should have?"	Canada (%)	U.S. (%)	Total (%)
No rights at all	4.6 (N = 50)	6.4 (N = 66)	5.5 (N = 116)
Survival: Right to sufficient food, water, and shelter for survival	51.5 (N = 563)	57.7 (N = 594)	54.5[a] (N = 1,157)
Comfort: Right to sufficient food, water, and shelter for safety, comfort, and freedom from pain	73.7 (N = 806)	71.9 (N = 741)	72.8 (N = 1,547)
Right to companionship and socialization	58.7 (N = 642)	61.6 (N = 634)	60.1 (N = 1,276)
Right to exercise and freedom of movement sufficient to sustain mental and physical health	62.2 (N = 680)	62.9 (N = 648)	62.5 (N = 1,328)
Right to respect and dignity	24.8 (N = 271)	26.3 (N = 271)	25.5 (N = 542)
Procedural rights: Legal rights to have a guardian and seek protection of their welfare in court	12.7 (N = 139)	13.3 (N = 137)	13.0 (N = 276)

[a]Chi square significant at 0.004 level.

governments must act as stewards to accommodate their welfare. Of the total respondents, 31.7 percent agreed with the statement "Human progress requires the use of other species as we see fit" (which identifies animals as an object of human dominion), suggesting that these respondents do not consider animal welfare to be as important as human welfare.

To measure support for the identification of animals as subjects of human stewardship or as autonomous beings, Table 3.3 provides the multiple response frequencies for the question "What rights, if any, do you think animals should have?" The majority of the responses in both nations indicated support for rights to protect the welfare of animals and a need for human stewardship against acts of cruelty. In defining human stewardship and responsibilities for animal welfare, more than 70 percent of respondents said that animals have the right "to sufficient food, water, and shelter for safety, comfort, and freedom from pain." A majority of respondents (Canada: 62.2 percent; United States: 62.9 percent) also felt that animals have the right "to exercise and freedom of movement sufficient to sustain mental and physical health." The "right to sufficient food, water, and shelter for survival" was cited by 51.5 percent of Canadian and 57.7 percent of U.S. respondents and was the only statistically significant difference reported. Although the right to respect and dignity was proposed by some animal legal rights activists, less than one-third of respondents agreed (Canada: 24.8 percent; United States: 26.3 percent), and only 12.7 percent of Canadians and 13.3 of Americans felt animals deserved procedural rights to defend their "legal rights to have a guardian to seek protection of their welfare in court." Nonetheless, at the other end of the rights spectrum, only 4.6 percent of Canadian and 6.4 percent of U.S. respondents expressed the human dominion identification or that animals have no rights at all.

Respondents who were companion animal caregivers were significantly more likely than those who were not to regard animals as deserving human stewardship or procedural legal rights. As reported in Table 3.4, we collapsed responses to the question "What rights, if any, do you think animals should have?" into categories of human dominion (no rights), welfare and stewardship responsibilities (companionship, health, comfort, freedom of movement for animals, and so forth), and procedural legal rights and dignity. The evidence is that cat and dog caregivers are more likely to support animal welfare and stewardship or procedural rights than are persons who do not care for an animal or who have other kinds of pets. Additionally, all groups of respondents were more likely to support welfare and stewardship (59.0 percent) than legal rights (30.9 percent) or no rights and human dominion (10.1 percent.). Significant differences in these findings did not appear between Canadian and U.S. respondents.

We then examined whether an association existed between demographic variables and human dominion, stewardship and welfare, and legal rights. No significant relationship existed between respondent age and support for animal welfare laws or legal rights in either country. However, higher income was significantly associated with support for animal legal rights. In Canada 45.5 percent of respondents with an income of more than $100,000 supported legal rights, and in the United States 40.7 percent

TABLE 3.4 *Companion Animal Caregiving and the Social Identities of Animals*

Animal Cared For	Human Dominion: No Rights (%)	Welfare and Stewardship: Responsibilities for Companionship, Comfort, and Freedom of Movement (%)	Autonomy: Rights to Dignity and Legal Procedural Rights (%)
No animal	17.2	55.2	27.6
Dog	7.0	59.3	33.8
Cat	8.4	58.4	33.1
Both cat and dog	5.5	64.4	30.1
Other animal	16.7	57.7	25.6
Total	10.1 (N = 192)	59.0 (N = 1,116)	30.9 (N = 585)

Note: Chi square = 49.54; df = 8; sig. = 0.000.

supported autonomy. Respondents with an income lower than $100,000 were more likely to support animal welfare responsibilities than procedural rights and autonomy. Significantly more male than female respondents assigned procedural legal protection to animals (Canadian males: 33.3 percent, U.S. males: 32.4; compared to Canadian females: 29.8 percent, U.S. females: 32.2). Female respondents were more likely than male respondents to assign welfare protection to animals (Canadian females: 66.8 percent, U.S. females: 63.3; compared to Canadian males: 54.0 percent, U.S. males: 48.5). Place of residence (farm, other rural area, suburban, urban) was not significantly associated with support for animal welfare or legal rights in either nation.

The survey data support the historical and quantitative evidence that people assign different social identities to animals. Additionally, the data analysis indicates that people in Canada and the United States most frequently support the identification of animals as subjects of human stewardship and welfare, and they support humans' legal accountability for the basic needs of cats, dogs, and horses and their protection against cruelty. Respondents showed much less support for the identification of animals as subjects of human dominion and, conversely, as autonomous beings with rights guarded by humans. Nevertheless, the assignment of conflicting identities to animals creates a basis for political struggles among alternatives that appear on the pet policy agenda.

Normative Values and the Treatment of Animals: Survey Data

Although Americans and Canadians tend to support the identification of animals as objects of human stewardship for whom they should be legally accountable, their treatment of animals reflects their normative values about animal cruelty. Because religion plays an important role in the formation of both moral and ethical values and attitudes toward a range of public policies in North America, religious guidance, as found in denominational texts and clerical guidance, might be associated with a person's assignment of a social identity to animals. Also, beliefs about human existence convey a normative stance that might be associated with the treatment of animals.

Organized Religion and the Treatment of Animals

How does affiliation with organized religious influence people's support for the identities of animals, such as dominion, welfare, and legal rights? Religious and normative ethics and attitudes about animals have had a complex interconnection throughout modern history.[23] On one hand, humans have projected attitudes shaped by contact with animals into religious doctrine and normative guidance about the appropriate or cruel treatment of animals.[24] There is conflicting religious guidance about the ethical and legal treatment of animals. For example, some Christians cite biblical passages that assert human dominion over other animals, such as one that states mankind is to possess "dominion over the fish of the sea, and over the birds of the air, and over cattle, and over all the wild animals of the earth, and over every creeping thing that creeps upon the earth."[25] Other Christians cite biblical passages that reject this position and assert, "for the fate of humans and the fate of animals is the same; as one dies, so dies the other. They all have the same breath, and humans have no advantage over the animals; for all is vanity."[26] Indeed, in recent years some Christian writers have articulated a theological justification for animal rights and for the avoidance of animals' suffering based on the overarching message of the Gospels.[27] The unsettled normative status of the treatment of animals provides a context in which we can empirically assess the connections between public perspectives on normative values, religious adherence, and support for animal welfare laws or legal rights.

In the past the linkage between organized religious affiliation and the social identification of animals has received only limited attention. A study of data from surveys conducted in the United States in 1993 and 1994 has shown that the interplay of religious values and gender influences how the American public views the ideology of animal legal rights. Specifically the study found that support for animal legal rights was not associated with fundamentalist religious values such as a literalist interpretation of the Bible, but support for animal legal rights was negatively associated with organized religion. Also, the study found correlations of a more pantheistic spirituality with support for animal legal rights.[28] Further analysis of this survey data confirmed that church attendance had a significant negative association with support for animal legal rights,[29] and the frequency of church attendance was more important than religious denomination in decreasing support for animal legal rights.[30] A small study of American undergraduate students found that religious fundamentalists and creationists were the least supportive of animal legal rights.[31] Other studies employing survey data have found that American animal legal rights activists tend to be ethical absolutists and are less likely to hold ethical positions associated with organized religion than the general population.[32] However, research studies conducted in Australia, the United Kingdom, and the United States have found that measures of gender, income, animal ownership, age, race, and contribution to animal interest groups were significantly associated with religious or moral perspectives about animal legal rights.[33] Therefore, despite the limited nature of these studies, it is possible that these measures influence the effect of religious tenets on a person's social identification of animals.

To explore further the association of organized religion with the assignment of a social identity to pets, we used data from our multinational Internet survey. However, the great diversity of religions mentioned by respondents, each with a small number of adherents, made detailed

TABLE 3.5 *Organized Religious Affiliation and the Social Identities of Animals*

Religious Affiliation	Human Dominion: No Rights (%)		Welfare and Stewardship: Responsibilities for Companionship, Comfort, and Freedom of Movement (%)		Autonomy: Rights to Dignity and Legal Procedural Rights (%)	
	Canada	U.S.	Canada	U.S.	Canada	U.S.
Catholic	6.6 (N = 19)	11.9 (N = 32)	62.4 (N = 181)	57.0 (N = 154)	31.0 (N = 90)	31.1 (N = 84)
Protestant	6.8 (N = 16)	13.9 (N = 46)	64.1 (N = 150)	57.3 (N = 189)	29.1 (N = 68)	28.8 (N = 95)
Other	3.0 (N = 1)	2.6 (N = 1)	66.7 (N = 22)	63.2 (N = 24)	30.3 (N = 10)	34.2 (N = 13)
None	8.2 (N = 26)	10.4 (N = 22)	60.4 (N = 192)	57.0 (N = 154)	31.4 (N = 100)	31.8 (N = 67)

examination of religious adherence very difficult, especially with regard to Islam (2 respondents of 1,951), Judaism (60 respondents), Hinduism and Buddhism (14 respondents total), Mormonism (28 respondents), and the many denominations and beliefs within Protestant Christianity. Consequently, we collapsed the denominational differences into four categories: Roman Catholic Christians, Protestant Christians, other religious affiliations, and no religious affiliation. Although these categories only reflect general commitments to patterns of organized religious beliefs, they permit some distinction among major theological differences.

Table 3.5 reports the association of religious affiliation with the measure of the social identification of animals. The data indicate that in most categories the influence of organized religion on the social identification of animals varies little between Canada and the United States. About three-fifths of respondents both with and without a religious affiliation supported the identification of animals as objects of human welfare and stewardship and deserving of comfort, companionship, and freedom of movement. About a third of respondents supported the identification of animals as autonomous subjects with legal rights and a degree of equality. However, when compared to Canadians, approximately twice as many

American Roman Catholics, Protestants, and persons with no religious affiliation identified animals as subjects of human dominion with no rights. Yet, overall affiliation with an organized religion did not appear to be related to individuals' social identification of animals.

However, we offer a caveat about Protestants' identification of animals. Most mainstream Protestant denominations (Anglican/Episcopal, Presbyterian, United Methodist, Evangelical Lutheran, United Church of Canada) and several smaller denominations (Religious Society of Friends [Quakers], Christian Science, Seventh-Day Adventist, Jehovah's Witnesses) expressed a concern for animal welfare in their official doctrines. We therefore assume that persons affiliated with these faiths might support animal rights and animal welfare legislation. However, the biblical literalist theology of some evangelical Protestant Christian denominations, especially Southern Baptist and Assembly of God (the largest Pentecostal denomination), often inclines persons affiliated with them to express the themes on human domination of animals found in numerous Old Testament passages.[34] A Spearman's Rho correlation analysis of adherence to evangelical religious values with attitudes about animals found a positive relationship between evangelical religious values and anti-animal altitudes and a negative relationship between evangelical religious values and pro-animal attitudes.

Beliefs about Human Existence and the Identities of Animals

Although adherence to an organized religion is one measure of the normative commitments of individuals, we independently posed a question about beliefs about human existence (ontology) on our multinational Internet survey. The categories of responses were as follows:

- "Man was made in God's image and given dominion over all the earth" (11.9 percent of sample; Canada: 8.0 percent; United States: 16.1 percent)
- "Humans evolved over many eons and are now able to use nature for their own purposes" (1.7 percent of sample; Canada: 1.2 percent; United States: 2.3 percent)
- "Man was created by God and was given the responsibility to care for

all the earth" (33.4 percent of sample; Canada: 28.7 percent; United States: 38.4 percent)
- "All creatures are formed of the same spirit and fit together into the oneness of being" (10.3 percent of sample; Canada: 12.1 percent; United States: 8.4 percent)
- "Humans evolved but our continued existence requires us to live within and show respect for the earth and all its inhabitants" (42.7 percent of sample; Canada: 50.0 percent; United States: 34.9 percent)

The distribution of these responses indicates that beliefs about existence that express human dominion or control of the earth and its beings receive little support. However, the evidence is that Americans rest their concern for human responsibility for the earth significantly more on a faith in God as a source of values than do Canadians.

Table 3.6 presents the associations between the respondents' beliefs about existence and the measure of social identities of animals for Canada and the United States. As with organized religion, there is limited variation between Canadian and American respondents in most categories. Greater support for the beliefs that "man was created by God and was given the responsibility to care for all the earth," "all creatures are formed of the same spirit and fit together into the oneness of being," and especially for the statement that "humans evolved but our continued existence requires us to live within and show respect for the earth and all its inhabitants" exists among respondents in both countries who identify animals as subjects of human welfare and stewardship or as autonomous beings. Greater support for the beliefs that "man was made in God's image and given dominion over all the earth" and "humans evolved over many eons and are now able to use nature for their own purposes" exist among respondents who regard animals as subjects of human dominion with no rights. Also, Americans are more likely than Canadians to believe that "man was made in God's image and given dominion over all the earth" and "humans evolved over many eons and are now able to use nature for their own purposes."

As Table 3.6 shows, beliefs about existence tend to coincide with the social identities that people assign to animals. Evangelical religious adherence is associated with greater support for human dominion over animals,

TABLE 3.6 *Beliefs about Existence and the Social Identities of Animals*

Belief about Existence	Human Dominion: No Rights (%)		Welfare and Stewardship: Responsibilities for Companionship, Comfort, and Freedom of Movement (%)		Autonomy: Rights to Dignity and Legal Procedural Rights (%)	
	Canada	U.S.	Canada	U.S.	Canada	U.S.
Man was made in God's image and given dominion over all the earth	23.7 (N = 18)	33.6 (N = 49)	53.9 (N = 41)	44.5 (N = 65)	22.4 (N = 17)	21.9 (N = 32)
Humans evolved over many eons and are now able to use nature for their own purposes	33.3 (N = 4)	42.9 (N = 9)	41.7 (N = 5)	33.3 (N = 7)	25.0 (N = 3)	23.8 (N = 5)
Man was created by God and was given the responsibility to care for all the earth	5.2 (N = 14)	2.7 (N = 2)	65.4 (N = 176)	61.8 (N = 220)	29.4 (N = 79)	30.9 (N = 110)
All creatures are formed of the same spirit and fit together into the oneness of being	1.9 (N = 2)	2.7 (N = 2)	63.9 (N = 69)	57.3 (N = 43)	34.3 (N = 37)	40.0 (N = 30)
Humans evolved but our continued existence requires us to live within and show respect for the earth and all its inhabitants	5.8 (N = 26)	5.9 (N = 19)	60.8 (N = 273)	60.2 (N = 194)	33.4 (N = 150)	33.9 (N = 109)

and measures of values associated with human dominion over animals are greater in the United States than in Canada.

Public Values and the Pet Politics Policy Agenda

To what extent do Americans and Canadians support animal welfare policies? During the consideration of revisions to the law regulating commercial dog kennels, Pennsylvania state representative Dwight Evans remarked, "What divides us are those who sincerely believe that dogs are equivalent to livestock and those who see it differently: that dogs are man's best friend."[35] Although contending social identities of animals and varying norms of cruelty create a basis for political struggles, what are the linkages of the differing social identities and normative values about pets with popular legal and policy preferences?

Public Opinion and Policies That Affect Pets: Quantitative Data

To begin to describe public opinion about the policies that affect companion animals, we rely on data generated by our multinational Internet survey. Table 3.7 reports the survey results on overall frequency of popular support for selected animal policy proposals. We selected these policies because they have generated attention or political action during the past decade. The policy proposals selected for analysis largely reflect the political struggle among animal welfare interest groups seeking stewardship of pets and limitations on animal cruelty and the proposals of animal legal rights–oriented groups to free animals from subjection and enact legal protection of their identity, businesses that treat animals as a commodity, and persons fearful of injuries from pets.

Several of these proposals would regulate some acts of cruelty, irresponsibility, and excessive breeding that result from human ownership and sale of animals as a commodity, such as kennel licensing and inspections designed to ensure the health and safety of dogs at commercial breeding facilities and consumer protection legislation ensuring the health of pets sold by commercial establishments (pet lemon laws). Measures such as bans or limitations on the scientific experimentation and laboratory use

TABLE 3.7 Support for Companion Animal Policies

Policy	Support (%)		Neutral/Unsure (%)		Opposed (%)	
	Canada	U.S.	Canada	U.S.	Canada	U.S.
Ban on permanent tethering or caging	71.0 (N = 755)	65.3 (N = 648)	13.6 (N = 145)	18.0 (N = 179)	15.4 (N = 163)	16.7 (N = 165)
Ban on animal research for non-medical commercial purposes	71.6 (N = 763)	60.1 (N = 598)	13.1 (N = 140)	18.6 (N = 185)	15.3 (N = 163)	20.3 (N = 213)
Ban on animal research when an alternative exists	78.4 (N = 834)	68.3 (N = 683)	9.2 (N = 98)	16.0 (N = 160)	12.4 (N = 131)	15.6 (N = 156)
Extension of cruelty legislation to protect research animals	71.0 (N = 764)	62.4 (N = 618)	18.2 (N = 193)	21.4 (N = 212)	9.8 (N = 104)	16.3 (N = 163)
Kennel licensing and inspections	92.2 (N = 981)	89.9 (N = 898)	5.2 (N = 55)	6.5 (N = 65)	2.6 (N = 28)	3.6 (N = 36)
Consumer protection law for purchases of pets	85.4 (N = 907)	81.4 (N = 813)	9.9 (N = 105)	13.0 (N = 130)	4.6 (N = 49)	5.6 (N = 56)
Differential licensing fees for unaltered animals	69.7 (N = 736)	64.2 (N = 636)	18.2 (N = 192)	20.9 (N = 207)	12.1 (N = 128)	15.0 (N = 148)
Bans on particular breeds of dogs	46.1 (N = 491)	35.2 (N = 349)	26.1 (N = 278)	36.9 (N = 366)	27.9 (N = 297)	27.8 (N = 276)

of animals, including cats and dogs, bans or limitations on commercial product testing using animals, and the replacement of animal testing with computerized simulations or in vitro studies[36] endeavor to respect the legal rights of animals and restrict their use as a commodity. Animal stewardship motives have encouraged differential licensing fees for unaltered animals in an attempt to reduce the number of abandoned and euthanized cats and dogs and bans on the outdoor tethering and continuous confinement of animals by chains or similar restraints. Although these policy proposals support pet welfare or legal rights, breed-specific laws or bans assume dogs are property. They are designed to ban the possession of specific kinds of dogs, such as pit bulls, as a public safety measure.

Our survey showed that there is considerable support for all of these animal welfare and legal rights policies—between 70 and 80 percent of respondents (see Table 3.7). Kennel licensing, a welfare measure that affects commercial breeders but that does not directly affect the vast majority of pet owners or caregivers, finds the most support among respondents. However, breed-specific bans, which have the potential to affect a large number of pet owners and the public, have the least support.

Demographic Features of Support for Pet Policies

To examine more closely whether specific national populations or demographic groups support or oppose certain policies, we cross tabulated the policies with the age, income, gender, and location of residence of respondents. The statistically significant findings are as follows:

- Canadians are more likely than Americans to support the adoption all of the policies included in our analysis.[37]
- Females are more likely to support the adoption of all of the selected policies except breed bans.
- Persons with greater income are less likely to support bans on nonmedical research using animals.
- Older persons are less supportive of bans on nonmedical research using animals, even when alternatives are available.
- Older and wealthier persons are more likely to oppose the protection for research animals by anti-cruelty laws.

- Older persons are more likely to support puppy protection laws.
- Older persons are more likely to support breed bans.
- People who earn more than $100,000 a year are most likely to oppose puppy protection laws.
- Older persons are more likely to support differential licensing of neutered and non-neutered pets.
- Location of respondent's residence, including residence on a farm or in a rural area, was not a significant factor in support for or opposition to any policy.

In addition to these laws and policies that affect the treatment of pets, the survey also disclosed that age more generally influences how people would treat animals usually not held as pets. For example, to a statistically significant degree:

- Older persons are less likely to support restrictions on factory farms.
- Older and wealthier persons are less likely to support extension of anti-cruelty laws to poultry.

Finally, we examined whether there was an association between cat or dog caregivers and policy preferences:

- Cat owners significantly supported differential licensing of neutered and non-neutered pets, restrictions on factory farms, extension of anti-cruelty laws to poultry, bans on nonmedical research using animals, and the protection of research animals by anti-cruelty laws.
- Dog owners significantly supported bans on nonmedical research using animals, the protection for research animals by anti-cruelty laws, and a ban on permanent tethering or caging of pets. However, owning a dog was not significantly associated with differential licensing of neutered and non-neutered pets, restrictions on factory farms, extension of anti-cruelty laws to poultry, kennel licensing and inspections, and consumer protection law for purchases of pets.

These findings imply that a support for policies that encourage animal welfare, stewardship, or legal rights might find increasing support as younger persons socialized to care for or respect animals over time become a larger portion of the population. The findings also confirm previous studies and anecdotal evidence that indicate the greater commitment of women to pet stewardship and animal legal rights. However, living with a pet, especially a dog, does not incline a person to be more supportive of most companion animal and other anti-cruelty policies.

Social Identity, Beliefs about Existence, and Support for Policies

Cross tabulations of the measure of social identity with policy preferences reported in Table 3.8 revealed that a significant majority of respondents who identified animals as objects of stewardship or as autonomous beings overwhelmingly supported all policies examined except breed bans. Again except for breed bans, persons who identified animals as subjects of human dominion offered far less support for all of the policies. However, a majority of persons who identified animals as subjects of human dominion did support kennel regulation and inspection and puppy lemon laws. Breed bans were not significantly associated with any social identity that respondents assigned to animals.

Cross tabulations of the measure of social identity with beliefs about existence showed that persons who agree with the statements "Man was made in God's image and given dominion over all the earth" and "Humans evolved over many eons and are now able to use nature for their own purposes" are significantly less likely to support bans or regulation of tethering and caging, bans on nonmedical or commercial research using animals, and bans on the research use of animals when an alternative is available. However, persons who agreed with these statements of belief exhibited more support for kennel licensing and puppy protection laws than for other policies, but nonetheless they supported them less than persons who agreed with the statements "Man was created by God and was given the responsibility to care for all the earth," "All creatures are formed of the same spirit and fit together into the oneness of being," and "Humans evolved but our continued existence requires us to live within and show respect for the earth and all its inhabitants." Support for breed bans was not significantly related to any of the statements of belief about existence.

• • •

TABLE 3.8 *Support for Policies and the Social Identification of Animals*

Policy	Respondents with a Specific Social Identification of Animals Indicating Very Likely or Somewhat Supportive of Policy (%)		
	Human Dominion: No Rights	Welfare and Stewardship: Responsibilities for Companionship, Comfort, and Freedom of Movement	Autonomy: Rights to Dignity and Legal Procedural Rights
Ban on permanent tethering or caging	32.0 (N = 57)	61.0 (N = 797)	71.5 (N = 419)
Ban on animal research for non-medical commercial purposes	27.8 (N = 50)	69.7 (N = 784)	69.6 (N = 410)
Ban on animal research when an alternative exists	36.1 (N = 65)	75.2 (N = 847)	80.3 (N = 473)
Extension of cruelty legislation to protect research animals	23.5 (N = 42)	70.4 (N = 788)	72.9 (N = 429)
Kennel licensing and inspections	73.9 (N = 133)	92.4 (N = 1041)	93.3 (N = 550)
Consumer protection law for purchases of pets	60.1 (N = 110)	85.8 (N = 962)	83.5 (N = 509)
Differential licensing fees for unaltered animals	45.3 (N = 81)	68.4 (N = 765)	71.4 (N = 416)
Bans on particular breeds of dogs	45.1 (N = 83)	40.2 (N = 450)	40.4 (N = 237)

Overall the survey revealed that a majority of respondents in both nations support policies that aim to enhance the welfare or legal rights of pets and other animals. The only policy not finding majority support was breed-specific bans. As with the examination of social identity and normative values, the findings on support for laws and policies revealed a population inclined to offer at least diffuse or generalized support for the welfare of pets.

Social Identities, Norms, and Pet Policy: Breed-Specific Legislation in Ontario

Our survey data provide a snapshot of public opinion about the legal and political treatment of pets. However, the survey responses do not offer detailed evidence of how people talk about animals. Although the data reveal diffuse popular support for animal welfare policies, they do not capture respondents' specific expressions about the treatment of animals. To offer a fuller description of public opinion, in this section we employ documents associated with the adoption of a law banning the ownership of pit bulls and other breeds of dogs in Ontario.

After discussions with various interests and other "consultations,"[38] in 2004 the Liberal Party government proposed the breed ban in Bill 132,[39] a series of amendments to the Ontario Dog Owner's Liability Act[40] and Animals for Research Act.[41] The Liberals sought a variety of restrictions on dog owners, restrictions on the use of dogs in research, and a ban on the ownership of American Pit Bulls, pit bull–type dogs, Staffordshire Bull Terriers, American Staffordshire Terriers, and dogs with "an appearance and characteristics" that are "substantially similar" to such breeds of dogs. During January and February 2005 a Subcommittee of the Ontario Legislative Assembly held a series of public hearings on the proposed amendments.[42] The transcript of the hearings on the breed-specific legislation in general and specifically on the "breed ban" provides a wealth of information about perceptions of the identity of dogs and popular norms, and it serves as a primary source for the following analysis.

What is important in the Ontario testimony about dogs? Legislative hearings allow persons to tell a story freely using real or imaginary knowledge and assumptions about the identity and behavior of people and animals, basic moral beliefs, their conception of the legitimate use of political power, and their predictions and desires for the future. Their testimony can illustrate how people articulate and connect identities, ethical norms, and legal assumptions to constitute their view of the human–animal relationship.[43] As people discuss dogs and relate their stories, they talk about the meaning of their world, compare their beliefs and knowledge to others, and draw on past experiences and cultural knowledge to fashion distinctive identities of dogs.⁴⁴ The examination of their stories therefore provides detail about the identity of dogs and how people define the legitimacy of related moral and political practices toward the animal.⁴⁵

Dogs as Nuisance Property

The story about some breeds of dogs presented by the proponents of the Ontario breed ban rested on the assumption that the "other"—the pit bull and other breeds—can be identified as a distinctive category of nuisance property that poses a distinctive risk to public safety.⁴⁶ The witnesses then constructed the pit bull as an antisocial or criminal category of property. Because it was dangerous nuisance property that could not be put to good use, it could be seized from owners and destroyed (as with illegal drugs or child pornography). However, by proposing that the dog be seized they were placing part of the blame for the danger and social cost of pit bull behavior on the dog rather than the owner.

Several of the witnesses at the Ontario hearing defined pit bulls as dangerous nuisance property with no legitimate use. For example, Louise Ellis described the horror of an allegedly unprovoked pit bull attack on her child in graphic terms. She asserted that the pit bull had "actually eaten part of her face" and then turned to rip a huge gash in the arm of a girlfriend of the owner. Ellis then explained that "dogs are not human. It is an animal. It has the brain of an animal." Additionally, she explained that humans could not "predict what their animal will do, or better yet, what they won't do."⁴⁷ The dog thus was a risk to innocent humans, it possessed no useful purpose, and the dog and its owner were outlaws.

Many witnesses in the Ontario breed ban hearing also spoke of the pit bull and other dogs in terms that implied they were not just a nuisance but a danger to social order and outside the law. Mark Fox contended that "When you breed a [pit bull] to be a superior killer, the breeding will eventually break down regardless of how caring and careful the owners are."⁴⁸ As Diane Porquet alleged, "pit bulls were created and bred to kill other dogs, not to become household pets."⁴⁹ Ronald Jeroy claimed that the breeds listed in the bill presented "a real danger to police officers who are trying to uphold the law."⁵⁰ The Toronto Police Chief, Julian Fantino, testified that criminals used pit bulls "as weapons." They were the "dog of choice for many criminals." Criminals used them "as an extension of their intimidation tactics on people." He also reported on four incidents when police officers serving warrants confronted pit bulls and one incident in which they had to shoot a dog. He concluded that "pit bulls pose a very serious, very real and legitimate threat to the safety of the public and to our police officers."[51] Bruce Miller buttressed Fantino's testimony with three stories of pit bull threats or attacks on police officers. He regarded such incidents as becoming more prevalent as the pit bulls became "weapons of choice" for criminals. The ban, he concluded, would "help ensure community safety."[52]

Reinforcing the public safety purpose of the breed ban, several witnesses employed the concept of a right to personal security to explain their support for the breed ban. Tom Kirby asserted that pit bulls were "designed" to be "aggressive," "tenacious," "unrelenting," and "ferocious." Because of these characteristics, "the right of individuals to live free from harm is jeopardized every time a pit bull walks by." He then concluded that "responsible citizens must stand shoulder to shoulder and stop the absurd notion that a few people have a right to place my safety and my children's safety in check just because they want a dog."[53] Adding to the dramatic explanation of the danger of dogs, George Scott described a lengthy pit bull attack on him, his wife, and their dog. Scott asserted that, unlike other dogs, pit bulls "bite you and hold on for as long as they want."[54] Kitchener Councillor Berry Vrbanovic added: "This is an issue of public safety, pure and simple. We have seen too many examples of pit bulls which are a time bomb waiting to go off. We have seen case after case of unprovoked, unpredictable and vicious attacks, and they need to stop."[55]

When Ontario Attorney General Michael Bryant testified, he connected several of the themes of the previous public testimony. In his statement in support of the breed ban, Bryant provided a story with a plot that (1) "pit bulls are inherently dangerous." Having established their identity, he assessed that (2) "fewer pit bulls are going to mean fewer pit bull attacks. Fewer pit bulls are going to mean fewer people victimized by pit bulls." (3) He found support for this assertion in the experiences of municipalities with a breed ban. (4) He claimed that the ban was moral. Without the ban there will be more pit bulls in pounds, more subjected to euthanasia, and more victims, so "Where is the humanity in that?" (5) He thought that the ban was reasonable and efficient because judges and prosecutors had enough information to define the breeds and municipalities would see more income from fines. (6) The result would be "public safety."[56]

What political meaning do these stories resting on the identification of the dog as the object of human dominion offer? The testimony indicates that humans should be allowed to not only treat pit bulls as a nuisance but to criminalize and banish them. Because the pit bull is a criminal, the law automatically frees persons of any sense of ethical responsibility for its welfare or its lawfulness as property. Because it cannot reverse its fate at the hands of a vengeful legal power, the banned dog is left to suffering, banishment, or a quickly forgotten death and disposal. People adhering to the idea of human dominion feel no guilt in supporting policies that elicit the suffering or death of the dog.

Benevolence and Dogs

During the Ontario hearing, dog breeder Peter Archer stated," In our society the dog is an integral part of the picture of the family."[57] The treatment of the dog as a family member is often identified by benevolence and tinged with nostalgic affection. Reflecting the identity of benevolent relationships of humans and pets given currency during the nineteenth century, for some witnesses the dog served as a companion engaged in an affectionate relationship with humans. For veterinary technician Michelle Holmes, "banning a breed is like banning a particular race or religious group from this province. These pit bulls are beloved family members."[58] Lieutenant Colonel Mike Dabros testified that he opposed the ban and felt that he was "fighting for our family's way of life as we know it against our own government" and that the law allowed the government to "come into our home and criminalize our way of life with absolutely no basis for doing so." The threat, he argued, was to his effort to have his children "experience the joy of growing up around dogs." He then described the mutual affection of his dogs and his children "almost as siblings."[59] Additionally, some witnesses described the affectionate qualities of the proposed breeds to be banned by the bill. The pit bull "represents all to me that is good," stated Squibbs Mercier. "They are true, honest, loyal, smart, and brave friends. They give me strength when I have none. They are the essence of my life," and "a loving family member."[60] As these statements indicate, the speakers assumed that legality and governmental policy in general must function to foster affectionate ties between caretaker and pet. They want laws to penalize those persons who would turn the naturally affectionate nature of companion animals toward violence.

The Dog as Commodity

During the hearings several persons assumed that dogs are a commodity providing income or status. For example, dog club president Ms. Mike Macbeth sought to protect the economic interest of the breeders of purebred dogs in the value of dogs as a commodity. Citing the benevolent qualities of purebreds, she claimed that puppy mills operating "in appalling conditions for profit" had produced the pit bull, "a type of mongrel" that bit more often than purebreds. Her desire was for legislation to control the "rogue breeders" and criminals who bred or owned the pit bull.[61] Dog breeder and control officer Sandy Briggs pointed out that purebred dog owners spent "billions of dollars a year in purchasing breeding stock." However, she claimed that the bill and "media hype" about dog bites threatened the revenue from puppy sales that breeders invested in events, training, supplies, insurance, travel, veterinary services, educational seminars, and dog clinics.[62]

Other witnesses sought the protection of revenues from dog-related events. For example, Sandra Alway asserted the bill would end the showing of breeds—and the income from breeding winning dogs. Also, if the breeds entered or transited Ontario, she argued that the ban would permit the seizure of the breeds and penalize responsible owners.[63] Glenn Hamilton of the North American Flyball Association argued against the breed ban. Although he recited a list of reasons for his organization's opposition to the ban, he concluded by asserting the negative economic impact of the bill. Arguing that it would end competition in his sport, he claimed that the ban would eliminate an estimated $4 million in revenue for the travel industry and governments that rented fields and arenas.[64] Finally Louis McCann, representing the pet industry, noted that the ban would increase costs for shelters, influence some owners not to seek veterinary care, and impose costs on dog breed registries.[65]

The testimony of the witnesses employing the commodity identity also reveals that they never discussed dogs in ethical terms. Assigned the identity of commodity, the dog is an object destined to subjection. Although the law entitles the dog to a core biological life, such as protections against cruelty, the dog has a life that is denuded of other entitlements. Its character is recognized as commodity rather than as a conscious being to which humans bear a degree of accountability.

Stewardship of Animal Welfare

During the Ontario hearings some witnesses proposed to grant the dog an identity as a possessor of identifiable interests that humans must respect. Their testimony presented the identity of human stewardship of the welfare of dogs and a concomitant desire to secure legalized accountability in human–companion animal relations. First, they tried to expose the pretensions, irrationality, rigidity, ridiculousness, arbitrariness, scientific inaccuracies, or foibles of the proponents of the breed ban. Then they offered a corrective expressed as the legalized accountability of dog caretakers.

Lois Jackson's testimony ridiculed the proposed breed ban and sought its replacement with laws that require human stewardship. The themes of her testimony—that the ban entrenched a "culture of fear between dogs and humans," was "simplistic" and "predisposed to open-ended interpretation, retaliatory in nature and biased," and that pit bulls were not "ticking time bombs" or "inherently dangerous"—found more specific iteration in the comments of other witnesses.[66] As Dianne Singer testified, the "proposed legislation appears to be based on urban myth and emotion."[67] Often the witnesses pointed out a humorous event: the inability of Attorney General Bryant to identify a pit bull in an array of dog pictures presented by a reporter.[68]

The opposition parties in the Ontario Legislative Assembly drew on and expanded these various arguments to offer a counterplot to the government's arguments for the breed ban. Progressive Conservative Party spokesman Joseph Tascona argued that breed-specific legislation is a "lazy-man approach to dealing with dog enforcement and dangerous dogs."[69] New Democratic Party spokesman Peter Kormos contended that the issue was "rife with mountebankery from the onset" and a product of the Liberals' "obsession with cheap publicity stunts."

Many witnesses offered an alternative version of legalized accountability: a dangerous dog law that criminalized owners or other persons who induced any breed of dog to attack. Unlike a breed ban, which blames the dog for misdeeds, the dangerous dog law proposal makes owners responsible for the behavior and welfare of their dog. Nonetheless, the legalized stewardship required of caregivers does not proffer positive rights or entitlements for the dog.

The Missing Identity: Animal Legal Rights

During the legislative debates on the Ontario breed ban, all participants neglected one possible identity for dogs. The witnesses and opposition parties did not employ an identity that drew upon the idea of an entitlement of rights for animals as a legal means to establish accountability for the behavior of pets and to prevent the elimination of some breeds of dogs. The idea of animal legal rights played little role in the struggles. There was no use of the discourse of rights or an effort to identify the dog as an autonomous rights-bearer. There also was not general opposition to the ban from other rights-oriented groups. Consequently the animal legal rights identity played little role in the political struggle about the breed ban.

Outcome

In the end, the Ontario Liberal Party defeated all efforts of the opposition parties to amend or reject the breed ban bill. The Legislative Assembly adopted the bill with only minor amendments made to clarify the original language of the bill.[70] The outcome reveals how humans often cast a blind eye to the passive cruelty created by their legal choices about pets. By assuming the pit bull is a dangerous piece of property, attention focused on the violence of some dogs, not on the violence trained into the dogs by humans or the violence of law that promises the extermination of the breed. In the Assembly humans' fear of these dogs, expectations about their behavior, and recognition of them as disposable property trumped any ethical concerns. This victimization of the dog was not a legislative concern.

The legislative majority was able to claim they had enacted a popular and functional policy. By ignoring the violence of their policy and ignoring or talking past persons who offered another identity for dogs, they could claim it was an efficacious solution to a public safety problem and averted a risk with minimal costs. Indeed, the law simplified the regulation of dangerous dogs. It casually inflicted legalized violence on a breed of dogs, dogs which would be destroyed outside of public view so it would be unlikely that the public would be appalled by their death. The law, consequently, imposed minimal accountability on humans and shifted the costs of reprisal for dog attacks to the dog.

CONCLUSION

This chapter has addressed the question: What is the meaning of pets for the public in contemporary Canada and the United States? Although the survey data and case study of a policy debate illustrate considerable support for a political agenda with proposals designed to improve the treatment of companion animals, the data and analysis of public attitudes about companion animals recounted in this chapter indicate deep-seated variations in the identities and normative values that the public uses to define the meaning of pets in Canada and the United States. Policies that reflect the identification and normative valuation of pets as subjects of human dominion, nuisance property, or commodity do not find widespread support. However in some instances, as with the Ontario breed ban, they find vocal and politically successful supporters who control the decisions of policymaking institutions. The consequence is that, despite diffuse support for animal welfare policies, conflicts about the political agenda exist and political struggles about pet law and policy will emerge and can persist.

Also, as illustrated by the hearings in Ontario, the proponents of the different identities of dogs tend to talk past one another. There occurred a breakdown in communication as the participants drifted into what Robin Wagner-Pacifici has identified as "discursive excess" or exaggeration and extremism of terms.[71] Such discursive excess makes conflict resolution difficult and freezes policy action unless, as transpired in the Ontario Legislative Assembly, one party or interest dominates policymaking institutions.

Yet, despite the persistence of conflict, there is a shared identification and common pattern of discourse among people evincing different identifications of cats, dogs and horses. Especially as illustrated in the competing stories of the persons testifying before the Ontario Legislative Assembly, all speakers framed dogs as subjects of a degree of human discretion. Almost all constituted dogs as property, commodity, or a subject of human stewardship. Regardless of their social identity or human understandings of animal cruelty, companion animals were not recognized as fully autonomous beings during the arguments about public policies that affect them. Finally, both the data and the case study offer further evidence that the depiction of widespread support for an animal rights movement lacks justification. The animal law and policy agenda is dominated by a struggle among people who support benevolent care or humane stewardship of animals versus people who categorize companion animals as either property or a commodity. Discussion of animal rights is thus closer to the fringe than the center of the political struggle about pet laws and policies.

NOTES

1. An exception is Scott Vollum, Jacqueline Buffington-Vollum, and Dennis R. Longmire, "Moral Disengagement and Attitudes about Violence toward Animals," *Society and Animals* 12 (2004): 210–35.
2. "Agenda" is defined as in John Kingdon, *Agendas, Alternatives, and Public Policies*, 2nd ed. (New York: HarperCollins, 1995), 4.
3. M. Kent Jennings and Richard G. Niemi, *The Political Character of Adolescence: The Influence of Families and Schools* (Princeton: Princeton University Press, 1974); Ellen S. Cohn and Susan O. White, *Legal Socialization: A Study of Norms and Rules* (New York: Springer-Verlag, 1990); June Louin Tapp and Felice J. Levine, "Legal Socialization: Strategies for an Ethical Inquiry," *Stanford Law Review* 27 (1974): 1–72.
4. Edward O. Wilson, *Biophilia* (Cambridge, MA: Harvard University Press, 1984).

5. Paul Shepard, *Thinking Animals: Animals and the Development of Human Intelligence* (New York: Viking Press, 1978); Paul Shepard, *The Others: How Animals Made Us Human* (Washington, DC: Island Press, 1996); Harriet Ritvo, "The Emergence of Modern Pet-Keeping," in *Animals and People Sharing the World*, ed. Andrew N. Rowan. (Hanover, NH: University Press of New England, 1988), 13–31; Yi-Fu Tuan, *Dominance and Affection: The Making of Pets* (New Haven: Yale University Press, 1984).
6. Leslie Irvine, *If You Tame Me: Understanding Our Connection with Animals* (Philadelphia: Temple University Press, 2004), 18–56.
7. Stephen R. Kellert and Miriam O. Westervelt, *Children's Attitudes, Knowledge and Behaviors Toward Animals* (Washington, DC: U.S. Dept. of the Interior, Fish and Wildlife Service, 1983); Stephen R. Kellert, *The Value of Life: Biological Diversity and Human Society* (Washington, DC: Island Press, 1996), 46–51.
8. Gail F. Melson, *Why the Wild Things Are: Animals in the Lives of Children* (Cambridge, MA: Harvard University Press, 2001), 32–70, 132–58.
9. Aline H. Kidd and Robert M. Kidd, "Children's Attitudes toward Their Pets," *Psychological Reports* 57 (1985) 15–31; Aline H. Kidd and Robert M. Kidd, "Factors in Children's Attitudes Toward Pets," *Psychological Reports* 66 (1990) 775–86; Aline H. Kidd and Robert M. Kidd, "Social and Environmental Influences on Children's Attitudes toward Pets," *Psychological Reports* 67 (1990) 807–18.
10. Frank R. Ascione, *Children and Animals: Exploring the Roots of Kindness and Cruelty* (West Lafayette, IN: Purdue University Press, 2004), 61, and generally 25–139.
11. Stephen R. Kellert and Joyce K. Berry, *Knowledge, Affection and Basic Attitudes toward Animals in American Society* (Washington, DC: U.S. Dept. of the Interior, Fish and Wildlife Service, 1980), 129–30.
12. Kellert, *Value of Life*, 10–26.
13. Kellert, *Value of Life*, 11–14; Kellert and Berry, *Knowledge, Affection and Basic Attitudes toward Animals*, 41–48.
14. Kellert and Berry, *Knowledge, Affection and Basic Attitudes*, 42–128; S. Plous, "Psychological Mechanisms in the Human Use of Animals," *Journal of Social Issues* 49 (1993): 11–52.
15. Kellert and Berry, *Knowledge, Affection and Basic Attitudes toward Animals*, 42–128.
16. Kellert, *Value of Life*, 24–26.
17. Kellert and Berry, *Knowledge, Affection and Basic Attitudes toward Animals*, 42–128.
18. Ruth M. Beatson and Michael J. Halloran, "Humans Rule! The Effects of Creatureliness Reminders, Mortality Salience and Self-Esteem on Attitudes

towards Animals," *British Journal of Social Psychology* 46 (2007): 619–32; Pamela Carlisle-Frank and Joshua M. Frank, "Owners, Guardians, and Owner-Guardians: Differing Relationships with Pets," *Anthrozoös* 19 (2006): 225–42; Shelley L. Galvin and Harold A. Herzog, Jr., "Ethical Ideology, Animal Rights Activism, and Attitudes toward the Treatment of Animals," *Ethics and Behavior* 2 (1992): 141–49; Harold A. Herzog, Jr., "'The Movement is My Life': The Psychology of Animal Rights Activism," *Journal of Social Issues* 49 (1993): 103–19; Harold A. Herzog, Jr., "Gender Differences in Human-Animal Interactions: A Review," *Anthrozoös* 20 (2007): 7–21; Sarah Knight et al., "Science versus Human Welfare? Understanding Attitudes toward Animal Use," *Journal of Social Issues* 65 (2009): 463–83; Charles W. Peek, Nancy J. Bell, and Charlotte C. Dunham, "Gender, Gender Ideology, and Animal Rights Advocacy," *Gender and Society* 10 (1996): 464–76; Tania D. Signal and Nicola Taylor, "Attitudes to Animals and Empathy: Comparing Animal Protection and General Community Samples," *Anthrozoös* 20 (2007): 125–30; Nicola Taylor and Tania D. Signal, "Pet, Pest, Profit: Isolating Difference in Attitudes towards the Treatment of Animals," *Anthrozoös* 22 (2009): 129–35.

19. On justifications for cruelty, see Frank R. Ascione and Kenneth Shapiro, "People and Animals, Kindness and Cruelty: Research Directions and Policy Implications," *Journal of Social Issues* 65 (2009): 569–87; Clifton P. Flynn, "Acknowledging the 'Zoological Connection': A Sociological Analysis of Animal Cruelty," *Society and Animals* 9 (2001): 71–87; Maria Vaca-Guzman and Arnold Arluke, "Normalizing Passive Cruelty: The Excuse and Justifications of Animal Hoarders," *Anthrozoös* 18 (2005): 338–57. On attitudes toward cruelty policies see Bill C. Henry, "Empathy, Home Environment, and Attitudes toward Animals in Relation to Animal Abuse," *Anthrozoös* 20 (2006): 17–34; Judith C. Oleson and Bill C. Henry, "Relations among Need for Power, Affect and Attitudes toward Animal Cruelty," *Anthrozoös* 22 (2009): 255–65; Valerie K. Sims, Matthew G. Chin, and Ryan Yordon, "Don't Be Cruel: Assessing Beliefs about Punishments for Crimes Against Animals," *Anthrozoös* 20 (2007): 251–59.
20. American Veterinary Medical Association, *U.S. Pet Ownership and Demographics Sourcebook (2012)*, (Schaumburg, IL: American Veterinary Medical Association, 2012), 14, 26, 42.
21. Matthiaas Schonlau, Ronald D. Fricker, Jr., and Marc N. Elliott, *Conducting Research Surveys via E-mail and the Web* (Santa Monica, CA: Rand, 2002), xv.
22. The complete survey is posted at http://slate.wvu.edu/r/download/183680.
23. John Passmore, "The Treatment of Animals," *Journal of the History of Ideas* 36 (1975): 195–218; Paul Waldau, "Seeing the Terrain We Walk Features of the Contemporary Landscape of 'Religion and Animals,'" in *Communion of Subjects:*

Animals in Religion, Science, and Ethics, ed. Kimberly Patton and Paul Waldau (New York: Columbia University Press, 2006), 40–61.

24. See Katherine Wills Perlo, *Kinship and Killing: The Animal in World Religions* (New York: Columbia University Press, 2009).

25. Genesis 1:26 (New Revised Standard Version); see also Genesis 9:2, Leviticus 1–10 (New Revised Standard Version); Gary Steiner, *Anthropocentrism and its Discontents: The Moral Status of Animals in the History of Western Philosophy* (Pittsburgh, University of Pittsburgh Press, 2005), 38–92, 112–52.

26. Ecclesiastes 3:19 (New Revised Standard Version); see also Laura Hobgood-Oster, *Holy Dogs and Asses: Animals in the Christian Tradition* (Urbana: University of Illinois Press, 2008).

27. Andrew Linzey, *Animal Gospel* (Louisville, KY: Westminster John Knox Press, 2000); Jay B. McDaniel, *On God and Pelicans: A Theology of Reverence for Life* (Louisville, KY: Westminster John Knox Press, 1989); Sallie McFague, *The Body of God: An Ecological Theology* (Minneapolis: Augsburg Fortress, 1993); Paul Waldau, *The Specter of Speciesism: Buddhist and Christian Views of Animals* (New York: Oxford University Press, 2002); Stephen H. Webb, *On God and Dogs: A Christian Theology of Compassion for Animals* (New York: Oxford University Press, 1998).

28. Charles W. Peek, Mark A. Konty, and Terri E. Frazier, "Religion and Ideological Support for Social Movements: The Case of Animal Rights," *Journal for the Scientific Study of Religion,* 36 (1997), 429–39.

29. Corwin R. Kruse, "Gender, Views of Nature, and Support for Animal Rights," *Society and Animals,* 7 (1999): 179–98.

30. Colin Jerolmack, "Tracing the Profile of Animal Rights Supporters: A Preliminary Investigation," *Society and Animals* 11 (2003), 245–63.

31. Jamie L. DeLeeuw et al., "Support for Animal Rights as a Function of Belief in Evolution, Religious Fundamentalism, and Religious Denomination," *Society and Animals* 15 (2007), 353–63.

32. Shelley L. Galvin and Harold A. Herzog, Jr., "Ethical Ideology, Animal Rights Activism, and Attitudes toward the Treatment of Animals," *Ethics and Behavior* 2 (1993), 141–49; S. Pious, "An Attitude Survey of Animal Rights Activists," *Psychological Science* 2, no. 3 (1991): 194–96.

33. Kruse, "Gender, Views of Nature, and Support for Animal Rights," 179–98; Peek, Konty, and Frazier, "Religion and Ideological Support"; A. Miura, J. W. S. Bradshaw, and H. Tanida, "Childhood Experiences and Attitudes towards Animal Issues: A Comparison of Young Adults in Japan and the UK," *Animal Welfare* 11, no. 4 (2002): 437–48; Signal and Taylor, "Attitudes to Animals and Empathy," 47–57; Karl L. Wuensch and G. Michael Poteat, "Evaluating the Morality of Animal Research: Effects of Ethical Ideology, Gender, and Purpose," *Journal of Social Behavior and Personality* 13 (1998): 139–50.

34. "Religious Statements on Animals," Humane Society of the United States, accessed Apr. 21, 2008, http://www.humanesociety.org/about/departments/faith/facts/statements/; Lewis Regenstein, *Replenish the Earth: A History of Organized Religion's Treatment of Animals and Nature—Including the Bible's Message of Conservation and Kindness toward Animals* (New York: Crossroad, 1991), 130–42, 147–65, 168–74; Robert D. Woodberry and Christian S. Smith, "Fundamentalism et al: Conservative Protestants in America," *Annual Reviews in Sociology* 24 (1998): 25–56.
35. Amy Worden, "Clock Ticks for Kennel Law," *The Philadelphia Inquirer*, Sept. 14, 2008.
36. For discussions of alternatives to animal testing, see "@Altweb: The Global Clearinghouse for Information on Alternatives to Animal Testing" (http://altweb.jhsph.edu/) and *ALTEX: Alternatives to Animal Experimentation* (http://altweb.jhsph.edu/altex/), Johns Hopkins University Center for Alternatives to Animal Testing, accessed Feb. 27, 2014.
37. Ban on permanent tethering or caging, bans on animal research for nonmedical commercial purposes, bans on animal research when alternatives exist, extension of cruelty legislation to protect research animals as well as pets, kennel licensing and inspections, consumer protection law for purchases of pets, differential licensing fees for unaltered animals, and bans on particular breeds of dogs.
38. Letter from Michael Bryant, attorney general, Province of Ontario, to Susan Hunter and Richard Brisbin, West Virginia University (Aug. 1, 2006) (on file with the authors).
39. 38:1, Bill 132, Public Safety Related to Dogs Statute Law Amendment Act, 2005, 38 Legislative Assembly (Ont. 2004) sec. 2 [Hereinafter *Hearings*].
40. *Revised Statutes of Ontario*, 1990, Chap. D.16.
41. *Revised Statutes of Ontario*, 1990, Chap. A.22.
42. 38:1, Bill 132, Public Safety Related to Dogs Statute Law Amendment Act, 2005, Background Information, 38 Legislative Assembly (Ont. 2005) [Hereinafter *Hearings*] (not paginated, cited by speaker).
43. Clifford Geertz, *The Interpretation of Cultures* (New York: Basic Books, 1973), 27–28.
44. Clifford Geertz, *Local Knowledge: Further Essays in Interpretive Anthropology* (New York: Basic Books, 1983), 170–75.
45. John Brigham, *The Constitution of Interests: Beyond the Politics of Rights* (New York: New York University Press, 1996), 20–27.
46. *Hearings* (testimony of Ronald Jeroy).
47. Ibid. (testimony of Louise Ellis).
48. Ibid. (testimony of Mark Fox).
49. Ibid. (testimony of Diane Porquet).
50. Ibid. (testimony of Ronald Jeroy).

51. Ibid. (testimony of Toronto Police Service, Julian Fantino). For scholarly discussion of the association of pit bulls with criminality, see Jaclyn E. Barnes et al., "Ownership of High-Risk ('Vicious') Dogs as a Marker for Deviant Behaviors," *Journal of Interpersonal Violence* 21 (2006): 1616.
52. *Hearings* (testimony of Police Association of Canada, Bruce Miller).
53. Ibid. (testimony of Tom Kirby).
54. Ibid. (testimony of George Scott; see also testimony of Peter Orphanos).
55. Ibid. (testimony of City of Kitchener, Barry Vrbanovic).
56. Ibid. (statement by the Minster and responses, Michael Bryant).
57. Ibid. (testimony of Peter Archer).
58. Ibid. (testimony of Michelle Holmes).
59. Ibid. (testimony of Mike Dabros). Compare Jessica Greenebaum, "It's a Dog's Life: Elevating Status from Pet to 'Fur Baby' at Yappy Hour," *Society and Animals* 12 (2004): 117–35.
60. *Hearings* (testimony of Staffordshire Bull Terrier Club of Canada, Squibbs Mercier).
61. Ibid. (testimony of Barrie Kennel and Obedience Club, Mike Macbeth).
62. Ibid. (testimony of Sandy Briggs).
63. Ibid. (testimony of Golden Horseshoe American Pit Bull Terrier Club, Sandra Alway).
64. Ibid. (testimony of North American Flyball Association, Glenn Hamilton).
65. Ibid. (testimony of National Companion Animal Coalition, Lewis McCann).
66. Ibid. (testimony of Animal Aide Association of St. Thomas-Elgin, Lois Jackson).
67. Ibid. (testimony of Animal Aide Association of St. Thomas-Elgin, Lois Jackson; testimony of Dianne Singer).
68. See "Michael Bryant's Pit Bull Ban Interview," accessed Oct. 5, 2015, https://www.youtube.com/watch?v=PVaJpFHed9A, for the interview of Attorney General Bryant.
69. 38:1, Bill 132, Public Safety Related to Dogs Statute Law Amendment Act, 2005, Debates and Progress, Standing Committee on the Legislative Assembly, Feb. 10, 2005, (statement of Joseph Tascona).
70. 38:1, Bill 132, Public Safety Related to Dogs Statute Law Amendment Act, 2005, Current Status: Royal Assent received Chapter Number: S.O. 2005 C.2. Some of the terminology in the Amended Act is clarified by Dog Owners' Liability Act, Ontario Regulation 157/05, Amended to O. Reg. 434/05, Pit Bill Controls.
71. Robin Wagner-Pacifici, *Discourse and Destruction: The City of Philadelphia versus MOVE* (Chicago: University of Chicago Press, 1994), 143–45.

4

The Formation of a Pet Policy Agenda: Activists and Organized Interests

Although the public assigns identities to companion animals, ascribes normative values to them, and debates their legal status, people must engage in civic and political actions for an issue about pets to reach the political agenda. In this chapter we answer the question: How do activists and organized interests shape the political agenda that affects the lives of cats, dogs, and horses? To answer this question we will discuss why people engage in civic actions that influence the lives of companion animals. Then we will turn to an exploration of the formation of social networks and nonpolitical civic organizations that influence the treatment of cats, dogs, and horses. Finally we will inquire into the influence of the agenda-setting activities of political activists, interest groups, and coalitions of organized interests on policy issues that affect pets.

ACTIVISTS AND ACTIVISM

There is no empirically rigid distinction between the less and more politically active individuals and organizations engaged in setting the pet policy agenda. Engagement in the many activities and organizations of society is best described as arrayed on a continuum along which only some individuals or groups engage in acts of political voice or undertake direct actions such as campaign contributions, lobbying, publicity campaigns, or litigation to influence government.[1] At the other end of the continuum are civic activists who engage in voluntary nonpolitical activity or participate in organizations that do not take stands on policy matters, seek the exercise of governmental authority, or pursue social benefits or economic profits from government.[2]

To engage in political or civic activism, persons need *motivation* and a *capacity* to pursue an interest. As noted in chapter 3 the motivation to act in ways that affect the lives of pets might originate during childhood socialization or through interaction with and attachment to animals. However, the motivation or incentive to *act* on matters related to the lives of companion animals could stem from any of the following:

1. A *material incentive* or "tangible rewards; that is, benefits that have a monetary value or can easily be translated into ones that have." For example, persons or corporate interests might find increased income if they breed and sell pets.
2. A *solidary incentive* or gratification that has "no monetary value and cannot easily be translated into one that has." The reward comes from the socializing, congeniality, identification, status, or social distinction provided by group activity people might enjoy when, for example, they have their dogs compete in an agility contest, show cats at fairs, or use horses for trail riding.
3. A *purposive incentive,* providing gratification that is intangible but derived "in the main from the stated ends of the association rather than from the simple act of associating. These inducements are to be found in the supra-personal goals of the organization, "which do not benefit the members in any direct or tangible way."[3] Persons with a purposive incentive can fulfill their connection to companion animals when they volunteer at animal shelters, foster abandoned cats, or rescue horses from slaughter. They can join associations with an avowed political aim such as the passage of laws to end greyhound racing. Sometimes accompanied by anger at the treatment of animals,

their purposive intentions become rigid. The members envision themselves as true believers or saviors. "In this case, flexibility as to goals is reduced by the moral or sacrosanct quality with which they become imbued."[4]

Evidence suggests that the capacity to act might be influenced by two factors: knowledge acquired from others (family, educators, associational and religious leaders, members of social networks) who provide information, indicate the benefits of engagement in an activity or animal-oriented organization, and recruit them for service in the organization; and resources, such as an individual's free time, money, opportunities for engagement on their own or through an established organization, and personal skills that relate to interactions with animals (such as physical ability to handle animals or to perform tasks that affect animals). In particular scholars have linked socioeconomic status to the capacity to act civically and politically.[5]

CIVIC ACTIVISM

Limited information exists about the motivations and capacities of persons active in nonpolitical civic companion animal activities. Much of the activity is simply economic support for animal-related organizations that seek to improve the welfare of pets. Of respondents to the multinational survey described in chapter 3, 30.7 percent indicated contributions to animal welfare or legal rights–focused organizations (Canada: 26.2 percent; United States: 35.6 percent). Also, a study reported that volunteers in U.S. animal benevolent or welfare organizations typically are female, white, pet-owning, heterosexual, employed, childless, married or partnered, Democrat-leaning, between the ages of 40 and 59, have an income between $50,000 and $99,999, are Protestant, and are motivated by a need to act on important values related to animals.[6] Pet rescue volunteers tend to be overwhelmingly apolitical females who do not seek political change in the welfare or rights of animals. Instead, they are motivated to change "the mindset of individuals by educating potential dog guardians about the dangers of irresponsible breeders and pet shops, the importance of spay/neuter, and positive dog caretaking."[7] They therefore seek to reinforce "existing ties to like-minded people rather than opening new ones to people with different values."[8] These patterns among activists reflect a society-wide pattern of greater support for animal welfare and rights among women who express an egalitarian ideology.[9]

Based on our observations and interviews, the participants in civic companion animal activities vary in their efforts but are devoted to improving the lives of companion animals.[10] They identify cats, dogs, and horses as beings that deserve human benevolence. Consider these examples of companion animal activists, all white, middle class, and middle-aged:

- Sarah is a cat caregiver who has devoted her efforts for years to the collection and distribution of pet food to needy pet owners through food banks. She focuses her efforts on pet food drives, but she does not engage in pet rescue or any political activity related to pet welfare.
- Chloe operates a kennel where she raises and shows purebred dogs. As a member of a purebred dog club affiliated with the American Kennel Club, she undertook the responsibility of the club's rescue chair. At first she fostered abandoned dogs of the breed that she raised; however, over time she extended her concern to other abandoned dogs. She now assists other rescues to save several breeds and arrange their adoption. She does not engage in animal-related political activities.
- Wendy operates a horse rescue in a rural area of a Middle Atlantic state. Because of her love of horses, after military service she used her veteran's benefits to obtain a bachelor's degree in equine management. With parental encouragement she became interested in horse adoption. After adopting two horses and keeping them at a farm, she was able to purchase the horse farm from the estate of its owner. At the farm she now cares for more than twenty rescued horses and attempts to secure adoption for them. She relies on donations and adoption fees to support the farm, and she has no interaction with or financial support from public officials.
- Charlie loved a particular breed of dog and donated his considerable financial resources to groups that rescued that breed. After marrying a woman who liked a different breed, Charlie, along with his wife,

started adopting dogs. Within five years they expanded their efforts to create an animal shelter that took all varieties of animals—small dogs to horses. In these efforts they made no contacts with government or public officials.

Some activists, such as Sarah and Chloe, center their activity on a local organization. They do not network with other individuals or groups. However, as illustrated by Charlie's efforts, individuals concerned about pet welfare often find they need allies to advance their concerns. The result is sometimes the emergence of social networks or interest groups of like-minded people who engage in collective but nonpolitical efforts to influence the lives of pets.

SOCIAL NETWORKS

Social networks are loose associations, and often they exist to improve the lives of pets. Networks lack the formal leadership and structure that permits organized public relations, lobbying, or other political actions. Instead, networks are ad hoc or latent groups of volunteers who seek a collective good.[11] From observations and interviews of individuals, we have identified numerous networks of people who identify cats, dogs, and horses as beings deserving of benevolent treatment. Individuals attach themselves to networks in a variety of ways. For example, Bart collects, organizes, and disseminates information about animals in shelters needing rescue, the need for volunteers to transport an animal from a shelter to rescue group or adopter, and rescue groups needing help to pay the medical bills of dogs in their care. He began these activities as a breed rescuer and then gradually moved to administrative activities and became a central figure in a network. Alternatively, Jane's connections to rescue networks are more tangential. She reads Internet postings by rescue groups, on occasion has donated to groups, and in a few instances has cared briefly for animals in need of rescue.

Networks vary in the intensity of communications among affiliated individuals.[12] The core of many companion animal networks is often a group of less than a dozen volunteers who are active almost daily in rescue or other companion animal matters. They communicate their shared interests in person or via telephone, e-mail, or social media on a regular basis. Indeed, the advent of the Internet and social media such as Facebook have permitted a significant expansion of the geographical scale and membership of social networks concerned about companion animals.

Network operations often are unstructured. For example, transportation networks that transfer rescued dogs to new homes frequently have contact persons who function as communication nodes. They volunteer to contact potential transporters, but they possess few other leadership duties. In most instances volunteers use e-mail to set up a chain of drivers for the dog's journey. For example, transportation networks such as the Animal Rescue Superhighway use e-mail contacts among volunteers to arrange the shipment of shelter and rescue dogs to individuals who furnish them with permanent homes. At a predetermined location another person takes over a section of the journey to a new home. Most network activities are funded by the volunteers who transport the animals. Often the volunteers do not have any personal familiarity with each other, and they attach themselves to the network only by their commitment to find homes for rescued animals. The number and scale of transportation networks is difficult to estimate. Some networks specialize in specific breeds, while others move whatever dog or cat needs a ride. Some networks rely on volunteers who drive private vehicles; others rely on long-distance truckers or airline personnel. Transportation networks do not usually engage in organized political activities.[13] Some have morphed into commercial enterprises referred to as "retail rescue." For example, Rescue Road Trips is a limited liability corporation whose volunteers acquire dogs from shelters in Southern states, prepare their medical certificates for transport, and ship them on a regular schedule by truck to the Northeast.[14]

ANIMAL-ORIENTED NONPOLITICAL ORGANIZATIONS

The recognition of the shared benefit can motivate people to join an organized interest, including interest groups, for-profit and nonprofit corporations, religious bodies, and other stakeholder organizations, with a collective objective.[15] Unlike a social network, an organized interest possesses a formal membership, a leadership selected from or by the members, and specific objectives. It then develops the capacity—the knowledge and resources—to secure its objective. Many organized interests avoid direct political activity.

Motivations and Incentives

What are the motives and incentives to act together as an organization and pursue a collective objective? Membership is often fluid, but most commonly members ally because of a shared motive or incentive.[16] The incentive for the formation of an organized interest can be material, solidary, or purposive.

Material Motivation or Incentive

The organized interests that possess a material objective, treat companion animals as a commodity, and avoid political activity are rare. Most trade associations and profit-seeking corporations in the pet business, such as dog wholesalers, pet stores, breeders, horse tracks, and stables, will engage in political activity related to the regulation, taxation, or subsidization of their operations. However, some businesses that treat pets as a commodity remain largely unregulated and receive no subsidies. For example, in states without kennel licensing laws there is no regulation of many cat or dog breeders who operate small kennels. The government's neglect of these breeders means that they do not generally need to defend their interests in the political realm. Kennel clubs promote and protect the value of the breed as a commodity without any political activity, unless their interests are threatened. For example, the Boston Terrier Club of Canada aims to "educate members and the public at large in the benefits of purebred Boston Terriers and responsible breeding practices and encourage participation by conducting licensed specialty shows, sanction matches, obedience trials, exhibitions and boosters under the rules of the Canadian Kennel Club."[17] As with affiliate members of the American Kennel Club, however, these usually inactive clubs will lobby forcefully against laws or regulations which threaten their ability to use their animals as they choose.

Solidary Motivation or Incentive

The solidary incentives for companion animal group membership include the benefits from socializing, congeniality, interaction, and identification with companion animals. Many solidary organizations have little contact with public officials. For example, the North American Flyball Association's "purpose is to promote the rules for amateur Flyball competition, to train and approve judges, to sanction Flyball tournaments, to promote interest in the sport of Flyball, to encourage national and international Flyball competition, and to confer titles of excellence."[18] The U.S. Dog Agility Association registers and certifies dogs for agility contests and oversees agility tournaments. Aimed at the promotion of social interaction among dog trainers and dogs, neither of these groups has any legislative or regulatory objectives that affect animals.

Purposive Motivation or Incentives

Many organizations' members join groups to express their benevolence and bring changes in lives of companion animals. However, these groups usually avoid political activity. In the United States, a group's reason for avoiding political actions is often its desire to maintain a status as a not-for-profit organization. The federal Internal Revenue Code (26 U.S.C. § 501(c)(3)) provides that these organizations do not have to pay federal income tax. Many states have provisions similar to the federal rule and exempt such organizations from taxation. Also, by making contributions to these organizations deductible from personal income tax, the federal and many state tax codes encourage donations to them. Groups lose these benefits if they spend "substantial" sums, 20 percent of the organization's budget, on legislative or executive agency lobbying and engage in direct and indirect participation in partisan political campaigns. The Canada Not-for-Profit Corporations Act (S.C. 2009, c. 23) and related regulations of the Canada Revenue Agency free most nonprofit organizations from taxation.[19] The activities of nonprofit companion animal groups must produce a public benefit as determined by the Canada Revenue Agency. These benefits can include education on animal issues, animal health programs, rescue, and sheltering, and efforts to "uphold the administration and enforcement of animal welfare laws by, for example, collection of evidence of animal abuse and alerting enforcement agencies to these cases." The groups cannot further the interests of a political party, support a party or candidate for public office, or lobby any level of government in Canada or another country.[20]

Despite the provisions that permit some political activity by companion animal groups, many groups simply avoid interactions with public agencies and officials. They justify this choice as a way to protect their not-for-profit status. A more important incentive, however, is the perceived economic benefit of the avoidance of politics. Because most civic groups rely on donations for funding, it is rational for them to maximize donations by ensuring donors that they only help animals and do not take positions on controversial policy issues. Indeed, in interviews two humane organizations said they would not support legislation because it might offend donors.[21] Finally, many smaller companion animal organizations do not have professional accountants within their membership and find tax issues to be frightening. They prefer to avoid politics completely.

To benefit pets, purposive animal welfare groups therefore often adopt one of two approaches. Groups with members who interact directly with companion animals illustrate the first approach. For example, Animal Friends in Pittsburgh, Pennsylvania, operates a spacious animal shelter for surrendered cats, dogs, and rabbits, provides a spay/neuter initiative that offers low- or no-cost spay and neuter surgeries to low-income pet owners, and assists feral cat colony caretakers and shelters without spay/neuter programs. It supplies low cost rabies inoculations, canine training for shelter animals, pet-assisted therapy for assisted living homes, and grief counseling for those whose pet dies. Also, it provides an array of animal education programs and animal-themed parties for children. Its only contact with government is through the receipt of abandoned pets from animal control officers and filings of cruelty reports by their humane officers.[22]

A multitude of local humane societies, rescue organizations, and shelters operated by private organizations exhibit a similar purposive objective while avoiding political action. Instead, they define their purpose as saving animals from abandonment and abuse. For example, Boston Terrier Rescue is a coalition of state and local groups of volunteers who watch for Bostons at risk, offer temporary foster homes to them, and work to find them new homes.[23] North East Rottweiler Rescue and Referral of Rhode Island rescues unwanted and abandoned Rottweiler dogs and places them in permanent homes. It also promotes responsible ownership by providing free educational services such as pre-adoption counseling, behavior evaluations, and breeder, trainer, and insurance referrals."[24] Rat Terrier Rescue Canada rescues and fosters Rat Terriers in private homes and attempts to find permanent homes for Rat Terriers that have been abused, neglected, or abandoned.[25]

Illustrative of a second approach are groups, often with a larger membership, that provide education on pet care and engage in fundraising to support animal efforts of other organizations, including food and medical or other care. They do not, as an organization, directly care for animals. For example, the group Speaking of Dogs in Toronto, Ontario, does not interact directly with animals. Instead, it offers seminars on how to assess and prepare shelter and rescue dogs for adoption, understanding nutritional health, animal communication, dog–child safety, how dogs communicate with each other, and positive training techniques. It publishes a directory of rescue groups and shelters and arranges medical assistance and foster care for abandoned and puppy mill dogs. It does not engage in any political activity.[26] The Mountaineer Spay Neuter Assistance Program (M-SNAP) of West Virginia provides assistance to pet caregivers "who honestly need help to spay or neuter the pets or feral cats in their care." The assistance is provided by a voucher program to veterinarians to compensate for the spaying or neutering of cats and dogs by local veterinarians. M-SNAP also does not directly interact with animals, support legislation, or engage in political activity.[27]

By-product Activity

Many organized interests affect the treatment of companion animals as a by-product of incentives to protect other interests.[28] For example, as we describe in chapter 6, the purposive incentive to protect the value of their real estate induced homeowners in Lancaster County, Pennsylvania, to become concerned about the noise and dirt generated by nearby kennels. Consequently the homeowners came to recognize the adverse conditions that dogs suffered in the kennels and sought out ways to protect them.

Coalitions and Interactions among Purposive Civic Groups

Nonpolitical companion animal groups do not always act independently. Individuals can be members of several groups and promote cooperation among these groups. Also, groups can interact with or assist other groups in support of a shared objective. For example, Boston Terrier Rescue Net assists small Boston Terrier rescue groups with the extraordinary medical expenses of dogs in their care. Funding for the care is derived from donations to the Rescue Net that it then distributes to partner rescue groups.

A much larger coalition is Best Friends Animal Society. It began as a coalition of more than seventy-five small rescue groups and shelters in Utah that decided they could do better with placing animals if they went together to hold large adoption days in central areas within the state. Soon it established Best Friends Animal Sanctuary in Kanab, Utah, and began to rescue animals all over the United States. Eventually it grew into the largest no-kill animal sanctuary in the United States. As a coalition, Best Friends coordinates locally sponsored super adoption events at which multiple animal groups get together in "a free, fun, festival-like atmosphere" to adopt out hundreds of animals during a limited period of time, and it operates adoption centers in Salt Lake City and Los Angeles that collaborate on pet adoptions with local private and public shelters. Best Friends also operates a Guardian Angel program for monthly donors and corporate, business, in-kind, and foundation partners who donate funds that are distributed as grants to local nonprofit rescue groups and shelters and other nonprofit animal organizations across the United States.[29]

Capacity

Despite the broad range of civic companion animal activity, many networks and groups that engage in the stewardship of companion animals and rescue abandoned pets confront a "collective action problem." Theorists of interest group behavior have noted that large, diffuse groups of people, such as individuals concerned about companion animals, lack the capacity—especially the resources—to provide selective benefits or diffuse knowledge in ways that induce large numbers of people to undertake joint action on an issue.[30] Such groups differ from those with an economic interest in companion animals who support profitmaking by members.

For example, although Labrador Retrievers are the most common breed of dog in Canada and the United States, Labrador Retriever rescue groups are often starved for resources (as are most organizations devoted to animal rescue) because Labrador owners cannot be coerced to donate to such groups. Rescue activists cannot provide selective benefits, such as money or the protection of income, for existing owners of the breed or companion animal supporters. Capacity to rescue, the groups' objective, thus depends on the time devoted by volunteer activists and the limited income from adoption fees, donations, and the sale of breed-related merchandise.[31]

Additionally, our interviews have disclosed that assumptions and prejudices curb the capacity to act. Many welfare activists stated that they have avoided political action because they feel that elected officials are uncaring about animals and that they would not listen to them. This attitude was reinforced when an activist contacted a local animal control officer, city official, or state representative and received no response. When asked if they had attended local government meetings, few rescue group respondents said they had. Only two local rescue group members had attended a state legislative session, and others had only met local elected officials if the official visited their rescue organization or attended a meeting they also happened to attend. Rescue group members admitted to not attending public forums on any issue or even reading information about candidates for office. At the local level, rescue group members were generally uninformed about politics and generally did not know names of local or state officials.[32]

The Political Meaning of Civic Activism

Although they avoid political action, the civic activists and civic interest groups concerned about the treatment of pets contribute to the formation of an agenda for political action focused on issues of companion animals and the appropriate control of pets. By their very existence and their acts of benevolence these activists and interests draw attention to problems, foster a social identity for pets, and communicate ethical concerns about the treatment of pets. Nonpolitical animal-oriented activists and groups may not try to get to the political table and have a voice in the selection of policies, but they construct a climate of opinion and educate the public about the appropriate treatment of pets, and in so doing they lay the groundwork for potential political conflict.

Finally, civic networks and organizations devoted to companion animals supplement governmental activities that affect the lives of cats, dogs, and horses. In particular the groups that collect abandoned and injured animals, operate shelters, spay/neuter pets, and provide health services to pets relieve government—and taxpayers—of the costs of activities that benefit the health and security of the public. Indirectly these activities reduce the pressure for governments to adopt and fund companion animal law and policies. Paradoxically, civic action can limit the issues that appear on the political agenda and reduce the extent of political struggles about the treatment of pets.

POLITICAL INTERESTS AND THE PET POLITICS AGENDA

Although civic activists and organizations indirectly contribute to the formation of the policy agenda, the details of policy proposals and their promotion depends in large measure on the activities of organized political interests. To understand the role of organized political interests in the pet politics arena it is necessary to examine (1) organizational policy objectives and motivations; (2) motives of their membership and their leadership; (3) the capacities of their leaders; (4) their selection and conduct of political activities; and (5) the willingness of the organized interest to enter into coalitions with other groups in pursuit of its objectives.[33]

Political Motivations

Why would a group organize for political action to influence the treatment of pets? The emergence of political action from interest group members' initial nonpolitical motivations is illustrated by the history of the American Society for the Prevention of Cruelty to Animals (APSCA). As noted in chapter 2, the social identification of animals changed in the early nineteenth century and greater concern and respect for cats, dogs, and horses and other animals developed. This concern provided a purposive incentive for activists, such as Henry Bergh, to organize the ASPCA to combat cruelty toward animals. Having adopted a broad motivation or mission and defined the mission as national in scope, the organization sought to enlist an inclusive membership. Its leadership offered incentives such as humane education programs and the sheltering of strays, but some potential members sought coercive action to deter animal cruelty. To acquire the support of these potential members and afford them a benefit, the leadership pursued laws that granted legitimacy to ASPCA anti-cruelty prosecutions. Soon the group leaders engaged in the publicity, litigation, and lobbying tactics commonly deployed by American interest groups to alert people to recognize animal cruelty, to characterize its immorality, and to enact laws in exchange for the support of its membership.[34] However, members remained primarily dues payers with limited influence over the leadership's decisions.

Alternatively, if the motivation of individuals is a broad political objective, such as the enhancement of the income of farmers, the incentive to support policies that protect the breeding and use of pets as a commodity is a by-product of the group's broader objective.[35] For example, the American Farm Bureau Federation and its state and local affiliates have a broad objective: "The purpose of Farm Bureau is to make the business of farming more profitable, and the community a better place to live. Farm Bureau should provide an organization in which members may secure the benefits of unified efforts in a way which could never be accomplished through individual effort." Consequently, along with political activism on a range of issues, including the immigration of farm laborers, pesticide use, estate taxation, and trade with Russia, as a by-product of its agricultural concerns the leadership of the Farm Bureau has engaged in public relations campaigns, electoral activities, and lobbying against commercial canine kennel regulation and legislation banning horse slaughter. Fearful that restrictions on commercial dog breeders and horse ranchers might encourage animal welfare groups to seek a range of potentially costly regulation of animal husbandry practices, Farm Bureau leaders and lobbyists have undertaken such political actions to protect these businesses against regulation. In these circumstances, the group's effort to influence companion animal issues is an aspect of efforts to protect the profits of its farmer and agribusiness membership.[36]

Members, Leaders, and Shared Motives

In general, strong moral commitments to animal welfare or legal rights movements motivate political activists. In several respects political activists resemble civic activists. As with nonpolitical civic activism, political "voice" on issues through collective activity is more common among individuals with a higher social status, a status affected by education and income, and a family tradition of civic activism. For example, in the 1950s the organizers of the Humane Society of the United States (HSUS) were well-educated individuals who had long participated in influential roles in other animal welfare organizations.[37] Recent evidence shows that animal welfare activists are white, middle-class, and less religious than the general population and attend closely to publications and other sources of information about animals. Women are more likely than men to be animal advocates regardless of their age, educational level, or political views or the place they were raised.[38]

From an ethnographic study of twenty-seven female animal policy activists, Emily Gaarder defined a range of conditions that contribute to an individual's reorientation from civic activities into political activism. Her study indicates that the political motives of many of these female activists often originated when they were children in contact with animals or witnesses to the abuse and neglect of animals. When they experienced specific injuries to companion animals or acquired knowledge of the abuse of animals, other women became active as adults.[39] In varying degrees they attributed their motivation for political activism to female instincts, their personal experience of inequities, or their assigned social role, but all recognized the importance of politics for the treatment of animals.[40]

The female political activists also acquired distinctive capacities. They developed psychological skills to deal with their critics and law enforcement, a repertoire of responses to defend their political positions, and the personal skills, confidence, and self-esteem necessary to convey their positions to others. When engaged in organized political activities they often left leadership to males and used their capacities in staff and support positions. In these positions they undertook fewer confrontational actions, downplayed their emotions about animal abuses, and offered rational arguments even when single-minded in support of animal welfare or legal rights law and policies.[41]

Our observations and interviews with political activists support the findings of Gaarder.[42] However, we also have found that a range of political activism exists. It extends along a continuum from persons who are occasionally politically active, usually in local or state political arenas, to the professional national group leaders, lawyers, and lobbyists. As in other studies, in our observations and interviews we have largely encountered grassroots political activists and group leaders who are female, white, and middle-aged and who had experience in nonpolitical animal welfare organizations. For example:

- Mathilda is a Canadian who raises pedigree American Staffordshire Terriers. A breed that is readily trained, these terriers can become docile, loving companions or turned into aggressive fighters. Legislative efforts in several municipalities and provinces to ban ownership of the breed as part of a broader ban on reputedly dangerous "pit bull–type dogs" encouraged her to communicate her concerns with networks of breeders and owners of the breed and networks of largely nonpolitical animal welfare activists. Eventually Mathilda and other activists founded a national interest group with the primary mission of opposing laws banning specific breeds. Elected an officer of the group, she testified against proposed breed ban laws before legislators in both her home area and in other provinces, worked to secure donations to her cause, engaged in letter writing and public relations actions, and participated in the formation of a coalition of groups that challenged the Ontario provincial breed ban in court.
- Jane, a resident of a Middle Atlantic state, has cared for animals since childhood. After raising her children, she and her husband acquired a show dog who soon won championship status. Encouraged by persons they met at dog shows, they began to breed pedigree dogs. Within

a few years their hobby breeding had produced several champions. As an upshot of their dog show contacts they also began to rescue and foster a few dogs of the breed. After the death of her husband Jane abandoned breeding and established a small nonprofit group to rescue the specific breed and to foster small numbers of dogs of all breeds on her rural property. Always politically attentive, her rescue activities and networks led her to join and then assume leadership roles in animal welfare groups. On behalf of these groups she has occasionally contacted and lobbied local and state legislators about animal welfare, written letters to newspapers on pet cruelty matters, spoken to a conference of government officials about animal laws, and met with representatives of local, state, and national groups to coordinate lobbying and public relations campaigns to change state animal cruelty laws and to secure the enforcement of existing laws.

- Abby, a Midwesterner, also has cared for animals since childhood. As her children grew older she began to volunteer at a city government–operated animal shelter. Finding decrepit conditions at the shelter, she began to work with animal welfare groups and engage in discussions with local officials about improvements at the shelter. Eventually the lobbying and media disclosures about the shelter induced the city to construct a new shelter. In the meantime Abby's political activity drew the attention of the leadership of the dominant local political party. With their encouragement she won a seat on the city council. In this position she has continued to press for improvements in animal control personnel and law enforcement and revisions in the city's animal control ordinance.

These examples and those of Gaarder illustrate the motives and activities of local political activists and group leaders committed to improving the welfare of pets. However, among the state and national groups that address animal issues, group leaders are often professional lobbyists or lawyers. They are also more likely to be male.[43] Unlike activists such as Jane or Abby, they often have not had extensive direct contact with problems in the care of cats, dogs, and horses. They often describe animals in legalized terms rather than speak about their personal relationship with individual animals. By distancing themselves from emotional concerns about the welfare of cats, dogs, and horses and constructing pets' injuries as a problem with the law, these activists' motive is to try to encourage a political "realism" that places law and politics at the center of discussions of the welfare of pets and creates a sense of shared mission.

For example, the national leadership of HSUS consists of individuals with limited direct connection with the problems faced by those who care for abandoned and abused pets. Instead, its leaders have experience in federal and state legislative and administrative agency lobbying, management of ballot initiatives, public relations, broadcasting, and advertising, law, financial management, management of state or national organizations, and veterinary and environmental science.[44] The leaders and spokespersons for national groups and coalitions are often male; many have degrees in political science, public relations, or a related field. They understand the workings of government and possess a core belief in the need to compromise and achieve some form of legality for the treatment of pets. Typical of these leaders is Wayne A. Pacelle. Soon after he graduated from Yale University with a degree in environmental studies and history, Pacelle, moved to Washington, DC. He quickly became executive director of the small staff at the Fund for the Animals. In 1994 he accepted the leadership of HSUS, where he supervises a staff of more than 100 lawyers, scientists, public relations experts, and lobbyists.[45]

HSUS also employs representatives to collect information, publicize animal welfare issues, and lobby in the American states. In accord with Gaarder's findings about political activists in more subordinate positions, these individuals tend to be females who have had close associations with animals since childhood. Although a few are employed without significant experience in animal policy matters, many have had experience in nonpolitical local humane and rescue groups or service as an animal control officer. A few are attorneys or professional lobbyists. They report that such experiences caused them to apply for state representative positions.[46]

As with animal welfare groups, interest groups that engage in the commercial use of companion animals tend to have a professional leadership. For example, the activities of Alexander M. Waldrop, president and chief executive officer of the National Thoroughbred Racing Association

(NTRA), include racing integrity, legislative advocacy, marketing and promotion of the sport and management of issues of national significance to thoroughbred horse racing. Additionally he is connected to other groups concerned about the protection of horses as a commodity. He is a trustee of the American Horse Council and an associate member of the International Masters of Gaming Law. An attorney, he has practiced law in Louisville and served as general counsel of Churchill Downs, the home of the Kentucky Derby.[47]

Groups or coalitions of groups that undertake political action to protect the commercial use of animals also tend to employ professionals with limited current contact with animals on an as needed basis. For example, a coalition of groups seeking to defend the slaughter of horses has employed a team headed by former Texas congressman Charles Stenholm. Stenholm, the former senior Democrat on the House Agriculture Committee, is a senior policy advisor with the Washington, DC, law firm whose clients have included agribusinesses and agricultural coalitions. His team has included John W. Bode, a U.S. Department of Agriculture (USDA) official in the Reagan and Bush I administrations; John Block, former agriculture secretary in the Reagan administration; Brent Gattis, a former staffer for House Agriculture; and Sally Donner, a longtime representative of Altria and General Foods Corporations.[48]

The Capacity of Leaders

Political activists play a role in policymaking, but the political capacity of group leadership is critically important for animal-oriented groups.[49] To be successful, leaders must possess *political knowledge and skills*. They must be capable of listening, accepting responsibility, providing support to other group members, efficiently and effectively organizing group activities, and communicating the group's message to a range of audiences. Organized interests' leaders can act as entrepreneurs and often endeavor to shape public opinion in ways that allow them to "sell" the value of pet policy proposals to public officials through lobbying and electoral endorsements. They need to communicate with other group members to learn their policy preferences and resolve differences among organizational members. At the same time they must be capable of spotting opportunities—"policy windows"—for having their group's policy proposals receive serious consideration by the officials who make laws and regulations.[50] To exploit such opportunities they must develop access to public officials, provide useful expertise and information to friendly officials, and persist in arguing against policies offered by rival groups.[51] Leaders also must determine whether to act independently or to cooperate or ally with other interest groups and public officials and agencies who display an interest in similar animal policies.

In addition to knowledge of the political process, often the leadership's capacity to mobilize people into an organization with a collective political objective requires *resources* of money and recognition. Leaders often must identify and court resource providers. National interest groups attentive to pet policy, such as HSUS or the American Farm Bureau Federation, have dues-paying membership and a professional fundraising staff to secure resources. However, many animal welfare groups have a small membership and no professional staff and are financially burdened.[52] Also, all animal welfare groups rely on the resources that donors or patrons provide.[53] Patrons can be individuals, foundations, or governments. For example, the patronage of the motion picture celebrity Doris Day provided the resources and an objective for the establishment of the Doris Day Animal League (affiliated with HSUS since 2006).[54] Besides wealthy or highly visible individuals, patrons might include celebrated activists, foundations, corporations or corporate partners such as pet food companies, and social organizations such as riding or kennel clubs. Canadian and U.S. governments also give grants to assist some groups with specific programs, such as spay/neuter programs, and fund private groups that implement anti-cruelty law, as with the Massachusetts, New York, and many Canadian SPCAs.[55]

Leaders also will undertake efforts to structure how the public and public officials perceive animals in order to enhance group resources. For example, Arnold Arluke has argued that leaders of humane organizations use media and other public relations campaigns to show that their organizations have the capacity to provide a happy ending for abused pets. In so doing they validate their existence, collect resources, and gather support for their campaigns and programs.[56] Likewise groups that support horse slaughter stress that the humane disposal of unwanted horses is better for the horse than their abandonment or starvation. For these group leaders it is important that death and passive cruelty remain masked unless useful to organizational maintenance.

Political Activities

What political actions do organized interests undertake to influence the officials who formulate and implement public policies? To understand how these interests affect pets in Canada and the United States, in Table 4.1 we categorize the representative set of organized interests with animal-related policy objectives that we discuss along two dimensions: (1) motivation of members as defined by primary group mission and (2) capacity, which we define as the organizational structure and resources a group possesses and the range of political activities of the group.

Materially Motivated Groups

Political action by groups to protect a vested commercial interest in animals as a valuable commodity is common in North America.[57] There are groups composed of companion animal owners or breeders who identify their animals in terms of their commercial value as well as scientific research groups and commercial firms that employ companion animals for research on pharmaceuticals and other products.

For example, the American Quarter Horse Association believes "End-of-life issues for horses are personal and should remain the right of the individual horse owner. AQHA opposes abolishing the option of horse processing until there are other provisions to take care of more than 150,000 horses that meet that end each year."[58] The South Dakota Farm Bureau lobbies and supports candidates who support its position that "the current practice of slaughtering horses in the United States is a humane and effective way of utilizing horses and should remain in effect" and who oppose "the use of animal rights curriculum in schools."[59] The North Carolina Sporting Dog Association states it was formed "to oppose animal rights legislation proposed to the NC General Assembly. Since then, we

TABLE 4.1 Examples of Incentives and Activities of Animal-Oriented Political Organizations

Political Capacity	Organizations with Primarily Material Motivation	Organizations with Primarily Solidary Motivation	Organizations with Primarily Purposive Motivation
Organizations with Focused Objective and Limited Resources			
		U.S. Polo Assn.	Ban Ohio Dog Auctions
		American Paint Horse Assn.	United Against Puppy Mills
		Masters of the Foxhounds Assn.	Dog Legislation Council of Canada
Organizations with Multiple Objectives and Greater Resources			
Animal Welfare			American Society for the Prevention of Cruelty to Animals
			Animal Legal Defense Fund
			Doris Day Animal League
			Humane Society of the U.S.
Animal Rights			People for the Ethical Treatment of Animals
			Animal Liberation Front
			In Defense of Animals
			Nonhuman Rights Project
Commodity Protection	American Farm Bureau Federation		Iowa Pet Breeders Assn.
	American Kennel Club		Missouri Pet Breeders Assn.
	American Quarter Horse Association		Oklahoma Assn. Pet Professionals
	American Pet Products Association		National Thoroughbred Racing Assn.
	Maryland Horse Breeders Assn.		American Veterinary Medical Assn.
	North Carolina Sporting Dog Assn.		Sportsmen's and Animal Owners' Voting Alliance
	South Dakota Farm Bureau		
Advocacy Coalitions	Horse Welfare Alliance of Canada		Canadian Horse Defence Coalition
	Utah Farm Bureau Federation		Metroplex Animal Coalition
			West Va. Federation of Humane Organizations

have been fighting continuously against animal rights legislation promoted by HSUS, PETA [People for the Ethical Treatment of Animals], and other radical animal rights groups."[60] The American Kennel Club (AKC), which represents purebred commercial dog breeders, has taken positions against state and local legislation that would increase license fees or impose limitations on dog breeding kennels, against mandatory spay/neuter laws, and in support of the use of dogs in medical research.[61] A trade association, the American Pet Products Association has a Government and Regulatory Affairs Department with lobbyists who advocate, monitor, and respond to legislation and regulations that affect pet-related businesses such as the availability of pharmaceuticals for pet illnesses.[62]

Groups with material motivations and economic capacity often have the advantage of campaign money, lobbyists, access to regulatory agencies, and public relations skills that allow easy access and influence over the policymaking process.[63] For example, commercial agricultural interests have secured political influence through contact with legislators and consultation with public agencies in efforts to secure regulations that treat companion animals in terms of their usefulness for various human endeavors.[64] The American Farm Bureau Federation's ACT program assists members in making direct contact with elected officials.[65] Commercial interests also have influence through support for the electoral campaigns of members of congressional and state legislatures, especially agriculture committee members, through the creation of political action committees (PACs). Examples include the American Kennel Club PAC and the AKC Canine Legislation Support Fund, the Maryland Horse Breeders PAC, and the American Quarter Horse Association's PAC.[66] In the United States these PACs can spend largely unregulated sums to support candidates who espouse the advancement of the groups' interests.[67]

Groups with Solidary Motives

Most animal-oriented organized interests with a solidary motivation avoid political activity. However, a few will support the political activities of advocacy coalitions that possess a political objective. For example, the United States Polo Association functions to promote and develop the sport of polo. In particular it sponsors and referees polo tournaments for its members. However, because of concern about the fate of older polo ponies, it has affiliated with coalitions that oppose efforts to ban horse slaughter, such as the Unwanted Horse Coalition and the American Horse Council, and that support programs for the welfare of unwanted horses.[68] Other interest groups whose members engage in social and recreational activities with their horses, such as the American Paint Horse Association, Masters of Foxhounds Association and Foundation, and United States Hunter Jumper Association, have also affiliated with the Unwanted Horse Coalition.[69]

Purposive Groups

The range of the policy objectives of animal-oriented groups can be located along a continuum from groups focused on a single policy objective, to groups with multiple objectives, to coalitions of groups. Many of the groups have adopted a direct strategy and use legislative and administrative agency lobbying or litigation to shape pet policy. Other groups have developed an "indirect" strategy. The members of these groups either engage in public relations campaigns to build mass public support for a policy or support candidates for office or ballot measures that affect the treatment of companion animals. Alternatively, as is common with some animal legal rights groups, they may engage in peaceful civil disobedience or violate the law by engaging in acts of violence toward property or people in an effort to alert the public of the need for certain pet polices.[70]

Specific Issue–Focused Purposive Political Interests

The motivation of many organized interests is the elimination of a specific problem. To address the problem they often concentrate on the use of one form of political action. For example, the Coalition to Ban Ohio Dog Auctions (CBODA) organized to stop the sale of puppies raised in commercial kennels in North Central Ohio. It determined that it could avoid legislative battles by placement of an initiative to ban dog auctions on the election ballot.[71] United Against Puppy Mills organized in Lancaster County, Pennsylvania, to lobby for state legislation to better regulate commercial kennels. Successful in this effort, it continues to expand kennel regulation through lobbying local zoning boards and the state legislature as well as distributing information about puppy mills to mobilize support for its lobbying efforts.[72] The Dog Legislation Council of Canada is a national organized interest that aims to eliminate breed-specific dog ownership bans. To regulate dangerous dogs it instead "supports the implementation and enforcement of zero-tolerance dog licensing, zero-tolerance leash laws, and heavy fines for non-compliance" and "financial repercussions for those owners whose dogs, when not in compliance with existing laws, cause injury to a human being or to another animal." Its activities have included litigation and lobbying to overturn the breed ban law in Ontario and prevent breed bans elsewhere.[73]

Multiple Issues–Focused Purposive Political Interests: Animal Welfare

The purposive animal-oriented group whose motivation is to affect public policy on multiple issues usually employs a direct strategy. Many of these groups express their efforts with reference to the stewardship identification. For example, active in Canada and the United States, the Animal Legal Defense Fund (ALDF) has utilized litigation and amicus curiae briefs to promote the welfare of companion animals in specific cases of abuse.[74] It also developed drafts of legislation and law-related publicity for lobbying efforts on behalf of animals. The Doris Day Animal League has engaged in petition drives and publicity in an effort to prevent the use of companion and other animals in commercial product testing, to push for control of puppy mills and horse slaughter, and to garner support for a federal Animal Bill of Rights.[75] Fund for the Animals has also used a litigation strategy, but largely on issues affecting wildlife rather than pets.[76]

Other interest groups have even more comprehensive agendas. As the oldest of the politically active multiple issues purposive interest groups, the ASPCA initially worked to enact anti-cruelty laws for a wide range of animals, including wildlife and exotic species. Today for companion animals its political agenda contains multiple objectives and activities. It campaigns at the federal, state, and local levels to enact felony animal cruelty laws and end dogfighting, puppy mills (commercial dog breeding operations that neglect the well-being of the dogs), animal hoarding, euthanasia of unwanted cats and dogs in gas chambers, soring of horses, horse slaughter, and double-deck trailer horse transportation. Also, it provides resources to animal shelters, low-cost pet vaccination programs, and information to assist the reporting of cruelty. It operates various animal health services and provides grief counseling to caretakers who lose pets. In support of its objectives it employs lobbyists around the country, and it encourages direct communication with legislators by its members. These activities are coordinated through a Legislative Services unit at its New York City headquarters, and it has additional legislative lobbyists and public relations personnel stationed regionally. The APSCA also possesses the authority to act as a humane law enforcement agency in New York City.[77]

HSUS is another example of a multiple issues purposive animal-oriented interest group. Founded in 1954, HSUS adopted an anti-cruelty agenda that gradually led it into supporting a wide range of public policies that affect many animal species. By aiming at the recognition and reduction of animal cruelty, HSUS has sought responsible stewardship of animals. It has not engaged in the care of animals, and it has not sought rights and legal personhood for animals. Rather, with the language of stewardship, HSUS has pursued a series of policy objectives though political actions. From early efforts in lobbying for the passage of the Humane Slaughter Act of 1958, HSUS incrementally added publicity and lobbying efforts to secure laws that protect agricultural animals, research animals, and wildlife against cruelty and abuse. It also expanded a range of humane education programs and publications and videos about animal care aimed at the general public and children. In its early years HSUS provided financial and technical assistance to animal shelters. However, more recent publicity and lobbying efforts have aimed at the adoption of laws to require painless euthanasia of companion animals, regulation of pet stores, pet sales, and breeding kennels, the humane transport of animals, and felony prosecution of acts of animal cruelty and dogfighting. HSUS also has sought policies to protect feral cats, prevent and penalize animal hoarding, ban greyhound racing, and assure proper veterinary care of pets.[78]

With its wide range of policy objectives, HSUS has adopted the institutional structure of the typical national interest group. Headquartered in Washington, DC, it has a professional staff of about 100 employees. The staff serves in several divisions, including programmatic divisions that address companion animal, laboratory animal, wildlife, and agricultural animal issues and administrative units devoted to field investigations of cruelty, humane education, disaster relief, international affairs, and membership services and internal management. It has regional or state offices under the centralized oversight of its Washington headquarters.[79]

Founded in 1957, the Canadian Federation of Humane Societies serves as an advocate for changes in laws that affect a wide variety of animals. For its members, who are provincial or local humane interest groups, it issues publications to inform member societies about "emerging animal welfare issues, training and funding opportunities, and best practices in animal sheltering, humane education and advocacy." It administers a fund to support animal welfare work in Atlantic Canada, communicates its position statements on a wide range of animal welfare issues, and lobbies for change in the drafting of laws that govern animal cruelty and transportation. It also serves as a member of several animal welfare advocacy coalitions.[80]

Multiple Issues–Focused Purposive Political Interests: Animal Legal Rights

In support of the principles of animal legal rights, several multiple issues focused purposive political interest groups have employed a strategy in which they try to influence public policy through legislative lobbying or litigation. For example, the Nonhuman Rights Project engages in litigation "to change the common law status of at least some nonhuman animals from mere 'things,' which lack the capacity to possess any legal right, to 'persons,' who possess such fundamental rights as bodily integrity and bodily liberty, and those other legal rights to which evolving standards of morality, scientific discovery, and human experience entitle them."[81]

Other groups have adopted an indirect strategy in which members either engage in peaceful civil disobedience or resist and violate the law by engaging in acts of violence toward property and people. These groups often view the struggle for animal rights as a moral crusade.[82] Activists of the Animal Liberation Front (ALF), In Defense of Animals (IDA), and People for the Ethical Treatment of Animals have adopted direct action and civil disobedience and, in a few instances, more violent tactics such as the illegal entry of animal testing facilities and assaults on persons wearing fur in Canada and the United States.[83] These groups have often derided more modest efforts at the improvement of the regulation of animal owners and breeders.[84]

In Defense of Animals has used less spectacular protests and legal action in an effort to prevent or reduce the uses of animals such as cats and dogs in scientific experiments and to ban puppy mills.[85] The notoriety of their actions has made them a significant contributor to the policy struggles surrounding animal rights, partially because they stirred academic criticism of the ideas of animal legal rights. More significantly the tactics of small, anonymous groups, including direct action such as trespass on the property of agribusiness and assaults on consumers of animal-originated products, have galvanized political opponents of animal welfare and rights laws such as the scientists, farmers, hunters, and the communities that are economically dependent on animal production.[86] PETA has used the exposure of abuses of animals and other forms of publicity to create negative publicity for companies that sell animals as a commodity or use them in experiments. Its list of accomplishments illustrates the exposure of a wide range of abuses of animals and subsequent changes in the treatment of animals by private concerns. However, other than lawsuits against a few firms and exposures of abuses that resulted in governmental investigations, PETA does not tout legislative or other policy changes among its successes.[87]

Single and Multiple Issues–Focused Purposive "Commodity" Interests

The political activity of organized interests that identify cats, dogs, and horses as a valuable commodity often emerges as a by-product of a desire to protect a profit-generating business or profession.[88] For example, commercial breeder associations such as the Iowa Pet Breeders Association, the Missouri Pets Breeders Association, and Oklahoma Pet Professionals engage in lobbying on regulatory and licensing issues that affect the operations of their business, and they engage in public relations campaigns to convince the public that they do not operate puppy mills but do sell healthy animals.[89] The National Thoroughbred Racing Association has a Legislative Action Campaign that addresses a range of federal and state issues that affect the profitability of the horse racing industry, including gambling regulations, federal regulation of concentrated animal feeding, regulation of the medication of horses, the taxation of the industry including rules on the depreciation of racehorses, and the immigration of stable workers. To advance its positions on these issues, the association engages in lobbying and, through a PAC, provides campaign contributions to legislators.[90] As a by-product of its professional attention to animal welfare, the American Veterinary Medical Association operates a Governmental Activities Division that lobbies Congress and monitors regulatory agencies, and it supports a PAC that addresses a number of federal and state issues that affect companion animals' health and welfare.[91] With these groups animal welfare legislation, such as expanded kennel regulation and horse slaughter bans, is a concern when it poses costs to breeder or racing industries.

In addition to seeking political support for their business, interest groups that identify animals as a valuable commodity will engage in programs to undercut support for animal welfare groups. Individual activists have initiated campaigns to deter corporations from partnerships with or donations to animal welfare groups such as HSUS. These campaigns often attract the support of interest groups.[92] The Sportsmen's and Animal Owners' Voting Alliance (SAOVA) seeks "to elect politicians who will oppose the 'Animal Rightist' (AR) threat to our rights as Americans." It states it studies "governmental candidates in all states to identify those who understand and resist the AR threat, as well as those who are in the pocket of the Animal Rightists." Its list of its opponents includes a range of interests that support animal welfare and animal legal rights.[93]

A consequence of direct action by animal legal rights groups has been that groups with an economic interest in animals, such as the Farm Bureau, and agribusinesses have lobbied for laws to curtail the activism of animal legal rights interest groups. In the United States the animal commodity interests have supported the passage of the U.S. Animal Enterprise Terrorism Act.[94] They have lobbied U.S. state legislatures to secure the passage of laws that extend the limits on the activism of groups such as ALF and PETA. The laws make it a criminal offense for persons to enter without permission or conceal themselves in an animal facility closed to the public with the intent to disrupt operations, vandalize, or cause physical damage to the property.[95] Additionally, groups with an economic interest in animals have pressured state legislatures to adopt "ag-gag" or anti-whistleblower laws.[96] They have pursued legislation to permit civil libel, defamation, and personal injury suits against animal legal rights and welfare groups that criticize or surreptitiously collect and distribute information about the alleged abuse of animals, including cats, dogs, and horses. Although passed primarily to protect farmers who raise animals for food, several states have laws, which could be applied to the rearing of companion animals, that lower standards for civil liability and allow for punitive damages and attorney's fees for plaintiffs alone, regardless of the case's outcome. However, the constitutionality of these laws is undergoing court challenge on First Amendment grounds.[97] Nonetheless, the passage of laws hostile to the campaigns of animal legal rights groups suggests these groups have not reshaped law and policy in ways that significantly improve the treatment of pets.

Political Activities Assessed

The examples that we offer illustrate the diverse range of policy objectives and political activities of the organized interests concerned about cats, dogs, and horses. Yet, most of the groups aim at either laws or policies that offer governmental support for companion animal welfare or the retention of laws and policies that regard animals as a commodity subject to human control. Although groups in support of animal legal rights or, alternatively, an unfettered human control of pets exist, such groups have tended to criticize laws and policies and other groups from the "outside" rather than engage in lobbying and other direct contacts with public officials. Consequently, there often exists a bipolar political conflict in which the key participants are animal welfare groups and others who view animals as commodity or subject, such as breeders, kennel operators, horse slaughterhouses, and the like.

Advocacy Coalitions

The large number of groups active in attempts to set the pet policy agenda provides an incentive for interests to seek out allies who can aid a group in securing governmental officials' recognition of their concerns. Constituted by *sets* of private and public organizations and interest groups who share particular beliefs and who are actively concerned with a policy problem, an *advocacy coalition* seeks to coordinate its participant groups and organizations to realize a shared set of policy goals and other political benefits over time.[98]

Varieties of Coalitions

In recent years a number of advocacy coalitions have formed to address concerns about the welfare of pets. Some coalitions consist of a relatively stable set of interest groups and have a coalitional leadership. For example, in Hillsborough County, Florida (Tampa area), a small number of activists invited more than one hundred interested organization representatives and individuals to hear a presentation about coalitions elsewhere. They then engaged in small working groups, met at later conferences, and collected information to plan the next steps they could undertake. Soon a coalition of dozens of animal welfare interest groups and rescue organizations emerged that supported the expansion of shelter, spay/neuter, and feral cat control programs. This coalition, Tampa Pets, also established a board of directors consisting of representatives of various organizations and private citizens. It continues to lead efforts to secure local government funding of improved animal control services and grants from national organized interests.[99] Tampa Pets has permitted small, resource-starved animal welfare groups to engage in political action that they could not afford on their own.

Other coalitions are event specific. After a major dogfighting ring was broken, HSUS and the APSCA joined forces with American Humane Association and Best Friends Animal Society to help the Humane Society of Missouri compile evidence and care for and transport more than five hundred animals to shelters. Within months of Hurricane Katrina, the American Humane Association announced the formation of the National Animal Rescue and Sheltering Coalition, which included, among others, ASPCA and HSUS. The coalition struck agreements with various federal agencies and set up frameworks for animal protective groups' response to national disasters and other crisis situations.

Shared Beliefs

What conditions influence whether an animal-oriented group engages in advocacy coalition formation in pursuit of its policy preferences? The concept of advocacy coalitions presupposes that groups that are members of a coalition share a "core belief system" or shared motives and policy objectives.[100] These beliefs, which might include a specific social identification of companion animals and specific norms about cruelty, serve as glue that allows organized interests to join and stick together in a coalition.[101] They also affect whether an animal welfare interest group willingly works with other groups.

For example, the Canadian Horse Defence Coalition membership consists of a range of disparate groups and businesses, including the Grand Royal Equestrian Centre, Horse Protection Society of BC, Horse-Canada, Horse Harbor Foundation, Horsemen's Benevolent and Protective Association of Canada, Horsemen Helping Horsemen, Humane Society, Jardin Estate Jewelry and Antiques, and LongRun Thoroughbred Retirement. It is united solely by identification with humane stewardship of horses and support for a law to prevent the slaughter of horses for food.[102]

Coalitions of interest groups and corporations that identify animals as a valuable commodity often are the result of an industry or trade association's effort to shape or defend a public policy. For example, as a coalition of farmer and rancher businesses, corporations, and county agricultural associations, the Utah Farm Bureau Federation supports a wide range of policies designed to increase the profitability of farming and ranching. It claims "strong relationships" with a host of state and federal agencies and interest groups that presumably allow it to influence policymaking. However, it also has lobbied to protect agribusiness from tort litigation, trespass, and interference with operations by animal welfare and legal rights interest groups. To that end it has secured a law to protect ranchers against animal welfare group efforts to inquire into their treatment of horses, and, possibly, commercial dog kennels.[103]

Barriers to Coalition Formation

Barriers exist that can prevent coalition formation among groups that practice animal stewardship or seek legal rights for animals. One barrier is that most animal welfare groups compete for attention and money for specific policy changes. This contest creates a barrier to coalition formation because the groups vigorously present and protect their own individual projects and successes, often while sniping at others. The groups' competition for resources also has blocked the notion of cooperation.[104]

Activists interviewed by the authors indicated that emotional attachments to animals pose another barrier to coalition formation. Persons in animal welfare groups often see themselves as "saviors" of victims. Their incentive to help animals is extremely personal. This incentive was particularly clear in an interview with the director of a no-kill shelter for cats and dogs. She renamed her shelter as a sanctuary and said that only one or two other people can even begin to understand what she does. To work with others in a larger group or coalition actually, she finds, diminishes the individual psychological benefit. In particular work on coalition activities that do not provide any individual benefit to animals made no sense to her. She would devote their time to helping individual animals—an effort for which they receive praise from the community and love from the animal.[105]

Some groups will often choose not to work together because they believe that joint action would impede the organization's special mission. For example, because of its support of euthanasia and its controversial protest tactics, PETA has not formed coalitions with other groups. PETA members possess a clear-cut purposive incentive and identify companion animals as autonomous, rights-bearing beings whose welfare should be separated from human desires.[106] This viewpoint has distanced them from the large number of animal welfare groups that encourage the human stewardship of cats, dogs, and horses.

A lack of skilled leadership is another barrier to coalition formation. For a coalition to survive, its leaders need to acquire and process information about a constantly changing political universe and adjust their political actions to offset any challenges generated by new political circumstance. Coalition leaders who fail to learn how to engage in political tactics to achieve their objectives cannot maintain an effective coalition.[107]

Finally, political barriers to coalition formation exist.[108] Various legal impediments serve as disincentives to advocacy coalition action, such as the laws that restrict certain forms of political contributions and activities by nonprofit coalitions. Second, the threat of opposition to an advocacy coalition can discourage it from lobbying or other tactics. For example, the mere perception that there will be untenable costs created by the agribusiness and breeder coalitions can dissuade an animal welfare coalition to press for kennel regulation.[109]

Assessment of Advocacy Coalitions and the Pet Politic Agenda

Although advocacy coalitions exist in the realm of companion animal policy, more commonly coalitions form around a broader range of policies affecting animals, including wildlife and animal husbandry policies. However, for a variety of reasons that we have identified, advocacy coalitions in support of animal welfare appear to be difficult to establish and maintain. This context thus creates further difficulties for persons and groups committed to the placement of animal welfare proposals on the political agenda.

THE INFLUENCE OF ORGANIZED INTERESTS' AND COALITIONS' ACTIVITIES

In this chapter we addressed the question: How do activists and organized interests influence the political agenda that affects the lives of cats, dogs, and horses? The evidence is that organized interests have actively attempted to influence the pet politics agenda in Canada and the United States in several ways, but the extent of group influence cannot be readily empirically measured. However, in subsequent chapters we will detail further the influence of group activities on cat, dog, and horse policymaking in six distinctive ways.

1. Groups Define the Political Nature of Problems

The primary concern of any organized interest is to control the definition of problems the government can resolve. The aim of the interest is to have public officials frame and prioritize problems in ways that support the interest's policy objectives. These efforts at agenda control involve information control.[110] The assumption is that if public officials do not hear about a point of view, they will not act to represent that view. Therefore the interest can use the media, distribute professional or scientific information, and engage in public relations campaigns to generate attention to an issue. Often the interest defines efforts to shape the political agenda as "campaigns." As we will detail in chapter 6, animal welfare groups have endeavored to use public relations campaigns and lobbying to define the characteristics of puppy breeding and draw attention to their version of proper breeding practices from legislators and regulators. Other groups' campaigns we will recount include efforts to secure anti–horse slaughter laws, spay/neuter laws, control of feral cat populations, and campaigns contesting breed bans. However, groups can act to prevent attention to a problem or to debunk assertions of a need for a policy change. For example, later chapters will discuss how Farm Bureaus and other agricultural groups have sought to prevent the passage of kennel regulation and anti–horse slaughter laws. Constructing a message about the economic costs of changes, the radicalism of their opponents, and, with horses, the harm done to animals, they have communicated the benefits of the legal status quo.

2. Groups Generate Policy Proposals

Organized interests can define solutions to policy controversies. These policy proposals are best stated as reasonable and legitimate solutions stated as legislative or regulatory proposals. Chapters 6 and 7 will depict how animal welfare and commodity-oriented groups have deployed the social identities of pets and definitions of cruelty to argue that the kennel licensing and horse slaughter proposals they offered were the most reasonable policy alternatives. Chapters 8 and 9 will assess competing claims about the reasonableness of competing policies to control feral cats and allegedly dangerous dogs.

3. Groups Influence Policymaking by Public Officials

The capacity of organized interests to shape animal-oriented policies is greatly dependent on their ability to direct lawmakers and regulators to what the group defines as the salience of an issue and its idea of what constitutes accurate knowledge about it.[111] Interests therefore must practice attention-creating activities, including communications with and the lobbying of legislators and agency rule makers, endorsements and financial contributions for the campaigns of elected officials, the use of consultants to bolster the credibility of their demands, and the invitation of legislators and regulators to conferences and social events. Organized interests that have long-standing interactions with public officials possess an advantage in the attention-creating process. As we will detail in chapters 6 and 7, in their desire to increase the profits of their agribusiness and farmer membership, U.S. agricultural groups have supported the commercial pet breeding industry and the slaughter of horses for human consumption. As organized interests long active in lobbying for a major industry in many states and in possession of money for electoral contributions, they have acquired influence with legislators and executive agency officials. On the other hand, as noted in this chapter, many animal-oriented groups avoid efforts to influence public officials or assume or determine that their nonprofit status precludes lobbying and electoral support of legislators.

In the United States, the institutional structure of politics abets the legislative influence of some groups. For example, in Congress and most state legislatures, animal-related issues fall within the jurisdiction of an agriculture committee. Members of the committee are often legislators with numerous constituents engaged in the agricultural economy and concerned with farm income. As we note in chapters 6 and 7, agriculture committee members and their staff draft legislation. The drafting process often occurs with formal hearings and consultation with agricultural interest groups, producer trade associations, and agribusiness and farmer constituents, as well as with consultations with executive branch administrators of the USDA or state agriculture departments. If this process occurs over time and other interests fail to interact with legislators, a "subgovernment" or "iron triangle" or "policy domain" can emerge. In these contexts legislators, agricultural officials, and agricultural interests design policies to serve mutual goals such as the desire for profitable uses of dogs and horses.[112] Finally, because these agricultural interests' allies among legislators and public officials control veto points in the legislative process, they can create a bias toward the policy and legal status quo. Indeed, one quantitative study has shown that they "appear to have been effective in opposing changes and preventing animal rights groups from bringing about legislative change."[113]

In Canada the federal and provincial parliamentary systems require that groups focus lobbying, appearances at legislative hearings, and other communication efforts on the members who serve in the Cabinet and as committee chairs.[114] As the discussion of the debate about breed-specific legislation in Ontario in chapter 9 illustrates, this practice helps shape animal law. Groups also contribute to campaigns and rally the public to contact legislators.[115]

Although agency rulemaking occurs in a slightly different context, groups with expertise and long-standing patterns of interaction with administrators can influence rulemaking. Legislative delegation of rulemaking authority to executive branch agencies in U.S. federal and state governments affords administrators in both countries the power to flesh out the meaning of laws and devise policies for their implementation. Sometimes these administrators can make decisions that support certain legislators and groups that treat animals as a commodity. For example, in chapter 7 we describe how the USDA has continued to support horse slaughter. Despite opposition from Congress as a whole, the USDA agreed with a range of meat producing firms, their interest group allies, and legislators from the Western states to continue slaughtering horses for human consumption.[116] In Canada groups submit their policy proposals to the federal and provincial cabinet ministers with jurisdiction over the issue and liaison and consult with key agency personnel.[117] For example, in 2010 the New Brunswick SPCA engaged with government ministers and agencies to toughen standards of care in kennels, pet stores, shelters, and other pet establishments.[118]

Groups with limited resources and knowledge often find it difficult to convert the concerns of members into legislation. For example, although one of the larger, wealthier, and more visible national animal welfare groups, in each state HSUS usually employs only one representative to address state and local animal welfare legislation and rulemaking. As noted in this chapter, some small or local animal welfare groups might also not know the appropriate political venue in which to present their proposal. However, the size of a group's or coalition's membership and the accompanying recognition of its name seem to influence officials. For example, Mahalley Allen has found that greater state membership in the HSUS had a "positive and statistically significant influence on state adoption of animal cruelty felony laws. State adoption of these felony laws rose as the state's level of HSUS members increased."[119]

4. Groups Propose Ballot Propositions

Organized interests can propose legislation through the initiative and referendum process that exists in several American states. Although the costs of advertising and contacting voters for support to file a petition for a referendum and, if successful, to draw voter attention and support for a referendum can be costly, it can allow interests to avoid veto points such as legislative opponents allied with opposing interests. As we will discuss in chapter 6, despite opposition from agricultural interests, animal welfare groups used this approach successfully to secure kennel regulation in Missouri.

5. Groups Employ Litigation to Induce Policy Change

When judges in Canada and the United States decide private lawsuits that affect the treatment of cats, dogs, and horses, they develop policy that influences the treatment of pets. Lawsuits afford judges the opportunity to clarify animal-related legislation and administrative rules, modify or reconstruct traditional common law standards about the treatment of pets, and devise and impose remedies that can change human behavior toward cats, dogs, and horses. In brief, judges make pet policy when they decide these cases. As indicated in studies by Helena Silverstein and Steven Tauber, in a small number of cases organized interests, including the ALDF, HSUS, PETA, and Nonhuman Rights Project, have attempted to use civil litigation to induce the judiciary to establish policies to protect the welfare or legal rights of animals.[120] These groups' attorneys often have developed specialist knowledge about animal legal issues not common among most attorneys.

Animal-oriented interest group litigation has addressed a range of issues that confront diverse animal species, but it has only incidentally developed policies or clarified statutes in ways that specifically protect the welfare or legal rights of cats, dogs, and horses. Additionally, no study has examined empirically the variables associated with litigation about the welfare or legal rights of cats, dogs, and horses. Nonetheless, from Tauber's empirical studies of samples of U.S. group litigation for animal species in general, some important evidence about group litigation and animal policy change can be garnered.

First, Tauber's examination of U.S. state appellate court decisions has found that "statistical evidence demonstrates that the presence of animal advocacy groups statistically improves the chance of a pro-animal decision in the more important ... cases" that seek to overturn statutes, precedents, or regulations that harm animals. He also has found that "animal advocacy groups are more likely than individual litigators to take the more difficult 'aggressive' cases." This "aggressive" or change-oriented approach toward the law is especially evident among some groups that seek an autonomous identity for animals, such as the Nonhuman Rights Project.[121] Nonetheless, both the groups and individual litigants lose the majority of the cases that seek to change the meaning of the law in favor of animal welfare or legal rights. Animal interest groups fare much better when their litigation aims at the enforcement of existing laws that benefit animals. Finally, state decisions favor an interest group's effort to protect an animal more frequently in states without a popularly elected appellate court and with a more liberal public.[122]

Second, because of rules of standing to sue, such as the requirement that a human suffer a direct injury, Tauber's examination of U.S. federal litigation has found that animal welfare and legal rights groups can face a legal barrier to initiating their case. Additionally, federal government opposition to animal litigators reduces the chance of litigation that results in an outcome favorable to animal welfare. However, Tauber has found that judges appointed by a Democratic president are more likely to support animal welfare than Republican presidential appointees.[123] Also, he concludes that the federal judiciary "generally does a good job protecting humane officers against retaliation and the rights of animal activists to seek information on how institutions use animals."[124]

Finally, Tauber has reported that litigation sparks media coverage of animal issues. However, he has found that, although media coverage of animal advocacy litigation introduces the public to legal issues that affect animals, it "does not increase favorable coverage of the animal advocacy movement or highlight the mistreatment of animals." Instead, he finds that nonconfrontational protests draw more attention to animal issues than does litigation.[125]

Because civil litigation by animal welfare and legal rights interest groups is a case-by-case, piecemeal method with a limited chance for policymaking in specific jurisdictions, as Tauber's studies imply often it can only produce incremental change in law and policies that govern the treatment of cats, dogs, and horses. Although Tauber's studies concern litigation about animals in general and not just cats, dogs, and horses, the studies suggest that groups can more likely succeed in the advancement of policy change beneficial to animals in some circumstances.

6. Groups Influence the Implementation of Law and Policy

The enactment of a law does not mean that it will be effectively enforced. Unless administrators have knowledge of their legal duties, are committed to implementing and enforcing a law, and have the resources—personnel and facilities necessary for enforcement—the law might become only a symbol of concern about a recognized political problem. As we will discuss in subsequent chapters, groups can exert pressure on legislators' appropriation of funds for enforcement and administrators' motivation and capacity to enforce laws that affect companion animals. However, as we also will recount, absent group attention or action there can be selective enforcement or inaction by the administrators designated to enforce these laws.

Group Influence Often Extends Political Struggles Rather than Results in Policy Change

In line with other evidence about policy change, in subsequent chapters we present evidence that pet politics will remain a field of political conflict. In this struggle, as we will recount further in these chapters, not all kinds of groups and coalitions exert significant influence on the political agenda.[126] Additionally, group influence on the political agenda is not proportional to popular support for policies. A skillfully led group can convert their reputation into influence over legislative or administrative action. The evidence presented in chapter 3 indicates broad popular support for animal welfare and stewardship and normative values and policies protective of animal welfare. Yet, as we will recount in subsequent chapters, commodity-oriented groups can use historically developed connections to legislators and bureaucrats and their resources for lobbying, public relations, and donations to election campaigns to offset or suppress the diffuse and often ill-organized efforts or groups devoted to the protection of pet welfare. These connections result in a reputation for power for the commodity-oriented groups. For example, in 2005 West Virginia legislators listed the Farm Bureau, Sporting Dog Association, Charles Town Races (horse racing), and Greyhound Owners and Breeders Association—all groups that regard cats, dogs, or horses to be a commodity—to be among the 60 most influential interest groups in the state. No animal welfare or legal rights–oriented group made the list.[127]

Although changes in pet law and policy do occur, they are more likely to be incremental changes than dramatic shifts in policy. For example, a study of HSUS influence on state anti-cruelty law found that while its members had a clear influence on "the development and diffusion of animal cruelty felony laws in the states, … its strength in the states may not play a role in shaping the stringency of those laws."[128] However, if animal welfare groups can mobilize the diffuse supporters of their policy objectives through exposure of abuses and the conveyance of new knowledge or understanding of the plight of pets, dramatic policy change is possible.

INTEREST GROUPS AND THE POLITICAL FUTURE

Regardless of assessments of their political influence and success, it should be expected that animal welfare or legal rights groups will continue the struggle to constitute the pet law and policy agenda. They assume that changes in external events and the political environment can induce variations in the successful pursuit of their political agenda. They have faith that a segment of the public might shift its motives for joining a group and the capacity of a group might expand because of leadership changes and increases or decreases in monetary and other resources. At the same time the attentiveness of public officials to the efforts of animal-oriented groups might alter. Other issues and new events, crises, or knowledge can change the priority of pet policies on the overall political agenda. The consequence is an unstable animal policy agenda and shifting support for a variety of pet policies.

NOTES

1. On the political actions of groups, see Frank R. Baumgartner and Beth L. Leech, *Basic Interests: The Importance of Groups in Politics and Political Science* (Princeton, NJ: Princeton University Press, 1999); Kay Lehman Schlozman and John T. Tierney, *Organized Interests and American Democracy* (New York: Harper and Row, 1986).
2. Sidney Verba, Kay Lehman Schlozman, and Henry E. Brady, *Voice and Equality: Civic Voluntarism in American Politics* (Cambridge, MA: Harvard University Press, 1995), 40–42, 49–84; Kay Lehman Schlozman, Sidney Verba, and Henry E. Brady, *The Unheavenly Chorus: Unequal Political Voice and the Broken Promise of American Democracy* (Princeton, NJ: Princeton University Press, 2012), 10–13.
3. Peter B. Clark and James Q. Wilson, "Incentive Systems: A Theory of Organizations," *Administrative Science Quarterly* 6 (1961): 134–37; James Q. Wilson, *Political Organizations* (Princeton, NJ: Princeton University Press, 1995), 195–201.
4. Clark and Wilson, "Incentive Systems," 147.
5. On civic activism see Verba, Schlozman, and Brady, *Voice and Equality*, esp. 417; and also Nancy Burns, Kay Lehman Schlozman, and Sidney Verba, *The Private Roots of Public Action: Gender, Equality, and Political Participation* (Cambridge, MA: Harvard University Press, 2001), 61–98; Hahrie Han, *Moved to Action: Motivation, Participation, and Inequality in American Politics* (Stanford: Stanford University Press, 2009); Hahrie Han, *How Organization Develop Activists: Civic Associations and Leadership in the 21st Century* (New York: Oxford University Press, 2014); Schlozman, Verba, and Brady, *Unheavenly Chorus*, 18–24, 174.
6. Sandra L. Neumann, "Animal Welfare Volunteers: Who Are They and Why Do They Do What They Do?," *Anthrozoös* 23 (2010): 351–64. For case studies of civic activists who engage in pet rescue, see Karin Winegar, ed., *Saved: Rescued Animals and the Lives They Transform* (Cambridge, MA: Da Capo Lifelong, 2008). See also an older study, Wesley V. Jamison and William M. Lunch, "Rights of Animals, Perceptions of Science, and Political Activism: Profile of American Animal Rights Activists," *Science, Technology, & Human Values* 17 (1992): 438–58.
7. Jessica Greenebaum, "'I'm Not an Activist!': Animal Rights vs. Animal Welfare in the Purebred Dog Rescue Movement," *Society and Animals* 17 (2009): 301.
8. Andrei S. Markovits and Robin Queen, "Women and the World of Dog Rescue: A Case Study of the State of Michigan," *Society and Animals* 17 (2009): 340.
9. Charles W. Peek, Nancy J. Bell, and Charlotte C. Dunham, "Gender, Gender Ideology, and Animal Rights Advocacy," *Gender and Society* 10 (1996): 464–78.
10. Pseudonyms are used in this section.

11. Mancur Olson, Jr., *The Logic of Collective Action: Public Goods and the Theory of Groups* (New York: Schocken Books, 1965), 50–51.
12. James M. Jasper, *The Art of Moral Protest: Culture, Biography, and Creativity in Social Movements* (Chicago: University of Chicago Press, 1997), 175.
13. For examples, see California Rescue Railroad, accessed July 19, 2012, http://home.earthlink.net/~gmckenzie1/joincarr.htm; Canine Underground Railroad, accessed Mar. 4, 2014, http://beingstray.com/dogs/canine-underground-rescue-transport-sites/; Operation Roger Truckers Pet Transport, accessed July 19, 2012, http://operationroger.rescuegroups.org/.
14. Nancy E. Halpern, "The Phenomenon Called 'Retail Rescue,'" May 20, 2014, accessed Oct. 5, 2014, http://animallaw.foxrothschild.com/2014/05/20/the-phenomenon-called-retail-rescue/; Rescue Road Trips LLC, accessed Mar. 4, 2014, http://www.rescueroadtrips.com/.
15. See Schlozman and Tierney, *Organized Interests and American Democracy*, 10. See also Baumgartner and Leech, *Basic Interests*, 25–30.
16. Olson, *The Logic of Collective Action*, 2, 5.
17. "Club Info," Boston Terrier Club of Canada, accessed June 28, 2013, http://www.bostonterrierclubofcanada.com/index.asp?ID=7.
18. "NAFA Corporate Information," NAFA, accessed July 18, 2012, http://www.flyball.org/nafa.html.
19. Interpretation Bulletin IT83R, Canada Revenue Agency, accessed May 14, 2014, http://www.cra-arc.gc.ca/E/pub/tp/it83r3/it83r3-e.html.
20. Promotion of Animal Welfare and Charitable Registration, Canada Revenue Agency, accessed May 14, 2014, http://www.cra-arc.gc.ca/chrts-gvng/chrts/plcy/cgd/nmlwlfr-eng.html; Political Activities, Canada Revenue Agency, accessed May 14, 2014, http://www.cra-arc.gc.ca/chrts-gvng/chrts/plcy/cps/cps-022-eng.html.
21. Confidential interviews by Susan Hunter, Feb. 2008.
22. Friends Caryl Gates Gluck Resource Center, accessed July 18, 2012, http://www.thinkingoutsidethecage.org/site/c.elKWIeOUIhJ6H/b.8580187/k.E854/Our_Namesake_The_Caryl_Gates_Gluck_Resource_Center.htm; Confidential interview and observation by Richard A. Brisbin, Jr., and Susan Hunter, Aug. 21, 2010.
23. "About Us," Boston Terrier Rescue, accessed October 8, 2015, http://www.btrescue.org/about.html.
24. "About North East Rottweiler Rescue & Referral, Inc.," North East Rottweiler Rescue & Referral, accessed July 18, 2012, http://www.rottrescue.org/about_nerr.html.
25. Rat Terrier Rescue Canada, accessed Feb. 11, 2014, http://www.ratterrierrescue.ca/.

26. "About Us," Speaking of Dogs, accessed Feb. 11, 2014, http://speakingofdogs.com/about-us/.
27. M-SNAP, accessed July 18, 2012, http://www.m-snap.org; "2011 Annual Report," Mountaineer Spay Neuter Assistance Program, accessed July 18, 2102, http://www.m-snap.org/MoreAboutM-SNAP.htm.
28. On by-product organized interests, see Olson, *The Logic of Collective Action*, 132–65.
29. Best Friends Animal Society, accessed Jan.22, 2014, http://bestfriends.org/; Confidential interview by Susan Hunter, Feb. 2009.
30. Olson, *The Logic of Collective Action*, passim; E. E. Schattschneider, *The Semi-Sovereign People: A Realist's View of Democracy in America* (New York, Henry Holt, 1960).
31. See Labrador Retriever Rescue, accessed Jan. 22, 2014, http://lrr.org/.
32. Confidential interviews by Susan Hunter, Feb. 2009.
33. See Baumgartner and Leech, *Basic Interests*, 25–30.
34. See Diane L. Beers, *For the Prevention of Cruelty: The History and Legacy of Animal Rights Activism in the United States* (Athens: Swallow Press/Ohio University Press, 2006), 20–92.
35. Terry M. Moe, *The Organization of Interests: Incentives and the Internal Dynamics of Political Interest Groups* (Chicago: University of Chicago Press, 1980), 74–75; Olson, *The Logic of Collective Action*, 132–35.
36. "We Are the Farm Bureau," American Farm Bureau Federation, accessed May 21, 2009, http://www.fb.org/index.php?action=about.home; Confidential interview by Susan Hunter and Richard A. Brisbin, Jr., Oct. 25, 2013. See also William P. Browne and Allan J. Cigler, eds. *U.S. Agricultural Groups: Institutional Profiles* (Westport, CT: Greenwood Press), 23–27.
37. Bernard Unti, *Protecting All Animals: A Fifty-Year History of the Humane Society of the United States* (Washington, DC: Humane Society Press, 2004).
38. Corwin R. Kruse, "Gender, Views of Nature, and Support for Animal Rights," *Society and Animals* 7 (1999): 179–98.
39. Emily Gaarder, *Women and the Animal Rights Movement* (New Brunswick, NJ: Rutgers University Press, 2011), 21–33. On adult activists and events more generally, see James M. Jasper and Jane D. Poulsen, "Recruiting Strangers and Friends: Moral Shocks and Social Networks in Animal Rights and Anti-Nuclear Protests," *Social Problems* 42 (1995): 493–512.
40. Gaarder, *Women and the Animal Rights Movement*, 41–86.
41. Ibid., 61–86.
42. Pseudonyms are used in this section. The information is from interviews conducted by the authors, 2005, 2009, 2011, and 2013.
43. Gaarder, *Women and the Animal Rights Movement*, 87–116.

44. "Leadership," Humane Society of the United States, accessed July 23, 2012, http://www.humanesociety.org/about/leadership/?credit=web_id66433060.
45. "Wayne Pacelle," Humane Society of the United States, accessed July 23, 2012, http://www.humanesociety.org/about/leadership/executive_staff/wayne_pacelle.html.
46. Confidential interviews by Susan Hunter, 2008–2009.
47. "Alexander M. Waldrop," International Masters of Gaming Law, accessed Jan. 23, 2014, http://www.gaminglawmasters.com/member/830.
48. Judy Sarasohn, "Merger Adds to Humane Society's Bite," *Washington Post*, Sept. 7, 2006; "Agriculture," Olsson, Frank, Weeda, Terman, Matz, P. C., accessed July 2, 2013, http://www.ofwlaw.com/CM/PracticeAreaDescriptions/Agriculture.asp.
49. Robert Salisbury, "An Exchange Theory of Interest Groups," *Midwest Journal of Political Science* 13 (1969): 17–19; James Q. Wilson, *Political Organizations* (Princeton, NJ: Princeton University Press, 1995), 195–201.
50. John W. Kingdon, *Agendas, Alternatives, and Public Policies*, 2nd ed. (New York: HarperCollins College Publishers, 1995), 179–86; Moe, *The Organization of Interests*, 36–72.
51. Salisbury, "An Exchange Theory of Interest Groups," 11–15.
52. Compare Jeffrey M. Berry, *Lobbying for the People* (Princeton, NJ: Princeton University Press, 1977) with Lisa Young and Joanna Everitt, *Advocacy Groups* (Vancouver: UBC Press, 2004), 73–76.
53. Jack L. Walker, *Mobilizing Interest Groups in America: Patrons, Professions, and Social Movements* (Ann Arbor: University of Michigan Press, 1991), 75–102; Anthony J. Nownes, "Patronage and Citizen Groups: A Reevaluation," *Political Behavior* 17 (1995): 203–21.
54. "About Us," Doris Day Animal League, accessed May 29, 2012, http://www.ddal.org/about/.
55. For Canadian groups, see A. Paul Pross, *Group Politics and Public Policy*, 2nd ed. (Toronto: Oxford University Press, 1992), 203–11; Young and Everitt, *Advocacy Groups*, 76–82.
56. Arnold Arluke, *Just a Dog: Understanding Animal Cruelty and Ourselves* (Philadelphia: Temple University Press, 2006), 147–81.
57. Lawrence Finsen and Susan Finsen, *The Animal Rights Movement in America: From Compassion to Respect* (New York: Twayne Publishers, 1994), 94, 98–106, 153–78; Harold D. Guither, *Animal Rights: History and Scope of a Radical Movement* (Carbondale: Southern Illinois University Press, 1998), 132–62, 221–32.
58. "AQHA Advocacy," American Quarter Horse Association, accessed Oct. 8, 2015, http://www.aqha.com/advocacy.

59. South Dakota Farm Bureau, accessed July 18, 2012, http://www.sdfbf.org/.
60. "Frequently Asked Questions," North Carolina Sporting Dog Association, accessed July 18, 2012, http://www.ncsportingdog.org/faq.htm.
61. See "Canine Legislation Position Statement: Breeding Restrictions," American Kennel Club, accessed July 18, 2012, http://www.akc.org/pdfs/canine_legislation/position_statements/Breeding_Restrictions.pdf; "Canine Legislation Position Statement: Use of Dogs in Research," American Kennel Club, accessed July 18, 2012, http://www.akc.org/pdfs/canine_legislation/position_statements/Use_of_Dogs_in_Research.pdf; "AKC 2012 Legislative Successes," American Kennel Club, accessed July 18, 2012, http://www.akc.org/governmentrelations/2012_successes.cfm.
62. "APPA Backgrounder," American Pet Products Association, http://americanpetproducts.org/about_backgrounder.asp.
63. See Mark A. Smith, "The Mobilization and Influence of Business Interests," in *The Oxford Handbook of American Political Parties and Interest Groups*, ed. L. Sandy Maisel and Jeffrey M. Berry (New York: Oxford University Press, 2010), 451–67.
64. On the influence of agricultural groups on legislation, see William P. Browne, *Private Interests, Public Policy, and American Agriculture* (Lawrence: University Press of Kansas, 1988), 41–63, 89–129; William P. Browne, *Cultivating Congress: Constituents, Issues, and Interests in Agricultural Policy* (Lawrence: University Press of Kansas, 1995), 65–130.
65. "ACT Agricultural Contact Team," American Farm Bureau Federation, accessed July 18, 2012, http://www.fb.org/legislative/fbact.
66. "Donations," American Kennel Club, accessed July 18, 2012, http://www.akc.org/governmentrelations/legislation_donations.cfm; "Political Action Committee," Maryland Thoroughbred, accessed July 18, 2012, http://marylandthoroughbred.com/cms/index.php/news-events/bulletin/archived-bulletins/15; "AQHA Political Action Committee," American Quarter Horse Association, accessed July 18, 2012, http://www.aqha.com/About/Content-Pages/About-the-Association/Advocacy/AQHPAC.aspx.
67. Schlozman, Verba, and Brady, *The Unheavenly Chorus*, 312–443.
68. United States Polo Association, accessed July 20, 2012, http://www.uspolo.org/; United States Polo Association, "Mission," accessed November 23, 2015, http://www.uspolo.org/about/mission.
69. "Current Unwanted Horse Coalition Member Organizations," Unwanted Horse Coalition, accessed July 20, 2012, http://www.unwantedhorsecoalition.org/?id=4&s=3.
70. On these tactics, see Baumgartner and Leech, *Basic Interests*, 148–55; Schlozman and Tierney, *Organized Interests and American Democracy*, 128–345.

71. Coalition to Ban Ohio Dog Auctions, accessed July 19, 2012, http://www.banohiodogauctions.com/Legislation.html.
72. "About Us," United Against Puppy Mills, accessed July 19, 2012, http://unitedagainstpuppymills.org/about-us/.
73. "About the DLCC," Dog Legislation Council of Canada, accessed July 19, 2012, http://www.dlcc.ca/aboutus.html; Confidential interviews by Richard A. Brisbin, Jr., and Susan Hunter, Sept. 2006, Halifax, Nova Scotia.
74. Finsen and Finsen, *The Animal Rights Movement in America*, 91–92; "About Us," Animal Legal Defense Fund, accessed Nov. 9, 2009, http://www.aldf.org/section.php?id=3.
75. Guither, *Animal Rights*, 46–56; "Campaigns," Doris Day Animal League, accessed Nov. 9, 2009, http://ddal.org/act-for-animals/.
76. Finsen and Finsen, *The Animal Rights Movement in America*, 87–90; "History of the Fund for the Animals," The Fund for Animals, accessed Nov. 9, 2009, http://fundforanimals.org/about/history.html.
77. "About Us" APSCA, accessed July 20, 2012, http://www.aspca.org/About-Us; "Programs and Services," APSCA, accessed July 20, 2102, http://www.aspca.org/about-us/programs-and-services.
78. Unti, *Protecting All Animals*, 2–5, 16–18, 26–30, 41–181.
79. Ibid., 7, 15,18–26, 34, 182–87.
80. "About the CFHS," Canadian Federation of Humane Societies, accessed Aug. 10, 2012, http://cfhs.ca/info/who_we_are.
81. Nonhuman Rights Project, accessed Sept. 30, 2014, http://www.nonhumanrightsproject.org/.
82. James M. Jasper and Dorothy Nelkin, *The Animal Rights Crusade: The Growth of a Moral Protest* (New York: The Free Press, 1992), 26–55; "What Is the ALF?," Animal Liberation Front, accessed Nov. 9, 2009, http://www.animalliberationfront.com/ALFront/WhatisALF.htm.
83. Steven Best and Anthony J. Nocella II, "Behind the Mask: Uncovering the Animal Liberation Front," in *Terrorists or Freedom Fighters? Reflections on the Liberation of Animals*, ed. Steven Best and Anthony J. Nocella II (New York: Lantern Books, 2004), 9–63; Finsen and Finsen, *The Animal Rights Movement in America*, 62–71, 76–81, 98–107; Guither, *Animal Rights*, 48–50, 56–57; Jasper and Nelkin, *The Animal Rights Crusade*, 29–38. See also "The ALF Primer," Animal Liberation Front, accessed October 29, 2009, http://www.animalliberationfront.com/ALFront/ALFPrime.htm; "Animal Liberation Front Actions-Canada," http://www.animalliberationfront.com/ALFront/Actions-Canada/alfcanada.htm; "PETA's History: Compassion in Action," accessed October 28, 2009, http://www.peta.org/about-peta/learn-about-peta/history/. See also Mark R.

Hawthorne, *Striking at the Roots: A Practical Guide to Animal Activism* (Ropley, UK: O Books, 2008).
84. Jasper and Nelkin, *The Animal Rights Crusade,* 26–70
85. "Campaigns," In Defense of Animals, accessed Nov. 9, 2009, http://www.idausa.org/#campaigns.
86. See Finsen and Finsen, *Animal Rights Movement in America,* 98–106, 153–78; Guither, *Animal Rights,* 132–62, 221–32.
87. "PETA's Milestones for Animals," PETA, accessed Feb. 11, 2014, http://www.peta.org/about-peta/milestones/.
88. Olson, *The Logic of Collective Action,* 132–65.
89. Iowa Pet Breeders Association, accessed July 20, 2012, http://www.iowapetbreeders.com/; Missouri Pet Breeders Association, accessed July 20, 2012, https://www.mpbaonline.org/; Oklahoma Pet Professionals, accessed July 20, 2012, http://www.okpp.org/.
90. "Legislative," National Thoroughbred Racing Association, accessed July 20, 2012, http://www.ntra.com/en/legislative/.
91. "Advocacy," American Veterinary Medical Association, accessed July 23, 2012, https://www.avma.org/Advocacy/.
92. See for example, "Farmers Sway Companies to End HSUS Sponsorship," Mar. 26, 2010, Ohio Farm Bureau, accessed July 20, 2012, http://ofbf.org/news-and-events/news/707/; HumaneWatch.org, accessed July 20, 2012, http://humanewatch.org/. HumaneWatch does not list information to determine whether it can be classified as an interest group or is a website run by a few activists.
93. Sportsmen's and Animal Owners' Voting Alliance, accessed July 20, 2012, http://saova.org/.
94. 18 *United States Code* §§ 43 ff.
95. For a summary of these laws, see Cynthia Hodges, "Detailed Discussion of State Animal 'Terrorism'/Animal Enterprise Interference Laws," Animal Legal and Historical Center, Michigan State University, accessed Jan. 24, 2014, http://www.animallaw.info/articles/ddusstateecoterrorism.htm.
96. See "Ag-Gag Laws at the State Level," ASPCA, accessed Jan. 24, 2014, http://www.aspca.org/fight-cruelty/advocacy-center/ag-gag-whistleblower-suppression-legislation/ag-gag-bills-state-level; Examples of the laws are *Kansas Statutes Annotated* §§ 47-1825 ff.; *Montana Code Annotated* §§ 81-30-101 ff.; *Utah Statutes* § 76-6-112.
97. These laws can be accessed at "Food-Disparagement Laws: State Civil & Criminal Statutes," Coalition for Free Speech, accessed Jan. 24, 2014, http://cspinet.org/foodspeak/laws/existlaw.htm. One suit about the constitutionality of these laws resulted in a summary judgment and directed verdict for

the party (media personality Oprah Winfrey), who had allegedly disparaged a commercial animal group and firms: see Texas Beef Group v. Winfrey, 11 F.Supp.2d 858 (N.D. Tex. 1998); Texas Beef Group v. Winfrey, 201 F.3d 680 (5th Cir., 2000). More recently, Animal Legal Defense Fund v. Otter, 2015 LEXIS 102640 (U.S. Dist. Ct., Ida. 2015) held that an ag-gag law is a violation of the First Amendment. See also "Judge Strikes Down Idaho 'Ag-Gag' Law, Raising Questions for Other States," National Public Radio, accessed Aug. 4, 2015, http://www.npr.org/sections/thesalt/2015/08/04/429345939/idaho-strikes-down-ag-gag-law-raising-questions-for-other-states; Steven C. Tauber, *Navigating the Jungle: Law, Politics, and the Animal Advocacy Movement* (New York: Routledge, 2016), 98.

98. Paul A. Sabatier, "An Advocacy Coalition Framework of Policy Change and the Role of Policy-Oriented Learning Therein," *Policy Sciences* 21 (1988): 129–68; Paul A. Sabatier and Hank Jenkins-Smith, "Policy Change over a Decade or More," in *Policy Change and Learning: An Advocacy Coalition Approach*, ed. Paul Sabatier and Hank Jenkins-Smith (Boulder, CO: Westview Press, 1993); Paul A. Sabatier and Hank Jenkins-Smith, "The Advocacy Coalition Framework: Assessment, Revisions, and Implications for Scholars and Practitioners," in *Policy Change and Learning*.

99. Francis E. Hamilton, "Leading and Organizing Social Change for Companion Animals," *Anthrozoös* 23 (2010): 277–92; "Our Coalition," Tampa Pets, accessed Jan. 22, 2014, http://tampapets.org/about.php.

100. Sabatier, "An Advocacy Coalition Framework," 144; Sabatier and Jenkins-Smith, "Policy Change over a Decade or More," passim.

101. Paul A. Sabatier and Christopher M. Weible, "The Advocacy Coalition Framework: Innovations and Clarifications," in *Theories of the Policy Process*, 2nd ed., ed. Paul A. Sabatier (Boulder, CO: Westview Press, 2007), 197; Matthew Zabonte and Paul Sabatier, "Shared Beliefs and Imposed Interdependencies as Determinants of Ally Networks in Overlapping Subsystems," *Journal of Theoretical Politics* 10 (1998): 477–78.

102. "Coalition Supporters," The Canadian Horse Defence Coalition, accessed July 23, 2012, http://defendhorsescanada.org/home/coalition-supporters.

103. "About Us," Utah Farm Bureau Federation, accessed July 24, 2012, http://www.utahfarmbureau.org/public/657/about-us/; "2011–2012 Farm Bureau Policy Book," Utah Farm Bureau Federation, accessed July 24, 2012, http://www.utahfarmbureau.org/public/768/legislative-action/policy-implementation. The law is *Utah Code Annotated* § 17-41-403.

104. Sharon L. Peters, "Animal Welfare Groups Put Cooperation to Work; It's Not Always Been the Case," *USA Today*, Nov. 25, 2009, 4D.

105. Confidential interviews by Susan Hunter, Feb. 2009.

106. Ibid.
107. Anthony E. Brown and Joseph Stewart, Jr., "Competing Advocacy Coalitions, Policy Evolution, and Airline Deregulation," in *Policy Change and Learning: An Advocacy Coalition Approach*, 101.
108. Edella Schlager, "Policymaking and Collective Action: Defining Coalitions within the Advocacy Coalition Work," *Policy Sciences* 28 (1995): 255–58; Sabatier and Weible, "The Advocacy Coalition Framework," 196.
109. Matthew A. Crenson, *The Un-politics of Air Pollution: A Study of Non-decisionmaking in the Cities* (Baltimore, Johns Hopkins Press, 1971), 177–84.
110. See Frank Baumgartner, "Interest Groups and Agendas," in *The Oxford Handbook of American Political Parties and Interest Groups*, ed. L. Sandy Maisel and Jeffrey M. Berry (New York: Oxford University Press, 2010), 521–24.
111. Baumgartner, "Interest Groups and Agendas," 525. On the importance of information in the policymaking process, see Bryan D. Jones and Frank R. Baumgartner, *The Politics of Attention: How Government Prioritizes Problems* (Chicago: University of Chicago Press, 2005).
112. On the legislative drafting of agriculture policies, see Browne, *Private Interests, Public Policy, and American Agriculture*, 41–63, 89–129; Browne, *Cultivating Congress*, 65–130.
113. Brenda J. Lutz and James M. Lutz, "Interest Groups and Pro-animal Rights Legislation," *Society & Animals* 19 (2011): 261–77, esp. 272.
114. Pross, *Group Politics and Public Policy*, 140–47, 167–68; Young and Everitt, *Advocacy Groups*, 88–95.
115. Pross, *Group Politics and Public Policy*, 166–75. Young and Everitt, *Advocacy Groups*, 104–11.
116. On administrators and agricultural policy, see Browne, *Cultivating Congress*, 133–60.
117. Pross, *Group Politics and Public Policy*, 174–54; Young and Everitt, *Advocacy Groups*, 95–101.
118. "N.B. Government Toughens Regulations for Kennels, Pet Stores, Animal Shelters," *The News*, June 1, 2010, accessed July 2, 2011, http://www.ngnews.ca/News/Canada---World/2010-06-01/article-1215456/N.B.-government-toughens-regulations-for-kennels,-pet-stores,-animal-shelters/1.
119. Mahalley D. Allen, "Laying Down the Law? Interest Group Influence on State Adoption of Animal Cruelty Felony Laws," *Policy Studies Journal* 33 (2005): 443–57.
120. Helena Silverstein, *Unleashing Rights: Law, Meaning, and the Animal Rights Movement* (Ann Arbor: University of Michigan Press, 1996), 123–59; Tauber, *Navigating the Jungle*, 54–60.

121. Nonhuman Rights Project, accessed July 30, 2012, http://www.nonhumanrights project.org; Steven Wise, discussion with Richard A. Brisbin, Jr., and Susan Hunter, Oct. 18, 2008.
122. Steven Tauber, "The Influence of Animal Advocacy Groups in State Courts of Last Resort," *Society and Animals* 18 (2010): 58–74, esp. 69; Tauber, *Navigating the Jungle*, 126–65.
123. Tauber, *Navigating the Jungle*, 73–125; Steven Tauber, "The Ability of Animal Advocacy Organizations to Overturn Regulatory Decisions in Federal Court" (paper presented at the Annual Meeting of the Law and Society Association, Boston, MA, May 30–June 2, 2013); Steven Tauber, "Animal Advocacy Groups in U.S. District Courts" (paper presented at the Annual Meeting of the Law & Society Association, Minneapolis, MN, May 29, 2014–June 1, 2014).
124. Tauber, *Navigating the Jungle*, 113.
125. Steven Tauber, "The Impact of Animal Advocacy Litigation on Press Coverage" (Paper presented at the Annual Meeting of the Midwest Political Science Association, Chicago, Illinois, Apr. 3–6, 2008); Steven Tauber, "The Impact of Group Litigation on Press Coverage of Animal Advocacy Issues," (Paper presented at the Annual Meeting of the Law and Society Association, Denver, Colorado, May 28–31, 2009); Tauber, *Navigating the Jungle*, 126–65.
126. Bias in interest group influence, the contingency of influence, and the power of the status quo mark the findings of interest group studies: see E. E. Schattschneider, *The Semi-Sovereign People: A Realist's View of Democracy in America* (New York, Henry Holt, 1960); Baumgartner, "Interest Groups and Agendas," 519–20, 530; Beth L. Leech, "Lobbying and Influence," in *The Oxford Handbook of American Political Parties and Interest Groups*, ed. L. Sandy Maisel and Jeffrey M. Berry (New York: Oxford University Press, 2010), 534–51.
127. Richard A. Brisbin, Jr., et al., *West Virginia Politics and Government*, 2nd ed. (Lincoln: University of Nebraska Press, 2008), 78–79.
128. Allen, "Laying Down the Law?," 449, 451.

5

Making Pet Policy: Anti-cruelty Laws

The widely publicized incarceration of star professional football player Michael Vick on federal felony animal abuse charges in 2007 illustrates an often neglected trend in American and Canadian law during the past three decades. To "put a bite in the law" since the 1990s, federal and many provincial, state, and local governments added or amended animal cruelty laws to enhance penalties for companion animal welfare abuses. Stimulated by the efforts of organized interests, these efforts at policy change are the result of a series of political conflicts about the proper treatment of companion animals. In this chapter we first describe the scope of existing anti-cruelty laws in Canada and the United States. Then we offer an assessment of the fruits of the recent political struggle about the adoption of anti-cruelty laws that affect cats, dogs, and horses by addressing the question: What political and social factors are associated with the companion animal anti-cruelty laws that are currently in place in the American states and Canadian provinces?

THE SCOPE OF ANTI-CRUELTY LAWS

Anti-cruelty laws govern a wide range of human actions that affect cats, dogs, and horses. These laws govern sadistic cruelty, such as torment and inflictions of physical suffering, other forms of abuse leading to death, the fighting of animals, and acts that demonstrate passive cruelty such as abandonment, letting a pet run at large, negligent care and shelter, keeping the pet in an enclosed vehicle, failure to vaccinate for rabies, maintaining a diseased animal, tethering, and unregulated breeding. However, laws also impose duties on owners and penalize them for negligence, such as laws that require people to prevent their pets from damaging property and injuring persons, other pets, and wildlife. Laws require the licensing and spaying or neutering of pets and obligate caregivers to protect the public against dangerous animals, habitually noisy pets, and unsanitary disposal of pet feces. Finally, there are laws that regulate the use of pets in experiments and the sale of cats, dogs, and horses at pet stores, other retail establishments, and auctions.[1]

United States Federal Laws

Various U.S. federal laws regulate cruelty directed at companion animals. The Animal Welfare Act was the first and, as amended, the most comprehensive federal statute passed dealing directly with animal welfare issues. The statute allows the Secretary of Agriculture to "promulgate standards to govern the humane handling, care, treatment, and transportation of animals by dealers, research facilities, and exhibitors." The Act defines "dealer" in part as a person who transports, buys, or sells any animal "for research, teaching, exhibition, or use as a pet" for compensation. It excludes from the definition of dealer a retail pet store that does not sell "animals to a research facility, an exhibitor, or a dealer." The Act defines "exhibitor" to include carnivals, circuses, and zoos, but it excludes fairs, livestock shows, rodeos, and dog and cat shows. Standards must include requirements "for animal care, treatment, and practices in experimental procedures to ensure that animal pain and distress are minimized." The

Act also requires every research facility to establish an Institutional Animal Committee of at least three members to review practices involving pain to animals and filing a report with the U.S. Department of Agriculture (USDA). Other provisions ban the importation of dogs in ill health and prohibit animal fighting, the buying, selling, and training of animals to fight, interstate transportation of fighting dogs, and the use of the mail to facilitate animal fights.[2] Regulations promulgated by the USDA spell out the details of these protections.[3] They are enforced by USDA inspectors. The Act also allows the U.S. Justice Department to seek and federal judges to issue injunctions against dealing in stolen animals or placing the health of an animal in serious danger in violation of the Act.

Passed in response to pressure from agribusiness, the Animal Enterprise Terrorism Act makes it a crime to travel in interstate or foreign commerce, or use the mail or any facility in interstate or foreign commerce: "(1) for the purpose of damaging or interfering with the operations of an animal enterprise; and (2) in connection with such purpose—(A) intentionally damag[ing] or caus[ing] the loss of any real or personal property ... [or] (B) intentionally plac[ing] a person in reasonable fear of the death of, or serious bodily injury to that person, a member of the immediate family ... of that person, or a spouse or intimate partner of that person." The statute defines "animal enterprise" as: (1) a commercial or academic enterprise that uses or sells animals or animal products for profit, food or fiber production, agriculture, education, research, or testing such as a breeding kennel or riding stable; (2) an animal shelter, pet store, breeder, circus, rodeo, or other lawful competitive animal event; or (3) any fair or similar event intended to advance agricultural arts and sciences.[4] The damage to the enterprise can include loss of food production or farm income and any other economic damage resulting from the offense. The law also protects any entity or person and his or her family members with an association to an animal enterprise.

The Twenty-Eight Hour Law provides that "a rail carrier, express carrier, or common carrier (except by air or water), a receiver, trustee, or lessee of one of those carriers, or an owner or master of a vessel transporting animals" across state lines, "may not confine animals [such as cats, dogs, or horses] in a vehicle or vessel for more than 28 consecutive hours without unloading the animals for feeding, water, and rest." It also provides that "animals being transported shall be unloaded in a humane way into pens equipped for feeding, water, and rest for at least 5 consecutive hours." The statute "does not apply when animals are transported in a vehicle or vessel in which the animals have food, water, space, and an opportunity for rest." Violation of this statute allows the U.S. Justice Department to bring a civil action against the violator and seek a penalty for each violation.[5]

Adopted after the Hurricane Katrina disaster, the Pet Evacuation and Transportation Standards Act authorizes federal disaster assistance in the "rescue, care, shelter, and essential needs" of "household pets and service animals," requires the director of the Federal Emergency Management Agency (FEMA) to develop "plans that take into account the needs of individuals with pets and service animals prior to, during, and following a major disaster or emergency." It also allows FEMA to "make financial contributions … to the States and local authorities for animal emergency preparedness purposes, including the procurement, construction, leasing, or renovating of emergency shelter facilities," and requires that FEMA approve state and local emergency preparedness operational plans that account for the needs of household pets and service animals prior to, during, and following a major disaster or emergency.[6]

The Lacey Act protects wild animals, birds, and fish from injury to themselves or their nests.[7] The Animal Damage Control Act directs the USDA to determine, demonstrate, and promulgate the best methods of eradication, suppression, or control of animals injurious to agriculture, horticulture, forestry, and animal husbandry. This law affords government the authority to control or eradicate feral cats and wild dogs, an authority used by the military.[8]

The Dog and Cat Protection Act makes it unlawful to import into or export any dog or cat fur product or to engage in interstate commerce in any dog or cat fur product.[9] Other federal laws provide for the adoption of military dogs,[10] permit the keeping of service dogs and common household pets in public housing,[11] criminalize the injury of federal law enforcement dogs and horses,[12] and regulate interstate wagering on horse races.[13]

Various federal laws affect the treatment of horses. The Horse Protection Act makes it a crime to exhibit, or transport for the purpose of exhibition, any "sore" horse, which refers to a horse intentionally injured to alter its gait. The Secretary of Agriculture is authorized with enforcement power.[14] The Wild Free-Roaming Horses and Burros Act makes it a crime to remove from the public lands any wild free-roaming horse or burro without authority from the Department of the Interior or the USDA, convert the animal to private use without authority from the department, maliciously cause its death or harassment, process its remains into commercial products, or sell it if it is maintained on private or leased land.[15] Several federal laws offer the *potential* to influence the treatment of horses. The Commercial Transportation of Equines to Slaughter Act provides that the USDA can issue guidelines for the regulation of food, water, and rest during the commercial transportation of equines for slaughter within the United States. The Humane Slaughter Act outlines the methods of slaughter that are deemed to be "humane," and thus appropriate for use in slaughtering animals.[16] The Animal Health and Disease Research Act, enacted to promote "the improved health and productivity of domestic livestock, poultry, aquatic animals, and other income-producing animals which are essential to the Nation's food supply," can regulate the treatment of horses bound for slaughter.[17] Because Congress has refused to fund the inspection of horse meat for human consumption in yearly appropriations acts, none of these laws currently affect horses.[18] Efforts to expand federal criminal laws that establish broader regulation of commercial kennels and kennel sales, a proposed Puppy Uniform Protection and Safety Act,[19] a proposed Pet Safety and Protection Act,[20] and a law to end the inspection of horses slaughtered for human consumption remain on the congressional agenda. Rejected by Congress in 2014, the King Amendment, an effort by agricultural interests to nullify state laws setting standards for agricultural production, could have resulted in the preemption and preclusion of the enforcement of state anti–puppy mill and other companion animal anti-cruelty laws.[21] Interestingly both the enacted and proposed laws have generally received bipartisan support in the Senate, while most opposition to new proposals has come from House Republicans and Senators and House members from the Southeastern and Rocky Mountain states.[22] Legislation adopted in 1999 making it a crime to knowingly create, sell, or possess any visual or audio depiction of animal cruelty with the intention of placing the depiction in interstate or foreign commerce for commercial gain was found to unconstitutionally abridge the First Amendment freedom of speech by the Supreme Court.[23] Consequently, unless the action is regulated under a carefully drawn federal or state law that specifically defines acts of cruelty and defines a compelling governmental interest in the regulation of the action, companion animals can be injured or killed in expressive acts such as the "stomp videos" filmed by sexual fetishists.

U.S. State and Local Laws

States and their county and municipal subunits have passed most other anti-cruelty legislation. These laws criminalize the sadistic abuse of cats, dogs, horses, and other animals, including the malicious killing or torture of these animals, animal fighting, restrictive tethering and confinement, and bestiality, and passive harms such as the failure to provide adequate nutrition and health care, unsanitary living conditions, and animal abandonment. State and local laws supplement federal legislation on the use of animals in scientific experiments and commercial product testing, commercial breeding kennels, and the transportation and slaughter of animals for human consumption. State and local laws also regulate or require the spaying and neutering of pets, the operations of animal shelters, the means of euthanasia employed by shelters, the control of roaming and feral cats, the ownership of selected breeds of dogs, and provide for pet trusts and probate laws that affect the disposition of pets of deceased caregivers. Most states permit their local governments the option to adopt additional measures such as penalties for the hoarding of animals and zoning laws that affect kennel and horse facilities and animal ownership. To further regulate the possession of animals, states and localities have adopted dog license and, infrequently, cat license requirements. Some of these requirements impose higher fees on unneutered or "intact" animals.

Congress has left the intrastate retail sale of pets, hobby breeders, public animal shelters, private animal shelters, and boarding kennels to state regulation and adjudication in state courts. Twenty-seven states regulate some aspects of the operation of pet stores and other retail pet businesses. These businesses often have to meet standards on licensing, food, water, and sanitation, housing including temperature, lighting, and ventilation, and veterinary care. Most of these laws prohibit the sale of unweaned animals. Nebraska requires the training of store employees, and California law specifies pet socialization or interaction with other animals and humans for personal attention or play.[24] To ensure that these businesses sell healthy animals, several states have passed puppy and, sometimes, kitten protection laws, or so-called puppy lemon laws, that require the sellers of puppies and kittens to guarantee their health and freedom from congenital abnormalities.

Exceptions to these laws exist. The First Amendment protections of freedom of speech and the free exercise of religion, accepted agricultural practices, and game laws permit specific acts that injure or cause the death of animals.[25] For dogs, cats, and horses the range of these exceptions is rather narrow. Unless a state or local law is neutral and generally applicable to all persons and religions, the free exercise of religion prohibits governments from banning the abuse or slaughter of companion animals in the rites of specific religions except by a narrowly drawn ordinance not motivated by religious convictions that serves a compelling governmental interest.[26]

State laws normally permit the treatment and training of dogs and horses to follow accepted animal husbandry practices, including the administration of pharmaceuticals, tail docking, the use of lures and whips, and other means of training cats, dogs, and horses for breed shows, agility contests, racing, rodeos, circuses, and other forms of public display. Accepted veterinary and research purposes are also often exempt from aspects of federal and state anti-cruelty laws.

Additionally, U.S. states have adopted laws that extend the limits on the disruptive activities of animal legal rights groups such as the Animal Liberation Front (ALF). As noted in chapter 4, several states have adopted so-called ag-gag laws. These laws make it a criminal offense for persons to enter without permission or conceal themselves in an animal facility closed to the public with the intent to disrupt operations, vandalize or cause physical damage to the property, including animals, records, and equipment, duplicate records or electronically record activity at the facility, free animals from confinement, or make allegedly false statements about the operation of an animal facility.[27] These laws can deter groups that seek to expose abuses at kennels and horse stables and training facilities. As noted in chapter 4, suits that challenge the constitutionality of ag-gag laws as an infringement on freedom of speech have succeeded only in one instance.[28]

State and local governments often engage in cooperation with federal agencies. For example, state and local police can cooperate with federal agencies in the enforcement of horse transportation laws. Also, most American states have adopted laws that govern equine activity liability (which protect equine professionals by eliminating the risk of lawsuits for injuries arising out of activities involving horses).[29] However, few states supplement U.S. federal laws that regulate cruel methods of killing horses, unsafe horse transportation, and the drugs administered to horses. States also do not regulate horse rescue organizations or the practices of tripping (a rodeo practice in which horses run fast and then are lassoed and taken to the ground), poling (forcing a horse to jump by hitting its legs), or soring (the deliberate injury of a horse's legs or hooves to produce an unnatural gait).[30]

Thoroughbred, quarter horse, harness, and other forms of racing are legal in all states.[31] State laws govern at-track and off-track betting, the licensing of tracks, owners, and jockeys, the conduct of races, veterinary inspection of animals, and disposition of winnings and revenues.[32] Most states with racetracks with betting ban the administration of a limited list of drugs to horses. However, because there are more than eight hundred known performance enhancing drugs and behavioral modifiers, prohibition and detection of them is problematic.[33]

Animal welfare and animal legal rights organizations have expressed considerable concern about the limitations in the state laws that govern the conduct of dog and horse racing and about state efforts to enforce regulations. Of special concern are cruelty or abuses in the conditions for breeding, housing, and training racing animals, the immaturity of horses that are raced, the use of drugs and stimulants to facilitate their ability to race, nerving, or the removal of nerves so horses can run pain free, and the disposition of horses and dogs that have outlived their racing lives.[34] An investigation by reporters for the *New York Times* estimated that twenty-four horses die each day at U.S. race tracks and thousands of others are injured. Their reportage associated many of the deaths and injuries with the administration of drugs to the horses.[35] Also, unwanted horses often end up exported to Mexican or Canadian slaughterhouses. Food safety advocates believe that the meat of many of these horses contains drugs administered for racing that can harm humans.[36]

A number of states permit pari-mutuel wagering on greyhound racing. There are greyhound tracks in seven states, most of which are affiliated with casinos to permit betting on races. Greyhound simulcast betting exists in thirteen states. Thirty-eight states ban commercial dog racing.[37] Dogs that underperform or are injured and cannot race are commonly put down.[38]

Canadian Laws

The Canadian Federation of Humane Societies asserts that Canada has "a dismal record when it comes to protecting animals from cruelty, abuse and neglect."[39] Overall, most federal and provincial anti-cruelty laws are both less extensive and less detailed than those of the United States. Canadian federal anti-cruelty law appears as a property crime in sections of the Criminal Code adopted in 1892 and modestly amended thereafter. As a consequence of the treatment of animals as property, in a widely cited 1978 case a Québec judge recognized the "animal is inferior to man," "humans have a privileged position," and that humans could cause pain to animals when necessary to service human needs and well-being.[40]

After the governing Liberal Party requested "consultations" to improve federal animal anti-cruelty law in 1999, fifteen bills were introduced to the House and Senate and there were forty-two separate debates on proposed changes in the law. All but one of the bills failed to pass. The failed bills primarily attempted to increase penalties for cruelty and other animal offenses, elaborate language that defined animal offenses, and move animal crimes out of the property law section of the Criminal Code. Progressive Conservative, Canadian Alliance, and Bloc Québécois opponents of the bills alleged they would cause a dangerous humanization of animals and adversely affect or criminalize the existing practices of farmers, hunters, fishermen, and trappers. Bill proponents countered that the proposed legislation would satisfy public demands that government curtail animal abuse as a threat to civic order, mistreatment of sentient beings, and inhumane behavior. The one bill passed, in 2008, retained animals in the property section of the Code and failed to recognize them as sentient beings but increased penalties for cruelty.[41]

As a result of the 2008 amendment the current provisions of the Criminal Code address a range of species using general language designed to punish persons engaged in "wilfully and without lawful excuse, killing maiming, wounding, poisoning, or injuring dogs, birds, or animals that are not cattle," and "wilfully permitting to be caused, unnecessary pain suffering, or injury to an animal or bird,"[42] as well as companion animal abandonment and dogfighting. Because Parliament has failed to amend and clarify the language of these provisions,[43] litigation has resulted about the meaning of *willfulness* and *unnecessary pain and suffering*. Interpretation of these words has generally favored human domination of animals. Commentary and case law also suggest that, unless there is extreme violence or sadistic behavior, many prosecutions under the Act are not treated as serious crimes.[44]

Canada permits horse slaughter for human consumption. The processing of horses is regulated by the Health of Animals Act 1990[45] and the Meat Inspection Act 1985[46] and supplemented by regulations adopted and enforced by the Canadian Food Inspection Agency to ensure the humane treatment of horses during their transport and slaughter.[47] Other federal laws have a marginal influence on companion animals. The Commission created by the federal National Capital Act, which provides for the regulation of property in the greater Ottawa area, has adopted regulations on where people can take pets and how they are to be controlled.[48] The federal Animal Pedigree Act permits the incorporation of associations to define and protect the value of specific breeds of animals, including dogs and horses, but it does not affect the welfare of animals.[49]

The anti-animal cruelty sections of the Canadian Criminal Code overlap some of the offenses made illegal by provincial and territorial law.[50] Every province and territory has animal protection laws and anti-cruelty laws. Because most of the provincial laws include specific standards of care for cats, dogs, and horses, they usually afford stronger protections against the abuse of animals than does the federal Criminal Code. The anti-cruelty laws of the Canadian provinces vary significantly in the definition of cruelty, animals protected, and enforcement mechanisms. The variations include different definitions of the protected species, when an animal is abandoned or "in distress," "generally accepted practices" in treatment of animals, investigative, seizure, and enforcement powers, inspection institutions, and penalties.[51]

In cases of animal abuse enforcement, officials may choose to lay charges under the provincial or territorial law, the Criminal Code, or both. Canadian pet stores and commercial breeding kennels are loosely or simply not regulated by the provinces. There is no provincial regulation of feral cats. Wagering on horse racing is legal in all provinces, but the country has only nine tracks. Drugs administered to race horses are regulated by the Canadian Pari-Mutuel Agency (CPMA), a special operating agency within the federal ministry of Agriculture and Agri-Food.[52] The scope of protections for pets and regulation of their care and control under municipal bylaws varies greatly across Canada. Some cities, such as Calgary, have extensive animal protection bylaws and enforcement agencies. Other cities employ Societies for the Prevention of Cruelty to Animals to elaborate and implement their bylaws. Pet protection in rural areas and communities is often more limited and the bylaws primarily address nuisance dogs.

WHAT INFLUENCES THE ADOPTION OF U.S. STATES' ANTI-CRUELTY LAWS?

As indicted in the previous section, the American states have adopted anti-cruelty laws and laws with the most direct effect on the lives of cats, dogs, and horses. To analyze the reasons for the states' adoption of companion animal anti-cruelty laws, we assume that the political preferences of the public and the social and economic characteristics of a state's population will influence the range of anti-cruelty laws adopted by that state. Because both animal welfare and animal control and commodity usage laws are constantly changing, this analysis is associated with the range of laws in place as of January 1, 2014.

To account for the influence of political and socioeconomic conditions and institutions on state legislation, we analyze the influence of three sets of variables on the existence of several companion animal laws in the states. The first set considers political influences on state anti-cruelty laws. To create these variables we relied on a range of evidence from public opinion surveys and studies of elite politics that indicates that individuals who categorize themselves as liberal and who prefer Democratic state and federal officeholders have more frequently supported public welfare laws and "new" minority rights claims. We assume that individuals with these political values might also be willing to increase welfare or rights protections that affect animals. However, because hunters often perceive that gun control adversely affects their interest in sports associated with the destruction of animals, opposition to gun control policies might signal a lower level of commitment to the protection of animal life. Therefore, to account for the association of politics in a state with animal welfare and legal rights laws and policies we included four variables in the analysis: (1) a state political liberalism index (2004),[53] (2) Democratic membership in the state legislature (2013),[54] (3) percentage of the state's vote for Barack Obama in 2012,[55] and a (4) a gun control index that measures the extent of state legislation that imposes restrictions on gun owners (2004).[56]

Second, we propose that various social and economic variables might affect legislative adoption of animal welfare and protection laws. We assume that states with larger populations who employ animals for economic gain, such as farmers, or whose economic conditions are affected by farming, such as rural residents, will be less likely to favor the forms of governmental regulation of animals that might create costs for themselves or their community. However, states with larger numbers of urban, white, wealthier, and better educated persons might be more protective of animals and comfortable with the legalistic ideology upon which concern for animal welfare and rights laws rest.[57] Also, religious affiliation might affect an individual's commitment to care for animals. Therefore, with reference to the analysis of organized religious adherence and attitudes toward animals discussed in chapter 3, we theorized that states with a higher percentage of Evangelical Christians and Mormons might have reduced support for animal welfare and rights laws. To analyze these potential associations, we used measures of (5) the mean per capita income of state residents (2007),[58] (6) the percentage of university graduates in a state,[59] (7) the percentage of the white population in the state,[60] (8) the percentage of the state population residing in rural areas (2010),[61] and (9) the state population's percentages of farm operators,[62] as well as (10) the Evangelical Christian and Mormon percentage of the state's population (2008).[63]

Third, given our findings about support for animal policies in chapter 4, we assume that personal contact with companion animals might be associated with stronger animal welfare or rights laws. Therefore we included the percentage of (11) pet, (12) cat, and (13) dog owners in the state in the analysis (2011).[64] To capture the extent of the treatment of animals as a commodity within a state, we included the number of federally licensed (14) breeding kennels and (15) dealers in a state (2005).[65]

We then conducted an analysis of the association of these variables with state companion animal anti-cruelty laws.[66] The state animal laws and policies protective of animal welfare or legal rights that we have chosen to include are: (1) enabling legislation for cat licensing;[67] (2) required spay or neuter for adopted shelter animals;[68] (3) differential licensing for unaltered dogs or cats;[69] (4) a ranking of the comprehensiveness of kennel regulation requirements;[70] (5) a ranking of the comprehensiveness of anti-tethering laws;[71] (6) the existence of a law banning the use of gas chambers for euthanasia;[72] (7) a rating of the comprehensiveness of a ban on dog racing and betting;[73] (8) a ranking of the comprehensiveness of a ban on dogfighting;[74] (9) a ranking of the comprehensiveness of bans on the acquisition of animals from shelters for research purposes;[75] (10) a ranking of the comprehensiveness of horse protection laws—laws about tripping, transportation, and slaughter;[76] (11) the existence of a puppy lemon law;[77] and (12) the existence of laws that require humane care in pet shops.[78] As a law that permits the treatment of pets as nuisance property we included (13) a ranking of the scope of statewide breed-specific legislation.[79] As a measure of laws that treat animals as a commodity we included (14) state passage or legislative consideration of ag-gag laws.[80] For comparative purposes, to examine anti-cruelty laws that affect other animals we included a measure of (15) the comprehensiveness of anti-cockfighting laws.[81] Also, to provide a more complete assessment of state anti-cruelty laws we used (16) the rankings of the protectiveness of state anti-cruelty laws compiled by (17) the Humane Society of the United States (HSUS) and (18) the Animal Legal Defense Fund (ALDF).[82] Table 5.1 provides a list of many of these laws to illustrate how they vary in adoption by each state. Found in subsequent chapters, Table 6.1 contains information about state kennel licensing and inspection laws, Table 6.2 lists state puppy protection laws, and Table 8.1 lists state spay/neuter laws.

TABLE 5.1 *Anti-cruelty Laws in the U.S. States, 2014*

State	Dog Racing Illegal[a]	Cat Licensing[b]	Tethering[c]	Prohibit BSL
Alabama				
Alaska	Xx			
Arizona				
Arkansas		X		
California	Xx	X	Xx	X
Colorado	X	X		X
Connecticut	X		Xx	X
Delaware	Xx		Xx	
Florida	Xx			X
Georgia	Xx			
Hawaii	Xx		X	
Idaho	X	X		
Illinois	Xx		X	X
Indiana	Xx		X	
Iowa				
Kansas	Xx			
Kentucky	Xx			
Louisiana	Xx	X	X	
Maine	Xx	X	X	X
Maryland	Xx	X	X	
Massachusetts	X	X	Xx	X
Michigan	Xx	X	X	
Minnesota	Xx	X		X
Mississippi	Xx			
Missouri	Xx			
Montana	X			

ALDF, Animal League Defense Fund; BSL, breed-specific legislation; HSUS, Humane Society of the United States.

[a] X refers to states in which dog racing is illegal; Xx refers to states in which both racing and betting on races are illegal.

[b] X refers to states that allow cat licensing; Xx refers to states in which cat licensing is required.

[c] X refers to states in which tethering is restricted by type; Xx refers to states in which tethering is limited by time and type.

[d] X refers to states which require spay/neuter of shelter animals; L refers to states with lower licensing fees for altered animals.

[e] 1 indicates states with felony for active participation; 2 indicates felony for spectating; 3 indicates felony for possession of fighting implements; 4 indicates cockfighting, also a felony.

Shelter Spay/ Differential Licensing[d]	Animal Fighting[e]	Cruelty ALDF Ranking[f]	Horse Protection Laws[g]	HSUS Rank[h]
	1,2,3	43		46
	1,3,4	42		41
XL	1,2,3,4	10	STD	7
X	1,3,4	21		38
XL	1,3	5	STD	1
X	1,2,3,4	8		7
L	1,2,3,4	27	S	12
XL	1,2,3,4	15		22
X	1,2,3,4	14	ST	17
	1,3,4	33	S	33
	1,2,3	32		25
	1,3,4	39		49
L	1,2,3,4	1	ST	3
	1,3,4	9		38
	1,3,4	49		24
X	4	14		35
	1,3	50		43
L	1,2,3,4	16		18
XL	1,3,4	4	T	10
	1,3,4	40	D	15
L	1,2,3,4	19	D	4
XL	1,2,3,4	3		20
	1,3,4	18		34
	1,2,3	28	SD	49
L	1,3,4	35		42
X	1,3,4	29		37

[f] ALDF rankings use only cruelty provisions for their ranking—whether forfeiture required, psychological counseling mandated, cross-referral required, level of felony provisions.

[g] S refers to a ban on soring; T refers to a ban on tripping (a rodeo practice); D refers to a ban or restriction on double-decked trailers for transport of horses.

[h] HSUS ranking of states on animal protection laws. These laws cover all animals and include animal fighting, agriculture laws, transportation, spay/neuter, kennel licensing, puppy protection.

Continued.

TABLE 5.1 Anti-cruelty Laws in the U.S. States, 2014—cont'd

State	Dog Racing Illegal[a]	Cat Licensing[b]	Tethering[c]	Prohibit BSL
Nebraska	Xx	X		
Nevada	X		Xx	X
New Hampshire		X		
New Jersey	Xx			X
New Mexico	Xx	X		
New York	Xx			
North Carolina	Xx			X
North Dakota	X			
Ohio	Xx			
Oklahoma	Xx			X
Oregon	X		Xx	
Pennsylvania	Xx			X
Rhode Island	Xx	Xx	Xx	X
South Carolina	X	X		
South Dakota	X			
Tennessee	Xx	X		
Texas		X		X
Utah	Xx	X		
Vermont	Xx		X	
Virginia	Xx	X	X	X
Washington	Xx			X
West Virginia		X		
Wisconsin		X		
Wyoming		X		

ALDF, Animal League Defense Fund; BSL, breed-specific legislation; HSUS, Humane Society of the United States.

[a] X refers to states in which dog racing is illegal; Xx refers to states in which both racing and betting on races are illegal.

[b] X refers to states that allow cat licensing; Xx refers to states in which cat licensing is required.

[c] X refers to states in which tethering is restricted by type; Xx refers to states in which tethering is limited by time and type.

[d] X refers to states which require spay/neuter of shelter animals; L refers to states with lower licensing fees for altered animals.

[e] 1 indicates states with felony for active participation; 2 indicates felony for spectating; 3 indicates felony for possession of fighting implements; 4 indicates cockfighting, also a felony.

Shelter Spay/ Differential Licensing[d]	Animal Fighting[e]	Cruelty ALDF Ranking[f]	Horse Protection Laws[g]	HSUS Rank[h]
	1,2,3,4	20	T	27
X	1,3,4	23	T	21
L	1,2,3,4	22		12
L	1,2,3,4	36	S	6
X	1,2,3	47	T	26
XL	1,4	38	D	4
	1,2,3,4	30		40
X	1,3,4	45		48
	1,2,3	25		30
X	1,3,4	34	T	30
L	1,2,3,4	2	T	2
XL	1,2,3,4	37	D	12
X	1,4	11	TD	18
	1,3	41	T	46
	1,3	48		50
X	1,3	12		23
	1 4	26	S	27
X	1,3	44		43
L	1,2,3,4	24	D	15
X	1,2,3,4	13		10
	1,2,3,4	7		7
X	1	6		30
L	1,3,4	31		35
	1,3,4	46		43

[f] ALDF rankings use only cruelty provisions for their ranking—whether forfeiture required, psychological counseling mandated, cross-referral required, level of felony provisions.

[g] S refers to a ban on soring; T refers to a ban on tripping (a rodeo practice); D refers to a ban or restriction on double-decked trailers for transport of horses.

[h] HSUS ranking of states on animal protection laws. These laws cover all animals and include animal fighting, agriculture laws, transportation, spay/neuter, kennel licensing, puppy protection.

What Does the Analysis of U.S. Anti-cruelty Law Find?

To measure the association between the independent variables and state laws we employed Spearman correlation analysis with scalar and ordinal variables and cross tabulations with Chi square tests of significance for nominal variables when appropriate. Because the large number of variables (thirty-three) precludes the presentation of findings in easily readable tables, the following list summarizes the statistically significant findings of the analysis.

Political Conditions in a State
- Greater state political liberalism is associated with a state's adoption of animal welfare laws, including differential licensing for unaltered animals, more anti-tethering laws, more comprehensive kennel regulation, a more comprehensive ban on the acquisition of animals from shelters for research purposes, more horse protection laws, and the adoption of puppy lemon laws and laws requiring humane treatment of animals by pet stores. Political liberalism also is associated with other measures of state legislation to protect animals, such as more comprehensive anti-cockfighting laws and a higher ranking for animal protection on the HSUS and ALDF scales.
- The presence of a greater number of Democrats in the state legislature is associated with the adoption of state animal welfare laws, including differential licensing for unaltered animals, more anti-tethering laws, more comprehensive kennel regulation, a more comprehensive ban on the acquisition of animals from shelters for research purposes, more horse protection laws, and the adoption of puppy lemon laws and laws requiring humane treatment of animals by pet stores. More Democrats in the state legislature is also associated with a higher ranking for animal protection on the HSUS and ALDF scales and less frequent state passage or discussion of ag-gag laws.
- A greater percentage of the state vote for Barack Obama in 2012 is very strongly associated with the adoption of state animal welfare laws, including differential licensing for unaltered animals, more anti-tethering laws, more comprehensive kennel regulation, a ban on

dog racing, a more comprehensive ban on the acquisition of animals from shelters for research purposes, more extensive horse protection laws, and the adoption of puppy lemon laws and laws requiring humane treatment of animals by pet stores. Additionally, a larger percentage of state vote for Obama is associated with other measures of state legislation to protect animals, such as more comprehensive anti-cockfighting laws and a higher ranking for animal protection on the HSUS and ALDF scales.

- A state's adoption of less restrictive gun laws is associated with the existence of more comprehensive statewide breed ban legislation. Also, these states with less restrictive gun laws have less comprehensive kennel regulation, a less comprehensive ban on the acquisition of animals from shelters for research purposes, fewer horse protection laws, and the failure to adopt puppy lemon laws and laws requiring humane treatment of animals by pet stores. States with less restrictive gun laws also have fewer anti-cockfighting laws and a lower rank on the HSUS animal protection scale.

Socioeconomic Characteristics of a State

- Higher mean per capita income in a state is associated with the adoption of animal welfare laws, including differential licensing laws for unaltered dogs, more comprehensive kennel regulation, a more comprehensive ban on the acquisition of animals from shelters for research purposes, more horse protection laws, and the adoption of puppy lemon laws and laws requiring humane treatment of animals by pet stores. Higher income is associated with less comprehensive statewide breed ban legislation. Higher mean income is also associated with other measures of state legislation to protect animals, such as more comprehensive anti-cockfighting laws and a higher ranking for animal protection on the HSUS scale.
- A greater percentage of college and university graduates in a state's population is associated with the adoption of animal welfare laws, including differential licensing laws for unaltered dogs, more comprehensive kennel regulation, a more comprehensive ban on the acquisition of animals from shelters for research purposes, more extensive horse protection laws, and the adoption of puppy lemon

laws and laws requiring humane treatment of animals by pet stores. Greater education is also associated with a lack of statewide breed ban legislation and with other measures of state legislation to protect animals, such as more comprehensive anti-cockfighting laws and a higher ranking for animal protection on the HSUS scale.

- A greater white population in a state is associated with the lack of a law banning the use of gas chambers for euthanasia, less extensive horse protection laws, and the passage or discussion of ag-gag laws.
- A greater percentage of rural population in a state is associated with the existence of more comprehensive statewide breed ban legislation and the existence of less comprehensive anti-tethering laws, no law banning the use of gas chambers for euthanasia, less comprehensive horse protection laws, and the failure to adopt puppy lemon laws and laws requiring humane treatment of animals by pet stores. States with a greater percentage of rural population also have less comprehensive anti-cockfighting laws and a lower rank on the HSUS animal protection scale.
- More farm operators as a percentage of the state population is associated with the existence of a more comprehensive statewide breed ban legislation and the passage or discussion of ag-gag laws. These states are less likely to have differential licensing and have less comprehensive anti-tethering and horse protection laws, and fail to adopt puppy lemon laws and laws requiring humane treatment of animals by pet stores. States with more farm operators also have less comprehensive anti-cockfighting laws and a lower rank on the HSUS animal protection scale.
- When compared to farm operators, the percentage of Evangelical Christians in a state's population is more strongly associated with the lack of a law banning the use of gas chambers for euthanasia, a less comprehensive ban on the acquisition of animals from shelters for research purposes, statewide breed ban legislation, and the passage or discussion of ag-gag laws. These states are less likely to have differential licensing, have less anti-tethering and horse protection laws, and fail to adopt puppy lemon laws and laws requiring humane treatment

of animals by pet stores. States with a greater percentage of Evangelical Christians also have less comprehensive anti-cockfighting laws and a lower rank on the HSUS animal protection scale.

Relationships with Animals within the State

- More pets in households in a state is associated with the lack of a puppy lemon law and laws requiring humane treatment of animals by pet stores. However, it is associated with the passage of statewide breed ban legislation.
- More cats in households in a state is modestly associated only with support for more comprehensive horse protection laws.
- More dogs in households in a state is associated with a lack of differential licensing, less comprehensive kennel regulation, a less comprehensive ban on the acquisition of animals from shelters for research purposes, less comprehensive horse protection laws, and the lack of a puppy lemon law and laws requiring humane treatment of animals by pet stores. The presence of dogs in households in a state is also associated with less comprehensive anti-cockfighting laws and a lower rank on the HSUS animal protection scale. However, dog ownership is associated with the passage of statewide breed ban legislation.
- More federally licensed breeders in a state is associated with less comprehensive kennel regulation, less comprehensive anti-tethering laws, a less comprehensive ban on the acquisition of animals from shelters for research purposes, and the passage or discussion of ag-gag laws. More federally licensed animal dealers in a state is associated with less comprehensive kennel regulation and the passage or discussion of ag-gag laws.

No Associations

- No political, socioeconomic, or animal status variable was significantly associated with enabling legislation for cat licensing, required spay or neuter for adopted shelter animals, the rating of the comprehensiveness of a ban on dog racing and betting, or a ranking of the comprehensiveness of a ban on dogfighting.

∙ ∙ ∙

In many ways these findings are not surprising. States with a population that is more liberal, higher income, and better educated and with more urban and suburban residents have more comprehensive companion animal as well as other animal anti-cruelty laws, such as those measured by cockfighting laws and the ALDF and HSUS indices. States with populations that are more conservative, whiter, rural, and Evangelical Christian have weaker companion and other animal welfare laws and stronger laws that treat pets as a commodity and some dogs as nuisance property. Although the states with more licensed breeders and dealers have significantly weaker kennel regulation and lower costs for these business owners, the presence of pets in households in a state is often not associated with the state's adoption of companion animal welfare laws.

More confounding are the associations between animals in the household and state legislation. We had anticipated that a greater percentage of state population residing with pets in general or with a cat or dog would incline that state to adopt strong animal protection laws. Yet, with the odd exception of laws more protective of horses, that was not the case. One reason appears to be that the presence of a cat in a household is not associated in any significant direction with the measures of state liberalism, higher income, college education, and more urban and suburban residency. Overall cat owners apparently are a diverse population with a variety of policy preferences.

Also, as noted above, the presence of dogs in a household is not associated with support for many animal welfare laws. The reason appears to be that the presence of a dog in a household is significantly associated with political conservatism as measured by the political liberalism index, percentage of Democrats in the state legislature, percentage of vote for Obama, and the gun index. Dog owners are also significantly associated with the states with lower income populations, fewer college graduates, more rural residents, and a greater proportion of farmers, breeders, and Evangelical Christians. These features of dog owners in a state's population appear to cancel any support for strong animal welfare laws that stem from residing with dogs.

WHAT INFLUENCES ARE ASSOCIATED WITH CANADIAN PROVINCIAL ANTI-CRUELTY LAWS?

The anti-cruelty laws of the Canadian provinces do not vary significantly in the definition of cruelty, animals protected, and enforcement mechanisms. The variations are far less about the range of substantive legal protections (kennel laws, use of animals in research, spay/neuter laws, and so forth) than about the specific definitions of the protected species, when an animal is abandoned or "in distress," "generally accepted practices" in the treatment of farm animals, and the details of investigative, seizure, and enforcement powers, inspection institutions, and penalties.[83] Because several policy, cultural, legal, and institutional differences exist between Canada and the United States that might affect the adoption of companion animal anti-cruelty legislation, such as much more restrictive gun ownership laws, a different political party system, and the use of Westminster parliamentary institutions in Canada, we modified our selection of variables. To account for the association between political variables and provincial animal laws we included the most recent percentage of provincial legislative vote for the (1) Liberal, (2) Progressive Conservative, and (3) New Democratic (NDP) parties[84] and (4) the percentage of the federal vote in the province for the Progressive Conservative Party in 2011.[85] Social and demographic variables included in the analysis include the province's (5) median family income (2010),[86] (6) white population percentage (2011),[87] (7) rural population percentage (2011),[88] (8) farm operators as percentage of the population (2006),[89] and (9) percentage of the population with a university degree (2007).[90] Unfortunately no data on companion animal ownership in the provinces exists, and there is no federal licensing of breeders and dealers.

The small number of provinces ("cases") and little variation in their laws hampers the statistical analysis of Canadian laws. The only anti-cruelty legal variable with some variance was the comprehensive ranking of the protectiveness of provincial anti-cruelty laws compiled by the ALDF.[91] The association of provincial political and socioeconomic variables with this measure of anti-cruelty laws produced little significant variance among provinces on all but one political and no socioeconomic variable.

A greater percentage of provincial votes for the New Democratic Party (a social democratic party) is associated with a higher ranking on the ALDF scale. Since a vote for the NDP is effectively a surrogate for political liberalism, it appears that in Canada, as in the U.S. states, provinces with a greater number of political liberals more eagerly support animal welfare and animal legal rights laws.

CONCLUSIONS

The scope of these laws varies, and, as described in this chapter, the federal laws of the Canada and the United States differ strikingly in the protection they afford cats, dogs, and horses. State and provincial anti-cruelty laws also vary markedly in the protection of the welfare of pets. To account for the differences we addressed the question: What political and social factors are associated with the companion animal anti-cruelty laws that are currently in place in the American states and Canadian provinces?

Although in chapter 3 we found broad support for policies and laws that protect pets, the analysis in this chapter finds that, at present, state and provincial laws that protect pet welfare against cruelty are associated with the presence of more politically liberal political values in a state's and province's population. In the United States a more urban population that has a higher mean income and a greater percentage of college graduates also is associated with the adoption of more laws to protect pets from cruelty. However, the extensiveness of the presence of pets in households in a state or province is not associated with stronger anti-cruelty laws. Consequently, legal accountability for the protection of cats, dogs, and horses from cruelty is developing through political struggles influenced by liberal political ideology, party affiliation, and socioeconomic attachments. In these jurisdictions organized animal welfare interests have had the most success in securing their legislative agenda. Therefore, the construction of what some people would regard as a more humane world for pets must account for political and social interests in the pursuit of their objective. The following chapters detail several of these struggles.

NOTES

1. A list of these laws appears in Stephen Aronson, *Animal Control Management: A New Look at a Public Responsibility* (West Lafayette, IN: Purdue University Press, 2010), 267–70, 276.
2. 7 *United States Code* §§ 2131–2159. Anti–animal fighting provisions, also found in 19 *United States Code* § 49, were strengthened in 2014. Federal Agriculture Reform and Risk Management Act of 2013, H.R. 2642, U.S., 113th Congress (2013–2014) (Engrossed Amendment House—EAH), Sec. 12311.
3. Animal Welfare Act Regulations, 9 C.F.R. §§ 1.1–4.11.
4. 18 *United States Code* § 43.
5. 49 *United States Code* § 80502; Twenty-Eight Hour Law Regulations, 9 C.F.R. §§ 89.1–89.5.
6. 42 *United States Code* §§ 5170b(a)(3)(J), 5196(e)(4), 5196(j)(2), 5196b(g).
7. 18 *United States Code* §§ 41–47.
8. 7 *United States Code* §§426–426(c); Armed Forces Pest Management Board, *Technical Information Memorandum No. 37: Guidelines for Reducing Feral/Stray Cat Populations on Military Installations in the United States* (Washington, DC: Defense Pest Management Information Analysis Center, Walter Reed Army Medical Center, 1996).
9. 19 *United States Code* § 1308.
10. 10 *United States Code* § 2583.
11. Fair Housing Act, 42 *United States Code* § 3604; National Housing Act, 12 *United States Code* § 1701r-1.
12. Federal Law Enforcement Animal Protection Act, 18 *United States Code* § 1368.
13. Interstate Horse Racing Act, 15 *United States Code* § 57.
14. 15 *United States Code* §§ 1821–1831; Horse Protection Act Regulations, 9 C.F.R. §§ 11.1–12.10.
15. 16 *United States Code* §§ 1331–1340; Wild Free-Roaming Horses and Burros Act Regulations, 43 C.F.R. §§ 4700.0-1–4770.5.
16. 21 *United States Code* § 603(b); Humane Slaughter Act Regulations, 9 C.F.R. §§ 313.1–313.90.
17. 7 *United States Code* §§ 3191–3201.
18. U.S. Congress, Consolidated Appropriations Act, 2014, Sec. 745 (1).
19. Angela Ostrowski, "2013 Federal Legislative Review," *Animal Law* 20 (2014): 447–49.
20. Ibid., 440–42.
21. Ibid., 436–38; "Farm Bill Strengthens Animal Fighting Law, Omits Dangerous King Amendment," Humane Society of the United States, Jan. 27, 2014,

accessed Jan. 30, 2014, http://www.humanesociety.org/news/press_releases/2014/01/farm_bill_012714.html#.UuplIdMo74Y; Bill Hayworth, "Farm Bill Compromise Drops Steve King's Amendment," *Sioux City Journal.com*, Jan. 28, 2014, accessed Jan. 30, 2014, http://siouxcityjournal.com/blogs/politically_speaking/hayworth-farm-bill-compromise-drops-steve-king-s-amendment/article_01558893-e160-5578-8371-d671fada5029.html.

22. "Humane Scorecard," Humane Society Legislative Fund, accessed June 5, 2013, http://dev.hslf.org/our-work/humane-scorecard.html.
23. 18 *United States Code* § 48; United States v. Stevens, 559 U.S. 460, 130 S.Ct. 1577 (2010).
24. "The Current State of Pet Shop Laws," Born Free U.S.A., accessed Mar. 7, 2014, http://www.bornfreeusa.org/b4a1_petshoplaws_currentstate.php.
25. See Joan E. Schaffner, *An Introduction to Animals and the Law* (New York: Palgrave MacMillan, 2011), 22–70.
26. Church of the Lukumi Babalu Aye v. City of Hialeah, 508 U.S. 520 (1993); David M. O'Brien, *Animal Sacrifice and Religious Freedom: Church of the Lukumi Babalu Aye v. City Of Hialeah* (Lawrence: University Press of Kansas, 2004).
27. For a summaries of these laws, see Cynthia Hodges, "Detailed Discussion of State Animal 'Terrorism'/Animal Enterprise Interference Laws," Animal Legal and Historical Center, Michigan State University, accessed Jan. 24, 2014, http://www.animallaw.info/articles/ddusstateecoterrorism.htm; "Ag-Gag Bills at the State Level," ASPCA, accessed Jan. 24, 2014, http://www.aspca.org/fight-cruelty/advocacy-center/ag-gag-whistleblower-suppression-legislation/ag-gag-bills-state-level. For examples of these laws, see Animal Enterprise Protection Act, *Florida Statutes Annotated* § 828.40–43; Farm Animal, Crop, and Research Facilities Protection Act, *Georgia Code Annotated* § 4-11-30–35; Animal Research and Production Facilities Protection Act, *Illinois Compiled Statutes Annotated*, CH 720 § 215/1–215/9; Farm Animal and Field Crop and Research Facilities Protection Act, *Kansas Statutes Annotated*, §§ 47-1825–1830; Farm Animal and Research Facilities Protection Act, *Montana Code Annotated* §§ 81-30-101–105; Animal Research Facility Damage Act, *North Dakota Century Code Annotated* §§ 12.1-21.1-01–05; *Utah Statutes* § 76-6-112. For critical commentary on these acts, see Jen Girgen, "State Animal Use Protection Statutes: An Overview," *Animal Law* 18 (2011) 57–74; Jared S. Goodman, "Shielding Corporate Interests from Public Dissent: An Examination of the Undesirability and Unconstitutionality of 'Eco-terrorism' Legislation," *Journal of Law and Policy* 16 (2008): 823–75; Laura G. Kniaz, "Animal Liberation and the Law: Animals Board the Underground Railroad," *Buffalo Law Review* 43 (1995): 765–834; Kimberly E. McCoy, "Subverting Justice: An Indictment of the Animal Terrorism Act," *Animal Law* 14 (2007): 53–70; Rebecca K. Smith,

"'Ecoterrorism'?: A Critical Analysis of the Vilification of Radical Environmental Activists as Terrorists," *Environmental Law Review* 38 (2008): 537–76.
28. Steven C. Tauber, *Navigating the Jungle: Law, Politics, and the Animal Advocacy Movement* (New York: Routledge, 2016), 98; Animal Legal Defense Fund v. Otter, 2015 LEXIS 102640 (U.S. Dist. Ct., Ida. 2015); "Judge Strikes Down Idaho 'Ag-Gag' Law, Raising Questions for Other States," National Public Radio, accessed Aug. 4, 2015, http://npr.org/sections/the salt/2015/08/04/4.
29. See Krystyna M. Carmel, "The Equine Activity Liability Acts: A Discussion of Those in Existence and Suggestions for a Model Act," *Kentucky Law Journal* 83 (1994): 157.
30. "Horses: Related Statutes," Animal Legal and Historical Center, accessed July 13, 2011, http://www.animallaw.info/statutes/speciesstatutes/stsphorse.htm.
31. USA Horse Racing—Race Tracks, accessed Mar. 6, 2014, http://www.officialusa.com/stateguides/horseracingtracks/.
32. See for examples "Horse Racing Law Index," California Horse Racing Board, http://www.chrb.ca.gov/horse_racing_law_index.html; "Statutes and Regulations," Kentucky Horse Racing Commission, http://khrc.ky.gov/Pages/regulations.aspx; "Law and Regulations," Maryland Racing Commission, http://www.dllr.state.md.us/racing/law/.
33. On the number and names of performance enhancing drugs, see "Uniform Classification Guidelines for Foreign Substances and Recommended Penalties and Model Rule, July 2015" Association of Racing Commissioners International, Inc., accessed Oct. 14, 2015, https://drive.google.com/file/d/0B2HwTiDKu_FHd0JqQnBMOFZiRlU/view?pli=1.
34. See for example "Greyhound Racing FAQ," ASPCA, http://www.aspca.org/fight-cruelty/animals-in-entertainment/greyhound-racing-faq; "Greyhound Racing in the United States," Grey2K USA, accessed Mar. 6, 2014, http://www.grey2kusa.org/pdf/GREY2KUSANationalFactSheet.pdf; "The Facts about Greyhound Racing," Humane Society of the United States, Oct. 21, 2009, accessed Mar. 6, 2014, http://www.grey2kusa.org/pdf/GREY2KUSANationalFactSheet.pdf; "Long Odds for Survival for Greyhound Racing," Humane Society of the United States, http://blog.humanesociety.org/wayne/2014/03/long-odds-for-survival-for-greyhound-racing.html; "Bred to Death," The Horse Fund, accessed Mar. 6, 2014, http://www.horsefund.org/horse-racing-fact-sheet.php; "Horse Racing: America's Most Dangerous Game?," National Public Radio, accessed May 9, 2012, http://www.npr.org/2012/05/10/152363564/horse-racing-americas-most-dangerous-game.
35. Walt Bogdanich et al., "Mangled Horses, Maimed Jockeys," *New York Times*, Mar. 24, 2012, http://www.nytimes.com/2012/03/25/us/death-and-disarray-at-americas-racetracks.html?ref=waltbogdanich&_r=0.

36. Advocates have proposed that Congress pass a Safeguard American Food Exports Act.
37. "Take Action: State by State," Grey2K USA, accessed Mar. 6, 2014, http://www.grey2kusa.org/action/states.html.
38. For descriptions of these practices by animal welfare groups, see "Long Odds for Survival for Greyhound Racing," Humane Society of the United States, http://blog.humanesociety.org/wayne/2014/03/long-odds-for-survival-for-greyhound-racing.html; "Greyhound Racing FAQ," APSCA, http://www.aspca.org/fight-cruelty/animals-in-entertainment/greyhound-racing-faq.
39. "Federal Legislation," Canadian Federation of Humane Societies, accessed Mar. 7, 2014, http://cfhs.ca/law/federal_legislation/.
40. R v. Ménard (1978) 43 CCC (2d) 458. See also Bisgould, *Animals and the Law*, 57–71.
41. Lyne Létourneau, "Toward Animal Liberation? The New Anti-cruelty Provisions in Canada and Their Impact on the Status of Animals," *Theoretical Criminology* 40 (2003): 1041–55; John Sorenson, "Some Strange Things Happening in Our Country: Opposing Proposed Changes in Anti-cruelty Laws in Canada," *Social and Legal Studies* 12 (2003): 377–402; Antonio Verbora, "The Politics of Animal Anti-cruelty Legislation in Canada: An Analysis of Parliamentary Debates on Amending the Criminal Code" (M.A. Thesis, University of Windsor, 2012). Antonio Robert Verbora, "The Political Landscape Surrounding Anti-cruelty Legislation in Canada," *Society & Animals* 23 (2015): 45–67.
42. *Criminal Code, Revised Statutes of Canada,* 1985 C 46, c. 445, 445.1(1)(a).
43. See Lesli Bisgould, *Animals and the Law* (Toronto: Irwin Law, 2011), 87–96.
44. Bisgould, *Animals and the Law*, 75–87. Compare R v. Paul [1997] BCJ No 808 (Prov. Ct.), with R v. Connors, 2011 BCPC 24. For general criticism of Canadian animal law, see John Sorenson, *About Canada: Animal Rights* (Toronto: Fernwood Publishing, 2010).
45. 1990, c. 21; Health of Animals Regulations, C.R.C., c. 296.
46. *Revised Statutes of Canada,* 1985, c. 25 (1st Supp.); Meat Inspection Regulations, 1990, SOR/90-288.
47. "Safety of Horse Meat," Canadian Food Inspection Agency, accessed May 13, 2015, http://www.inspection.gc.ca/food/information-for-consumers/fact-sheets/specific-products-and-risks/meat-and-poultry-products/horse-meat/eng/1331217628360/1331225704619.
48. National Capital Act, *Revised Statutes of Canada,* 1985, c. N-4; National Capital Commission Animal Regulations, SOR/2002-164.
49. Animal Pedigree Act, *Revised Statutes of Canada,* 1985, c. 8 (4th Supp.).
50. *Criminal Code, Revised Statutes of Canada,* 1985, c. C-46, 445.1–447.1.
51. Bisgould, *Animals and the Law*, 103–18.
52. Canadian Pari-Mutuel Agency, Agriculture and Agri-Food Canada.

53. Virginia Gray et al., "Public Opinion, Public Policy, and Organized Interests in the American States," *Political Research Quarterly* 57 (2004): 415.
54. Calculated from data in Council of State Governments, *The Book of the States* (Lexington, KY: Council of State Governments, 2013).
55. "Presidential Election Results," NBCNews.com, accessed July 23, 2013, http://elections.nbcnews.com/ns/politics/2012/all/president/#.Ux8B_dPD_4Y.
56. Gray et al., "Public Opinion, Public Policy, and Organized Interests," 415. The gun index is derived from the existence of the number of thirty state laws that reflect a state's commitment to regulating firearms.
57. Indirect support for these associations is found in Steven Tauber, "State Legislators' Roll-Call Votes on Farm Animal Protection Bills: The Agricultural Connection," *Society and Animals* 21 (2013): 501–22.
58. "Personal Income Per Capita in Current Dollars, 2007," United States, Bureau of the Census, accessed July 15, 2013, http://www.census.gov/statab/ranks/rank29.html.
59. United States Census Bureau, *Statistical Abstract of the United States* (Washington, DC: Government Printing Office, 2012), 153.
60. Ibid., 25
61. "2010 Census Urban and Rural Classification and Urban Area Criteria," United States Census Bureau, accessed May 13, 2015, https://www.census.gov/geo/reference/ua/urban-rural-2010.html.
62. Calculated from United States Census Bureau, *Statistical Abstract of the United States* (Washington, DC: Government Printing Office, 2012), 541.
63. "Religious Landscape Survey: Maps, Religious Groups," Pew Research, Religion and Public Life Project, accessed June 18, 2013, http://religions.pewforum.org/maps.
64. Derived from tables in the American Veterinary Medical Association, *U.S. Pet Ownership and Demographics Sourcebook* (Schaumberg, IL: American Veterinary Medical Association, 2012).
65. Calculated from "Inspection Reports and License and Registration List," U.S. Department of Agriculture, accessed Mar. 22, 2013, https://acissearch.aphis.usda.gov/LPASearch/faces/CustomerSearch.jspx.
66. The identification of laws was compiled from a Lexis/Nexis search of state legislation and a CanLawII search of Canadian provincial legislation. We also used Animal Legal and Historical Center, Michigan State University, http://www.animallaw.info/; HSUS "Laws and Cases," Animal Legal Defense Fund, http://aldf.org/resources/laws-cases/; "State Legislation," Born Free USA, http://www.bornfreeusa.org/legislation_archive_state_map.php; "State Legislation," Humane Society of the United States, http://www.humanesociety.org/about/departments/legislation/state_animal_protection_laws.html#.UyHMbtPD_4Y.
67. Coded as state has law, state does not have law.

68. Coded as state has law, state does not have law.
69. Coded as state has law, state does not have law.
70. Coded as an ordinal measure of number of protective provisions in the law.
71. Coded as an ordinal measure of number of protective provisions in the law.
72. Coded as state has law, state does not have law.
73. Coded as an ordinal ranking of no racing or betting, betting only, racing, racing only, and betting on races.
74. Coded as an ordinal measure of number of protective provisions in the law.
75. Coded as state has law, state does not have law.
76. Coded as an ordinal measure of number of protective provisions in the law.
77. Coded as state has law, state does not have law.
78. Coded as state has law, state does not have law.
79. Coded as an ordinal measure: statewide ban, local option permitted by the state, no state law.
80. Coded as an ordinal measure: no law, legislative consideration of law, passage of law.
81. Coded as an ordinal measure of number of protective provisions in the law.
82. "2013 Ranking of State Animal Protection Laws Released," Humane Society of the United States, Jan. 6, 2014, accessed Jan. 16, 2014, http://www.humanesociety.org/news/press_releases/2014/01/2013-state-ranking-010613.html; "2013 U.S. Animal Protection Laws Rankings," Animal Legal Defense Fund, accessed Jan, 15, 2014, http://aldf.org/wp-content/uploads/2013/12/2013-United-States-Animal-Protection-Laws-Rankings.pdf.
83. Bisgould, *Animals and the Law,* 103–18.
84. "Party Leaders and Standings," Parliament of Canada. Accessed July 29, 2013, http://www.parl.gc.ca/parlinfo/compilations/provinceterritory/PartyStandingsAndLeaders.aspx.
85. "Electoral Results by Party," Parliament of Canada, accessed July 29, 2013, http://www.parl.gc.ca/parlinfo/compilations/electionsandridings/ResultsParty.aspx.
86. "Median Total Income, by Family Type, by Province and Territory," Statistics Canada, accessed July 29, 2013, http://www.statcan.gc.ca/tables-tableaux/sum-som/l01/cst01/famil108a-eng.htm.
87. "Visible Minority Population, by Province and Territory," Statistics Canada, accessed July 29, 2013, http://www.statcan.gc.ca/tables-tableaux/sum-som/l01/cst01/demo52a-eng.htm.
88. "Population, Urban and Rural, by Province and Territory," Statistics Canada, accessed July 29, 2013, http://www.statcan.gc.ca/tables-tableaux/sum-som/l01/cst01/demo62a-eng.htm.
89. "Farm Operators by Farm Type and Province," Statistics Canada, accessed July 29, 2013, http://www.statcan.gc.ca/tables-tableaux/sum-som/l01/cst01/agrc22a-eng.htm.

90. "Population 15 Years and Over by Highest Degree, Certificate or Diploma, by Province and Territory," Statistics Canada, accessed July 29, 2013, http://www.statcan.gc.ca/tables-tableaux/sum-som/l01/cst01/educ41a-eng.htm.
91. "2013 Canadian Animal Protection Laws Rankings," Animal Legal Defense Fund, accessed Feb. 24, 2014, http://aldf.org/wp-content/uploads/2013/07/2013-REPORT-canadian-rankings.pdf.

6

Making Pet Policy: Kennel Licensing Legislation

The commercial breeding of companion animals is a major business in North America. Puppies sell from a few hundred to thousands of dollars each. Although sometimes conducted as a hobby in the backyard by the owners of a few purebred dogs and cats, large breeding operations with hundreds of popular breeds of dogs — often called "puppy mills"—are not uncommon. The operators of these facilities often identify the animals as a commodity and subject them to passive cruelty. Some of them will provide the animals only with the limited care necessary to make them marketable. Often they invest as little money as possible in the physical condition and cleanliness of kennels, health, and feeding of dogs, keep dogs in cages, breed the females as frequently as possible, sell or auction the puppies, and kill females who cannot breed or the unmarketable puppies that result from excessive breeding.

Canadian federal law places few specific requirements on commercial kennels, and the judiciary has issued few opinions that affect kennel operations.[1] The authority to regulate kennels has therefore passed to the provinces or their municipalities. Although engaged in interstate commerce, because of provisions in the U.S. federal Animal Welfare Act (AWA), many American commercial breeding operations are establishments defined as "retail pet stores" that sell dogs directly to the public without federal supervision or, until Internet sales were banned by the adoption of a United States Department of Agriculture (USDA) regulation in September 2013, on the Internet.[2] However, because federal law does not preempt additional forms of state regulation, the states and their local governments possess authority to regulate these facilities, too. This chapter details the development of commercial pet breeding law and policies and examines the fate of recent efforts of animal welfare interests to enact laws to regulate the commercial breeding of dogs in several states.

U.S. FEDERAL LAWS AND COMMERCIAL KENNEL OPERATIONS

The U.S. Animal Welfare Act of 1966 as amended governs selected aspects of commercial dog and cat breeding. The AWA requires that certain commercial breeders be licensed by the USDA. Breeders must keep records about the purchase, sale, transportation, identification, and previous ownership of animals. The USDA's Animal and Plant Health Inspection Service (APHIS) inspectors can investigate and inspect the records of canine breeding kennels. They can enforce rules about handling, housing, feeding, watering, sanitation, ventilation, shelter from extremes of weather and temperatures, adequate veterinary care, cage size, number of animals in a cage, and, for dogs, exercise. There is no limit to the number of dogs a breeder can have, and there is no age limit for breeding dogs or rules on how long they can be in a facility. The AWA requires that a breeder must hold an animal for five business days before sale. However, the amended AWA does not require the federal inspection of retail pet stores, sales through classified ads, breeder sales at flea markets, the operations and sale of animals by public and private animal shelters, or the operations and sales of "hobby" breeders who have three or fewer breeding female dogs. The AWA also does not require that dogs and cats live a quality life in a kennel, and inspectors make sure only that breeders are adhering to the minimum standards set forth by the AWA.[3]

Although they are veterinarians or animal health technicians trained by APHIS, fewer than 120 personnel regulate the approximately 6,000 licensed kennels that sell dogs wholesale or in litter lots and the 4,000 licensed research facilities, zoos, and circuses, as well as the ports and airports through which animals are imported.[4] There is no significant federal effort to locate and penalize operators of unlicensed breeding kennels. If federal inspectors acquire information about unlicensed facilities, they turn the information over to state or local inspectors, if they exist.[5] A 2010 report by the Office of the Inspector General of the USDA found that the Animal Care unit's enforcement process was ineffective against problematic dealers because it relied on education and cooperation rather than enforcement actions. The report noted that many inspectors did not document violations properly to support enforcement actions. It found that APHIS inspectors' New Penalty Worksheet allowed the agency to assess minimal penalties that did not deter violators and that APHIS misused guidelines to lower penalties for AWA violators.[6] Although the federal judiciary has permitted citizens to sue the USDA to demand enforcement of AWA provisions, such suits about kennels are apparently quite rare.[7] The limitations in federal legislation and the weaknesses in the enforcement effort have therefore contributed to a shift in the debate about commercial animal breeding policy to the states.

STATE AND PROVINCIAL KENNEL LAWS

The American states have a mix of laws that affect the operations of canine breeding kennels. As an indication of the saliency of the issue, more than twenty states have adopted or revised kennel laws during the past decade. Yet, as Table 6.1 indicates, some states have no kennel laws and some states' laws cover only retail or commercial operations. Kennel inspections, standards for the care of animals, and the restrictions on the number of dogs at a kennel are not always a part of the law. In the states with commercial kennel laws, mandatory inspections to enforce the law are conducted by a state Department of Agriculture inspector, as in Georgia; the Department of Health, as in New Jersey; or by agents of the county commission as in New York. In other states, inspections are made upon complaint by a humane officer or citizen, but there are no mandatory inspections. Thirty states have various humane care requirements in their kennel laws.[8]

As identified in Table 6.1, Canadian provincial law places few specific requirements on commercial kennels, and the judiciary has issued few opinions that affect kennel operations.[9] For example, peace officers in Alberta can conduct warrantless searches during ordinary business hours of any premises other than a private dwelling where animals are kept for sale, hire, or exhibition or any vehicle used to transport animals to inspect the animals and enforce anti-cruelty law. However, there is no schedule for regular inspections or specific requirements for operations of commercial kennels.[10] Prince Edward Island and Saskatchewan require that kennels follow *A Code of Practice for Canadian Kennel Operations* published by the Canadian Veterinary Medical Association, but they have no inspection process.[11] Newfoundland and Labrador also require that kennels comply with *A Code of Practice for Canadian Kennel Operations* as well as *A Code of Practice for Canadian Cattery Operations*, but there is no inspection requirement.[12] In British Columbia the Farm Practice Protection Act[13] prevents litigation about or regulation of normal farm practices at operations that include breeding pets or operating a kennel. However, Manitoba licenses and has requirements for kennel operations,[14] and New Brunswick specifically provides for the licensing and inspection of commercial kennels.[15]

As identified in Table 6.2, a minority of states have specific consumer protection or puppy purchaser laws with a variety of provisions. Only municipal bylaws and a very limited body of case law provide for consumer protection in the sale of dogs in Canada.[16] The U.S. states' laws regulate sales by commercial breeders and act as an indirect check on breeder practices. For example, as New York law states, its purpose is "safeguarding the public and insuring the humane treatment of such animals by guaranteeing the good health of such dogs or cats in the course of such transactions, or providing other alternatives to the consumer."[17] As in New York, most puppy lemon laws require puppies sold by pet dealers to be healthy and free of congenital abnormalities. A veterinarian's certification of health is normally required. If the animal turns out to be ill or unfit, the consumer has a right to return the animal and receive a refund of the purchase price.

Alternatively, in some states the consumer has a right to retain the animal and receive reimbursement from the pet dealer for the services of a licensed veterinarian. The law can also require that the pet be vaccinated against diseases such rabies. Misrepresentation of the condition of the animal can result in criminal penalties.[18] As with other consumer protection laws, the burden is on the consumer to file a complaint with the appropriate agency—usually the state's attorney general.[19]

POLITICS AND THE ADOPTION OF KENNEL LEGISLATION

How has politics influenced the adoption of these laws and extension of the legal accountability required of commercial pet breeders? To address this question, we examine policymaking activity in five states: Pennsylvania, Virginia, Ohio, Missouri, and West Virginia. The information about events in these states indicates the importance of politics in shaping the treatment of pets.

Pennsylvania

As commercial dairy farming declined and the demand for farmland increased, the costs associated with profitable farming induced many southeastern Pennsylvania farmers, especially the Amish of Lancaster and Chester counties, to begin commercial dog breeding. By 2000 there were reportedly more than 240 kennels with more than 27,000 dogs in Lancaster County alone. Although since 1982 Pennsylvania had regulated commercial kennels under its Dog Law, problems associated with commercial breeders continued to draw the attention of local animal welfare groups and residents. State law required only licensing and basic maintenance of breeding facilities, not extensive records of health and welfare, veterinary care, or provisions for exercise. The state's Bureau of Dog Law Enforcement reported it was understaffed. In interviews with reporters, some breeders indicated that the dog was little more than a commodity, and the state's Farm Bureau and operators opposed any change in the law.[20]

TABLE 6.1 *State and Provincial Kennel Licensing and Inspection Laws, 2013*

State or Province	No Kennel Laws	Laws Cover Retail or Commercial Kennels	Laws Cover Most Kennels	Inspection Provisions	Care of Animals Addressed in Law or Regulations
Alabama	x				
Alaska	x				
Arizona			x	x	
Arkansas	x				
California		x			x
Colorado			x	x	x
Connecticut		x			x
Delaware			x	x[a]	x
Florida	x				
Georgia		x		x[b]	x
Hawaii	x				
Idaho	x				
Illinois		x		x	x
Indiana		x			x
Iowa		x		x[a]	x
Kansas		x		x[a,b]	x
Kentucky	x				
Louisiana		x			
Maine		x		x	x
Maryland		x		x[a]	
Massachusetts		x		x[a]	x
Michigan		x		x[b]	x
Minnesota	x				
Mississippi	x				
Missouri		x		x	x
Montana	x				
Nebraska		x		x	x
Nevada		x		x[a]	x
New Hampshire		x		x	x
New Jersey		x		x[a]	x
New Mexico	x				x
New York		x		x	
North Carolina	x				

TABLE 6.1 *State and Provincial Kennel Licensing and Inspection Laws, 2013—cont'd*

State or Province	No Kennel Laws	Laws Cover Retail or Commercial Kennels	Laws Cover Most Kennels	Inspection Provisions	Care of Animals Addressed in Law or Regulations
North Dakota	x				
Ohio		x		x	x
Oklahoma		x		x	x
Oregon		x		x	x
Pennsylvania			x	x	x
Rhode Island		x		x	x
South Carolina	x				
South Dakota	x				
Tennessee		x		x[a]	x
Texas		x		x	x
Utah	x				
Vermont			x	x[a]	x
Virginia		x		x	x
Washington		x			x
West Virginia		x		x[a]	
Wisconsin		x			x
Wyoming	x				
Alberta				x[a]	
British Columbia	x[c]				
Manitoba		x			
New Brunswick		x		x[a,b]	x
Newfoundland & Labrador			x		x
Northwest Territories	x				
Nova Scotia				x[a]	
Nunavut	x				
Ontario	x				
Prince Edward Island			x		x
Quebec		x			x
Saskatchewan			x	x[a]	x
Yukon	x				

[a] Optional.
[b] New kennels.
[c] Except for sled dogs.

TABLE 6.2 *State and Provincial Puppy Protection and Lemon Laws, 2014*

State or Province	No State or Provincial Law	State Law, with Maximum Recovery Amount	State Law Allows Reimbursement of Veterinary Bills	State Law with Seller Disclosure Provisions
Alabama	x			
Alaska	x			
Arizona		x	x	x
Arkansas		x	x	
California		x	x	x
Colorado	x			
Connecticut		x	x	x
Delaware		x	x	
Florida		x	x	x
Georgia	x			
Hawaii	x			
Idaho	x			
Illinois		x	x	
Indiana	x			
Iowa	x			
Kansas	x			
Kentucky	x			
Louisiana	x			
Maine		x	x	
Maryland				
Massachusetts		x		
Michigan				x
Minnesota		x	x	x
Mississippi	x			
Missouri	x			
Montana	x			
Nebraska		x	x	
Nevada		x	x	
New Hampshire		x		x
New Jersey		x	x	x
New Mexico	x			
New York		x	x	x

TABLE 6.2 *State and Provincial Puppy Protection and Lemon Laws, 2014—cont'd*

State or Province	No State or Provincial Law	State Law, with Maximum Recovery Amount	State Law Allows Reimbursement of Veterinary Bills	State Law with Seller Disclosure Provisions
North Carolina	x			
North Dakota	x			
Ohio	x			
Oklahoma	x			
Oregon		x	x	
Pennsylvania		x	x	x
Rhode Island		x	x	x
South Carolina		x	x	x
South Dakota	x			
Tennessee	x			
Texas	x			
Utah	x			
Vermont		x	x	x
Virginia		x		x
Washington	x			
West Virginia	x			
Wisconsin	x			
Wyoming	x			
Alberta	x			
British Columbia	x			
Manitoba	x			
New Brunswick	x			
Newfoundland & Labrador	x			
Northwest Territories	x			
Nova Scotia	x			
Nunavut	x			
Ontario	x			
Prince Edward Island	x			
Quebec	x			
Saskatchewan	x			
Yukon	x			

What events precipitated kennel regulation becoming an issue on the political agenda? When commercial breeders sought zoning variances to operate or expand kennels, local political struggles about dog breeding escalated. Neighbors of kennels complained at zoning board hearings that the zoning variances that permitted the operation of kennels had created disruptive barking, automobile traffic, and problems associated with the disposal of dog waste, disposal of dead dogs, and the treatment of puppies. Some townships refused the variances; others cited some kennels for violations of existing zoning laws, while others considered efforts to devise zoning requirements to prevent the expansion of commercial breeding in their jurisdiction. Local animal welfare activists also met with state legislators and representatives of the Bureau of Dog Law Enforcement to voice their concerns. The group Main Line Animal Rescue of Valley Forge, led by Bill Smith, erected a billboard along the Pennsylvania Turnpike with the organization's Internet address and the slogan, "Welcome to Lancaster County, Home to Hundreds of Puppy Mills." It mailed postcards with the same slogan to seniors groups who toured Amish country. Formed in 2005, the Lancaster County group United Against Puppy Mills, undertook public demonstrations and erected signs to protest the operation of commercial kennels, contacted politicians, and established a connection to the Humane Society of the United States (HSUS) effort to end puppy mills. During the 2005 mayoral race in the city of Lancaster, the Republican Party erected signs and mailed flyers accusing the Democratic candidate of being a lawyer for puppy mill operators.[21]

Meanwhile, animal welfare legislation languished in the state's General Assembly. Animal welfare groups had only three registered lobbyists at the state capital, and the only one with a salary commuted twice a month from Washington, DC. In comparison to hunting and farming interests, animal welfare groups had little money to donate to legislators' elections. However, Governor Edward Rendell (D) recognized that his state had one of the highest concentrations of kennels in the United States and that these facilities often operated to the detriment of the dogs. Taking a personal interest in the issue, he created an ad hoc advisory panel of animal welfare group leaders, animal researchers, dog breeders, farmers, police officers, veterinarians, pet shop owners, legislative staffers, and officials of the Agriculture Department and the Attorney General's Office to recommend changes in animal welfare laws. Then in May 2006 he dismissed all fourteen members of the official Dog Law Advisory Board for not being "proactive." During the summer of 2006 an investigator hired by the ad hoc board produced a video of dogs in cages with wire mesh flooring that had injured their paws, filthy cages and animals, dogs exposed to wind and rain, puppies hidden from inspectors, dogs running endlessly on treadmills for exercise, and overcrowded cages at fifteen of twenty-five kennels in three counties.[22]

Under pressure from organized interests and their leaders, including Marsha R. Perelman, an American Society for the Prevention of Cruelty to Animals (ASPCA) board member and a supporter of his campaigns, Rendell and his staff spent several months in the selection of a special deputy secretary for the Bureau of Dog Law Enforcement with experience as a prosecutor and a humane society officer, a special prosecutor for dog law enforcement, a special enforcement compliance team, a new sixteen-member Dog Law Advisory Board, and regulatory changes to stiffen penalties for abuse. The proposed regulatory changes required the exercise of dogs, provisions for the lighting, ventilation, heating, and sanitation of kennels, health and safety rules, improved record keeping, and civil penalties for violations of the regulations. The new Dog Law Advisory Board held public hearings on a draft of the proposed regulations in late 2006 and into 2007. Often engaging in emotional outbursts with welfare advocates, breeders appeared at the hearings to object to the costs of the required upgrades in many kennels. One Board member noted that the participants offered two versions of the identity of dogs: "as pets" versus "as less similar to children and more as a field of corn." Hobby and show breeders also complained that proposed regulations failed to address their interests. At the same time the number of inspections and citations by the Bureau of Dog Law Enforcement increased dramatically. Despite enforcement efforts, the limited legal training of dog wardens and problems with the effectiveness of inspections remained.[23]

Pennsylvania requires that proposed regulations undergo review by state legislative committees and the Independent Regulatory Review Commission. The Commission primarily employs cost-benefit analysis to assess the effects of new regulations. In its report in May 2007, the Commission cited the regulations as too costly and recommended changes in the regulations to better differentiate among the size and type of kennels. Consequently the Dog Law Enforcement Bureau had to invest months in a revision of the regulations.[24]

In late 2007 Rendell decided on a second approach, and he notified the media that he would seek new legislation rather than administrative regulations to govern kennel operations. His staff recognized that various political interests might object to more extensive kennel regulatory legislation. To address potential opponents, during a five-month period they arranged a series of face-to-face meetings with various stakeholder interests to craft a draft of legislation. These negotiations included various humane societies, breed rescue groups, home breeders, and groups that use dogs for conformation, hunting, and sporting. However, the state's Farm Bureau and the Professional Dog Breeders Advisory Council refused to participate in the discussions. Individuals and organized interests filed more than 16,000 additional comments on the proposed law.[25] By consultation and getting stakeholder groups to commit to certain policy changes, officials in the Rendell administration deterred complaints and opposition to a new kennel law.

In April 2008, prior to the completion of Rendell's draft of legislation and without contact with his administration, talk show host Oprah Winfrey broadcast nationally two programs with undercover footage of abuses at commercial kennels in Lancaster County. Coupled with assistance from Winfrey's investigators and lobbying by the HSUS, the APSCA, United Against Puppy Mills, veterinarians, attorneys, and other animal welfare groups, in May 2008 a bipartisan group of state legislators held a press conference and rally in support of the Rendell proposals. Immediate opposition came from the U.S. Sportsmen's Alliance, a national organization that had already spent more than $200,000 to oppose kennel regulation laws, the Farm Bureau, and the Professional Dog Breeders Association.[26]

In May 2008 State Representative James Casorio (D-Irwin) introduced Rendell's proposed commercial kennel law in the state's House of Representatives. After approval by the House Agriculture and Rural Affairs Committee, it was bogged down by a series of more than two hundred amendments from Republicans to prevent Rendell from claiming credit for ending the abuses at kennels. The bill languished during the General Assembly's summer recess. However, Rendell kept up the pressure for its passage while both bill proponents and commercial breeders conducted rallies. A widely publicized incident in which a commercial kennel owner shot more than a hundred dogs because he thought it would be too costly to comply with a revised law also contributed to public support for the bill. On September 17 the House approved the bill. However, the Senate Agriculture and Rural Affairs Committee chair desired changes to allow kennels time to complete the construction of facilities that complied with a new law, and the committee amended the bill to ease standards on flooring, cage size, and climate control. Despite opposition to these changes from animal welfare groups, Rendell indicated that he would accept them. The Senate then passed the revised bill 49-1, the House concurred, and Rendell signed it on October 27 at a ceremony held at a rescue center.[27]

The final version of the revised dog law, called Act 119, created several classes of kennels, with each class defined by the number of dogs sold yearly and the number held in the kennel. The classes included commercial, dealer, pet shop, boarding, nonprofit, rescue network, research, and "private kennels" where dogs are kept or bred by their owner for the purpose of hunting, tracking, exhibiting in dog shows, or participating in performance events or field and obedience trials. The number of dogs determined the variable license fee imposed on the commercial operator. To be licensed any operator had to satisfy a series of requirements specified in the law, including standards on cage size, sanitation, construction, location, ventilation, access to potable water, and the isolation of females in heat and with puppies from other dogs. The kennel operators also had to report any animal cruelty convictions, undergo criminal background checks, keep records on the condition, breed, color, markings, sex, age, and sale or transfer of dogs and submit to inspections of their facilities to earn and retain their license. The operator had to arrange for a signed agreement with an attending veterinarian who would supervise physical examination and vaccination schedules, disease, pest, and parasite control, nutrition, and euthanasia for dogs at a kennel. The revised Dog Law provided a series of civil penalties for Dog Law violations.[28]

A provision in the law restructured the Bureau of Dog Law Enforcement in the state's Department of Agriculture. The law and regulations charged the Bureau with oversight of the enforcement of the Dog Law and the selection of state dog wardens. The law specified a training program for the wardens, and they received the same law enforcement powers as police officers and could carry firearms. Dog wardens were assigned to inspect each licensed kennel at least twice a year. They could order veterinarians to examine any dogs in the kennel. If refused entry to inspect a kennel they possessed the authority to apply for a search warrant. If a warden found a violation, a citation with fine or an order to cease and desist from operating the kennel, especially if unlicensed, could be issued. If endangered, dogs also could be impounded. The law provided administrative hearings for challenges to license revocations and associated fines and seizures of dogs. If they discovered violations of the state's animal cruelty law, dog wardens also could file criminal complaints.[29]

To assist dog wardens, the Bureau of Dog Law Enforcement established a tip line and an online complaint form for the public reporting of violations of the law. They also received reports of violations of the Dog Law from shelters, rescue groups, animal control officers, and humane officers. With the enactment of the revised law, the number of kennels significantly decreased. In large part the decrease appeared to be related to the costs of compliance with the law. Media publicity about legal actions against violators may have aided in causing the decrease.[30]

Other steps to implement the new Dog Law began immediately after its passage. Bureau employees contacted more than 1,400 kennel owners to inform them that only a veterinarian could euthanize their dogs and that they had to adhere to the time lines for kennel improvements included in the new law. The Bureau dedicated employees to answer phone calls from kennel owners, created a website, hosted two workshops on the new kennel application, and replied to a large volume of e-mail inquiries. It assigned a warden to become the first dangerous dog coordinator with responsibility to contact municipalities and courts to update a dangerous dog registry, ensure all requirements for these dogs are being met, find violators who had moved or sold the dangerous dog, and to inspect dangerous dogs. The Bureau hired two veterinarians with extensive dog and kennel experience to assess and monitor dog health and undertook extensive training of its personnel and expanded its record keeping.[31]

During 2009 the state amended the Dog Law to prevent owners and breeders of dogs from performing debarking, ear and tail docking, declawing, and caesarian sections on dogs. Initial efforts to weaken the revised

Dog Law failed. Federal judge Sylvia Rambo upheld the law against a challenge by three breeders and the Pennsylvania Dog Breeders Advisory Council. However, in 2010 the state modified regulations to permit pregnant and nursing dogs to live in cages with wire flooring and to limit unfettered access to outdoor exercise areas. In 2011 a group of rural Republican lawmakers, with the support of the American Kennel Club, proposed but failed to secure legislation to study what they regarded as the adverse economic consequences of the revised Dog Law. An observer noted that many legislators simply did not want to reopen the kennel issue. Many felt besieged by angry constituents during the consideration of the bill and feared that raising the issue again might only create a struggle that would dissatisfy enough constituents to damage their reelection chances.[32]

After coming into office in 2011, Governor Tom Corbett (R) replaced the head of the Bureau of Dog Law Enforcement. Although the new director pledged to aggressively enforce the law, animal welfare activists remained concerned that the enforcement of the law would be weakened by budget cuts.[33] A Dog Law Restricted Fund with income from dog and kennel licenses and civil penalties funded Bureau personnel and operating expenses, grants to shelters, and payments for dog and coyote damage to farm animals and property. Budget shortfalls resulted in a reassignment of Dog Law Restricted Fund revenues away from enforcement activity, personnel, and the dedication of a prosecutor to Dog Law violations. With the Dog Law Fund reduced, the interest it earned decreased, further strapping enforcement efforts. However, the new law did produce a significant decrease in the number of commercial kennels known to be legally operating. Certainly the revision of the kennel law eliminated the worst of the state's puppy mills and provided a better life for most breeders' dogs and their puppies.

Virginia

Variations in the Pennsylvania example of the legislative and gubernatorial politics of kennel regulation have occurred in other states, including Virginia and Ohio. In 2008 Virginia significantly revised its companion animal laws, including the sections addressing kennel and pet sales. Puppy mills had long existed in Virginia, but they had not drawn much public attention. However, a widely publicized 2007 fire at an Amish-run breeding operation in the rural southwestern section of the state that killed more than 200 dogs triggered attention to the need to change the law. After investigating the fire, the HSUS issued a scathing report about conditions at commercial kennels in southwestern Virginia. It noted that in addition to filthy and "deplorable" conditions, most of the puppy mills did not have the required USDA licenses. The same year authorities and animal welfare groups rescued more than 1,100 puppies from a breeding kennel in Carroll County and 115 puppies from a home in Washington County.[34]

In response, Delegate Bobby Orrick (R) introduced a kennel licensing and safety bill in the state's House of Delegates. It attracted support from the HSUS and the Virginia Animal Control Association. Opponents included the American Kennel Club, the Virginia Federation of Dog Clubs and Breeders, and various dog hunting groups. They appeared in force at legislative hearings on the bill. The bill squeaked out of the House Agriculture, Chesapeake and Natural Resources Committee, and eventually through the General Assembly. It easily won Senate approval. After the kennel bill passed, Governor Tim Kaine (D), accompanied by his rescued pit bull, not only signed it, he used his authority to put the law into action on January 1, 2009, six months ahead of what legislators had proposed. When the law went into effect the state inspectors immediately arrested and secured the conviction of a "notorious" puppy mill operator; however, some animal welfare organization spokespersons still thought that the law was underutilized.[35]

The result was a comprehensive extension of state law and regulations. Under the revised law a kennel is any establishment in which five or more canines, felines, or hybrids of either are kept for the purpose of breeding, hunting, training, renting, buying, boarding, selling, or showing. A commercial dog breeder is any person who, during any twelve-month period, maintains thirty or more adult female dogs for the sale of their puppies as companion animals. The law also requires that commercial dog breeders can keep no more than fifty dogs over the age of one year at any time for breeding purposes. However, a higher number of dogs may be allowed if approved by local ordinance after a public hearing. Any local ordinance may include additional requirements for commercial breeding operations.

Additionally, no commercial dog breeder can breed dogs without a valid business license issued by any locality.[36]

Unlike Pennsylvania's, the Virginia law did not provide for a state agency to regulate commercial breeders. The state veterinarian and his representatives (deputized veterinarians and their staff) possess the power to conduct inspections of any business premises where animals are housed or kept. The state veterinarian's representatives, any animal control officer, and any public health or safety official may respond to a complaint and without a search warrant investigate any violation of commercial kennel regulations. The investigation may include the inspection of the books and records of any commercial dog breeder, the inspection of any companion animal owned by the breeder, and the inspection of any place where animals are bred or maintained.[37]

However, using the term *adequate care,* the law fails to specify the required housing and treatment of animals. As interpreted by inspectors, *adequate care* or *care* means the responsible practice of good handling, production, management, confinement, feeding, watering, protection, shelter, transportation, treatment, and, when necessary, euthanasia appropriate for the age, species, condition, size, and type of the animal. It also means the provision of veterinary care when needed to prevent suffering or impairment of health. Therefore, each dog must receive adequate feed, water, shelter, space for movement, exercise, and veterinary care when needed. Any commercial dog breeder violating any provision of this article is guilty of a misdemeanor with a penalty of confinement in jail for not more than twelve months and a fine of not more than $2,500 or either or both.[38]

Using their zoning authority, some Virginia cities and counties have adopted stricter limitations on the number of dogs in kennels and special license fees. Most of these jurisdictions, such as Arlington, Hanover, and Prince William and cities such as Alexandria and Chesapeake, are urban or suburban communities. In addition to the kennel licensing, the state has adopted consumer protection provisions to require the sale of companion animals only from commercial dealers licensed by the USDA. If sold as a registered breed, the animal must have a pet history certificate with information that describes it, its parents, and its veterinary care history. The law also affords remedies for consumers who are not provided with this information or who are sold a diseased animal.[39] Consequently, despite a lack of a central state regulatory body and the regulation of only breeders with a more substantial number (fifty) of breeding dogs than states such as Pennsylvania, Virginia has controlled some breeders.

Ohio

For many years Amish farmers in northeastern Ohio raised thousands of dogs for sale across the Midwestern and Northeastern United States. Only recently has the state extended legal accountability to the commercial breeding of dogs.[40] Until late 2012 the core of its statutory requirements for kennels dated from 1953. However, complaints from purchasers of puppies, disclosures of abuses at kennels by rescue groups such as Central Ohio Dog Rescue, League to Save Ohio Strays, New Beginnings Animal Shelter, and Luv4K9s Dog Rescue, media exposes, and ongoing protests by animal activists against the Buckeye Dog Auction in Holmes County triggered efforts to change kennel and dog sales law.[41] Media outlets such as the Columbus *Dispatch* publicized abuses. At the local and state levels, officials' attention became focused on the sale and attempted relocation of a dog auction from Holmes to Geauga Counties in the northeastern section of the state. This event drew media attention and apparently caused the owners to keep the auction in Holmes County, the center of the breeding industry.[42] However, the Amish farmers in Holmes County and dog breeders who had located there from out of state pressured their county's representative, House Agriculture and Natural Resources Committee Chairman David Hall (R-Millersburg), to block state legislative action on a puppy mill law.

More political activity on puppy mills came about when state legislators proposed a kennel inspection law in 2009. One of its sponsors, Senator Jim Hughes (R-Columbus), said the bill sought to separate the bad from the respectable breeders. Support for it came from the ASPCA, HSUS, Columbus Dog Connection, a number of rescue groups and volunteer-run shelters, and, with less enthusiasm because of proposed veterinarian inspection requirements, the Ohio Veterinary Medical Association. However, the Ohio Association of Animal Owners, a group representing "people from every aspect of the animal industry: farmers, exotic animal owners, educators and exhibitors, dealers, medical researchers, game ranchers, pet stores, capture/transport specialists, and pet owners,"[43] asserted the bill's sponsors were "out to shut down dog breeding, period."[44] The bill failed to win legislative approval. Using another political tactic, in 2010 a political action committee composed of many local and statewide humane groups and the Coalition to Ban Ohio Dog Auctions (CBODA) began to seek signatures to place an initiative on the 2011 state ballot to ban the auction and raffle of dogs. The initiative gathered a considerable number of the required 120,700 signatures, especially after the release of a video showing cruelty to cattle at an Ohio farm.[45]

At this stage Governor Ted Strickland (D) reluctantly intervened. Asserting a desire to avoid a costly political battle that might pit humane organizations against farm groups, his office configured a compromise proposal. In the compromise the HSUS, Ohio SPCA, and Farm Bureau agree to improve kennel regulations and address other forms of animal cruelty while retaining the dog auctions.[46] However, despite the interest of legislative leadership in the passage of a bill, contention between various animal welfare and breeder groups resulted in the proposal bogging down in the state legislature. In December 2011 the chair of the Senate committee reported that he would not advance a bill unless the stakeholders could find common ground. An effort to broker a compromise collapsed.[47] The same month CBODA submitted its petition with 150,000 signatures to ban dog auctions to the state General Assembly. It was ignored. CBODA then filed to place the ban on the 2012 ballot for a referendum.[48] However, CBODA failed to raise the funds for the official certification of the 115,000 signatures on its initiative petition within the required 60 day period. The ballot measure was left in limbo.

Finally in February 2012 the Ohio Senate achieved a compromise on a modest version of kennel regulation legislation with less stringent requirements than the laws in Pennsylvania and Missouri.[49] The bill proposed a board to regulate "high volume breeders" who keep adult breeding dogs that produce at least nine litters of puppies in any given year and sell sixty or more adult dogs or puppies per calendar year.[50] The Senate bill also proposed to regulate pet retailers and rescue organizations. After some delay, in November the House passed the kennel licensing bill, and Governor John Kasich (R) signed it into law in December. The law requires the licensing, bonding, governmental inspection, and annual veterinary inspection of the high volume breeders. It specifies cage size and cleanliness and requires protective coated wire grid but not solid cage floors,[51] the "effective enrichment" of puppies, cleanliness, and access to exercise areas of unspecified size. Provisions address the record keeping, sale, and transportation of dogs by kennels. The law includes procedures for addressing complaints about breeders and injunctive relief and the assessment of civil penalties for violations. Another provision attempts to control dog auctions by requiring licenses and record keeping for pet retailers who "sell dogs at wholesale for resale to another or who sell or give one or more dogs to a pet store annually." The law compels the registration of canine rescue groups. Finally, the law prohibits anyone convicted of animal cruelty in the last twenty years from obtaining a kennel license.[52]

The law also created a Commercial Dog Breeding Advisory Board to assist the director of the Ohio Department of Agriculture in the promulgation of administrative rules on housing, nutrition, exercise, waste management, grooming, whelping, and other general care standards to be followed by breeders and retailers. The rules were approved by the state's Joint Committee on Agency Rule Review during the fall of 2013.[53] Because there will be six state inspectors for an estimated 3,000 kennels and not all counties have a humane officer or an officer dedicated to kennel oversight, complaints rather than inspections trigger most kennel inspections. Most regulations will not take effect until December 31, 2016. Although the law failed to ban dog auctions, in June 2012 operators held their last one in Holmes County.[54] Nonetheless, puppy sales reportedly still generate $9 million a year for the economy of Holmes County.

Missouri

Labeled the puppy mill capital of the United States by the HSUS, Missouri law "allowed dogs to be kept in wire enclosures only slightly larger than their bodies" and placed limits neither on the number of dogs that a breeder could own nor on the number of times that a dog could be bred without rest. Learning of abuses, in February 2009 the Humane Society of Missouri reported the conditions at a series of kennels to state Department of Agriculture officials and sheriff deputies, who then raided the facilities. The Humane Society used media reports to focus attention on abuses at the kennels, and they had some of the dogs found during one raid appear on the Oprah Winfrey show. The reports drew the attention of Governor Jay Nixon (D) and the state's Agriculture director, Jon Hagler. Hagler created a program called Operation Bark Alert, which allowed people to report unlicensed breeders directly to him by e-mail. State Attorney General Chris Koster (D), a strong supporter of animal welfare, initiated Prosecution Bark Alert to pursue criminal charges against kennel law violators. By August 2009 Koster's office claimed they had identified more than 170 unlicensed kennels, and their raids of kennels and a dogfighting ring continued. A state legislator also introduced a bill to tighten puppy mill regulations.[55]

In December 2009 a ballot initiative committee, Missourians for the Protection of Dogs, kicked off a campaign to use the initiative and referendum procedure provided by its state constitution to establish more extensive regulation of commercial kennels. An advocacy coalition, Missourians for the Protection of Dogs included numerous individuals and animal welfare organizations such as the Humane Society of Missouri, the Missouri Alliance for Animal Legislation, Central Missouri Humane Society, Humane Society of Southwest Missouri, Wayside Waifs, Best Friends Animal Society, the ASPCA, and the HSUS. The group's initiative proposition, initially titled as the Puppy Mill Cruelty Prevention Act, or Proposition B, required large-scale dog breeding operations to provide each dog under their care with sufficient food and clean water, veterinary care, sufficient housing and protection from the elements, cages with space to turn, lie down, and fully extend their limbs, regular exercise, and adequate rest between breeding cycles. The proposition also limited the number of female breeding dogs to fifty per facility, but it did not apply to breeders with ten or fewer intact female dogs. The proposition did not affect individuals who raised hunting dogs, livestock facilities, or animal rescue and shelter operators who are not involved in the commercial sale of puppies.[56]

To place Proposition B on the ballot, Missourians for the Protection of Dogs had to gather more than 100,000 valid signatures of registered Missouri voters. To assist in this effort, the HSUS donated $450,000 to Missourians for the Protection of Dogs. Support also came from public figures such as St. Louis Cardinals manager Tony La Russa, the wife of U.S. Senator Kit Bond, former Senator John Danforth, and various celebrities. By May 2010 the coalition had gathered nearly twice the number of signatures needed to have the proposition placed on the November ballot, and the state's secretary of state certified the signatures that August.[57]

Proposition B generated significant controversy. The Missouri Federation of Animal Owners, a group representing commercial kennel interests, filed suit to have the proposition removed from the ballot. The suit failed. In their press releases commercial breeders emphasized the regulations already on the books and noted that the proposition included no funding provisions for additional inspections. Breeders and an ad hoc group sponsored by conservative antiregulatory activists called Alliance for Truth took particular issue with the proposed prohibition on possessing more than fifty breeding dogs. They claimed that this would put good breeders out of business and cause the import of dogs from other states to skyrocket. Additional opposition, largely aimed at discrediting HSUS involvement in the proposition campaign, came from agricultural groups such as the Missouri Farm Bureau, Missouri Pork Association, Missouri Egg Council, the agricultural advocacy group Missourians for Animal Care Coalition, and the libertarian Calvary Group. These groups feared the kennel proposition might encourage initiatives to regulate the treatment of hogs, poultry, and cattle. Also, the Farm Bureau received important financial support from the Hunte Corporation, a firm in Goodman, Missouri, that purchased thousands of dogs from commercial breeders, warehoused them in a 100,000 square foot facility, and then sold them to retailers. The Missouri Veterinary Medical Association opposed the proposition as potentially ineffective and costly. Opponents also had friendly legislators introduce bills to undercut the vote on the proposal. However, proponents of the proposition replied by citing new incidents of significant abuses at kennels and evidence that dog breeders evaded taxes. With much of its support coming from urban and suburban precincts, the proposition ultimately passed by a narrow margin.[58]

Within a few days after the passage of Proposition B, several rural Republican state legislators announced that they would introduce legislation to amend or overturn the proposition. During the 2011 term the Missouri legislature considered several bills to modify Proposition B. Unlike in other states, in Missouri the legislative debate about puppy mills became both a rural–urban/suburban conflict and an ideological issue.[59] Animal welfare groups supported Senate Bill 95 to extend the law beyond commercial dog breeders. The bill would have imposed regulations on any person with more than ten female dogs over six months of age. It would additionally have eliminated the exemption for animal shelters and renamed the statute the Puppy Cruelty Prevention Act.[60] On the other hand, rural and small town Republican opponents of the proposition, some claiming the voters did not understand the proposition, introduced twelve bills and joint resolutions.[61] Senate Bill 4 and House Bill 94 proposed to repeal Proposition B in its entirety.[62] Senate Bill 113 proposed to weaken the law by eliminating the fifty-dog limitation, shortening the mandatory rest period between breeding cycles, and delegating the definition of "regular exercise," "sufficient housing," and "sufficient space" to the state's Department of Agriculture.[63] Eventually the legislature consolidated the provisions of Senate Bills 95 and 113 in committee. The consolidated version, House Bill 131, overturned significant provisions of Proposition B that regulated the number of dogs in kennels, defined the size of cages or pens, described the scope and frequency of veterinary examinations, required rest periods between breeding cycles, required ground-level heated cages, raised license fees, and created the misdemeanor of puppy mill cruelty. It passed the Senate by a vote of 20–14 and passed the House by a vote of 85–71.[64]

However, pressure from the Governor and the Department of Agriculture and the threat of a veto resulted in the introduction of a compromise, Senate Bill 161. Called the Canine Cruelty Prevention Act, Senate Bill 161 revised many of the Proposition B provisions such as yearly hands-on veterinary inspections and details on cage size while allotting breeders additional time to phase in some of the more expensive changes required such as solid flooring and outdoor exercise areas. Unlike Proposition B, Senate Bill 161 did not require limits on the number of breeding dogs at a kennel or specify periods between breeding cycles, and it placed a tax and $1.00 per animal fee on nonprofit animal shelters and rescue groups for every animal held or transferred, up to $2,500 per year. Small, nonprofit volunteer shelters and rescues viewed this tax as an effort to penalize their efforts. Enforcement, assigned to county prosecutors until Proposition B, was left to the state's Department of Agriculture. House members approved the new legislation 108–42, and the Senate voted 24–10 to pass it.[65]

Senate Bill 161 divided the animal welfare community, receiving the endorsement of the Humane Society of Missouri but drawing opposition from the HSUS and the APSCA. Immediately a group of legislators urged Governor Jay Nixon to reject the compromise and sign House Bill 131. Governor Nixon, however, signed the compromise bill (the Canine Cruelty Prevention Act, Senate Bill 161) into law.[66] The state then modified existing administrative regulations to guide enforcement of the law.[67]

After the passage of the law a number of Missouri kennels closed and Attorney General Koster took action against a number of commercial breeders. However, during the 2012 and 2013 sessions the legislature failed to repeal the transfer fee on nonprofit shelters and rescue groups and to provide for the licensing of only legitimate shelters and rescue groups. The HSUS, Dogwood Animal Shelter of Osage Beach, and Stray Rescue of St. Louis then challenged the tax in court but lost. Several agricultural groups proposed a constitutional amendment to protect farmers against potentially unfair regulations and a "right for farmers and ranchers to engage in modern farming and ranching practices." Because dogs are legally an agricultural commodity in Missouri, the proposal might further hamper efforts to regulate commercial dog breeders. At the 2014 primary election the voters narrowly approved the proposition (50.12 percent to 49.88 percent). Agricultural groups also supported legislation to toughen the requirements to place propositions on the ballot. However, a federal suit by dog breeders challenging the kennel law was not pursued.[68]

Despite the consistent opposition from breeders and agricultural interest groups and some weakening of the puppy mill initiative law, a significant reduction in the number of federally licensed kennels has occurred in Missouri. In 2012 the state attorney general's Canine Cruelty Prevention Unit reported actions that resulted in the rescue of more than 5,500 animals.[69] The extent to which unlicensed breeding facilities operate remains uncertain. Firms that broker pets, such as the Hunte Corporation, remained unregulated by the new state law.

West Virginia

Until 2013 kennel law in West Virginia addressed only the registration of facilities. Although revised on several occasions, the core of the law dated from 1951.[70] Despite the publicized disclosure of the massive abuse of companion animals at the Star Ridge Center in Preston County in 2006 and the Whispering Oaks Kennel near Parkersburg in 2008, efforts to regulate mass commercial breeding initially did not gain much political traction in the state.[71] The state representative of the HSUS ranked puppy mills lower on its organization's lobbying efforts than the regulation of exotic animals and support for spay/neuter programs. However, by cooperating with members of the Federation of Humane Organizations of West Virginia (FOHO), the state representative of the HSUS had on occasion lobbied for kennel regulation. Nonetheless only a few state legislators joined to sponsor a stricter commercial kennel law.[72] With other issues and other animal welfare issues on the agenda of a legislature that is constitutionally restricted to a sixty-day session and in which the party leadership directs the flow of business, the legislature often placed animal welfare on a political back burner. Additionally, the two statewide elected officials who might influence the legislative agenda, Governor Earl Tomlin (D), who was affiliated with greyhound racing, and Commissioner of Agriculture Gus Douglass (D), who did not regard the administration of companion animals breeding as agriculture, never voiced an interest in the puppy mill issue. Despite the limited support from the executive branch, during the 2010 session, the House of Delegates passed a bill to regulate kennels with more than fifty dogs. It was not considered by the Senate.[73]

During the 2012 session several members again introduced bills to regulate commercial kennels.[74] A bill passed the Senate that would have required the licensing of commercial breeding kennels with more than eleven unsterilized adult dogs by county commissions, basic health standards for dogs in the kennels, and the twice a year inspection of these kennels by county animal control officers or law enforcement personnel. Unlike other states, it assigned enforcement to local officials and agencies with other duties rather than a single statewide regulatory agency. However, the bill did not reach the floor of the House of Delegates. It was opposed by the Farm Bureau and the American Kennel Club, which hailed its defeat as a victory.[75]

Nonetheless, despite some complaints from animal welfare groups that its language was nebulous and that it would not stamp out illegal puppy mills, a bill introduced in 2013 with provisions similar to the 2012 bill passed.[76] Although not as specific as Pennsylvania law and regulations, it required heating of kennels, solid flooring, no stacking of cages, and access to exercise. However, it excluded from regulation commercial breeders who kept dogs exclusively for the purpose of herding or guarding livestock, hunting, tracking, exhibiting in dog shows, participation in performance events or field and obedience trials, and greyhound kennels registered with the state's Racing Commission. Legislators designed the exclusions to offset opposition from the Farm Bureau, sportsmen's groups, and the greyhound racing industry. No state agency was created to license or develop rules for the operation of kennels, and the state devoted no fiscal resources to its implementation. County commissions were to issue permits to operate a kennel at a fee of $250 or less that they could set. The bill required breeders with a permit to meet basic sanitation, shelter, solid cage flooring, and exercise requirements for dogs, obtain a permit to operate, and sell dogs only as household pets. Violators could face misdemeanor charges and fines or a required "improvement period not to exceed one year upon such terms and conditions as the judge or magistrate may determine" and dismissal of charges if improvements occurred.[77] It was signed by Governor Tomblin on April 11, 2013. To date only ten county commissions have adopted legislation to license and inspect the commercial kennels regulated by the act.

ASSESSMENT OF POLICY INITIATIVES

What do these case studies about puppy mill legislation indicate about the making of animal welfare law? In most American political contexts it can be assumed that there exists a bias against policy change. The concept of path dependency indicates that in many political contexts policy stasis accompanied with occasional incremental policy adjustments is the norm.[78] What then induced policy change in commercial kennel operations in some states?

Table 6.3 summarizes the political struggles and decisions in the five case studies. First, the recognition of a problem with existing policy must occur.[79] In all five states the disclosure of significant harms at puppy mills triggered attention to the abuses that occurred at commercial kennels. Initially the recognition of problems often occurred at the local level. In each state a mix of media reporting of its investigations, local complaints, and state regulatory inspections especially focused attention on the abuses at kennels and the inadequacy of governmental regulations and inspections.

Next, interest groups sought policy change. Utilizing reports of abuses, anti-cruelty groups at the state and local levels, such as United Against Puppy Mills in Pennsylvania, Missourians for the Protection of Dogs, CBODA in Ohio, and, in a less visible role, FOHO in West Virginia, further heightened attention to what they considered to be cruelty in the operations of these businesses. Also, to induce lawmakers to think about puppy mills and thus open a window for policy change, the role of policy entrepreneurs was critical.[80] These individuals included organized interest spokespersons, legislators, and administrative officials.

Nonetheless the arguments about the costs of established policy succeeded only when there was policy leadership. Since studies of state politics have shown the power of governors in the creation of a policy agenda, the designation of policy priorities, the use of staff and other appointees to draft policy proposals, the ability to propose a budget and other legislation, and the potential to influence legislators, this is not a surprising finding.[81] Pennsylvania Governor Rendell, Virginia Governor Kaine, and Missouri Attorney General Koster drew attention to the need for the intensified regulation of commercial kennels. In particular Rendell used the visibility of his office to keep attention to the issue alive and assert the need for it even when legislative progress on it slowed.[82] In Missouri, Governor Nixon, who had avoided a role in the initiative process but who supported raids on problem puppy mills, intervened after the passage of legislation to retain regulations found in the initiative proportion.

Legislative leadership also matters. In Ohio, where the governors stood apart from the issue, and in West Virginia, where governors ignored pressures for kennel regulation and the elected commissioner of agriculture opposed change in kennel laws, legislators kept the issue on the political agenda.[83] In Pennsylvania, Virginia, and West Virginia, key

TABLE 6.3 *Conditions Influencing the Expansion of Kennel Regulation*

Activity	Pennsylvania	Virginia
Precipitating or focusing events "trigger"	Media reported multiple abuse cases	Media reported abuse case Events in other states
Primary organized groups for policy change	United Against Puppy Mills, with HSUS and ASPCA assistance	HSUS Virginia Animal Control Association
Initial administrative action	Investigations by Dog Law Advisory Board and Bureau of Dog Law Enforcement	Limited
Public opinion	Rallies by kennel regulation supporters	Muted
Local legislation	Zoning laws	None
Opposition	Pennsylvania Breeders Association Farm Bureau American Kennel Club	American Kennel Club Virginia Federation of Dog Clubs and Breeders Sportsmen's groups
Legislative leadership	Support under pressure from governor	Support
Executive leadership	Significant leadership role	Significant support
Later events	Some reduction in enforcement funding but no core provisions	

legislative leaders and committee chairs sought intensified regulation. In West Virginia legislative leaders acted even when little support for kennel regulation came from the governor or the commissioner of agriculture. However, breeder regulation initially did not pass in Ohio, Missouri, and West Virginia, where the Farm Bureau and agribusiness and sportsmen interests quickly found allies when majority party leaders assigned bills about kennel regulation to legislative agriculture committees. Only

Ohio	West Virginia	Missouri
Media reported abuses at dog auctions and exotic animal facility	Media reported abuse case Events in other states	Multiple media reported abuse cases, with national coverage
Ban Ohio Dog Auctions	West Virginia Federation of Humane Organizations	Missourians for the Protection of Dogs (coalition of humane organizations)
None	No state administrative efforts	Raids of kennels by Department of Agriculture
Largely muted Humane Lobby Day rally	Quiescent	Proposition adopted by public ballot
None	None	Support for state regulation
Ohio Association of Animal Owners Farm Bureau	Sportsmen's groups American Kennel Club	Missouri Federation of Animal Owners Missourians for Animal Care Coalition Alliance for Truth
Support	Support	Support
Support for compromise law	No support	Support from governor Action from attorney general
		Significant limitations made in initial law

continued support from legislators in key leadership positions resulted in legislative action that overcame opposition or brokered compromises with the organized opposition.

The case studies of commercial kennel legislation presented in this chapter illustrate the importance of specific political contexts in shaping political struggles about the development of legalized accountability as a means of protecting companion animals from breeders' passive cruelty. In each state particular conjunctures of events, media coverage, organized interest activity, policy entrepreneurship by key public officials, and, in particular, sympathetic executive and legislative policy leaders contributed to the nature of a political struggle between proponents of animal welfare and commodity-oriented groups and pet businesses. Yet, even in the states with more intensive inspection laws and regulations such as Pennsylvania, the funding of inspection efforts can constrain efforts to root out illegal kennels and improve licensed operations. As with other governmental programs, the effective implementation of kennel regulation depends on the continuing willingness of legislators to appropriate funds to ensure legalized accountability with a bite.

NOTES

1. See Lesli Bisgould, *Animals and the Law* (Toronto: Irwin Law, 2011), 129–33.
2. 7 *United States Code* § 2132(f). For general information, see "Questions and Answers on Animal Care's Regulation of Commercial Animal Dealers," USDA Animal and Plant Health Inspection Service, accessed Aug. 7, 2012, http://www.milestonesetters.com/uploads/faq_animal_dealers.pdf. On the ban on Internet sales, see "USDA Restores Important Check and Balance on Retail Pet Sales to Ensure Health, Humane Treatment," USDA Animal and Plant Health Inspection Service, accessed Aug. 7, 2012, http://www.aphis.usda.gov/newsroom/2013/09/pdf/retail_pet_final_rule.pdf.
3. 7 *United States Code* §§ 2134, 2135, 2140, 2143, 2146; 9 *Code of Federal Regulations*, chap. 1, Animal and Plant Health Inspection Service, Department of Agriculture, §§ 3.1–12; "Licensing and Registration under the Animal Welfare Act: Guidelines for Dealers, Exhibitors, Transporters, and Researchers," USDA Animal and Plant Health Inspection Service, accessed Aug. 7, 2012, http://www.aphis.usda.gov/animal_welfare/downloads/aw/awlicreg.pdf.
4. "Animal Care: Compliance Inspections," USDA Animal and Plant Health Inspection Service, Feb. 2012, accessed Aug. 7, 2012, http://www.aphis.usda.gov/publications/animal_welfare/content/printable_version/fs_compliance_inspection.pdf.
5. Confidential interviews by Susan Hunter, 2009.
6. *Animal and Plant Health Inspection Service Animal Care Program Inspections of Problematic Dealers*, U.S. Department of Agriculture, Office of Inspector General, Audit Report 33002-4-SF, May 2010, accessed Aug. 7, 2012, http://www.usda.gov/oig/webdocs/33002-4-SF.pdf.

7. Animal Legal Defense Fund v. Glickman, 943 F. Supp. 44 (D.C. 1996); 130 F.3d 464 (D.C. Cir. 1998); 154 F.3d 426 (D.C. Cir. 1998).
8. Humane Society of the United States, "State Puppy Mill Laws," Feb. 2013, accessed May 28, 2013, http://www.humanesociety.org/assets/pdfs/legislation/state_puppy_mill_laws.pdf.
9. See Lesli Bisgould, *Animals and the Law* (Toronto: Irwin Law, 2011), 129–33.
10. Alberta, *The Animal Protection Regulations,* 2000, RRS c A-21.1 Reg.
11. Prince Edward Island, Companion Animal Protection Act, *Revised Statutes of Prince Edward Island,* 1988, c C-14.1; Saskatchewan, The Animal Protection Act, 1999, being chap. A-21.1, *Statutes of Saskatchewan,* 1999 as amended 2010, c.38, 5, 7.
12. Newfoundland and Labrador, Animal Health and Protection Act, *Statutes of Newfoundland and Labrador,* 2010, c A-9.1; Animal Protection Regulations, *Statutes of Newfoundland and Labrador,* 35/12; Animal Protection Standards Regulations, *Statutes of Newfoundland and Labrador,* 36/12, 6, 7; Canadian Veterinary Medical Association, *A Code of Practice for Canadian Kennel Operations,* 2nd ed., May 2007, accessed Aug. 25, 2012, https://www.canadianveterinarians.net/documents/Code-of-Practice-for-Canadian-Kennel-Operations; Canadian Veterinary Medical Association, *A Code of Practice for Canadian Cattery Operations,* 2009, accessed Aug. 25, 2012, https://www.canadianveterinarians.net/documents/a-code-of-practice-for-canadian-cattery-operations.
13. British Columbia, Farm Practices Protection (Right to Farm) Act, *Revised Statutes of British Columbia,* 1996, c.
14. Manitoba, *The Animal Care Act,* C.C.S.M. c A84.
15. New Brunswick, *The Animal Care Act,* C.C.S.M. c A84; *New Brunswick Regulation 2010-74 under the Society for the Prevention of Cruelty to Animals Act* (O.C 2010-299); General Regulation, *New Brunswick Regulation* 2000-4; Provincial Offences Procedure Act, *Statutes of New Brunswick,* 1987, c P-22.1.
16. Bisgould, *Animals and the Law,* 134–37; Montier v. Hall, 2002 ABQB 70; International Bio Research v. Richmond, 2011 B.C.S.C. 471.
17. *New York General Business Law* § 751.
18. See for example *Arizona Revised Statutes* §§ 44-1799–1799.09; *Florida Statutes Annotated* § 828.29; *New Jersey Statutes Annotated* §§ 56:8-92–96; *Vermont Statutes Annotated* §§ 4301–4304; *Virginia Code Annotated* §§ 3.2-6509–6517.
19. Humane Society of the United States, "Puppy Lemon Laws," accessed May 28, 2013, http://www.humanesociety.org/assets/pdfs/pets/puppy_mills/puppy_mill_lemon_law_chart_1.pdf.
20. "Area Breeder, Critics Keep Clashing over Raising Puppies," *Lancaster New Era,* Jan. 23, 2002.
21. This paragraph relies on John Friel, "Salisbury Board Rejects Two Kennel Requests," *Intelligencer Journal* (Lancaster, PA), Sept. 4, 2002; Dean L. Evans,

"Brecknock Township Taking Steps to Control Kennel Operations," *Intelligencer Journal* (Lancaster, PA), Sept. 24, 2003; Dean L. Evans, "Brecknock Targets Dog Breeders in Ordinance," *Intelligencer Journal* (Lancaster, PA), Nov. 4, 2003; Civia Katz, "Puppy Mill Foes Seek Support in Penn," *Intelligencer Journal* (Lancaster, PA), Nov. 10, 2003; "Kennel Plan Stirs Strong Opposition in West Hempfield," *Lancaster New Era,* Jan. 11, 2005; Civia Katz, "Penn Imposes Multiple Conditions on Large Dog Kennels," *Intelligencer Journal* (Lancaster, PA); Tom Knapp, "W. Hempfield Kennel Plan Gets Zoning Approval," *Lancaster New Era,* Feb. 9, 2005; "E. Earl Rejects Kennel Plan," *Lancaster New Era,* Sept. 20, 2005; Madelyn Pennino, "Change State Dog Laws, Activists Say," *Intelligencer Journal* (Lancaster, PA), Mar. 5, 2005; Kathy Boccella, "Sending a Big Message on County's Puppy Mills," *The Philadelphia Inquirer,* Mar. 21, 2005; Susan E. Lindt, "New Group Targeting Puppy Mills Hopes to Raise Awareness Today," *Intelligencer Journal* (Lancaster, PA), Apr. 30, 2005; Susan E. Lindt, "Activist Addresses Puppy Mill Foes," *Intelligencer Journal* (Lancaster, PA), Jun. 7, 2005; Daniel Burke and Tom Murse, "Rally Targets Puppy Mills Here," *Lancaster New Era,* Sept. 17, 2005; "Anti–Puppy Mill Group Meets Thurs.," *Lancaster New Era,* Sept. 20, 2005; "In March along Route 340, Animal Activists and Plain Operators of Puppy Mills Bark at Each Other," *Sunday News* (Lancaster, PA), Sept. 17, 2006. See also Amy Worden, "Doggedly Devoted to Saving Animals," *The Philadelphia Inquirer,* Nov. 1, 2007; "United Against Puppy Mills," *Intelligencer Journal* (Lancaster, PA), Apr. 12, 2008; Susan E. Lindt, "Campaign Goes to the Dogs," *Intelligencer Journal* (Lancaster, PA), Oct. 24, 2005; Dave Pidgeon, "City GOP Mail Plays up Gray Kennel Ties," *Intelligencer Journal* (Lancaster, PA), Nov. 2, 2005; Patricia Poist, "Puppy Mill Issue Nips at Gray," *Sunday News* (Lancaster, PA), Nov. 6, 2005.

22. This paragraph relies on Panel Discussion, "Pennsylvania's New Dog Law," Sixth Annual Animal Law Conference, Pennsylvania Bar Institute, Pittsburgh, PA, July 23, 2009; Confidential interview by Richard A. Brisbin, Jr., July 5, 2012; Amy Worden, "Animal Activists Get Harrisburg's Ear," *The Philadelphia Inquirer,* Jan. 9, 2006; Amy Worden, "Rendell Pledges to Amend Dog Law," *The Philadelphia Inquirer,* Mar. 26, 2006; "Activists Say Pa. Does Not Enforce Law against Puppy Mills," Associated Press State and Local Wire, May, 12, 2006; Amy Worden, "Rendell Dismisses Dog-Law Advisers," *The Philadelphia Inquirer,* May 12, 2006; "Governor Has Bite to Match His Bark," *Sunday News* (Lancaster, PA), May 14, 2006; John Grogan, "Video Intensifies Puppy Mill Iissue," *The Philadelphia Inquirer,* July 14, 2006.

23. This paragraph relies on Amy Worden, "Philly-Area Animal Advocate Named ASPCA Board Chief," *The Philly Dawg,* Aug. 18, 2009, http://www.philly.com/philly/blogs/pets/Philly-area_animal_advocate_named_ASPCA_board_chief

.html; "Group Wants for Law Enforcement under Separate State Agency," *Intelligencer Journal* (Lancaster, PA), Oct. 6, 2006; Amy Worden, "Rendell to Name Puppy-Mill Regulator," *The Philadelphia Inquirer,* Oct. 17, 2006; Kathleen Brady Shea, "Rendell Gives Dogs a Fair Shake," *The Philadelphia Inquirer,* Oct. 18, 2006; Susan E. Lindt, "Rendell Names New Pa. Dog-Law Enforcer," Associated Press State & Local Wire, Oct. 18, 2006; "Rendell Appoints Dog-Law Enforcers," *Intelligencer Journal* (Lancaster, PA), Oct. 19, 2006; Amy Worden, "New Pa. Dog Board Convenes," *The Philadelphia Inquirer,* Dec. 14, 2006; Amy Worden, "Breeders, Rescuers Speak Out at Meeting on Kennel Conditions," *The Philadelphia Inquirer,* Mar. 15, 2007; Larry A. Hicks, "Proposed Dog Law Hurts Hobbyists," *The York Dispatch,* Apr. 23, 2007; Amy Worden, "Pa. Begins 'Puppy Mill' Crackdown with Arrest," *The Philadelphia Inquirer,* Jan. 7, 2007; Amy Worden, "Dog Law Efforts Still Fall Short," *The Philadelphia Inquirer,* Aug. 14, 2007; Amy Worden, "Pa. Accused of Ignoring Kennel's Fatal Conditions," *The Philadelphia Inquirer,* Oct. 30, 2007.
24. Pa. Independent Regulatory Review Commission, Regulation #2–152: Dog Law Enforcement; Amy Worden, "Dog-law Plan Raises Hackles," *The Philadelphia Inquirer,* Mar. 7, 2007; Susan E. Lindt, "Commission: Dog Law Still Needs Work," *Intelligencer Journal* (Lancaster, PA), Apr. 18, 2007; John Hayes, "Dog Breeder Rules Rewritten," *Pittsburgh Post-Gazette,* Sept. 25, 2007; "Animal Welfare," *Morning Call* (Allentown, PA), Oct. 10, 2007.
25. Amy Worden, "Rendell to Push Broad Changes for Kennels," *The Philadelphia Inquirer,* Dec. 22, 2007; Brad Bumsted, "Rendell Insists on Kennel Reform," *Pittsburgh Tribune Review,* Jan. 22, 2008; "House Committee Advances Dog Law Legislation," US State News, June 25, 2008. For copy of a standard reply to comments, see e-mail from Jessie L. Smith, Deputy Secretary, Dog Law Enforcement, reproduced in *Materials for Sixth Annual Animal Law Conference,* Pennsylvania Bar Institute, Pittsburgh, PA, July 23, 2009, 122.
26. Amy Worden, "Oprah Takes Aim at Pa. Puppy Mills," *The Philadelphia Inquirer,* April 3, 2008; Letter from Edward G. Rendell to Oprah Winfrey, reproduced in Materials for Sixth Annual Animal Law Conference, Pennsylvania Bar Institute, Pittsburgh, PA, July 23, 2009, 123; Amy Worden, "Oprah Winfrey Will Back Revised Dog Law for Pennsylvania," *The Philadelphia Inquirer,* May 7, 2008; "Dogs at Capitol in Support of Puppy Mill Bill," *The Times-Tribune* (Scranton, PA), May 15, 2008; "Sportsmen's Groups Battle against State's Proposed Kennel Laws," *Republican & Herald* (Pottsville, PA), May 18, 2008; "Renewed Criticism over Pa. Dog Law Changes," Associated Press State and Local Wire, June 12, 2008.
27. "Memorandum, To: All House Members, From: Representative James E. Casorio, Jr., Apr. 29, 2008," reproduced in Materials for Sixth Annual Animal

Law Conference, Pennsylvania Bar Institute, Pittsburgh, PA, July 23, 2009, 124–25; Tom Barnes, "Amendments Stall State Puppy Mill Bill," *Pittsburgh Post-Gazette*, July 4, 2008; Amy Worden, "With Shootings in Mind, Rendell Touts Puppy Mill Bill," *The Philadelphia Inquirer*, Aug. 17, 2008; Richard Fellinger, "Puppy-Mill Bill Returns for Fall Session," *The Evening Sun* (Hanover, PA), Aug. 12, 2008; Amy Worden, "Clock Ticks for Kennel Law," *The Philadelphia Inquirer*, Sept. 14, 2008; Brad Bumsted, "Puppy Mill Reformers Rally Near Capitol," *Pittsburgh Tribune Review*, Sept. 17, 2008; Vinny Tennis, "Doggedly Determined," *Sunday News* (Lancaster, PA), Sept. 21, 2008; Letter to Michael Brubaker, Gibson Armstrong, Michael O'Pake, and Gerald LaValle from Edward G. Rendell, Oct. 2, 2008, reproduced in Materials for Sixth Annual Animal Law Conference, Pennsylvania Bar Institute, Pittsburgh, PA, July 23, 2009, 126–27; "Governor Rendell Praises House Passage of Dog Law Reforms," PR Newswire, Sept. 17, 2008; Susan E. Lindt, "State House OKs New Rules on Kennels," *Intelligencer Journal* (Lancaster, PA), Sept. 18, 2008; Jim Hook, "Puppy Mill Proposal Amended," *Public Opinion* (Chambersburg, PA), Sept. 26, 2008; Amy Worden, "Pa. Lawmakers Approve Overhauling Dog Law," *Philadelphia Inquirer*, Oct. 9, 2008; "Pa. New Dog Law Provides Better Protection for 'Man's Best Friend' says Gov. Rendell during Ceremonial Bill Signing," PR Newswire, Oct. 27, 2008.

28. 3 *Pennsylvania Statutes* §§ 459-101, 459-206–211; 7 *Pennsylvania Code* §§ 21.21–42.

29. 7 *Pennsylvania Code* Part II, Ch 21 ff. (2013); 3 *Pennsylvania Statutes* §§ 459-218, 459-220, 459-222, 459-224, 459-401, 459-901–903.

30. Pennsylvania Bureau of Dog Law Enforcement, Dog Law Complaint Form; Jon Hurdle, "2008 Law Leading to Crackdown on Pennsylvania Puppy Mills," *New York Times*, Aug. 18, 2009, A-12; Michael Rubinkam, "Activists, Officials Take on Puppy Mills," Associated Press, Jan. 10, 2010; Bob Stiles, "Breeders Dogged by Pennsylvania's New Laws," *Tribune-Review* (Greensburg, PA), Feb. 7, 2010; Michael Rubinkam, "New Pa. Law Putting Puppy Mills Out of Business," Associated Press, June 11, 2010.

31. Pennsylvania Department of Agriculture, *Report to the Pennsylvania General Assembly, Act 225 of 1982, as amended by Act 119 of 2008, The Dog Law*, Mar. 1, 2009, 1–10, accessed Aug. 21, 2012, http://www.agriculture.state.pa.us/portal/server.pt/gateway/PTARGS_0_2_24476_10297_0_43/AgWebsite/Files/Publications/DL2008.pdf.

32. "Gov. Rendell Signs Bill Protecting Dogs from Painful, Inhumane Procedures," US State News, Aug. 29, 2009; *Professional Dog Breeders Advisory Council v. Wolff*, 2009 U.S. Dist. LEXIS 83054; Ad Crable, "Judge Upholds Pa. Law on Dog Kennels," *Intelligencer Journal/New Era* (Lancaster, PA), Sept. 16, 2009;

Gil Smart, "Dog Law Revised, Activists Growl," *Sunday News* (Lancaster, PA), Sept. 5, 2010; Chris Toneri, "Dog Lovers Unleash Outrage over Changes to Pennsylvania Law," *Pittsburgh Tribune Review*, Sept. 12, 2010; Richard J. Lupinsky, Jr., "Commission Approves New Regulations for Pennsylvania Commercial Dog Kennels," *The Agricultural Law Brief*, Penn State Dickinson School of Law, Sept. 2010, http://law.psu.edu/_file/aglaw/September_2010.pdf; Amy Worden, "Lawmakers, AKC Declare War on PA Dog Law," *Philly Dawg*, Feb. 26, 2011; Gil Smart, "34 Breeding Kennels Left in County," *Sunday News* (Lancaster, PA), May 29, 2011; Confidential interview by Richard A. Brisbin, Jr., July 5, 2012.
33. Amy Worden, "Corbett Replaces Top Dog Law Enforcer, Restructures Bureau," *Philadelphia Inquirer*, June 15, 2011; "Pa.'s Top Dog Law Enforcer Replaced," Associated Press State and Local Wire, June 15, 2011; Bill White, "State Still Weakening Dog Law," *Morning Call* (Allentown, PA), Oct. 8, 2011.
34. Donna Alvis-Banks, "Humane Society Rips Virginia Pet Mills," *The Roanoke Times*, Nov. 2, 2007; "Puppy Mill: Carroll County Responds Quickly to Puppy Mill Uncovered in Hillsville, Virginia," Carroll County, Virginia, accessed Jan. 27, 2012, http://carrollcountyva.org/govt_template/animal_control.
35. Michael Sluss, "Dog-Breeding Measure Survives Panel," *The Roanoke Times*, Jan. 31, 2008, B10; Robin Starr, "Oversight Protects Consumers and Animals," *Richmond Times Dispatch*, Feb. 24, 2008, E-6; "Senate Toughens Law for Breeders," *The Roanoke Times*, Mar. 5, 2008; Michael Sluss, "Budget, Bills Changed Slightly: The Governor Altered Legislation on Payday Lending and Animal Welfare," *The Roanoke Times*, Apr. 15, 2008; Jim Nolan, "Animals to Get New Legal Protection: Kaine Signs Bills That Raise Penalty for Animal Fighting and Operating Puppy Mills," *Richmond Times Dispatch*, June 5, 2008, B-2; "Notorious Virginia Puppy Miller Sentenced Under Commonwealth's New Puppy Mill Law," Targeted News Service, July 13, 2009; Tony Gonzalez, "Dog-Support Groups Split over Va. Puppy-Mill Law," *Richmond Times Dispatch*, Dec. 10, 2009 B-02.
36. *Virginia Code Annotated* §§ 3.2-6507.1; 3.2-6507.2.
37. *Virginia Code Annotated* § 3.2-6507.3.
38. *Virginia Code Annotated* § 3.2-6507 ff.
39. *Virginia Code Annotated* §§ 3.2-6512–6514.
40. Information in this section was confirmed in a confidential interview by Susan Hunter and Richard A. Brisbin, Jr., Oct. 25, 2013.
41. Sheldon Ingram, "Action News Extra: Puppy Mills Investigated," WTAE, May 4, 2006, accessed Oct. 27, 2013, http://www.wtae.com/Action-News-Extra-Puppy-Mills-Investigated/-/9681798/7689320/-/y5thfkz/-/index.html; "Puppy Mill Capital, USA?," ABC News, Mar. 30, 2009, accessed Oct. 27, 2013, http://

abcnews.go.com/video/playerIndex?id=7194974; "Investigator: Dog Auctions Accused of Animal Cruelty," WKYC.com, July 9, 2012, accessed Oct. 27, 2013, http://www.wkyc.com/news/article/251383/0/Investigator-Sick-dogs-auctioned. A list of other media stories exists at "Media Releases," Coalition to Ban Ohio Dogs Auctions, accessed Oct. 27, 2013, http://www.banohiodogauctions.com/Media_Releases.html.

42. "Troubled Dog Auction Called Off in Ohio, Future Uncertain," Associated Press, Apr. 4, 2007.
43. OAAO, Ohio Association of Animal Owners, accessed Jan. 16, 2012, http://oaao.us/files/tri-fold.pdf.
44. Tim Tressler, "Is Puppy Mill Crackdown a Threat to All Breeders?," *Dayton Daily News*, Aug. 9, 2009, A14.
45. "In Response to IG Report, Group Calls for Ban on Ohio Dog Auctions," PR Newswire, June 2, 2010; David W. Jones, "Group Wants to See Improper 'Puppy Mills,' 'Dog Auctions' Regulated in Ohio," *The News Herald of Willoughby, Ohio*, Sept. 27, 2010; "Citizens-Initiated Statute (2012 Ballot Initiative) to Ban Ohio Dog Auctions," Coalition to Ban Ohio Dog Auctions, accessed Oct. 27, 2013, http://www.banohiodogauctions.com/Campaigns.html.
46. Julie Carr Smyth, "Animal Groups, Ohio Farmers Strike Deal on Cruelty," Associated Press State and Local Wire, July 1, 2010.
47. "Lawmakers Seek Consensus on Ohio Puppy-Mill Bill," Associated Press State and Local Wire, Dec. 2, 2011; Jim Siegel, "Puppy Mill Bill Might Move Forward; State Would Manage Licensing, Inspection of Breeding Sites," *Dayton Daily News*, Dec. 25, 2011.
48. Kathy Lynn Gray, "Group Claims Backing to Halt Dog Auctions; Coalition Submits 150,000 Signatures to Secretary of State," *Dayton Daily News*, Dec. 28, 2011, B3; Coalition to Ban Ohio Dog Auctions, "Initiated Statute (2012 Ballot Initiative) to Ban Ohio Dog Auctions," accessed Jan. 16, 2012, http://www.banohiodogauctions.com/Campaigns.html.
49. "Ohio Senate Clears 'Puppy Mill' Bill," Associated Press State and Local Wire, Feb. 2, 2012; "Animal Advocates Gather at Ohio Capitol to Lobby for Animal Welfare," Legislation, States News Service, Mar. 13, 2012.
50. Ohio Senate, 129th General Assembly, Senate Bill 130 (2012).
51. Wire flooring can injure a dog's feet and damage their teeth if chewed. It allows waste to drop, and therefore some operators might not feel compelled to clean it as regularly as solid flooring.
52. Ohio, 129th General Assembly, An Act to amend sections 955.02, 955.10, 955.12, 955.20, 955.26, and 1901.183 and to enact sections 956.01 to 956.18 of the Revised Code to regulate certain dog breeding kennels and dog retailers (2012).
53. *Ohio Administrative Code Annotated* 901:1-6-01-10 (2013); Eric Sandy,

"Proposed Puppy Mill Rules to be Voted Upon at Upcoming Committee Meeting," *Cleveland Scene*, Sept. 17, 2013, accessed Oct. 27, 2013, http://www.clevescene.com/scene-and-heard/archives/2013/09/17/proposed-puppy-mill-rules-to-be-voted-upon-at-upcoming-committee-meeting.

54. Eric Sandy, "Caged: How Ohio Politicians Keep the State's Puppy Mill Business Booming with Little Regulation," *Cleveland Scene*, July 24, 2013, accessed Oct. 27, 2013, http://www.clevescene.com/cleveland/caged-how-ohio-politicians-keep-the-states-puppy-mill-business-booming-with-little-regluation/Content?oid=3613836. For criticism of the regulations, see Laura Allen, "Hearing to be Held on Weak Proposed OH Puppy Mill Regulations," *Animal Law Coalition*, Sept. 17, 2013, accessed Oct. 27, 2013, http://animallawcoalition.com/oh-board-to-consider-puppy-mill-regulations/; Donna J. Miller, "Ohio dog Breeders Association Owns Shuttered Farmerstown Dog Auction," Jan. 5, 2012, *Cleveland.com*, accessed Oct. 28, 2013, http://blog.cleveland.com/metro/2012/01/ohio_dog_breeders_association.html.

55. T. J. Greaney, "'Puppy Mill' Proposition Divides State," *Columbia Daily Tribune*, A12 (Oct. 23, 2010), accessed Apr. 7, 2012, http://www.columbiatribune.com/news/2010/oct/23/puppy-mill-proposition-divides-state/; Confidential interview by Susan Hunter and Richard A. Brisbin, Jr., Oct. 22, 2013; "150 Dogs, Tiger Rescued from Missouri Dog Breeder," Associated Press Online, Feb. 19, 2009; Cheryl Wittenauer, "Woman Charged with Animal Abuse after Breeder Raid," Associated Press Online, Feb. 20, 2009; Kim Bell, "Tip from Buyer Led to Seizure of Dogs, Tiger: 208 Dogs Are Shipped to Humane Society in St. Louis; Tiger is Taken to Springfield, Mo., Zoo," *St. Louis Post-Dispatch*, Feb. 21, 2009, A5; Deb Peterson, "Rescued Dogs Get Their Day as Stars on Oprah," *St. Louis Post-Dispatch*, Feb. 21, 2009, A2; Cheryl Wittenauer, No title, Associated Press State and Local Wire, Feb. 25, 2009; "Rescue Groups Deal with Influx of Dogs," Associated Press State and Local Wire, Mar. 1, 2009; "Deputies Shoot Chimp, Then Find Squalid Puppy Mill," Associated Press, Apr. 2, 2009; Cheryl Wittenauer, "Mo. to Study Policy That Recycles Dogs to Auctions," Associated Press State and Local Wire, Apr. 9, 2009; Tim Talley, "Lawmaker to Purse Puppy Mill Bill," Associated Press State and Local Wire, May 27, 2009; Cheryl Wittenauer, "Missouri to Prosecute Unlicensed Dog Breeders," Associated Press State and Local Wire, June 29, 2009; "Mo. Announces Next Steps on Puppy Mill Crackdown," Associated Press State and Local Wire, June 29, 2009; "Koster: Some Dog Breeders Ducking Inspection," Associated Press State and Local Wire, Aug. 13, 2009.

56. "Missourians for the Protection of Dogs Launch Signature Drive to Prevent Puppy Mill Cruelty," Targeted News Service, Dec. 14, 2009; Missouri Secretary of State, 2010 Initiative Petitions Approved for Circulation in Missouri

Statutory Amendment to Chapter 273, Relating to Dog Breeders 2010-085, Version 1, accessed Aug. 1, 2013, http://www.sos.mo.gov/elections/2010petitions/2010-085.asp; Missouri Secretary of State, 2010 Initiative Petitions Approved for Circulation in Missouri Statutory Amendment to Chapter 273, Relating to Dog Breeders 2010-085, accessed Aug. 1, 2013, Version 2, http://www.sos.mo.gov/elections/2010petitions/2010-086.asp.

57. "Humane Society Pours $450,000 into Group Fighting to Shut Down Puppy Mills," *The Turner Report,* Jan. 7, 2010; Jake Wagman, "La Russa, Kit Bond's Wife Endorse Anti-Puppy Mill Measure," *Political Fix,* May 10, 2010; "Missourians for the Protection of Dogs Forms Advisory Board to Help Fight Puppy Mill Cruelty," Targeted News Service, May 10, 2010; "More than 170,000 Missouri Voters Sign Petition to Place Puppy Mill Initiative on November Ballot," Targeted News Service, May 3, 2010; Chris Blank, "2 Mo. Initiative Petitions Qualify for Ballot," Associated Press State and Local Wire, Aug. 3, 2010.

58. Virginia Young, "Dog Breeders Cry Foul over Prop B: They Say Wording on Anti-Puppy Mill Ballot is Biased; Judge Takes Case under Advisement," *St. Louis Post-Dispatch,* Aug. 10, 2010, A1; "Mo. Group Fights Dog Breeding Ballot Measure," Associated Press State and Local Wire, Aug. 10, 2010; Chris Blank, "Mo. Judge Upholds Dog Breeding Ballot Measure," Associated Press State and Local Wire, Aug. 13, 2010; Emily Younker, "Forum to Focus on Dog Breeder Proposal," *The Joplin Globe,* Apr. 5, 2010; Dennis Rich, "Puppies, Tax Initiatives to Top Ballot for November's General Election," *The Sedalia Democrat,* Aug. 7, 2010; Virginia Young, "Prop B Raises Stakes for Dog Breeders: Animal Activists in Missouri Push for Tougher Standards, but Opponents Say Better Inspections Are Needed, Not More Limits," *St. Louis Post-Dispatch,* Oct. 3, 2010, A1; A. G. Sulzberger and Malcolm Gay, "Old Foes Square Off over Issue of Puppies," *New York Times,* Oct. 31, 2010, 18; "Missourians for the Protection of Dogs Launches Radio Ad against Legislative Power Grab," Targeted News Service, May 4, 2010; Amy Worden, "Battle Rages in Missouri, Puppy Mill Capital of America," *Philly Dawg,* Sept. 24, 2010; T. J. Greaney, "Puppy Mill Restrictions Barely Pass, Prop B to Limit Dog Numbers," *Columbia Daily Tribune,* Nov. 3, 2010; Jim Suhr, "Mo. Measure on Puppy Mills Passes," Associated Press State and Local Wire, Nov. 3, 2010.

59. Tony Messenger, "Lawmakers Seek to Veto Voters' Will, Republican Wants to Repeal Dog Breeding Prop; Democrat Wants to Modify Earnings Tax Prop.," *St. Louis Post-Dispatch,* Dec. 3, 2010, A1; Dennis Rich, "Parson Foresees Changes, Not Repeal, on Puppy Mill Measure," *The Sedalia Democrat,* Jan. 15, 2011; Virginia Young, "Foes Hope to Muzzle Law on Dog Breeding: Some in Missouri House Join Effort to Repeal It," *St. Louis Post-Dispatch,* Jan. 26, 2011,

A1; "Effort to Repeal Mo. Dog Breeding Law Begins," Associated Press State and Local Wire, Jan. 25, 2011; Bill McCellan, "Here's a Solution to Cultural Divide," *St. Louis Post-Dispatch*, Mar. 7, 2011, A9.

60. Missouri, An Act to repeal section 273.345, R.S.Mo., and to enact in lieu thereof one new section relating to the Puppy Mill Cruelty Prevention Act, with an existing penalty provision, Senate Bill 95, 96th Gen. Assembly, 2011.
61. Missouri, Senate Bill 4; Senate Bill 95; Senate Bill 113; House Bill 94; House Bill 99; House Bill 100; House Bill 131; House Bill; House Joint Resolution 3; House Bill 332; House Joint Resolution 17 (96th General Assembly, 2011).
62. Missouri, An Act to repeal section 273.345, R.S.Mo., relating to dog breeders, Senate Bill 4, 96th General Assembly, 2011, http://www.senate.mo.gov/11info/pdf-bill/intro/SB4.pdf; Missouri, An Act to Repeal, section 273.345, R.S.Mo., relating to dog breeders. House Bill No. 94, 96th General Assembly.
63. Missouri, An Act to repeal section 273.345, R.S.Mo., and to enact in lieu thereof one new section relating to commercial dog breeders, with existing penalty provisions and an emergency clause, Senate Bill 113, 96th General Assembly, 2011.
64. Missouri, *Journal of the Senate*, 96th General Assembly, Mar. 10, 2011, 431–32; Missouri, *Journal of the House*, 96th General Assembly, Apr. 13, 2011, 1250–51; §273.345 *Revised Statutes of Missouri* (2013); Virginia Young, "Voters' Dog Law Closer to Repeal House Bill, Missouri Senate Votes to Undo Some of Prop B's Restrictions on Breeders Set to Take Effect in November," *St. Louis Post-Dispatch*, Mar. 11, 2011, A1; Chris Blank, "Mo. Lawmakers Approve Overhauling Dog-Breeding Law," Associated Press State and Local Wire, Apr. 13, 2011.
65. Missouri, Senate Bill 161, 96th General Assembly, 2011; Attorney General of Missouri, Tracking the Legislation: How did the Canine Cruelty Prevention Act change Prop B?
66. Virginia Young, "A Deal is Made on Dog Issue Farm, Animal Welfare Groups Agree on New Breeding Rules," *St. Louis Post-Dispatch*, Apr. 19, 2011; David A. Lieb, "Ag, Animal Groups Announce Deal on Mo. Dog Law," Associated Press State and Local Wire, Apr. 19, 2011; Jake Wagman, "Dog Breeding Compromise is Crumbling: Dozens of Lawmakers, Agriculture Industry Reps Press Nixon to Sign Earlier Bill to Roll Back Prop B," *St. Louis Post-Dispatch*, Apr. 19, 2011, A1; Chris Blank, "Mo. Gov. Nixon Signs Compromise Dog-Breeding Bill," Associated Press, Apr, 28, 2011.
67. *Missouri Code of State Regulations*, 2 CSR 30-9.010 ff. (2013).
68. "Number of Mo. Dog Breeders Dwindling," Associated Press State and Local Wire, Aug. 15, 2011; "Puppy Love Our View: House Bill Proposition B Compromise Appears to Be Reducing Puppy Mills," *St. Louis Post-Dispatch*, Oct. 13, 2011; Todd C. Frankel, "Howls in Dog Breeding Fight Fade: Deal

Altering Prop B Seems to Have Brokered Truce; But Impact is Felt as Many Breeders Quit," *St. Louis Post-Dispatch*, Apr. 27, 2012; Sue Sterling, "State Forces Animal Shelters to Pay Fee to Protect Animals," *The Daily Star-Journal* (Warrensburg, Mo.), Feb. 25, 2013; Missouri Right-to-Farm, Amendment 1 (August 2014), Ballotpedia, accessed Oct. 16, 2015, http://ballotpedia.org/Missouri_Right-to-Farm,_Amendment_1_(August_2014); accessed Oct. 16, 2015, http://ballotpedia.org/Missouri Right-to-Farm,_Amendment_1_(August_2014); Humane Society of the United States, Dogwood Animal Shelter, Inc., and Stray Rescue of St. Louis, Inc. v. Missouri, 405 S.W.3d 532 (Sup. Ct. Mo. 2013); see also "Mo. Lawmakers Pass Farm Constitutional Amendment," Associated Press State and Local Wire, May 14, 2013.
69. Attorney General Chris Koster, 2012 Annual Report, 6, accessed Aug. 9, 2013, https://archive.org/stream/2012AGOAnnualReport#page/n3/mode/2up.
70. Information in this section is from interviews with animal welfare organizations and state legislators conducted by Susan Hunter, 2005–2012; see also Susan Hunter, "Animal Welfare and Control Issues in West Virginia and the United States: Old Problems with New Answers," *West Virginia Public Affairs Reporter* 27 (2007): 1–14.
71. Brandy Brubaker, "Star Ridge Caretakers Charged with Animal Cruelty: Many Rescued Animals Need to be Adopted," *Dominion Post* (Morgantown, WV), July 13, 2006; "About 1,000 Dogs Rescued from West Virginia Kennel," Associated Press, Aug. 25, 2008.
72. Mannix Porterfield, "W.Va. Ranks 36th for Animal Protection Laws," *Beckley Register-Herald*, Dec. 31, 2010, 11B; Mannix Porterfield, "House Working on 'Puppy Mill' Legislation" *Beckley Register-Herald*, Jan. 31, 2011, 11B; Kate Coll, "W. Va, Humane Society Fighting for the Animals," *Bluefield Daily Telegraph*, Dec. 13, 2011.
73. Mannix Porterfield, "House Approves First Puppy Mill Rules," *Beckley Register-Herald*, Mar. 1, 2011.
74. West Virginia Legislature, House Bill 2015, Senate Bill 460 (2010).
75. "WV Victory: Restrictive Breeder Bill Defeated!," American Kennel Club, AKC News, Mar. 11, 2012, accessed July 18, 2012, http://www.akc.org/press-center/news/wv-victory-restrictive-breeder-bill-defeated/.
76. David Beard, "House Resolution Supports National Minimum Wage Raise," *The Dominion Post* (Morgantown, WV), Apr. 13, 2013, 3-A.
77. West Virginia Legislature, Senate Bill 437 (2013).
78. Paul Pierson, "Increasing Returns, Path Dependence, and the Study of Politics," *American Political Science Review* 94 (2000): 251–67.
79. See John W. Kingdon, *Agenda, Alternatives, and Public Policies*, 2nd ed. (Boston: Little, Brown, 1995), 90–144.

80. Ibid., 188–93; Morris P. Fiorina and Kenneth A. Shepsle, "Formal Theories of Leadership: Agents, Agenda Setters, and Entrepreneurs," in *Leadership in Politics: New Perspectives in Political Science*, ed. Bryan D. Jones (Lawrence: University Press of Kansas, 1989), 32–35.
81. Margaret Robertson Ferguson, "Chief Executive Success in the Legislative Arena," *State Politics and Policy Quarterly* 3 (2003): 158–82; Donald A. Gross, "The Policy Role of Governors," in *Gubernatorial Leadership and State Policy*, ed. Eric B. Herzik and Brent W. Brown (Westport, CT: Greenwood Press, 1991), 1–24; Thad Kousser and Justin H. Phillips, *The Power of American Governors: Winning on Budgets and Losing on Policy* (New York: Cambridge University Press, 2012), 74–134; Alan Rosenthal, *The Best Job in Politics: Exploring How Governors Succeed as Policy Leaders* (Los Angeles: CQ Press, 2013), 87–120.
82. See E. Lee Bernick and Charles W. Wiggins, "Executive-Legislative Relations: The Governor's Role as Chief Legislator," in *Gubernatorial Leadership and State Policy*, 73–97; Raymond Cox III, "The Management Role of the Governor," in *Gubernatorial Leadership and State Policy*, 59–69; Kousser and Phillips, *Power of American Governors*, 75–134; Rosenthal, *Best Job in Politics*, 121–92.
83. On the importance of governors in focusing attention to an issue, Kousser and Phillips, *Power of American Governors*, 74–102; Rosenthal, *Best Job in Politics*, 72–77.

7

Making Pet Policy: The Disposition of Unwanted Horses

Although in Canada and the United States a few horses serve as draft animals, assist ranchers and wildlife officers reach remote areas, and help urban police in crowd and traffic control, most horses provide recreational opportunities. Indeed, the American Veterinary Medical Association defines the horse as a companion animal.[1] Today horses provide for pleasure riding, activities at horse shows such as jumping and dressage, and racing. These recreational activities have a multibillion dollar impact on the North American economy.[2] However, when horses become unwanted because of age, illness, inability to race, neglect, or abandonment, a problem arises. What is to be done with "surplus" or unwanted horses?[3]

Unwanted recreational horses that have reached the end of their useful life for pleasure riding, showing, racing, or breeding often end up at livestock auctions. Because the burial of a deceased horse requires a plot of rural land and heavy equipment, euthanasia and carcass disposal for a horse can cost up to $500. Also, often these horses cannot be dumped at a shelter or rescue.[4] Consequently, the demand for horse meat means that owners can profit from the sale of an animal at auction to "kill-buyers" who sell it to a slaughterhouse.[5] As a form of passive cruelty, slaughter of a companion animal for meat and its consumption thus ensues.

Unlike anti-cruelty and kennel legislation, the slaughter of unwanted horses has a significant international political dimension. In this chapter we discuss the globally radiating effect of legislative and regulatory conflicts in Canada and the United States regarding the disposition of unwanted horses.[6] The existing studies of transnational regulatory legalization describe the organization and accountability of the cross-national administrative bodies and global regulatory networks currently in place.[7] However, none of these studies explains the messy conflict of the *emerging but incomplete* transnational regulation of activities such as the disposal of horses. An example of incomplete bottom-up transnational legalization, the disposal of horses appears to be a patchwork of "distributed administration" in which the choices of domestic legislators and regulatory agency personnel in one nation influence the legalized regulation of activity primarily occurring in other countries. Our argument therefore is that a patchwork of transnational regulations regarding the disposal of horses is developing incrementally from policymaking at the national and subnational government levels.[8] In these circumstances, how have the decisions of national regulators, in response to organized interests and legislators, influenced regulation by governments in other nations?[9]

To address the disposition of horses we employ a comparative analysis of the interaction of regulatory ideas and practices in Canada and the United States and two of their trading partners, the European Union and Mexico. Although Argentina, Brazil, Uruguay, Kazakhstan, and Mongolia are also exporters of large numbers of horses and horse meat, and although horse meat consumption is common in Russia, Japan, and China, these nations are not included in this study. As in previous chapters we examine the influence of social identity, normative values, and political institutions in constituting the transnational regulation of horses.

INTEREST GROUPS AND THE IDENTITY OF HORSES

In Canada, Europe, Mexico, and the United States, a political conflict between persons and organizations that identify the necessity of human stewardship of horses and others who identify horses as a marketable commodity exists. At present there is no "epistemic community" of experts and scientists attempting to shape public preferences and initiate transnational policy coordination.[10] Consequently there is no consensus, "no globalization of the mind" about the disposition of unwanted horses.[11]

Animal welfare groups have employed pictures and language to stress the suffering of unwanted horses shipped and slaughtered for meat and to contend that the reason for unwanted horses is excessive breeding.[12] Special interest groups that oppose horse slaughter, such as Americans Against Horse Slaughter, Equine Advocates, the Equine Protection Network, the Equine Welfare Alliance, and Wild for Life Foundation in the United States and the Canadian Horse Defence Coalition and Humane Society International/Canada, have advocated their positions at the national or subnational level.[13] Organized opposition to horse consumption also has appeared in France, such as the French League for the Protection of the Horse, the Fondation Brigitte Bardot, and the Center for the Protection of Equine Martyrs,[14] and in Belgium, such as GAIA, Global Action in the Interest of Animals.[15] Opposition to horse slaughter from groups such as the Fund for Horses, established in the United States, and World Horse Welfare, established in the United Kingdom, operate primarily at the national rather than transnational level.[16] Despite international conferences organized by the Humane Society of the United States (HSUS), no international advocacy group to coordinate an international campaign against horse slaughter has appeared.[17] Eurogroup for Animals, a coalition of 40 European animal welfare organizations, has supported the protection of horses during transportation but has not opposed the consumption of horse meat.[18]

The horse welfare groups have faced opposition from advocates for the identification of horses as a commodity. They identify horses as an agricultural product whose disposition as meat creates income for ranchers, truckers, and slaughterhouse employees while satisfying a consumer demand. The advocates of slaughter include a few well-funded and highly organized international corporations such as Chevideco NV, a Belgium corporation with operations in Argentina, France, Mexico, and Romania.[19] U.S. slaughter advocates are largely nationally or locally based agricultural organized interests, horse breeders, stable owners, and their allies among national and subnational publics. Larger umbrella groups with more than 150 member organizations such as the American Horse Council and its affiliated Unwanted Horse Coalition have not criticized horse slaughter for human consumption and have not shown an interest in policies outside of the United States.[20]

NORMATIVE VALUES AND THE CONSUMPTION OF HORSES

As with social identity, variations in normative values affect the conflict about treatment of horses. In particular the variance appears in norms about the passive cruelty associated with the consumption of horse meat, or hippophagy. A taboo, religious tenet, or social resistance to the consumption of horse meat has long existed. Ancient Roman civilization and Christianity, Islam, Judaism, and Buddhism proscribed the eating of horse meat except in unusual circumstances. Disgust toward the consumption of horse meat eventually produced a ban on its consumption by the Catholic Church in AD 732 and, much later, by several European governments.[21] The French Revolution (1789) brought a change in the disgust with and opposition to the eating of horse meat in Western Europe. In a country beset with famine, the poorer and army classes in France, Belgium, and sections of Germany seized horses and consumed much more horse meat. The French Revolution also enhanced the influence of Enlightenment ideas about science and nutrition. Early nineteenth-century French scientists conducted publicity campaigns to encourage the consumption of horse meat. By the end of the century the consumption of horse meat peaked in Western Europe. Although it is not a significant component of diets, today in France, Belgium, Italy, Russia, and several other European countries, people accept the consumption of horse meat. However, the continental European change did not affect the diets of English-speaking countries.[22]

The varying norms on horse meat consumption contribute to the conflicts about treatment of horses. In the United States, where the consumption of horse meat is largely taboo, there is an intense struggle about the ethics of the slaughter of horses for food. In the European context the struggle has focused less on the morality of eating horse meat and more on the development of norms to govern the purity of horse meat.

The legitimacy of the consumption of horse meat in Europe has meant that the normative concerns of anti-slaughter groups have seemed misguided to some European politicians. Nonetheless, efforts to impose a legislative ban on the consumption of horse meat in Italy suggest that the struggle about the disposal of unwanted horses can influence European politicians' behavior.[23] Regardless, normative differences about the consumption of horse meat continue to shape the struggle about the disposal of unwanted horses.

POLITICAL INSTITUTIONS AND LEGALIZED ACCOUNTABILITY

Engaging national and subnational institutions that regulate animal cruelty and the safety of meat, horse welfare organizations in Canada and the United States concerned about slaughter and the treatment of animals entered into a political struggle with organized interests, corporations, and constituents that accepted horse slaughter for human consumption. Soon transnational political contests developed among various interests about the disposition of unwanted horses.[24]

The Politics of Federal–State Struggle in the United States

Since 1970s the struggle about the disposition of unwanted horses in the United States has evolved into a political struggle about the federal government's role as a steward of horses and firms that slaughter unwanted horses.[25] However, the institutional structure of American federalism allows a conflict between federal and state and local governments to arise about a variety of policies, including methods of disposing of unwanted horses. States possess a variety of means to challenge, modify, subvert, and ignore federal statutes and regulations.[26] These options mean that state and local officials have the opportunity to define the social identity of horses and the set of normative values about the consumption of horse meat contrary to federal efforts to define legal accountability for the treatment of unwanted horses. So, what has occurred?

The United States Congress and the Disposition of Wild Horses

The American federal government has attempted to impose legalized accountability on the disposition of both wild and domesticated horses. Concern about the capture and slaughter of wild horses triggered lobbying for their protection by environmental interest groups in the late 1960s. In 1971 the U.S. Congress passed the Wild Free-Roaming Horses and Burros Act to protect wild horses on federal lands.[27] The Act curtailed the roundup of wild horses for slaughter and prevented ranchers from destroying them to preserve grazing land. The Act not only saved wild horses and burros from extinction, it resulted in the relatively rapid repopulation of the western wild horse ranges. The federal Bureau of Land Management (BLM) then devised a policy to round up a portion of the wild horse population for auction for recreational purposes. However, a proviso in the policy was that one year after adoption, wild horses and burros could be sold by the adopters for any purpose they desired. Other horses were simply kept corralled by the BLM or, especially if sick or lame, disposed of "in the most humane and cost efficient manner possible."[28]

In June 2005 Jon Porter (R-NV), Shelley Berkley (D-NV), and James Gibbons (R-NV) introduced the Wild Free-Roaming Horses and Burros Sale and Adoption Act of 2005, which would have allowed all horses not suitable for adoption to be sold for slaughter. Senators Harry Reid (D-NV) and John Ensign (R-NV) introduced a similar bill in the Senate. However, House and Senate committees buried this proposal for regulated wild horse slaughter.[29] In 2009 an alternative proposal, the Restore Our American Mustangs bill, designed in part to criminalize the commercial use of wild horses and burros, passed the House but died in the Senate.[30]

Meanwhile a section of the Wild Horses and Burros Act that limited the number of horses sold to a buyer each year to four made it uneconomical for buyers to seek wild horses for slaughter.[31] The BLM also adopted a rule preventing the sale of wild horses and burros for "commercial exploitation."[32] With sale for slaughter effectively prohibited and adoptions slowing, the BLM relocated many horses from overpopulated areas to eleven larger holding areas or "pastures" for long-term care.[33]

Congress and Domesticated Horse Slaughter

During the first decade of the twentieth century, people in the horse community sensed an increase in the number of unwanted domesticated horses. Because the ban on wild horse slaughter caused a decrease in the number of abattoirs that processed horse meat, U.S. horse slaughter declined from 113,000 animals in 1996 to a low of 42,000 in 2002, but the volume processed increased thereafter.[34] The reason for the post-2002 increase apparently was an increase in the number of unwanted domesticated horses. A 2009 Internet survey of horse owners and "stakeholders" by the Unwanted Horse Coalition reported the costs of care for a horse and the age and health of the horse contributed most frequently to it becoming unwanted. Often these horses were sold for slaughter to so-called killer-buyers. Sale for slaughter was economically rational. Horses could be sold for slaughter at often double the cost of disposal.[35]

The European and Asian demand for horse meat ensured that the slaughter plants were profitable enterprises. Also, organized interests allied with members of agriculture committees of Congress and state legislatures, including the American Farm Bureau and its subsidiaries, the National Cattlemen's Beef Association and its subsidiaries, the American Quarter Horse Association (AQHA), the American Association of Equine Practitioners (AAEP), and the American Veterinary Medical Association (AVMA), supported humane slaughter as a reasonable means for the disposal of unwanted domesticated horses.[36] The U.S. Department of Agriculture (USDA) supported these interests. At an advisory committee hearing in 2007 an official of the USDA's Food Safety and Inspection Service (FSIS) stated, "We have been consistently opposed to the legislative efforts to do away with horse slaughter."[37]

Except for meat inspection standards, few rules regulated domesticated horses sold for slaughter. The Humane Methods of Slaughter Act of 1978 amendments of 1996 allowed the USDA to register and regulate the commercial transportation of horses on direct trips to slaughterhouses.[38] After criticism of the USDA regulation effort from horse welfare groups, and a study by the Department, the USDA convened meetings of slaughter proponents, such as the American Horse Council, American Horse Protection

Association, and managers of slaughter plants and horse auctions, with the HSUS, the American Humane Association, and the American Association of Equine Practitioners to hammer out a consensus on new regulations.[39] Among the regulations adopted by the USDA were standards on the size and conditions of trailers, the care of horses during transit, and the requirement of an "Owner/Shipper Certificate—Fitness to Travel to a Slaughter Facility" certifying that a horse is fit for travel.[40]

The next significant legislative activity that affected horses occurred in 2004. Senator Conrad Burns (R-MT) introduced a rider into the 2004 Omnibus Appropriations Act. Unnoticed by other members of Congress, the rider passed into law when Congress adopted the Appropriations Act for the Department of Agriculture.[41] The rider allowed the BLM to auction wild horses to commercial enterprises. Some of the horses would then be taken to slaughter by commercial purchasers such as a Bouvry Exports horse feedlot in Shelby, Montana.[42]

Opponents of horse slaughter engaged in two legislative efforts to prevent the Burns Rider from becoming a permanent statutory requirement. First, frustrated by a minority of members who used institutional procedures and key committee positions to continue the Burns Rider's wild horse slaughter policy, in 2006 Senator Ensign introduced the American Horse Slaughter Act, a bill that went *beyond* the control of the slaughter of wild equines to create a prohibition on the slaughter of domesticated horses. Congressmen John Sweeney (D-NY) and Ed Whitfield (R-KY) introduced companion legislation in the House. They sought to ban all horse and other equines' slaughter for human consumption, the use of double-deck trailers to ship horses, and the movement, exhibition, or sale of "sore" horses or the use of chemical or mechanical means causing pain to horses' legs when they are moved. The bill passed the House in September 2006, but the Senate did not act on it. A variation of the bill was reintroduced in 2007, but again it failed to pass.[43] Also, when alerted to the Burns Rider by animal welfare groups, a bipartisan group of sixty-eight House members led by Nick Rahall (D-WV) and Ed Whitfield and Senators led by Robert Byrd (D-WV) attempted to repeal the rider and end the slaughter of all horses, not just wild horses. Their efforts were frustrated when the chair of the House

Committee on the Interior, Richard Pombo (R-CA), blocked consideration of the bill in committee.

Second, to avoid Pombo, a bipartisan group of House members led by Sweeney and John Sprat (D-SC) and Senators Ensign and Byrd devised another tactic. They secured an amendment to a 2006 appropriations bill to deny funding for the federal inspection of horse meat for sale as required by the Federal Meat Inspection Act of 1906 and the Federal Agriculture Improvement and Reform Act of 1996.[44] Horse meat from any source thus became unmarketable in the United States.[45]

Despite the denial of funding for inspection, the Bush administration's secretary of agriculture maintained that the USDA still possessed authority to permit U.S. horse slaughterhouses to hire their own private inspectors. Following administration policy, the USDA operated a "fee-for-service" inspection system for the antemortem inspection of horses by their personnel and publicly funded postmortem inspections of horse meat. Horse slaughter for export could therefore continue even when money for federal inspection was eliminated in the 2006 and subsequent appropriations bills.[46] However, the federal inspection ban and concurrent state laws had made slaughter economically unprofitable, and U.S. plants in Oregon, Connecticut, Idaho, Missouri, Nebraska, Ohio, South Carolina, and Virginia no longer processed horses.[47]

In 2009 Congress approved an agriculture appropriations bill that required the Government Accountability Office (GAO) to report on horse welfare in light of the closing of U.S. horse slaughterhouses. In response to the congressional requirement, the GAO examined the enforcement of the Humane Methods of Slaughter Act of 1978. In March 2010 it issued a report that addressed the inspection of 782 U.S. slaughterhouses by the FSIS. The report revealed considerable inconsistency in the enforcement of the Act and regulations of the USDA's FSIS adopted under authority delegated to FSIS by the Act. The report especially noted weaknesses in the training and oversight of FSIS slaughterhouse inspectors, a lack of staff, no provision of specific criteria for inspectors to determine violations, and a deficiency in the performance assessment of inspectors.[48] The report concluded that, when it existed, the FSIS poorly inspected antemortem horse slaughter.[49] Subsequently, in 2011, the GAO released another report specifically on the treatment of horses. Among its findings, it noted that since the end of horse slaughter in the United States the prices of horses had dropped markedly. It used interviews and scattered state reports to conclude that horse abuse and abandonment had increased.[50] The report concluded, in part:

> In light of the unintended consequences on horse welfare from the cessation of domestic horse slaughter, Congress may wish to reconsider the annual restrictions first instituted in fiscal year 2006 on USDA's use of appropriated funds to inspect horses in transit to, and at, domestic slaughtering facilities.[51]

These conclusions immediately generated criticism from various animal welfare interest groups who asserted the report was deliberately instigated to forestall Senate action on a proposed congressional ban on horse slaughter.[52]

In the meantime the federal ban on the inspection of horse meat encouraged the export of unwanted horses for slaughter. To control exports and the mistreatment of horses transported to slaughter abroad, Congressman Mark Kirk (R-IL) introduced the Horse Transportation Safety Act of 2009 that proposed to extend beyond horses shipped for slaughter the prohibition of the interstate transport of any horse in a double-deck truck. The bill failed to pass.[53] Likewise the proposed Prevention of Equine Cruelty Act of 2009, which required a fine and/or prison term of up to three years for possessing, shipping, transporting, purchasing, selling, delivering, or receiving any horse, horse flesh, or carcass for human consumption, failed to reach the floor of the Senate.[54] In another effort to end horse slaughter, in 2011, Senators Mary Landrieu (D-LA) and Lindsey Graham (R-SC) introduced the American Horse Slaughter Prevention Act of 2011 to prohibit "shipping, transporting, moving, delivering, receiving, possessing, purchasing, selling, or donation of horses and other equines for slaughter for human consumption."[55] House members introduced a companion bill. Both bills failed to receive committee support and a floor vote.

The intensity of the political struggles about horse slaughter only grew when, in November 2011, the rider banning the inspection of horse meat for human consumption was stripped out of the appropriations bill.[56] Instigated by Representative Jack Kingston (R-GA), chairman of the House agriculture spending subcommittee and supported by Senators Roy Blunt (R-MO) and Herb Kohl (D-WI) as an alleged jobs creation and animal welfare measure, it passed without drawing attention from the opponents of horse slaughter. Since U.S. horse slaughter operations had ended and Congress did not appropriate funds for horse meat inspection, the elimination of the rider had little immediate impact, but it did encourage the opponents of slaughter to push for the passage of the broad ban on horse slaughter included in the proposed American Horse Slaughter Prevention Act that, despite its introduction every year after 2006, had failed to pass. Also, in 2013 members of the Congressional Animal Protection Caucus introduced language to reinstate the ban on the appropriation of funds for the inspection of horse meat for human consumption and the Safeguard American Food Exports Act to end U.S. horse slaughter and restrict the exportation of horses for slaughter.[57]

In the interim, a group of Roswell, New Mexico, slaughterhouse and horse owners sought USDA approval to reinitiate horse slaughter. In late June 2013 the slaughterhouse won USDA approval for its operation, and its operators indicated the meat would be shipped to Europe. The USDA also undertook consideration of issuing permits for slaughter at plants in Iowa and Missouri.[58] USDA spokespersons indicted that they were legally bound to issue the permits if the slaughterhouse satisfied regulatory requirements. However, in response to a filing against the USDA by several anti-slaughter organizations, a U.S. District Court judge issued a temporary restraining order to prevent slaughter at the New Mexico, Missouri, and Iowa plants. The Iowa plant owners then decided not to pursue slaughter. Joined by the New Mexico and Colorado attorneys general, the anti-slaughter groups then sought an injunction.[59] After the challengers posted a $435,600 bond, a federal judge issued a temporary restraining order to prevent the plant from operating. However, on November 1, 2013, the federal judge removed the temporary restraining order on the New Mexico plant. The anti-slaughter parties then appealed the case.[60] Meanwhile a Missouri state judge delayed the opening of a horse slaughterhouse in Gallatin, Missouri, until a hearing on a suit challenging the issuance of a permit by the state's Department of Natural Resources that would allow the slaughterhouse to operate a lagoon where skinned horses would be washed.[61] However, the federal budget adopted in January 2014 reinstated the denial of funding for the USDA to inspect horse meat, and the plants never began to process horses.[62]

State and Local Efforts to Regulate the Disposition of Unwanted Horses

Federal policy has not preempted state action on the subject of horse slaughter. This situation has allowed state and local governments to enter the policy debate about the treatment of unwanted horses. With horse slaughter, several factors have induced an end to horse slaughter in several states. One factor is public opinion. Public opinion polls have shown high support for a federal ban on horse slaughter. In one recent poll 70 percent favored a ban and only 11 percent said they would consider eating horse meat if it were legal. More than 60 percent thought horse slaughter was already illegal. Only 6 percent of the general public considered horses to be livestock, 34 percent classified them as companion animals, and 57 percent defined horses as recreational and sporting animals. Even in Texas, a state with a significant number of unwanted horses, a poll revealed that 72 percent of voters opposed horse slaughter.[63] Second, federal interstate transport regulations and state regulations had made transport more expensive and slaughter less economically viable.

With political pressure mounting against horse slaughter, some states have considered legislation to ban the practice. In 1998 California voters passed Proposition 6, the first successful state initiative to ban the slaughter of horses for human consumption. The Save the Horses campaign, executed by the California Equine Council, convinced 59.4 percent of voters to criminalize the sale of horses for slaughter for human consumption.[64] California also banned the transportation of horses for slaughter for human consumption.[65] Mississippi and Oklahoma have banned the sale of horse meat for human consumption as well.[66] After intensive lobbying by animal welfare groups in 2007 the State of Illinois amended its Horse Meat Act to ban horse slaughter,[67] closing a DeKalb slaughterhouse where 60 employees processed from 40,000 to 60,000 horses a year. A federal court of appeals upheld the law,[68] and the DeKalb plant, the last remaining horse slaughterhouse operating in the United States, closed.[69] In 2012 New Jersey adopted a law with bipartisan support to ban horse slaughter for human consumption.[70] Other states that did not process horses, including Massachusetts and New York, also witnessed the introduction of bills to prohibit the transportation or slaughter of horses for human consumption.[71] Some local governments, such as Snohomish County, Washington, also banned the slaughter of horses for food.[72]

In Texas the conflict about horse slaughter pitted the slaughterhouse industry against the effect of slaughtering on the quality of life in a community. In Kaufman, Texas, the public and local officials had complained about the smell of the plant and the improper disposal of blood and waste products from the slaughtering process. They felt that these conditions adversely affected the value of their homes, also. State Representative Tony Goolsby (R) responded to the complaints about the horse slaughter plant by asking Texas Attorney General John Cornyn (R) whether the plant violated a 1949 state law that prohibited the sale of horse meat for human consumption.[73] Based on advice from the attorney general, district attorney Tim Curry successfully brought state criminal charges against the firm. During this litigation the USDA produced a 906-page document that disclosed innumerable acts violating regulations on the shipping, treatment, and method of slaughter of horses at a plant in Fort Worth.[74] Both the Kaufman and Fort Worth, Texas, facilities shut down after a federal court of appeals upheld the Texas law prohibiting the sale of horse meat.[75]

State Legislative Opposition to Federal Policy about Horse Slaughter

Despite the closure of horse slaughtering facilities, several, mostly Western, state legislatures have sought to reestablish the horse slaughter industry. Continuing state legislative efforts to permit horse slaughter offer evidence that the pro–horse slaughter lobbyists have managed to convince some state legislators that horses are suffering as a result of the inability to slaughter them for food. They claim that unusable horses are no longer property useful for recreation or work. The costs of burial or cremation of deceased horses has made it seem rational for some state legislators to support the horse slaughter industry even though the majority of the horses sent to slaughter are in good health.[76] Even though the plants that once operated usually employed fewer than 75 employees, slaughter also appeals to some legislators to offer the opportunity to create more jobs. Other legislators and groups argue that a liberty to slaughter is a worthy property rights, free market, or states' rights measure.[77]

Therefore, despite the successes of its opponents at the federal and state levels, the meat packing industry has found support for horse slaughter in Western states and states with a meat packing industry. For example, in 2009 the Montana legislature passed a bill to permit the operation of horse slaughter plants, which became law when the governor refused to sign or veto it. The bill was sold in part as a jobs creation measure, a snipe at federal regulatory powers, and a protection of private property rights. The law had no power because the state already had the authority to slaughter horses for human consumption and for sale to pet food companies, circuses, and zoos. The bill did not give the state the authority to export horse meat. To dissuade legal challenges to plant operations, the bill protected the developers of a slaughter plant from judicial injunctions to stop plant construction or operations because they created a nuisance or other harms, required persons engaging in legal action to prevent the operation of a plant to post a bond at the amount of 20 percent of the cost of the facility, restricted environmental license and permit challenges to plant operations, and required unsuccessful challengers of plant operations to pay the slaughterhouse firms' legal fees.[78]

Since 2007 other legislative initiatives or acts to allow or promote horse slaughter or horse meat sales have surfaced in Colorado, Idaho, Missouri, Nebraska, North Dakota, South Dakota, Tennessee, and Wyoming.[79] Of the states demanding that Congress allow horse slaughter for human consumption, only Idaho and Missouri had USDA-inspected horse slaughter facilities after 1985.[80] However, these states have horse auction businesses that would be adversely affected by a ban on horse transportation to slaughter or for export. Additionally, in support of these state legislatures the National Conference of State Legislatures adopted a resolution in support of the export of horses for slaughter.[81] Arizona, Arkansas, Kansas, Minnesota, Missouri, South Dakota, Tennessee, Utah, and Wyoming state lawmakers have passed resolutions instructing their congressional delegations to oppose federal horse transport legislation that would restrict the transport of horses for slaughter abroad.[82]

U.S. Politics and Horse Slaughter Policy: An Assessment

Because the United States remains a horse exporter, the U.S. federal and state political conflicts about horse transportation have transnational implications. Since the export of horses for slaughter is unregulated by the United States, inspection of exported meat remains less strict than regulations of domestically consumed meat,[83] and there is a lack of formal cooperation agreements on transportation with other nations, U.S. policies have affected the quality and quantity of the global supply of horse meat. Consequently, even though governments in the United States have acted to curtail horse slaughter, they have only incrementally induced policy change elsewhere.

The European Union

Countries in the European Union (EU), especially Belgium (by far the largest importer per capita), France, the Netherlands, Italy, and non-EU member Switzerland import significant quantities of horses for slaughter and horse meat for human consumption. In addition to North America, sources of horses have included newer members of the EU, such as Poland and Romania, Latin America, and countries in central Asia. By weight the most recent EU data indicate that horse meat was 1.1 percent of all meats consumed in Belgium, 0.3 percent of all meats consumed in France, and 1.2 percent of all meats consumed in Italy.[84]

The EU has regulated the importation, transportation, and health of the horses destined for dinner tables. These regulations reflect long-standing European concerns about the purity and labeling of many agricultural commodities rather than concern for animal welfare.[85] Opponents of the consumption of horse meat exist in countries across Europe, but only in the United Kingdom have they secured laws that ban the consumption of horses.[86]

EU legislation about the treatment of horses originated with administrators concerned about the safety of food, especially the Food and Veterinary Office in the Directorate General for Health and Consumer Affairs, committees of experts and civil servants, such as the Standing Veterinary Committee, and council working groups, part-time bodies composed of civil servants from member states. A 1990 directive of the European Economic Community's Council (renamed the Council of Ministers of the EU in 1999) set forth the basic rules for horse transportation and slaughter for all EU members. It required the inspection of imported horses prior to their entry into the EU and prohibited slaughter for horses with certain infectious diseases. Horses had to be transported in a clean and safe method. A 2005 regulation especially specified the health and safety conditions governing horse transport.[87]

A 2000 EU directive required the withdrawal of various veterinary medicinal products for six months before horses and other *equidae* (donkeys, burros) could be processed for food. Additionally, EU regulations banned the importation of horses treated with certain classes of antibiotics commonly used in racehorses in the United States.[88] The animals also had to meet a maximum residue limit for the medicinal products. The EU additionally required that exporting countries establish a program of controls to inspect for the presence of drugs in their horse meat bound for Europe. In 2004 an EU regulation expanded the amended 1990 directive on the health of imported horses. It established more rigorous standards for inspection and record keeping in countries exporting to the EU.[89]

By conducting a Europe-wide petition drive and letter writing campaigns, the interest group World Horse Welfare continued to press for stricter regulation of the transportation of horses to slaughter.[90] The interest group Eurogroup for Animals also has conducted a campaign to protect animals, including horses, during transportation within the EU.[91] Effective in 2010 the EU required lifetime "horse passports" (Equine Information Document, or EID) for all horses and other equines imported into its member nations. The passport is a smart card that documents a horse's pharmacological history to determine if it received banned drugs,[92] and all countries that export food animals to the EU are required to have systems in place that mirror the passport requirements of the EU. To guarantee the passport matches a specific horse, when it is issued a microchip is injected into the horse so a record of the horse's medical history can be logged into a database. In 2013 the EU required a Universal Equine Life Number and lifetime medication records for all horses slaughtered in non-EU countries before accepting imports of horse meat from those countries.[93] Additionally, the EU now requires that non-EU countries intending to export equine meat to the EU submit an action plan to its Food and Veterinary Office with a drug residue monitoring plan and provide annual updates of the plan and monitoring results.

However, there is some evidence of the ineffective enforcement of these regulations. A 2011 EU report documented poor inspection of equid animals prior to transport and threats to animal health during transport.[94] Additionally, there are reports of violations of health regulations. For example, undeclared horse meat of unknown safety also occurred in some meat products, such as sausages, in violation of the laws of some member states.[95] Political reaction in several countries caused the European Parliament and national legislatures and agencies to begin to modify meat labeling and safety standards.[96] Therefore, despite the horse passport, EU policymakers have yet to secure fully the quality of horse meat as a commodity, let alone address opponents of horse slaughter and consumption of horse meat who define it as cruelty. However, what the EU has done has transnational regulatory implications for horses exported from the United States and slaughtered in Canada and Mexico.

Canada

EU food safety regulations and the prospect of horse passports effectively induced many horse and horse meat exporter nations such as Canada to adopt regulations and establish or adapt their regulatory institutions. Regulations of horse transport and slaughter for human consumption in the United States and the EU rather than domestic political struggles have especially affected regulatory institutions and regulations in Canada.

As in the United States, in Canada a political struggle about the social identity of horses exists between groups committed to stewardship and those that regard horses to be a commodity. Save for a small portion of the Francophone population and some gourmands, Canadians have treated the consumption of horse meat as taboo. However, Canadian horse stewardship interest groups entered the slaughter policy arena somewhat later than those in the United States and have not achieved the same success.

The Canadian Horse Defence Coalition and other humane organizations have staged public protests and letter writing campaigns in support of an end to horse slaughter.[97]

Despite organized opposition and reports of cruelty and unsanitary conditions at Canadian horse slaughter plants,[98] the federal parliament and provincial legislatures have seldom faced significant organized pressure from stewardship groups to regulate the disposition of unwanted horses.[99] Indeed, the Horse Welfare Alliance of Canada, an alliance of provincial equine organizations, farm animal care groups, and other segments of the animal agriculture industry, especially has supported horse slaughter.[100] Bills to address horse slaughter through federal legislation prohibiting the export or import of horses or horse meat have failed to reach the floor debate stage.[101] Initially, regulation of horse transport to slaughter was left to the provinces. For example, Alberta contracted with the private Livestock Identification Services Ltd. to oversee intra-provincial transport from provincial horse auctions and feedlots to the Bouvry slaughterhouse in Fort Macleod and the Canadian Premium Meats plant in Lacombe.[102]

Because the provinces and the Canadian federal government lagged behind the United States and its states and municipalities in regulating horse transportation, the inspection of horse meat, and the elimination of horse slaughter, during the first decade of the twenty-first century Canadian slaughterhouses benefited from the shipment of unwanted horses from south of the border. Indeed, the export of U.S. horses to Canada for slaughter increased significantly when the U.S. Congress effectively ended horse slaughter.[103] In 2009 five plants in Canada imported 56 percent of the 93,812 horses slaughtered from the United States.[104] In that year 30 percent of Canadian horse meat, offal, and carcass exports went to France and 12 percent to Japan.[105]

When the EU announced the requirements of its horse passport system and it recognized that U.S. horses would not possess the documentation to satisfy the EU, Canadian officials acted. Using their existing range of institutional rulemaking powers, a federal agency, the Canadian Food Inspection Agency (CFIA) of the Ministry of Agriculture and Agri-Food, acted to regulate aspects of the disposition of unwanted horses. Unlike the United States, where the USDA and some members of Congress supported the production of horse meat for economic reasons and the Animal and

Plant Health Inspection Service and the Food and Drug Administration have not aggressively addressed the presence of pharmaceuticals in horse meat, the CFIA actions have placed significant restrictions on the transport and health of horses destined for human consumption. Because Canadian horse meat is almost all exported, the 2010 initiation of EU regulations governing the use of certain drugs in horses bound for slaughter was the primary inducement for the CFIA to adopt regulations on horse slaughter. Also, beginning in 2011, U.S. horses could enter Canada only at specific inspection points. The Canadian regulations appear to be influenced by a fear of a repeat of the costly curtailment of meat exports due to "mad cow disease," or bovine spongiform encephalopathy (BSE).[106] To protect the export market, the CFIA held stakeholder consultations and information sessions with representatives from Equine Canada, plant operators, and auction markets during the rule drafting process. The agency also considered how to identify the health of live horses imported from the United States.[107]

Today CFIA regulations require that inter-provincial and international transporters must provide feed, water, rest, and proper equipment to ensure the health and safety of the horses.[108] The owner of the horse bound for slaughter must fill out an Equine Identification Document (EID) that certifies that the horse has not been administered restricted drugs in the last six months. The CFIA therefore banned the marketing of meat from horses, mostly those used in racing and entertainment, given certain drugs. Records on drugs administered to the horse within six months of slaughter must be provided. However, despite these regulations, no system is yet in place to track the drugs administered to horses at other times. With horses imported from the U.S. the documentation is often scarce. Consequently, in 2015 the European Commission's Food and Veterinary Office released an audit report raising "serious concerns" about the reliability of controls on horses slaughtered in Canada for export of horse meat to the EU. Especially the report asserted that, "Whilst the CFIA puts the responsibility for follow-up of non-compliances largely on the shoulders of the slaughterhouses, the CFIA does not always fulfil [sic] its obligations for verifying and ensuring the effectiveness of the follow-up investigations and corrective actions. The CFIA is in this regard hampered by a lack of direct powers over primary producers and transient agents." The CFIA responded that it would undertake corrective measures.[109] Regardless of the adoption of these additional measures, Canadian exports of horse meat to Belgium and France had already declined significantly after 2009.

Mexico

Since the beginning of the elimination of horse slaughter in the United States and with the propagation of Canadian regulations of the health of horses sent to slaughter, Mexico has become more and more frequently a destination for unwanted American horses. Economically the Mexican option is an attractive way to avoid the U.S. and state bans on horse slaughter and Canadian regulations. Today Mexico reportedly slaughters more horses than any other nation except China.[110] The slaughter business persists in part because of the lack of influence of groups committed to the human stewardship of horses,[111] a willingness of a small portion of the Mexican population to consume horse meat as a cheap alternative to beef, and the availability of horses for processing and export.

The ineffectiveness of the political institutions assigned to regulate horse slaughter also has made Mexico into a hospitable environment for it. Despite a long history of regulation and management of the food supply, today Mexican law imposes few restrictions on horse slaughter and the sale, use, and export of horse meat.[112] Regulation of unaccounted numbers of clandestine butcher shops that supply local and, possibly, Asian markets is lax or nonexistent. The consequence is that much domestic Mexican horse meat often "reflects an extremely poor handling during slaughtering, evisceration and storage."[113]

Administrative oversight of the industry of large plants which export to European firms is conducted by the Secretariat of Agriculture and Livestock (Secretaría de Agricultura, Ganaderia, Desarrollo Rural, Pesca y Alimentacion or SAGARPA). The regulation of 1,500 municipal slaughterhouses falls to the Secretariat of Health (Secretaría de Salud or SSA). These agencies are supposed to certify that horse meat shipped to EU countries satisfies European food safety regulations. However, a 2010 investigation by the European Commission's Health and Consumers Directorate-General, Directorate F-Food, and Veterinary Office uncovered numerous deficiencies in the inspection of four Mexican plants and three collection centers that process horse meat for export to Europe. Especially there was no verification of documents about veterinary treatments and the drugs administered to horses and problems with hygiene during the processing of the horses.[114] The Mexican government has since adopted a requirement that horses imported for slaughter be microchipped, and border controls have been strengthened. A sworn statement on veterinary medical treatments is requested for all slaughter horses, no matter what their country of origin.

In 2012 the EU Health and Consumers Directorate-General again audited the processing of horse meat in Mexican abattoirs. Despite noting improvements in statistics, abattoir hygiene, and laboratory inspection procedures, the report concluded that "the systems in place for identification, the food chain information and in particular the affidavits concerning the non-treatment for six months with certain medical substances, both for the horses imported from the US as well as for the Mexican horses are insufficient to guarantee that standards equivalent to those provided for by EU legislation are applied." The report also noted that 80 percent of the horses processed for meat destined for the EU came from the United States and that border controls on many imported horses did not exist.[115]

However, in 2015 additional EU audits of food safety resulted in an EU ban on the importation of Mexican-processed horse meat.[116] Whether this decision will change the Mexican horse slaughter industry with regard to importation of U.S. horses remains uncertain. However, the Mexican case illustrates the potential transnational effects of EU food safety regulations and U.S. restrictions on horse slaughter. Poor documentation of the health history of horses imported from the United States might either curtail Mexican slaughter operations or induce Mexican firms to dump undocumented horse meat in markets such as China.

Assessment

Although in these nations the norms that defined the treatment of horses were in conflict, all participants employed legality in an effort to reinforce their vision of the correct status and treatment of horses. However, in seeking legalized accountability for the treatment of horses, the contesting parties confronted different lawmaking and regulatory institutions. In the United States the horse slaughter issue became a legislative matter. With minuscule consumption of tabooed horse meat, the quality of the meat, including its pharmaceutical content, never arose as an issue. At most decision points the USDA supported slaughter as a legitimate economic activity of benefit to ranchers and the horse industry. The development of regulations of slaughter and transportation to slaughter fell primarily to a bipartisan coalition of members of Congress and Senators and to state legislators sympathetic to animal welfare advocates and legalized accountability for the disposal of horses. For a period Congress prevented the inspection of horse meat for domestic consumption and forced slaughterhouses out of business, but it did not restrict the export of meat. A few state legislatures banned the sale of horse meat and prevented the operation of slaughterhouses. However, in Western states where animal advocates had far less political support, legislators sought to keep the industry alive to serve the export market.

In Canada, Mexico, and the EU a different regulatory context emerged that was far less concerned with animal welfare. In the EU the administration of pharmaceuticals to horses and the health of horses became of concern to administrators already designated with the duty of securing safe food. In a context marked by a lack of internal governmental support for slaughter, respect for administrative expertise, a weak legislature, fewer points of access to officials for organized interests, and limited opposition from member states and organized interests, the EU scientific committees and commission incrementally pushed forward transportation and horse meat quality regulations. These unelected administrators' extension of legalized accountability in the treatment of horses did not end horse slaughter. However, the EU regulations have had a transnational effect on the scope of regulation. In what has been called the *California Effect,* as a wealthy and politically powerful entity the EU forced exporter nations such as Canada and Mexico to adjust their regulations and regulatory procedures in ways that restricted the slaughter of horses imported from the United States. In Canada, because of a broad jurisdictional statute and concerns about both food safety and exports, the CFIA undertook this legalization task without legislative approval. Mexican officials found a need for greater legal accountability for the disposition of horse meat for the European export trade. Indirectly these actions have also affected the quality of horse meat exported to nations with enforced food safety standards for meat, such as Japan, and those with weaker regulatory systems, such as China.

THE RADIATING EFFECTS OF STRUGGLES ABOUT THE DISPOSITION OF UNWANTED HORSES

Despite the lack of public or private transnational regulatory and enforcement institutions, a homogenized transnational common law, or a model code for reference,[117] the upshot of regulation of horse slaughter in one nation has often been a change in the treatment of horses elsewhere. Despite struggles about the ethics of the consumption of horse meat and quite different institutional regulatory politics, legalized regulations and enforcement practices have begun to emerge from the disjointed but reciprocal interaction of Canadian, EU, Mexican, and U.S. subnational and national policy choices. Although the consequence is an ineffective enforcement of a patchwork of regulations, the trend is clearly toward a global harmonization of the regulation of horse slaughter. Law's territory thus is moving beyond the nation-state. However, whether this trend continues, a crystallization of regulation in legalized transnational animal regulatory institutions remains uncertain.[118] However, the passive cruelty of horse slaughter remains as yet off the transnational political agenda. Until demand for horse meat greatly decreases and the economic rationale for slaughter ebbs, unwanted horses will continue to be a commodity.

NOTES

1. American Veterinary Medical Association, *U.S. Pet Ownership and Demographics Sourcebook (2012)* (Schaumburg, IL: American Veterinary Medical Association, 2012).
2. See Ann M. Griffin, "Whoa Means Whoa—The Reinstitution of Horse Slaughter in the U.S. Is Not Necessary to Ensure Equine Welfare," *Journal of Animal and Natural Resources Law* 9 (2013): 5–7.

3. Many of the actions toward horses that we discuss apply to other *equidae,* including ponies, mules, donkeys, and burros.
4. Griffin, "Whoa Means Whoa," 22–26.
5. See Ibid, 28–29 on auctions.
6. The definition of *transnational* is derived from Robert Keohane and Joseph Nye, "Transgovernmental Relations and International Organizations," *World Politics* 27 (1977): 39–42.
7. See John Braithwaite and Peter Drahos, *Global Business Regulation* (Cambridge: Cambridge University Press, 2000); H. Patrick Glenn, "A Transnational Concept of Law," *in The Oxford Handbook on Legal Studies*, ed. Peter Cane and Mark Tushnet (New York: Oxford University Press, 2005), 851–59; Anne-Marie Slaughter, *A New World Order* (Princeton: Princeton University Press, 2004), 36–64; Thomas Hale and David Held, ed., *Handbook of Transnational Governance: Institutions and Innovations* (Malden, MA: Polity, 2011).
8. In this respect horse slaughter involves the export and import of national legal norms. See Gregory Shaffer, "Transnational Legal Process and State Change," *Law and Social Inquiry* 37 (2012): 233–34.
9. Miles Kahler, "Conclusion: The Causes and Consequences of Legalization," in *Legalization and World Politics,* ed. Judith Goldstein, Miles Kahler, Robert O. Keohane, and Anne-Marie Slaughter (Cambridge: MIT Press, 2001), 284–85.
10. Peter M. Haas, "Introduction: Epistemic Communities and International Policy Coordination," *International Organization* 46 (1992): 3.
11. Griffin, "Whoa Means Whoa," 35–40, outlines the conflicting views and lack of consensus. This situation stands in contrast to some other areas of transnational regulation; see H. W. Arthurs, "Globalization of the Mind: Canadian Elites and the Restructuring of Legal Fields," *Canadian Journal of Law and Society* 12 (1997): 219–46.
12. On the excessive breeding argument see Eryn Maria Pearson, "Horse Slaughter: A Conflict of Ethics, Economics, and Welfare," *Journal of Animal Law and Ethics* 4 (2011): 205–41.
13. "Welcome to Americans Against Horse Slaughter," Americans Against Horse Slaughter, accessed Mar. 7, 2012, http://www.americansagainsthorseslaughter.com/; "The Issues," Equine Advocates, accessed Mar. 1, 2012, http://www.equineadvocates.org/issues.php; "Horse Slaughter—An American Disgrace, Not a Necessary Evil," Equine Protection Network, accessed Mar. 7, 2012, http://equineprotectionnetwork.com/slaughter/sindex.htm; "End Horse Slaughter," Equine Welfare Alliance, accessed Mar. 7, 2012, http://www.humanesociety.org/issues/horse_slaughter/; Wild for Life Foundation, accessed Mar. 7, 2012, http://www.wildforlifefoundation.org/home.html; Canadian Horse Defence Coalition, accessed Mar. 7, 2012, http://www.defendhorsescanada.org/; "Horse

Slaughter," Humane Society International/Canada, accessed Mar. 7, 2012, http://www.hsicanada.ca/horses/horse_slaughter/.
14. Adam Sage, "Horses as Courses May End under French Pet Protection Bill," *The Sunday Times*, Dec. 26, 2009, accessed Aug. 18, 2011, http://www.timesonline.co.uk/tol/news/world/europe/article6968034.ece.
15. "Ban Latijns—Amerikaans paardenvlees," GAIA, accessed Aug. 18, 2011, http://gaia.be/nl/campagnes/ban-latijns-amerikaans-paardenvlees.
16. The Horse Fund, accessed Mar. 10, 2012, http://www.horsefund.org/; World Horse Welfare, accessed Mar. 10, 2012, http://www.worldhorsewelfare.org/.
17. "International Equine Conference Blasts Off in DC," Straight from the Horses Heart, accessed Mar. 7, 2012, http://rtfitchauthor.com/2011/09/27/international-equine-conference-blasts-off-in-dc/.
18. Eurogroup4Animals, accessed Mar. 10, 2012, http://eurogroupforanimals.org/.
19. "Chevidico Worldwide," Chevidico, accessed Mar. 7, 2012, http://www.chevideco.be/en/chevideco/wereldwijd.asp.
20. "Issues Affecting the U.S. Horse Industry," American Horse Council, accessed Mar. 1, 2012, http://www.horsecouncil.org/issues-affecting-us-horse-industry; "Own Responsibly," Unwanted Horse Coalition, accessed Mar. 1, 2012, http://www.unwantedhorsecoalition.org/?id=1.
21. Frederick J. Simoons, *Eat Not This Flesh: Food Avoidances from Prehistory to the Present*, 2nd ed. (Madison: University of Wisconsin Press, 1994), 180–88.
22. Simoons, *Eat Not This Flesh*, 188–91; Kari Weil, "They Eat Horses, Don't They? Hippophagy and Frenchness," *Gastronomica: The Journal of Food and Culture* 7 (2) (2007): 44–51.
23. F. Martuzzi, A. L. Catalano, and C. Sussi, "Characteristics of Horse Meat Consumption and Production in Italy," accessed Aug. 29, 2011, http://www.unipr.it/arpa/facvet/annali/2001/martuzzi.pdf; Nick Pisa, "Horse Meat Faces Ban in Italy," *The Telegraph*, Feb. 8, 2010, accessed Aug. 29, 2011, http://www.telegraph.co.uk/news/worldnews/europe/italy/7182202/Horse-meat-faces-ban-in-Italy.html.
24. Amy A. Quark, "Transnational Governance as Contested Institution-Building: China, Merchants, and Contract Rules in the Cotton Trade," *Politics and Society* 39 (2011): 3–39.
25. For a legal history of U.S. horses see Lafcadio H. Darling, "Legal Protection for Horses: Care and Stewardship or Hypocrisy and Neglect?," *Animal Law* 6 (2000): 105–27.
26. For example see R. McGreggor Cawley, *Federal Land, Western Anger: The Sagebrush Rebellion and Environmental Politics* (Lawrence: University Press of Kansas, 1993), 4–9, 71–91; Robert A. Mikos, "On the Limits of Supremacy: Medical Marijuana and the States' Overlooked Power to Legalize Federal

Crime," *Vanderbilt Law Review* 62 (2009) 1421–82; Jocelyn M. Johnston and Kara Lindaman, "Implementing Welfare Reform in Kansas: Moving, but Not Racing," *Publius: The Journal of Federalism* 28:3 (1998): 123–42; John D. Nugent, *How the States Protect Their Interests in National Policymaking* (Norman: University of Oklahoma Press, 2009); J. Mitchell Pickerell and Paul Chen, "Medical Marijuana and the Virtues of Federalism," *Publius: The Journal of Federalism* 38:3 (2008): 22–55; Paul Posner, "The Politics of Coercive Federalism in the Bush Administration," *Publius: The Journal of Federalism* 37:3 (2007): 391; Barry Rabe, "Environmental Policy in the Bush Era: The Collision Between the Administrative Presidency and State Experimentation," *Publius: The Journal of Federalism* 37:3 (2007): 422–29; Bryan Shelly, "Rebels and Their Causes: State Resistance to No Child Left Behind," *Publius: The Journal of Federalism* 38:3 (2008): 444–68; Joseph F. Zimmerman, *Congressional Preemption: Regulatory Federalism* (Albany: State University of New York Press, 2005).

27. U.S. Public Law 92-195; 16 *United States Code* §§ 1331 et seq.
28. 43 *Code of Federal Regulations* §§ 4700–4770.
29. U.S. House of Representatives, Wild Free-Roaming Horses and Burros Sale and Adoption Act of 2005, H.R. 2993 (109th Congress, 1st Sess.); U.S. Senate, Wild Free-Roaming Horses and Burros Sale and Adoption Act of 2005, S. 1273 (109th Congress, 1st Sess.).
30. U.S. Senate, Restore Our American Mustangs Act, S. 1579 (111th Congress, 1st Sess.).
31. 16 *United States Code* § 1333(b)(2)(B).
32. 43 *Code of Federal Regulations* 4770.1(e).
33. On BLM policy see U.S. Dept. of the Interior, Bureau of Land Management, "Prepared Remarks of BLM Director Bob Abbey at THE 'Summit of the Horse,' Las Vegas, Nevada, Tuesday, Jan. 4, 2011," accessed Oct. 13, 2015, http://www.blm.gov/wo/st/en/info/newsroom/extras/summitstatement.html.
34. Testimony of Liz Ross, Animal Welfare Institute, U.S. House of Representatives, Committee on the Judiciary, Subcommittee on Crime, Terrorism, and Homeland Security, *Hearing, Prevention of Equine Cruelty Act of 2008, and the Animal Cruelty Statistics Act of 2008*. July 31, 2008, 14. Approximately 900,000 horses die in the United States in any year; see Statement of Wayne Pacelle, Ibid., 92, submission at 369.
35. Catrin Einhorn, "Horses Spared in U.S. Face Death Across the Border," *New York Times* Jan. 11, 2008, accessed Aug. 18, 2011, http://www.nytimes.com/2008/01/11/us/11horse.html.
36. A list of pro-slaughter groups is found at "Wild Horse Haters & Horse Slaughter Promoters," accessed Oct. 17, 2015, https://whohateshorses.wordpress

.com/2011/03/28/do-you-know-who-supports-horse-slaughter/. For examples of the detailed policy positions of some of these groups, see "2014 NCBA Policy Book, AFP 1.11," National Cattlemen's Beef Association, accessed Oct. 16, 2015, http://www.beefusa.org/CMDocs/BeefUSA/Issues/2014%20NCBA%20 Policy%20Book.pdf; "Position on the Transportation and Processing of Horses," American Association of Equine Practitioners, accessed Mar. 16, 2010, http:// aaep.mediamarketers.com/position-transportation-processing-horses-i-327.html; "Unwanted Horses and Horse Slaughter FAQ," American Veterinary Medical Association, accessed Mar. 16, 2010, https://www.avma.org/KB/Resources /FAQs/Pages/Frequently-asked-questions-about-unwanted-horses-and-horse -slaughter.aspx.

37. Statement of Bryce Quick, Deputy Administrator, Food Safety and Inspection Service, Plenary Session, U.S. Dept. of Agriculture, National Advisory Committee on Meat and Poultry Inspection, Aug. 8, 2007, 63, accessed Feb. 14, 2011, http://www.fsis.usda.gov/wps/wcm/connect/fb138f2f-cfe2-46c6-8939 -0a0672e3431b/NACMPI_Transcript_080807.pdf?MOD=AJPERES.
38. Public Law 104–27 (1996), 7 *United States Code* § 1901.
39. C. L. Stull, "Evolution of the Proposed Federal Slaughter Horse Transport Regulations," *Journal of Animal Science* 79 (e. Supp.) (2001): E12–E15.
40. 9 *Code of Federal Regulations* 88.1-6 (adopted in 2001).
41. Consolidated Appropriations Act, 2005, U.S. Public Law 108-447, 262-63.
42. Bouvry Exports Calgary Ltd. is headquartered in Calgary, Alberta, and operates the largest horse slaughter facility in Canada at Fort Macleod, Alberta. Conditions at the Shelby feedlot in 2008, from which horses are held before shipment to Canada, are reported in "Investigation at the 'Slaughter' Horse Feedlot in Shelby, MT—External Report," Animals' Angels USA, accessed Sept. 5, 2011, http://www.kaufmanzoning.net/InvestigationShelbyMontanMay2008extera reportt.pdf.
43. U.S. House of Representatives, Horse Slaughter Prohibition Bill, H.R. 503 (109th Congress, 1st Sess., 2005); U.S. Senate, Virgie S. Arden American Horse Slaughter Prevention Act, S. 1915 (109th Congress, 1st Sess., 2005); U.S. House of Representatives, Bill to amend the Horse Protection Act to prohibit the shipping, transporting, moving, delivering, receiving, possessing, purchasing, selling, or donation of horses and other equines to be slaughtered for human consumption, and for other purposes (109th Congress, 2nd Sess., 2007); U.S. Senate, Bill to amend the Horse Protection Act to prohibit the shipping, transporting, moving, delivering, receiving, possessing, purchasing, selling, or donation of horses and other equines to be slaughtered for human consumption, and for other purposes, S. 311 (110th Congress, 1st Sess., 2007).

44. Agriculture, Rural Development, Food and Drug Administration, and Related Agencies Appropriations Act, 2006, U.S. Public Law 109-97, Section 794 (Nov. 10, 2005).
45. Bacterial diseases such as Salmonella can also be transmitted through horse meat that is contaminated during its processing, and horse livers and kidneys often contain levels of cadmium that make them unfit for human consumption; see C.O. Gill, "Safety and storage stability of horse meat for human consumption," *Meat Science* 71 (2005): 506–13.
46. Letter from members of Congress, *Hearing, Prevention of Equine Cruelty Act of 2008*, 370–74; Statement of Wayne Pacelle, U.S. House of Representatives, Ibid., 86; U.S. Dept. of Agriculture, FSIS Establishes Fee-For-Service Program for Ante-Mortem Inspection of Horses. The current inspection regulation is 9 *Code of Federal Regulations* § 354.19. FSIS also has cooperative agreements that assign meat inspection to state agencies in twenty-seven states, 9 *Code of Federal Regulations* § 321.1–2, the inspection must conform to or be "at least equal" to federal standards.
47. Sheila Johnson, USDA, e-mail message to Susan Hunter, June 2011.
48. U.S. Government Accountability Office, *Humane Methods of Slaughter Act: Actions Are Needed to Strengthen Enforcement*, GAO 10-203, Feb. 2010; Statement of Lisa Stames, Director, Natural Resources and Environment, U.S., Government Accountability Office, *Humane Methods of Slaughter Act: Weaknesses in USDA Enforcement*, GAO 10-487T, Mar. 2010.
49. Noted animal slaughter expert Temple Grandin of Colorado State University has stated publicly that 90 percent of all U.S. slaughterhouses fail to comply with federal regulations.
50. U.S. Government Accountability Office, *Horse Welfare: Action Needed to Address Unintended Consequences from Cessation of Domestic Slaughter*, GAO 11-228 (June 2011), 13–25, accessed Aug. 17, 2011, http://www.gao.gov/products/GAO-11-228.
51. Ibid., 44.
52. See "Animal Law Coalition Responds to GAO Horse Slaughter Report," accessed July 13, 2011, http://rtfitch.wordpress.com/2011/06/23/animal-law-coalition-responds-to-gao-horse-slaughter-report/; "GAO Study Wastes Time and Tax Dollars," Americans Against Horse Slaughter in Arizona, accessed July 13, 2011, http://arizona1-aahsbloggingupdates.blogspot.com/2011/06/gao-study-wastes-time-and-tax-dollars.html.
53. U.S. House of Representatives, Horse Transportation Safety Act of 2009, H.R. 305 (111th Congress, 1st Sess., 2009).
54. U.S. Senate, Prevention of Equine Cruelty Act of 2009, S. 727 (111th Congress, 1st Sess., 2009).

55. U.S. Senate, American Horse Slaughter Prevention Act of 2011, S. 1176 (112th Congress, 1st Sess., 2011).
56. U.S. Senate, Consolidated and Further Continuing Appropriations Act, 2012 (112th Congress, 1st Sess., 2011); U.S. Public Law 112-55.
57. U.S. House of Representatives, Safeguard American Food Exports Act of 2013 (113th Congress, 1st Sess., 2013).
58. John Glionna, "Horse Slaughter Plant Wins Tentative Approval in New Mexico," *Los Angeles Times,* June 28, 2013, accessed Oct. 13, 2015, http://articles.latimes.com/2013/jun/28/nation/la-na-nn-horse-slaughter-new-mexico-20130628.
59. Dan Flynn, "Agreement in Horse Slaughter Case: All Parties Want It to End," *Food Safety News,* Aug. 26, 2013, accessed Sept. 3, 2013, http://www.foodsafetynews.com/2013/08/agreement-comes-to-horse-slaughter-case-they-all-want-it-to-end/#.UiYkvF3D_4Y.
60. "Judge Clears Way for Domestic Horse Slaughter," *USA Today,* Nov. 1, 2013, accessed Oct. 13, 2015, http://www.usatoday.com/story/money/business/2013/11/01/judge-clears-way-for-domestic-horse-slaughter/3360471/.
61. "Judge Blocks Permit for Horse Slaughter Facility," *News Leader* (Springfield, MO), Aug. 5, 2013, accessed Sept. 3, 2013, http://www.news-leader.com/article/20130805/NEWS01/308050122/Judge-blocks-horse-slaughter-plant; Georgina Gustin, "Horse Slaughterhouse Plans Stalled in Missouri," *St. Louis Post-Dispatch,* Aug, 9, 2013, accessed Sept. 3, 2013, http://www.stltoday.com/business/local/horse-slaughterhouse-plans-stalled-in-missouri/article_56208bc0-9d98-562f-8356-8defce230e63.html.
62. Barry Massey, "Horse Slaughter Blocked by Federal Law," *USA Today,* Jan. 17, 2014, accessed Oct. 13, 2015, http://www.usatoday.com/story/money/business/2014/01/17/horse-slaughter-blocked-by-federal-law/4604929/; U.S. Senate, Consolidated Appropriations Act, 2014, Sec. 745 (1).
63. "Overview of Statewide Public Opinion Survey Report on Horse Slaughter 1997," "Overview of New York Statewide Public Opinion Survey Report on Horse Slaughter 1999," Survey Shows Texans Strongly Oppose Horse Slaughter May 2003," HOOFPAC Political Action Committee, accessed Aug. 17, 2011, http://www.hoofpac.com/polls/index.asp.
64. *California Penal Code* § 598c (2009). See also, Carolyn L. Stull, "California and the Unwanted Horse," in *Hearing, Prevention of Equine Cruelty Act of 2008,* 375–80.
65. *California Penal Code* §§ 597o, 597x, 598c, 598d.
66. *Mississippi Code Annotated* § 75-33-3 63; *Oklahoma Statutes Annotated* §§ 1-1135–1139.
67. 225 *Illinois Compiled Statutes* 635.
68. Cavel International, Inc. v. Madigan, 500 F.3d 551 (2007). See A. Bryan Endres

and Donald L. Uchtmann, "Survey of Illinois Law: Conservation, Energy and Food Developments in Agricultural Law," *Southern Illinois Law Journal* 32 (2008): 809–14.
69. See Pearson, "Horse Slaughter," 223–24.
70. New Jersey, Bills 2012–2013, A2023.
71. General Court of the Commonwealth of Massachusetts, 2011, Bill S.655, An Act Relative to Animals; New York State Assembly, 2009, Bill No. A03736.
72. Lornet Turnbull, "Snohomish County Council Bans Slaughter of Horses for Food," *Seattle Times*, Dec. 20, 2012, accessed Oct. 13, 2015, http://www.seattletimes.com/seattle-news/snohomish-county-council-bans-slaughter-of-horses-for-food/.
73. *Texas Agriculture Code Annotated* §§ 149.001–007 (2004). See Submission, Paula Bacon, Mayor of Kaufman, Texas, U.S. House of Representatives, *Hearing, Prevention of Equine Cruelty Act of 2008*, 365–68.
74. For the U.S. Department of Agriculture inspection documents and actions on the Fort Worth plant of the Beltex Corporation, accessed Mar. 10, 2011, http://www.kaufmanzoning.net/nov24/06-108-Records-A.pdf; http://www.kaufmanzoning.net/nov24/06-108-Records-B.pdf; http://www.kaufmanzoning.net/nov24/06-108-Records-C.pdf; http://www.kaufmanzoning.net/nov24/06-108-Records-D.pdf; http://www.kaufmanzoning.net/nov24/06-108-Records-E.pdf; http://www.kaufmanzoning.net/nov24/06-108-Records-F.pdf.
75. Empacadora de Carnes de Fresnillo, S.a. de C.V. v. Curry, 476 F.3d 326 (7th Cir. 2007).
76. See Laura Jane Durfee, "Anti-Horse Slaughter Legislation: Bad for Horses, Bad for Society," *Indiana Law Journal* 84 (2009): 353–71.
77. For a summary of these arguments see Testimony of Charles W. Stenholm, *Hearing, Prevention of Equine Cruelty Act of 2008*, 44–48;" Equines (H.O.R.S.E.) act," United Organizations of the Horse, accessed Oct. 16, 2015, http://www.unitedorgsofthehorse.org/equines-h-o-r-s-e-act; "New Alliance Unites Horse Owners," accessed Mar. 16, 2010, http://www.bloodhorse.com/horse-racing/articles/50745/new-alliance-unites-horse-owners; Christina Macejko, "AAEP Says Horse-Slaughter Bill Would Add to Neglect, Starvation," *DVM Newsmagazine* (Sept. 2008), 22.
78. Montana Legislature, House Bill No. 0418 (2009).
79. *Colorado Revised Statutes* §§ 39-22-3801–3804; Idaho Legislature, An Act Relating to Animals, 2010, Legislature of the State of Idaho, Sixtieth Legislature Second Regular Session 2010, Senate Joint Memorial No. 104, accessed Sept. 21, 2011; Missouri General Assembly, An Act to Amend Chapter 265, R.S.Mo., by Adding Thereto Eighteen New Sections Relating to Animal Agriculture, with a Penalty Provision (2010), House Bill No. 1747, 95th General Assembly; *Revised Statutes of Nebraska* § 54-1908 (2011); *North Dakota Century Code* § 36-21-19

(2009); § 54-01-28 (2011); South Dakota, Eighty-Third Session, Legislative Assembly, 2008, House Concurrent Resolution No. 1007; H.B. 1361; Tennessee General Assembly, An Act to Amend Tennessee Code Annotated, Title 43, Chapter 1; Title 44 and Title 53, Chapter 7, relative to horses (2009); House of Representatives Sixtieth Legislature of the State of Wyoming 2010 Budget Session, A Bill for an Act Relating to Livestock; Providing for the Disposal of Estrays, Livestock and Feral Livestock; Adding Definitions; Providing for the Disposal of Meat from Slaughter as Specified; Making Conforming Amendments; and Providing for an Effective Date. Enrolled Act No. 54.
80. Johnson, e-mail message to Hunter.
81. Conference of State Legislatures, Committee: Agriculture and Energy Policy, Horse Industry (2009), accessed Sept. 7, 2011, http://www.ncsl.org/default.aspx?tabid=18106.
82. State of Arizona, Senate, Forty-Ninth Legislature, First Regular Session, 2009, SCM 1001, a Concurrent Memorial Urging the United States Congress to Oppose Federal Legislation That Interferes with a State's Ability to Direct the Transport or Processing of Horses; State of Arkansas, 87th General Assembly, Regular Session, 2009, HCR 1004, House Concurrent Resolution, Requesting the Arkansas Congressional Delegation and the Congress of the United States to Support Horse Processing Facilities, House Concurrent Resolution No. 5004, Kansas State Legislature, accessed Sept. 27, 2011, http://www.kansas.gov/government/legislative/bills/2010/2009_5004.pdf; Minnesota House of Representatives, H.F. No. 840; Minnesota Senate, S.F. 133; Missouri State Senate, Senate Concurrent Resolution 8, Urges Congress to Support the Continuation of Horse Processing in the United States (2009); South Dakota, Eighty-Fifth Session, Legislative Assembly, 2010, *House Concurrent Resolution No. 1003*; South Dakota, Eighty-Fifth Session, Legislative Assembly, 2010, *Senate Concurrent Resolution No. 4;* House Joint Resolution 245, A Resolution Relative to the Transporting and Processing of Horses and Other Equine, Tennessee General Assembly (2009); State of Utah, House Joint Resolution 7, Equine Resources Joint Resolution, 2009 General Session; Original House Joint Resolution No. 8, *Session Laws of Wyoming*, 2009, 730.
83. U.S. Government Accountability Office, *Horse Welfare*, 32–37.
84. European Commission Health and Consumers Directorate-General, *Country Profile: Summary Data on Production, Consumption, and Trade of Food, Animals, and Plants: Belgium, 2013*, accessed Oct. 16, 2015, http://ec.europa.eu/food/fvo/country_profiles/details.cfm?co_id=BE; European Commission Health and Consumers Directorate-General Directorate F—Food and Veterinary Office, *Country Profile of France on Food and Feed Safety, Animal Health, Animal Welfare and Plant Health,* accessed Feb. 22, 2011, http://ec.europa.eu/food

/fvo/country_profiles/CP_france.pdf; European Commission Health and Consumers Directorate-General Directorate F—Food and Veterinary Office, *Final Country Profile of Italy on Food and Feed Safety, Animal Health, Animal Welfare and Plant Health,* accessed Feb. 22, 2011, http://www.salute.gov.it/portale/documentazione/p6_2_2_1.jsp?id=1259.

85. See Susanne Freidberg, *French Beans and Food Scares: Culture and Commerce in an Anxious Age* (New York: Oxford University Press, 2004).
86. Tom Rawstone, "How 5,000 Horses a Year Secretly Go to Slaughter," *Mail Online,* Jan. 10, 2008, accessed Aug. 29, 2011, http://www.dailymail.co.uk/news/article-507214/How-5-000-horses-year-secretly-slaughter.html#ixzz1WQqF6D5S.
87. Council Directive of 26 June 1990 on Animal Health Conditions Governing the Movement and Import from Third Countries of Equidae, 90/426/EEC; Directive 90/425/EEC; Directive 91/496/EEC; Decision 92/130/EEC; Directive 92/36/EEC; Decision 2001/298/EC; Decision 2002/160/EC; Regulation (EC) No 2003/806; Directive 2004/68/EC; Council Directive 91/628/EEC of 19 November 1991 on the Protection of Animals during Transport and Amending Directives 90/425/EEC and 91/496/EEC; Council Directive 95/29/EC of 29 June 1995 Amending Directive 90/628/EEC Concerning the Protection of Animals during Transport.
88. Directive 2001/82/EC of the European Parliament and of the Council of 6 November 2001 on the Community Code Relating to Veterinary Medicinal Products; Commission Regulation (EC) No 1950/2006 of 13 December 2006 Establishing, in Accordance with Directive 2001/82/EC of the European Parliament and of the Council on the Community Code Relating to Veterinary Medicinal Products, a List of Substances Essential for the Treatment of Equidae.
89. Corrigendum to Council Directive 2004/68/EC of 26 April 2004 Laying Down Animal Health Rules for the Importation into and Transit through the Community of Certain Live Ungulate Animals, Amending Directives 90/426/EEC and 92/65/EEC and Repealing Directive 72/462/EEC.
90. "Campaigning for Horse Welfare," World Horse Welfare, accessed Sept. 21, 2011, http://www.worldhorsewelfare.org/help-tomorrow/campaigning.
91. Europe Must Act on Horse Welfare," Eurogroup for Animals, accessed Oct. 16, 2015, http://www.eurogroupforanimals.org/our-issues/act4equines/.
92. Banned drugs are listed in Commission Regulation (EU) No 37/2010 of 22 December 2009 on pharmacologically active substances and their classification regarding maximum residue limits in foodstuffs of animal origin, *Official Journal of the European Union* 20.1.2010.
93. A summary of EU regulations affecting the importation of live horses is European Commission, Intra-Union Trade in and Imports of Equine Animals;

European Commission, Health and Consumers Directorate—Directorate D—Animal Health and Welfare, "General Guidance on EU Import and Transit Rules for Live Animals and Animal Products from Third Countries" (2010); and European Union, Imports of Animals and Food of Animal Origin from Non-EU Countries; Summaries of all regulations of horse meat imports are found at European Union, Importation of Fresh Meat Derived from Domestic and Wild Ungulate (Hoofed) Animals. See also Council Directive 2009/156/EC of 30 November 2009 on Animal Health Conditions Governing the Movement and Importation from Third Countries of Equidae, text with EEA relevance, 2010 OJL 192.

94. EFSA Panel on Animal Health and Welfare (AHAW), "Scientific Opinion Concerning the Welfare of Animals during Transport," *EFSA Journal* 9 (1) (2011): 1966; European Commission, *Report from the Commission to the European Parliament and the Council on the Impact of Council Regulation (EC) No 1/2005 on the Protection of Animals during Transport*, Brussels, 10.11.2011, COM (2011) 700 final.

95. See United Kingdom, Food Standards Agency, "Survey of Undeclared Horse Meat or Donkeymeat in Salami and Salami-Type Products," Dec. 2003. See also Laurence Norman, "European Police Smash Gang Trading in Illegal Horse Meat," *Wall Street Journal* (Apr. 25, 2015).

96. See "Commission Implementing Decision of 19 February 2013," *Official Journal of the European Union*, L48/23, 2013; "EU Sets Out Post-Horsemeat Food Standards Revamp," *EU Business*, May 7, 2013; "Scant Progress Made in EU Horsemeat Regulation," Aug. 9, 2013, accessed Oct. 4. 2013, http://horsetalk.co.nz/2013/08/09/scant-progress-made-eu-horsemeat-regulation/#axzz2rhYWGEcr.

97. See Ken Wightman, "Canadian Protestors Fight to Ban Horse Meat," Oct. 4, 2010, accessed Aug. 1, 2011, http://www.digitaljournal.com/article/298495; "Furor over Horse Meat on Top Chef Canada," May 16, 2011, accessed Aug. 1, 2011, http://www.cbc.ca/news/arts/story/2011/05/16/horse-meat-tvshow.html; Aleksandra Sagan, "Europe's Horsemeat Scandal Spurs Canadian Consumption," CBC News, Feb. 26, 2013, accessed Feb. 27, 2013, http://www.cbc.ca/news/canada/story/2013/02/22/can-horsemeat-europe-scandal-canada-foodie.html.

98. "2010—Chambers of Carnage—Investigation of Bouvry Exports and Richelieu Meats," Canadian Horse Defence Coalition, accessed Oct. 15, 2015, http://defendhorsescanada.org/investigations/chambers-of-carnage.

99. See the brief commentary on the issue at a federal parliamentary hearing, 39th Parliament, 2nd Session, Standing Committee on Agriculture and Agri-Food, Tuesday, June 17, 2008, 1000–1005, 1020 ff.

100. "About the Horse Welfare Alliance of Canada," accessed Aug. 16, 2011, http://www.horsewelfare.ca/about.
101. Parliament of Canada, Bill C-544 (2010), accessed Aug. 15, 2011, http://www.parl.gc.ca/HousePublications/Publication.aspx?DocId=4633655.
102. "Livestock Inspection," Livestock Identification Services Ltd., accessed Aug. 16, 2011, http://www.lis-alberta.com/legislation/livestock_inspection.aspx.
103. Horses Slaughtered in Canada, 2006–2014, accessed Oct. 15, 2015, https://canadianhorsedefencecoalition.files.wordpress.com/2015/02/2014_statistics_r.pdf.
104. The number of licensed plants is currently greater than the number actively processing horses; see Search the List of Federally Registered Meat Establishments and Their Licensed Operators, Canadian Food Inspection Agency, accessed Aug. 8, 2011, http://www.inspection.gc.ca/active/scripts/meavia/reglist/reglist.asp?lang=e.
105. Calculated from "Import and Export Reports: Red Meat Trade (Imports and Exports): Canadian Red Meat Trade Balance by County and Commodity" Agriculture and Agri-Food Canada, accessed Oct. 17, 2015, http://www.agr.gc.ca/eng/industry-markets-and-trade/statistics-and-market-information/by-product-sector/red-meat-and-livestock/red-meat-market-information-canadian-industry/imports-and-exports/?id=1415860000005. Some meat exported to France might have been reshipped to other European nations.
106. See "Mad Cow Disease and Canada's Cattle Industry," Parliament of Canada, Parliamentary Information and Research Service, prepared by Frédéric Forge, Science and Technology Division, Jean-Denis Fréchette, Principal, Economics Division, Revised 12 July 2005.
107. Dr. Martin Appelt, National Veterinary Program Manager, Meat Programs Division, Government of Canada, e-mail to Richard A. Brisbin, Jr., Oct. 6, 2011.
108. Health of Animals Regulations, XII. Transportation of Animals, *Consolidated Regulations of Canada*, c. 296 (2011); "Transporting Horses in Canada: Is That Animal Fit for the Trip?," Canadian Food Inspection Agency, accessed Aug. 6, 2011, http://www.inspection.gc.ca/animals/terrestrial-animals/humane-transport/horses/fit-for-the-trip/eng/1363747385631/1363747449156.
109. European Commission Directorate-General for Health and Food Safety Directorate F—Food and Veterinary Office, *Final Report of an Audit Carried Out in Canada from 02 to 15 May 2014*, accessed July 3, 2015, http://ec.europa.eu/food/fvo/audit_reports/details.cfm?rep_id=3442, 1, 10–17; *Competent Authority Response to the Report's Recommendations*, accessed July 3, 2015, http://ec.europa.eu/food/fvo/audit_reports/details.cfm?rep_id=3442.
110. United Nations Food and Agriculture Organization, FAOSTAT, accessed Feb. 14, 2011, http://faostat.fao.org/site/339/default.aspx.

111. The Mexican group AnimaNaturalis has shown concern about Mexican horse slaughter; see "Las carreras de caballos," AnimaNaturalis, accessed Sept. 30, 2011, http://www.animanaturalis.org/p/603/las_carreras_de_caballos.
112. NOM-008-ZOO-1994, Especificaciones zoosanitarias para la construcción y equipamiento de establecimientos para el sacrificio de animales y los dedicados a la industrialización de productos cárnicos (Animal Health Specifications for the Construction and Equipment of Establishments for the Slaughter of Animals and Those Designated for the Industrial Processing of Meat Products).
113. M. L. Pérez Chabela, G. M. Rodríguez Serrano, P. Lara Calderón, and I. Guerrero, "Microbial Spoilage of Meats Offered for Retail Sale in Mexico City," *Meat Science* 51 (1999): 279–82. See also Gary Gereffi and Joonkoo Lee, "A Global Value Chain Approach to Food Safety and Quality Standards," Paper prepared for the Global Health Diplomacy for Chronic Disease Prevention Working Paper Series (2009), accessed Feb. 27, 2012, http://www.cggc.duke.edu/pdfs/GlobalHealth/Gereffi_Lee_GVCFoodSafety1_4Feb2009.pdf, 35–36.
114. "Final Report of a Mission Carried Out in Mexico from 22 November to 03 December 2010 in Order to Evaluate the Operation of Controls over the Production of Fresh Horse Meat and Meat Products Intended for Export to the European Union as Well as Certification Procedures," European Commission Health and Consumers Directorate-General, Directorate F—Food and Veterinary Office, accessed Aug. 16, 2011, http://tuesdayshorse.files.wordpress.com/2011/05/fvo_inspection_report_horse_meat_mexico_dec_2010.pdf.
115. "Final Report of an Audit Carried Out in Mexico from 29 May to 08 June 2012 in Order to Evaluate the Operation of Controls over the Production of Fresh Horse Meat and Meat Products Intended for Export to the European Union as Well as Certification Procedures," European Commission Health and Consumers Directorate-General Directorate F—Food and Veterinary Office, http://*ec.europa.eu/food/fvo/act_getPDF.cfm?PDF_ID=11431*.
116. "Mexican Horse Meat Banned by EU," *Journal of the American Veterinary Medical Association* 246 (2015): 389–90.
117. Braithwaite and Drahos, *Global Business Regulation*, 578–601, argue for the value of model codes in the development of transnational regulatory and enforcement practices.
118. See Donal Casey and Colin Scott, "The Crystallization of Regulatory Norms," *Journal of Law and Society* 38 (2011): 76–95.

8

Making Pet Policy: Roaming and Feral Cats

When socialized through human contact early in life and living indoors with humans, cats often enjoy a comfortable and cozy existence.[1] However, unrestrained outdoor cats can create a range of potential nuisances. They prey on wildlife and carry diseases that affect other animals and people. They can harm other pets and create dirt and noise in urbanized areas. How then has government attempted to address the unrestrained breeding of cats, the fate of casually abandoned cats, and the problems that irresponsible treatment of cats can generate? In this chapter we examine and compare how governments in Canada and the United States have devised policies that define some cats as nuisance property and regulate them. Using case studies of policymaking about spay/neuter, pet limitation ordinances, roaming at large laws, and laws that affect the human care of feral cat colonies (groups of "wild" cats that are not socialized to accept human contact), we depict the complex political struggles across a range of jurisdictions about the definition and regulation of some cats as a nuisance. Although cats have received less attention from policymakers than have dogs and horses, through these case studies we examine how the identity of cats, ideas about cruelty, and political conditions have contributed to policies to regulate cats.

THE CAT: DOMESTICATED AND FERAL

North American law treats cats either as owned (domesticated) or feral. In the majority of U.S. states the statutory or the common law defines a domesticated cat as personal property. Various states and municipalities have adopted laws that specifically affect the definition and management of owned or domesticated cats. California, Maine, and Rhode Island have the most comprehensive statutes. California has legislated spaying and neutering requirements, differential license fees for spayed and neutered cats, and holding periods for impounded cats.[2] Maine addresses the seizure of stray cats and vaccination requirements.[3] Rhode Island's cat law is aimed at reducing the number of free-roaming domestic cats and feral cats through a mandatory spay or neuter requirement. It is the only state that requires cat ownership to be identifiable by a tag, collar label, tattoo, or microchip and that requires permits to breed cats.[4]

Calgary, Alberta, has passed a bylaw requiring licenses for domesticated cats which also requires that their ownership be identifiable.[5] License requirements exist in communities scattered across the United States, such as Victorville, California; Howard County, Maryland; Minneapolis, Minnesota; Elkins, West Virginia; several communities in New Jersey; Alexandria, Hampton, Chesapeake, Norfolk, and Virginia Beach, Virginia; Seattle, Washington; and Madison and Waukesha, Wisconsin. However, licensing laws are not a common means to control the fecundity of cats, feral cat damage, and the surplus of unwanted animals. Although the passage of licensing laws finds support among interest groups such as the American Bird Conservancy, most pressure to adopt them seems to come from informal groups of neighbors bothered by stray cats.[6] On the other hand, cat owners have often appeared in large numbers at local council meetings to oppose licensing.[7] To avoid fines, they claim that licensing cats would force owners to confine their cats and control what some owners regard as their cat's natural need to roam. The interest group Alley Cat Allies contends that cat licensing will increase the number of cats in shelters, where nationally the adoption rate is so low that most end up euthanized.[8]

A few jurisdictions, such as Virginia, define feral cats as companion animals. Rhode Island law specifies how they are to be treated.[9] In most locales, however, feral cats often exist in a legal limbo in which the law is silent about their existence, they are "nongame mammals,"[10] or they are categorized as wildlife. In these legal situations they are unprotected by domesticated or companion animal anti-cruelty laws.[11] If a feral cat is cared for by a human, its status is determined either by the judiciary or, in a few jurisdictions, a feral cat ordinance.[12]

Despite predation by coyotes in rural areas and demise by freezing in colder climates, a cat overpopulation problem exists in North America.[13] In the United States the number of "owned" roaming cats may exceed forty million, and there are perhaps fifty million or more abandoned and feral cats.[14] Several Canadian cities have reported significant numbers of feral cats.[15] Often, roaming, abandoned, and feral cats become a significant nuisance that threatens public health, public peace, and the ecosystem. Although often opposed by animal welfare organizations, historically the policy of many North American communities has been to deal with surplus, roaming, and feral cats by rounding them up and exterminating them.[16] The vast majority of cats captured or turned in and held at shelters have ended their lives there. To control the threats to public health and the ecology posed by the indiscriminate breeding of cats and a lack of caretaker control of breeding, local governments have also adopted policies that limit the possession of cats to a small number per household.

SPAY/NEUTER LAWS AND DOMESTICATED CATS

To manage animal populations and prevent abandonment, numerous jurisdictions, including most American states, have adopted a variety of spay and neuter laws for both cats and dogs. There are no state spay/neuter laws that mandate the sterilization of all pets. Rhode Island has adopted legislation which requires all cats to be spayed or neutered unless the caretaker purchases a $100 breeding permit.[17] Most spay/neuter laws require the sterilization or a promise to sterilize before the adoption of an animal from a pound, animal shelter, or companion animal rescue organization. Most laws also require a monetary deposit to ensure future sterilization of adopted animals, and the majority of the states provide for certain exceptions.[18] Table 8.1 provides details on these laws for the states and provinces.

Only a few municipalities—Los Angeles County, California; Las Vegas and North Las Vegas, Nevada; Dallas, Texas; Winnipeg, Manitoba—require that most cats in the possession of caretakers be spayed or neutered. A Winnipeg, Manitoba, bylaw requires that residents "ensure that, if the cat is over the age of six months, it is sterilized unless a valid license for an unsterilized cat has been issued for the cat."[19] A few exceptions to mandatory sterilization exist for ill animals, and a few states and municipalities make exceptions for animals used for breeding purposes and for cats returned to their owner. However, most spay and neuter laws only apply to cats that come into the possession of a government animal control agency or private shelter, humane, or rescue organization. Most strays therefore avoid spaying or neutering.[20] If captured, before the animal is released to an owner or adopter the cat must be sterilized, usually at the expense of the owner, adopter, or private rescue organization. Alternatively, usually with immature animals, the owner or adopter must post a refundable deposit and sign a sterilization agreement. Violations of these laws can result in fines for owners, adopters, or the agencies that release the animal to them. In some states there are publicly funded programs to educate the public about the benefits of having animals sterilized, and financial incentives such as lower license fees for sterilized dogs and cats have been implemented. Using fines collected for violations of these statutes and license fees, some states and provinces provide financial assistance or grants to local governments and private organizations that offer low-income people reduced-cost spay/neuter services.[21]

Because most spay and neuter laws affect only the cats that come into shelters managed by government or private welfare organizations, volunteer organizations to educate or assist cat and dog caretakers with spaying and neutering have appeared in several communities. However, in a few communities, such as Pittsburgh, Pennsylvania, the government has sponsored free spay/neuter programs for municipal residents.[22] Although they can help control cat populations, their efforts to spay and neuter companion animals require a proactive effort by caretakers. Firm evidence of the comparative effectiveness of the variety of these programs in controlling cat populations or shelter intakes of cats is lacking. One study examined spay/neuter programs in New Hampshire and Texas. It showed that in New Hampshire there was a significant decrease in cat intake and euthanasia at shelters; however, there was no decrease in dog intake or euthanasia. The study also assessed the impact of an Austin, Texas, free spay/neuter program by comparing shelter intake and euthanasia data from the targeted program areas versus areas without a program within the city. The findings demonstrated a significantly lower rate for dog and cat intake and euthanasia in the program areas.[23] A study of privately sponsored spay/neuter programs in five communities in Alabama, Arizona, California, Florida, and Utah found that low-cost spay/neuter programs raised total community spay/neuter levels. However, the study disclosed no clear results on the impact of total spay/neuter procedures on shelter intake.[24] Another study in one county in North Carolina indicated that the creation of a spay/neuter clinic leveled off a pattern of increasing euthanasia in cats in dogs at the county shelter and reduced the number of cats impounded.[25]

If comprehensive mandatory spay and neuter regulations might dent the number of unwanted cats, why have governments not adopted them? In part the answer is the assumption that people should be responsible for the breeding habits of their pets. The cat is not identified as an object of public stewardship. Additionally, officials seem reluctant to spend limited public resources to address what initially will be a costly number of surgical procedures. Finally, it appears that organized interests have not effectively brought pressure on officials to adopt such policies, and public officials have rarely acted as entrepreneurs to sell spay and neuter. In this policy void, volunteer groups have struggled to protect the welfare of cats.

POSSESSION LIMITATION LAWS AND HOARDING

Whatever the reasons for uncontrolled breeding, the surplus of cats and other pets has stimulated some jurisdictions to establish policies to control the hoarding of animals. Among companion animals, domesticated cats and dogs are the animals most commonly collected by hoarders. Hoarders

TABLE 8.1 *State and Provincial Spay/Neuter Laws, 2013*

State or Province	No Spay/Neuter Requirements	Spay/Neuter from Shelters	Other Spay/Neuter Laws	Low-Cost Spay/Neuter Funding	Differential Licensing[a]
Alabama		x		x	
Alaska	x				
Arizona		x		x	x[b]
Arkansas		x[c]			
California		x[c]		x	x
Colorado		x		x	
Connecticut		x		x[d]	x
Delaware		x[c]		x	x
District of Columbia		x[c]		x	x
Florida		x		x	
Georgia		x		x	
Hawaii	x				
Idaho	x				
Illinois		x		x	x
Indiana	x			x	
Iowa		x			
Kansas		x			
Kentucky				x	
Louisiana		x		x	x
Maine		x		x	x
Maryland				x	x[b]
Massachusetts		x		x	x
Michigan		x		x	x
Minnesota	x				
Mississippi	x			x	
Missouri		x		x	x
Montana		x			
Nebraska		x			
Nevada		x[c]		x	
New Hampshire				x	x
New Jersey		x		x	x
New Mexico		x		x	
New York		x		x[d]	x
North Carolina	x			x	
North Dakota		x			

TABLE 8.1 *State and Provincial Spay/Neuter Laws, 2013—cont'd*

State or Province	No Spay/Neuter Requirements	Spay/Neuter from Shelters	Other Spay/Neuter Laws	Low-Cost Spay/Neuter Funding	Differential Licensing[a]
Ohio				x	x
Oklahoma		x		x	
Oregon	x				x
Pennsylvania		x			x
Rhode Island			x[e]	x	x[b]
South Carolina		x		x	
South Dakota	x				
Tennessee		x		x	
Texas		x		x	
Utah		x		x	
Vermont				x[d]	x
Virginia		x		x	
Washington	x			x	
West Virginia		x			x
Wisconsin	x				x
Wyoming	x				
Alberta	x				
British Columbia	x				
Manitoba	x				
New Brunswick	x				
Newfoundland & Labrador	x				
Northwest Territories	x				
Nova Scotia	x				x[b]
Nunavut	x				
Ontario	x[f]			x[g]	x[b]
Prince Edward Island	x[f]				
Quebec	x				
Saskatchewan	x[f]				
Yukon	x				

[a]The differential is usually $5 to $10.
[b]Law permits local option.
[c]Requires animals to be altered before placement. Others accept a deposit and/or signed agreement, or promise.
[d]Vouchers given to adopters.
[e]Requires all cats and all publicly owned animals to be spayed/neutered.
[f]Except for dogs adjudged dangerous.
[g]Local option.

are individuals, most commonly females, who obsessively persist in accumulating and keeping large numbers of companion animals as domestic pets without the ability to properly house, feed, or care for their health. Sometimes offenders hoard a combination of cats, dogs, and other animals; however, often hoarders' actions result in the overcrowding of cats in a small space, malnourishment, filthy and unsanitary homes, the presence of dead animals, excrement, and insects, and a lack of veterinary care that results in the spread of disease.[26]

Cat hoarders often minimize the problems and living conditions of the animals while regarding their collection of animals as saintly, moral, or virtuous.[27] As one animal control officer has noted, "Collectors are blinded by love." They react to questions about why they hoard by statements such as, "I love them. I just try to help them. People I know love the cats, so they bring them to me. How can I say no?"[28]

Cat hoarding can result in complaints by neighbors, landlords, utility workers, social workers, police, firefighters, or local government code inspectors, who contact local animal control authorities. If there is probable cause to suspect a code violation, a search warrant might be sought by the authorities. The investigation by animal control and other local officers can result in criminal charges for animal cruelty or violations of housing and public health codes, civil orders that mandate changes in the number of animals and their care, the protection of children or seniors on the property, and mental health care for the hoarder. If charges are filed, they commonly are for misdemeanor or citation offenses, including violations of animal licensing, anti-cruelty, and rabies vaccination ordinances; health, zoning, and fire safety codes; wildlife statutes; or agriculture or market codes.[29] Prosecutors often do not file multiple cruelty charges against hoarders because they feel that they clog the system or present evidentiary problems related to the lack of a specific possession limitation ordinance. Before trial psychological evaluations are sometimes ordered, and a veterinarian may examine the animals and appear as a witness if there is a trial. Most defendants have their cases terminated with a bargained guilty plea or a verdict of guilt after a brief bench trial. Probation, fines, and limitations on cat ownership are the common penalties.[30]

Cats may be seized and assigned care in a variety of ways. Severely ill animals can be immediately destroyed, and other animals might be cared for temporarily by animal welfare groups or a public animal shelter as "evidence" in the case. After a decision in the case, cats can be adopted or destroyed. Private care for the animals after the closure of the case is almost always uncompensated. The locale of the hoarding can require disinfection or even demolition that often creates costs for public health agencies. In a few cases the hoarder has been able to secure the return of their cat as "property," and recidivism is not uncommon.[31] (Often the treatment of dog hoarding cases is similar. Because of costs and a lack of facilities, horses present more difficulties in the arrangement of care.)

To prevent the collection of cats by hoarders and avoid problems with the use of anti-cruelty and other laws in prosecutions, some communities in Canada and the United States have adopted animal ownership or possession limitation ordinances. Most ordinances limit the number of animals, and a few have restrictions on the size, place of residence, or physical condition of the cat or dog. For example, Los Angeles County, California, limits property owners to three cats, or up to five cats if all cats are spayed and neutered and live primarily indoors.[32] A Winnipeg bylaw states that without an "excess animal permit," "no person may own, harbour, keep, have in his or her possession, or have on a single parcel of land of which he or she is the occupant a total of more than six dogs and cats over the age of six months, of which no more than four may be dogs."[33]

A small number of U.S. states have adopted laws that more specifically address hoarding. Hawai'i has made it a misdemeanor when a person "intentionally, knowingly, or recklessly: (a) Possesses more than fifteen dogs, cats, or a combination of dogs and cats; (b) Fails to provide necessary sustenance for each dog or cat; and (c) Fails to correct the conditions under which the dogs or cats are living, where conditions injurious to the dogs', cats', or owner's health and well-being result from the person's failure to provide necessary sustenance."[34]

Illinois law defines a "companion animal hoarder" as "a person who (i) possesses a large number of companion animals; (ii) fails to or is unable to provide what he or she is required to provide under Section 3 of this Act

[Section 3 states the duties as the provision of water, food, shelter, veterinary care, and humane treatment]; (iii) keeps the companion animals in a severely overcrowded environment; and (iv) displays an inability to recognize or understand the nature of or has a reckless disregard for the conditions under which the companion animals are living and the deleterious impact they have on the companion animals' and owner's health and well-being." Persons who violate this law are guilty of a misdemeanor for the first offense; a second or subsequent violation is a felony. The judge also can order convicted persons to undergo a psychological or psychiatric evaluation and treatment at the convicted person's expense.[35]

To deter hoarding, in 2013 Oregon adopted legislation that provided for two degrees of criminal animal cruelty. Possible felony charges could be filed for neglect or cruelty if the individual had prior convictions for animal law violations, possessed more than ten animals, or committed the offense in the presence of a minor child. Persons could face enhanced penalties for the neglect of ten to forty and more than forty animals, and they could be prohibited from possession of animals. The law also provided penalties for hoarders who claimed to be rescue organizations but who failed to meet new licensing procedures.[36]

Pet owners have challenged U.S. cat and dog possession limitation laws in court. Litigation has resulted in support for such laws when the judge deemed them "reasonable" measures that promoted legitimate government goals such as public health and were supported by evidence that the limitation on number of pets served a governmental goal such as public health and disease prevention, public peace, or public safety.[37]

Canadian federal and provincial law does not directly address the issue of cat and dog hoarding. Federal law does not establish a possession limit or a standard of care, nor does it define negligence in the care of cats. Therefore, "given that there is no actual provision in Canadian law that addresses animal hoarding, it is difficult to get a sense of how often ... cases come to court and how they are dealt with."[38]

Despite the lack of federal and provincial law, some Canadian cites have adopted pet limitation bylaws. For example a Toronto bylaw states that "no person shall keep in any dwelling unit more than six of any combination of dogs, cats, ferrets and rabbits" and Vancouver, British Columbia, limits dog possession to three animals but does not limit the number of cats.[39] An analysis of the few published judicial opinions in hoarding cases found that they result in minor penalties and that evidence of benevolence or good intentions is a defense against more severe sentences. However, with police presence and a warrant, a cat in distress can be seized to relieve its distress.[40] No legal provisions exist for the payment of the costs to shelters for the care of companion animals seized as evidence in a hoarding case, and, unless relinquished as part of a sentence, seized animals remain the property of the hoarder.[41] Nonetheless, a British Columbia judge allowed the seizure of a hoard of feral cats to relieve their distress.[42] However, another British Columbia judge ordered a hoarder's cats returned because they were healthy and the seizure violated principles of procedural fairness.[43]

Although evidentiary problems, especially related to searches and seizures, affect the utility of the application of existing animal anti-cruelty laws, the lack of attention to the problem and blind eye cast by neighbors, public service workers, and public inspectors contributes to the existence of hoarding. If animal possession limitation laws might facilitate and stimulate actions against hoarders, why have most governments not adopted them? Since hoarding is often defined as a problem for local governments to address, the reason appears in part to be the lack of organized efforts to address the problem in most jurisdictions. Additionally, because hoarding incidents tend to draw attention infrequently and are often regarded as a mental health problem among humans, hoarding is not identified as the continuing direction of cruelty and abuse at animals that has stimulated organized interests' efforts and politicians' attention to campaigns designed to end puppy mills and horse slaughter.

CATS ROAMING AT LARGE

Whether domesticated or feral, roaming or abandoned domestic cats are regarded by many communities as nuisance property whose frequent breeding causes public health problems. Officials have adopted laws in an effort to manage this perceived threat. For example, Los Angeles County, California, regards roaming cats to be a menace to public health. County officials have linked cat fleas to the occurrence of typhus and have found evidence that cat feces has caused outbreaks of parasitic diseases, including toxoplasmosis, cryptosporidiosis, giardiasis, roundworm, and hookworm. When complaints from the public about cats occur, the Department of Public Health can cite the owner or lessee of the property where the cats live and order them to abate the cause of cat-borne diseases, limit the number of cats, or surrender the cats to Department of Animal Care and Control.[44] In many jurisdictions animal control officers can seize roaming cats without identification and permit humane disposal of the unclaimed cat after a few days.[45] Hampton, Virginia, makes it unlawful to permit any cat owned or kept by a person to run or go at large within the city unless the cat is spayed or neutered and properly licensed.[46] Winnipeg also requires cat licenses.[47] Judges have upheld these and related laws that permit the euthanasia of cats captured or trapped while roaming as rational exercises of regulatory powers.[48]

Another effort to control roaming cats is the cat leash or confinement law. For example, in Dallas, Texas, outdoor cats must be restrained by a handheld leash or in a fenced area or cage.[49] York County, South Carolina, requires a leash or confinement for all pets when they are outdoors.[50] Because it believes that these laws encourage the relinquishment of cats to shelters where they face likely euthanasia, the groups Cat Fanciers' Association and Alley Cat Allies oppose cat leash laws.[51] As in Barre, Vermont, local disputes about the adoption of cat leash laws have sparked spirited opposition from local cat fanciers.[52]

By and large laws to control roaming cats address the needs of the human population. A "right to roam" for domesticated cats has not made its way into North American law. Roaming cats have no independent legal rights. When a cat is injured or killed by another person while roaming, it is the owner who must file a lawsuit to recover damages. Traditional computation of damages for the loss of the cat is its market value—the amount of money someone would pay for the identical cat of the same, age, breed, and condition. Since most domesticated cats are of mixed breed, they have little or no market value and the owner is left without compensation. Whether legislative or judicial, public policy toward roaming domesticated cats therefore assumes the cat is a form of property subject to government regulation. Yet, many jurisdictions lack specific policies designed to make owners responsible for their cat. Instead, under their police power to protect public safety and health, governments have assumed the authority to capture and exterminate roaming domestic cats as a way to manage their roaming and excessive breeding.

FERAL CATS

Around 1900 the first organized efforts in the United States to protect the welfare of feral cats appeared. Today organizations such as the national group Alley Cat Allies and its local branches and Neighborhood Cats seek policies to protect feral cats.[53] Canadian groups, such as the Cat Action Team of Prince Edward Island, Cat Rescue Maritimes, and the Ottawa Humane Society, also have sought to protect roaming and feral cats from extermination.[54] Although cat-oriented groups pursue anti-cruelty and mandatory spay/neuter legislation, operate shelters or adoption programs, and conduct educational programs and distribute information about the proper care of cats, they have directly addressed the feral cat issue by sponsoring trap-neuter-release (TNR) programs.[55] These programs require that persons feed groups or colonies of feral cats on schedule at a specific location, trap them in large cages at the feeding site, assess their health and behavior, have the cats neutered, place the socialized stray ones for adoption, return the others to the site of trapping with ears tipped for recognition purposes, and provide oversight and feeding of the colony.[56] However, a TNR colony manger has written, "The success of TNR depends largely upon the motivation of a colony's caretakers—those who monitor the colony's members and attend to their daily needs."[57]

TNR and the Law

Although there is a lack of comprehensive data, in the United States probably most TNR programs function as either informal private associations or nonprofit corporations that have to comply only with federal tax laws. Most states and municipalities have not established laws or regulations of TNR programs. However, from our observations, it appears that more legalized accountability for these programs is emerging. In particular because of pressure from the organizations supporting TNR or complaints about feral cats, several communities have passed ordinances or bylaws that legalize and sometimes financially subsidize private organizations or individuals engaged in TNR.

Three types of TNR ordinances have been enacted in the United States: "(1) sponsor-based, which require caretakers to register their colonies with a private organization or individual acting as a sponsor of the TNR program, (2) caretaker-based, which require caretakers to register their colonies directly with the municipality or its agent, and (3) delegations of authority, which legalize TNR efforts and give a designated government agency the task of promulgating TNR program guidelines."[58] A sponsor-based ordinance requires that a colony caretaker register the colony with an eligible sponsor such as an animal welfare group, humane society, rescue group, or individual approved by the municipality. Groups or persons become sponsors by meeting certain requirements and submitting a letter of intent, as in Clark County, Nevada (Las Vegas), and Cook County, Illinois (Chicago), or through application to and approval by the municipality. Sponsors can help protect the privacy of caretakers and their colonies by holding information normally considered confidential, such as caretaker identities and colony locations. They can provide interested caretakers with the documentation necessary to receive public and private funding and offer training to caretakers. They can also act as mediators between caretakers and residents with complaints related to the colony and advise animal control about feral issues. Caretakers are responsible for trapping the cats, sterilization, and regular visits to provide food, water, and necessary veterinary care to the colony. Often, as in Cook County, they are required to provide sponsors with sterilization and vaccination records and information about the number of cats in the colony, the number of cats sterilized and vaccinated, the number of kittens born to colony cats and their disposition, and the number of cats that have died or otherwise ceased to be part of the colony. Animal control agencies can be charged with overseeing the performance of duties by the sponsor and caretaker and can have duties to protect colonies and address complaints about them. They can also enforce limitations on the size of colonies.[59]

Under a caretaker-based ordinance a colony caretaker must register the colony directly with the municipality or its animal control agency or apply to the municipality for a colony permit.[60] Often caretakers must provide their identity and colony location during the registration process. In addition, caretakers and animal control officers can be required to exercise the same duties as under a sponsor-based legislative scheme.

A third category of TNR ordinance assigns the regulation of TNR practices to a specific municipal agency. Rather than delineating caretaker or animal control agency responsibilities, an ordinance delegating authority generally approves the practice of TNR in the community and authorizes a municipal agency to promulgate guidelines or rules and oversee caretakers. Under the regulations caretakers and animal control officers can be required to exercise the same duties as under a sponsor-based legislative scheme. For example, a Baltimore (City), Maryland, ordinance delegates to its health commissioner the authority to regulate feral cats and feral cat caretakers. After a period of public comment, the commissioner used this authority to institute regulations governing responsibilities of caretakers, acceptable standards of care, and duties of animal control officers.[61]

Other legal issues have shaped or at least created legal uncertainty in the conduct of feral cat control and TNR programs. Statutes and ordinances are sometimes not clear about evidentiary assessments or penalties of caretakers who do not satisfy registration requirements for a colony, who fail to satisfy vaccination or sterilization rules, who fail to mark colony cats by tattoo or ear tipping, or who abandon a colony.[62] Questions exist about whether environmental protections laws and ordinances can make colony caretakers responsible if their cats prey on other species.[63] Since most TNR organizations do not carry liability insurance, TNR caretakers can also face personal injury or trespass litigation for their actions. In jurisdictions that both have and do not have feral cat laws, a very small number of cases consider whether a caretaker or person in some degree of control or "ownership" can be liable for tort damages caused by the feral cats. A California appellate court held that a nuisance and emotional distress claim, which was based on the defendants' alleged failure to cease activity that resulted in the attraction of feral and domestic cats to the plaintiffs' backyard, survived summary judgment.[64] In jurisdictions where feral cat keepers or caretakers are considered the cats' legal owners, keepers and caretakers may also be liable for damage caused by feral cats to property or persons. The key question is whether the caretaker has a duty to control a cat's behavior. Judges commonly find a duty only if the damages caused by a feral cat trespassing on property or injuring someone were reasonably foreseeable.[65] Determining when a feral cat caretaker may be criminally liable under anti-cruelty laws and other local laws for abandonment or failure to care adequately for a colony, or for failure to comply with license, vaccination, and spay and neuter laws for cats in the colony, has not been fully addressed by the courts.[66]

TNR Programs in Operation

Many TNR programs involve a few volunteers who manage one colony of less than a dozen cats. Although they network with other colony caretakers, they operate independently of any formal organization and often without government authorization or support. However, a few larger, formally organized programs exist. One of the largest is the New York City Feral Cat Initiative (NYCFCI). It is one of more than 150 members of the Mayor's Alliance for NYC's Animals, a 501(c)(3) nonprofit charity that is the umbrella organization for animal welfare in New York City. NYCFCI provides traps and cages for feral cat capture and arranges transportation of traps and cats; offers a variety of educational materials, an online newsletter, and advice by telephone; provides workshops on cat welfare and feral cat colony management, shelter, and health; provides referrals to spay/neuter programs and low cost veterinary services; and assists persons in the completion of no-fee TNR certification workshops or online TNR certification courses. Feral cat caretakers must sign adoption, foster, or caretaker and coach legal agreements with NYCFCI. They also are informed about New York laws on trespass, rabies vaccinations, and the establishment of ownership of cats.[67]

Another example of a large TNR organization is Save a Kitty Feral Cat Program, an incorporated nonprofit organization operating in more than a dozen counties in the Ohio River Valley of Ohio and West Virginia. Kandi Habeb started Save a Kitty in July of 2004. Today the group has dozens of people who feed colonies or support them in other ways. About sixty people are actively involved in feeding about one hundred colonies.

Each colony averages close to twenty cats, but some are bigger and some have only two or three cats.

Save a Kitty requires that persons who want to participate in managing a colony complete five forms, including an agreement that they will trap the cats, will transport them to a facility for spaying or neutering and vaccinations, and will not take animals to a shelter for euthanasia. They have to agree to feed and otherwise care for the cats on a regular basis. Some colony caretakers buy their own food, but the group will provide food if they can and it is needed. Some volunteers do not feed cats but instead provide food for particular colonies that others then use. A veterinarian holds clinics for the group and performs spaying and neutering on cats at her clinic.

Save a Kitty conducts public awareness education. They have a website and newsletter and they network with other groups. People often e-mail them for help regarding feral or stray cats and they receive referrals from animal control officers. Because they encounter problems with people harming cats, in one instance shooting them with bows and arrows, they post copies of the state law in various locations so people know they cannot kill cats. To protect colonies they do not publicize the location of the colonies and they try to keep a low profile about where they are feeding cats. When people complain about colonies, they move the cats.

A Florida study reported that most colony caretakers are overwhelmingly middle-age females who own more than one cat and who express sympathy or ethical concern toward cats.[68] For example, one woman in Parkersburg, West Virginia, reported that she became involved in Save a Kitty when she was asked to take a mother cat and kittens in the fall of 2004. Although the numbers fluctuate as cats are hit by cars, killed by dogs, or come to the colony in some way, she now has about seventeen cats in a colony adjacent to her property. Many cats in her colony were relocated from Athens, Ohio. A man was feeding about fifty cats in a trailer court but could not afford to continue. The Athens shelter contacted Alley Cat Allies, and Save a Kitty was the closest group that could help. Since she had a colony in place, she agreed to take twenty-one cats that had been caught in fifteen traps. Three were adopted, but eighteen joined her colony. She also has seven dogs and fosters dogs for a local shelter and a rescue group.

To support its caretakers Save a Kitty applies for grants, but it has not received any support from any of the local governments. It has received a

$2,000 grant from WV-SNAP (a West Virginia Federation of Humane Organiztions spay and neuter program), a $12,000 grant from the retailer PetSmart, small grants from the Petco Foundation, Wal-Mart Stores, the Humane Society of the United States, the governor's community participation grant program, and money from three state delegates' discretionary funds. Dinners, book sales, yard sales, bingo, and other events also support the organization. Because it had bad experiences with other "rescue" groups, originally the Humane Society that ran a local shelter did not assist Save a Kitty. However, after Save a Kitty proved its viability, the Humane Society shelter became supportive of its efforts. Although the shelter normally euthanizes cats after holding them for five days, it calls Save a Kitty when cats have an ear tip to indicate membership in a colony.

Save a Kitty has worked with West Virginia state legislators to introduce several different bills to help cats. It has sought a law to permit the registration of feral cat colonies. However, the state's Veterinary Commission does not support TNR, and the Department of Agriculture has in the past refused to support laws requiring it to deal with companion animal issues. The Veterinary Commission regulations of veterinarians affect TNR because they do not allow mobile spay and neuter vans to come into the state from outside and will only allow an in-state van to go one hundred miles from the base clinic. County commissioners have been more supportive of the organization. For example, one commissioner asked for donations to Save a Kitty in lieu of flowers when her mother died. And the local media has treated its efforts positively. In one county in which the group was active, a 2009 task force on animal issues recommended a license on cats, differential licensing for spayed and neutered pets, and direct support for Save a Kitty, but nothing has happened.[69]

Is TNR Successful?

As the experiences of Save a Kitty imply, TNR programs are not always popular and they have become a source of political struggles in some communities. Because of the waste, noise, and occasional property destruction feral cats create, residents often regard them to be a nuisance.[70] Other persons and several national wildlife interest groups believe that feral cats carry diseases harmful to their pets, kill songbirds, and damage wildlife habitats by killing the small mammals which serve as a food source for other mammals and birds. Regarding cats as an invasive species, interest groups such as the American Bird Conservancy and The Wildlife Society have campaigned against TNR.[71] Unlike groups such as Alley Cat Allies that adopt a frame of stewardship to protect the feral cat population, the anti-TNR groups utilize a more comprehensive frame that demands human stewardship of the broader environment.[72] In support of their position, these groups cite numerous scientific studies that find feral colonies, even if part of a TNR program, prey on wildlife, threaten some endangered species, and carry a higher rate of disease-causing pathogens. Additionally, they note findings that suggest the limited scope of most TNR programs, the inability of volunteers to devote enough time to colony management, the economic cost of trapping, neutering, and managing a colony, and the difficulty in trapping and neutering the 70 percent or more of cats necessary to reduce their population in an area mean that the effect of a program on the overall feral and roaming cat population can be isolated and often temporary.[73] But despite significant questions about the utility of TNR, limited evidence suggests these programs have reduced the problems associated with feral cats. An animal control officer in the area managed by Save a Kitty reported a reduction in the number of cats entering the shelter.[74] Caretakers have noted that the number of cats in their care diminish over time, but they cannot confirm the decline in numbers to be directly associated with neutering.[75]

At present TNR remains at best a localized and incomplete solution to the feral cat issue and related problems of cat overpopulation. TNR programs remain largely volunteer efforts that depend greatly on the energy of their members. Governments have authorized some TNR programs and provided occasional limited financial support, but most have not adopted any policies or regulations that give legitimacy or support to the programs. Feral cats, consequently, remain subject to the actions of their human neighbors and animal control officers as well as the vicissitudes of life in the wild.

CONCLUSION

Human neglect of cats has significantly contributed to a roaming, abandoned, and feral problem cat for humans. Organized interests have stimulated some policymaking efforts to address the problems associated with cats. But, save in a tiny number of municipalities, no comprehensive approach to address the source of the problem—an overpopulation of cats—has appeared. Instead, if they bother to address the cat population, governments continue to use euthanasia and policies that require human responsibility for the care of cats. Also, to protect cats individuals and organized interests have developed spay and neuter and TNR programs. However, these programs do not exist in many jurisdictions, and governments often lack the financial resources to serve the needs of cats in their community.

Given the very large number of pet cats, it is surprising that cat-related public policy conflicts seem to be more a managerial reaction to the noise, dirt, threat to wildlife, and other nuisances that cats might cause in public and private spaces rather than an effort to improve the lives of animals and guard them against forms of passive cruelty. Also, what is noticeable is the lack of organized interests using political tactics, such as lobbying and public relations campaigns, and the lack of policy entrepreneurship by both private individuals and, in particular, public officials to develop laws and policies to improve public responsibility for the treatment of cats. These conditions have deterred the development of legal changes to benefit the welfare of cats and have encouraged private stewardship to supplant the lack of law and policies. Consequently, the unwanted cat remains too often framed as a nuisance and a problem for humans and less as a victim in need of public as well as private efforts to ameliorate the hurts it suffers.

NOTES

1. Patrick Bateson, "Behavioural Development in the Cat," in *The Domestic Cat: The Biology of Its Behaviour*, 2nd ed., ed. Dennis C. Turner and Patrick Bateson (Cambridge: Cambridge University Press, 2000), 9–22; Sandra McCune, "The Impact of Paternity and Early Socialisation on the Development of Cats'

Behaviour to People and Novel Objects," *Applied Animal Behaviour Science* 45 (1995): 109–24; Michael Mendl and Robert Harcourt, "Individuality in the Domestic Cat: Origins, Development, and Stability," in *The Domestic Cat*, 47–64; Claudia Mertens, "Human–Cat Interactions in the Home Setting," *Anthrozoös* 4 (1991): 214–31.
2. *Annotated California Codes, Food and Agricultural Code* §§ 31751–31765.
3. *7 Maine Revised Statutes Annotated* §§ 3916–3919-C.
4. *General Laws of Rhode Island Annotated* §§ 4-22-1–22.10, 4-24-1–13.
5. *Bylaw Number 23M2006, Being a Bylaw of the City of Calgary Respecting the Regulation, Licensing and Control of Animals in the City of Calgary*, 4. Cat Licensing.
6. "Get the Facts about Cat Law," American Bird Conservancy, accessed July 20, 2013, http://abcbirds.org/wp-content/uploads/2015/05/GettheFactsabout CatLaw2011.pdf. An example of efforts to secure cat licensing is Tim O'Brien, "Stray Cat Boom Calls for a Fix," *Times Union* (Albany, NY), July 20, 2010, accessed Oct. 15, 2015, http://www.timesunion.com/local/article/Stray-cat-boom-brings-calls-for-a-fix-583266.php.
7. Jeff Mikorski, City Manager, Morgantown, WV, interview by Susan Hunter, Apr. 8, 2014.
8. "Cat Licensing: A License to Kill," Alley Cat Allies, accessed July 15, 2013, http://www.alleycat.org/page.aspx?pid=397.
9. *Virginia Code Annotated* § 3.2-6500; *Rhode Island Statutes* §§ 4-22-2, -5, -6, -8.
10. *Annotated California Codes. Fish and Game Code* §§ 4150–4151.
11. *Nebraska Revised Statutes* § 37-246-247.
12. For examples see *Connecticut General Statutes* § 22-339d; *Illinois Compiled Statutes* Ch. 510 § 5/35; and David Fry, "Detailed Discussion of Feral Cat Issues," Animal Legal and Historical Center, Michigan State University College of Law, 2010, accessed July 12, 2012, http://www.animallaw.info/articles/ddusferalcat2010.htm.
13. Irene Rochlitz, "Feline Welfare Issues," in *The Domestic Cat*, 208–11.
14. See Julie K. Levy and P. Cynthia Crawford, "Humane Strategies for Controlling Feral Cat Populations," *Journal of the American Veterinary Medical Association* 225 (2004): 1355.
15. "Feral Cats in the City of London," accessed Oct. 16, 2015, https://www.london.ca/residents/animal-services/ps-pet-protection/Pages/Feral-Cats-in-the-City-of-London.aspx; "Feral Cats—Public Meeting Report on CBC—MikeCohen.avi" (Côte Saint-Luc, Québec), accessed July 13, 2012, http://www.youtube.com/watch?v=5ipp6UuuN70; "Stray Cats a Big Problem" (Windsor, Ontario), Canada.com, accessed July 13, 2012, http://www.canada.com/windsorstar/story.html?id=4071c08b-415b-49a9-9804-c01a6d610518; Brodie Fellon,

"Toronto's War on Homeless Cats," Cnews, http://cnews.canoe.ca/CNEWS/Canada/2007/02/09/3569010-sun.html.

16. Verne R. Smith, "The Law and Feral Cats," *Journal of Animal Law and Ethics* 3 (2009): 7. See also Jennifer Fiala, "Feral Cat Crackdown Evokes Emotional Public Debate," *DVM: The Newsmagazine of Veterinary Medicine* 34 (2003): 1, 42; Jim Montavalli, "Kitty the Killer? The Raging Debate over Feral Cats," *E—The Environmental Magazine* 14, no. 5 (2003): 14, 22–25.

17. *Rhode Island General Laws* § 4-22-1.

18. "Summary Report: Mandatory Spay/Neuter Laws" was published by the American Veterinary Medical Association in November 2009 and can be found online at http://www.avma.org/advocacy/state/issues/sr_spay_neuter_laws.asp (accessed May 11, 2011).

19. City of Winnipeg, By-Law 92/2013, 18(1)(a) (2013).

20. "Missing the Target: Mandatory Spay/Neuter Legislation Fails to Reach Most Intact Cats," Alley Cat Allies, accessed July 15, 2013, http://www.alleycat.org/document.doc?id=240.

21. For overviews of these laws, see Cynthia Hodges, "Detailed Discussion of State Spay and Neuter Laws," Animal Legal and Historical Center, Michigan State University College of Law, accessed July 12, 2012, http://www.animallaw.info/articles/ddusspayneuter.htm#fn15; "Summary Report: Mandatory Spay/Neuter Laws," American Veterinary Medical Association, accessed July 12, 2012, http://www.avma.org/advocacy/state/issues/sr_spay_neuter_laws.asp. On the operations of state programs, see Sharon J. Secovich, "Case Study: Companion Animal Over-Population Programs in New Jersey, New Hampshire, and Maine and a New Program for Maine," accessed July 12, 2012, http://www.spayusa.org/assets/pdfs/study_three_state_programs.pdf. On Canada, see Simon Shields, "Establishing Low-Cost Spay-Neuter Services for Cats in Ontario," accessed Aug. 9, 2012, http://www.isthatlegal.ca/index.php?name=spay_neuter.dog_cat_control_ontario.

22. "City of Pittsburgh Spay/Neuter Program," City of Pittsburgh, accessed Oct. 24, 2014, http://www.pittsburghpa.gov/animalcontrol/spay_neuter.htm. The program is currently "on hold."

23. Sara C. White, Ellen Jefferson, and Julie K. Levy, "Impact of Publicly Sponsored Neutering Programs on Animal Population Dynamics at Animal Shelters: The New Hampshire and Austin Experiences," *Journal of Applied Animal Welfare Science* 13 (2010): 191–212.

24. Joshua M. Frank and Pamela L. Carlisle-Frank, "Analysis of Programs to Reduce Overpopulation of Companion Animals: Do Adoption and Low-Cost Spay/Neuter Programs Merely Cause Substitution of Sources?," *Ecological Economics* 62 (2007): 740–46.

25. Janet Scarlett and Naomi Johnston, "Impact of a Subsidized Spay Neuter Clinic on Impoundments and Euthanasia in a Community Shelter and on Service and Complaint Calls to Animal Control," *Journal of Applied Animal Welfare Science* 15 (2012): 53–69.
26. See Allison Estes and Tina Salaks, *Paw and Order: Dramatic Investigation by an Animal Cop on the Beat* (Laguna Hills, CA: BowTie Press, 2008), 32–43.
27. See also, Arnold Arluke, *Just a Dog: Understanding Animal Cruelty and Ourselves* (Philadelphia: Temple University Press, 2006), 85–114; Christiana Bratiotis, Cristina Sorrentino Schmalisch, and Gail Steketee, *The Hoarding Handbook: A Guide for Human Service Professionals* (New York: Oxford University Press, 2011), 110; Sue-Ellen Brown, "Theoretical Concepts from Self Psychology Applied to Animal Hoarding," *Society and Animals* 19 (2011) 175–93; Gary J. Patronek, Lynn Loar, and Jane N. Nathanson, *Animal Hoarding: Structuring Interdisciplinary Responses to Help People, Animals, and Communities at Risk* (Boston: Hoarding of Animals Research Consortium, 2006), 1; Randy O. Frost et al., "The Hoarding of Animals: An Update," *Psychiatric Times* Apr. 30, 2015, accessed Oct. 17, 2015, http://www.psychiatrictimes.com/addiction/hoarding-animals-update.
28. Estes and Salaks, *Paw and Order,* 39.
29. Victoria Hayes, "Detailed Discussion of Animal Hoarding," Animal Legal and Historical Center, Michigan State University College of Law, 2012, accessed July 11, 2012, http://www.animallaw.info/articles/ddushoarding.htm.
30. Colin Berry, Gary Patronek, and Randall Lockwood, "Long-Term Outcomes in Animal Hoarding Cases," *Animal Law* 11 (2005): 167–94.
31. See Ibid., 183–87; Lisa Avery, "From Helping to Hoarding to Hurting: When Acts of 'Good Samaritans' Become Felony Animal Cruelty," *Valparaiso University Law Review* 39 (2005): 815–58; Bratiotis, Schmalisch, and Steketee, *Hoarding Handbook,* 115–16, 126–36. For a legal decision supporting the seizure of animals, see Animal Legal Defense Fund v. Woodley, 640 S.E.2d 777 (N.C. 2007), appeal dismissed 652 S.E.2d 254 (N.C. 2007).
32. County of Los Angeles Departments of Public Health and Animal Care and Control, "County Policies Relating to Free-Roaming Cats," accessed May 16, 2012, http://file.lacounty.gov/dacc/cms1_197084.pdf.
33. City of Winnipeg, By-Law 92/2013, 25(2) (2013).
34. *Hawaii Revised Statutes* § 711-1109.6. Animal hoarding.
35. *Illinois Compiled Statutes Annotated* 510 ILCS 70/2.10, 70/3.
36. *Oregon Revised Statutes* §§ 87.159, 167.320, 167.322, 167.325, 167.330, 167.332, 167.347, 167.348.
37. See Joan E. Schaffner, *An Introduction to Animals and the Law* (New York: Palgrave MacMillan, 2011), 120–22; Rebecca F. Wisch, "Overview of Pet

Number Restrictions in Municipal Ordinances," Michigan State University College of Law, 2004, accessed July 31, 2012, http://www.animallaw.info/articles/ddusdognumberordinances.htm; Holt v. City of Sauk Rapids, 559 N.W.2d 444 (Minn. 1997). Gates v. City of Sanford, 566 So. 2d 47, 49 (D.C. Fla. 1990); People v. Strobridge, 339 N.W.2d 531, 535 (Mich. App. 1983); People v. Yeo, 302 N.W.2d 883, 885–86 (Mich. App. 1981); Downing v. Cook, 431 N.E.2d 995, 997 (Ohio 1982); Village of Carpentersville v. Fiala, 425 N.E.2d 33, 341 (Ill. App. 1981); State v. Mueller, 265 N.W. 103, 105–06 (Wis. 1936).

38. Kathryn M. Campbell, "The Paradox of Animal Hoarding and the Limits of Canadian Criminal Law," *Journal of Animal and Natural Resource Law* 9 (2013): 54.

39. *Toronto Municipal Code* § 349-4. Vancouver also bans keeping more than six hamsters, guinea pigs, tame mice, chinchillas, cats, rabbits, and other small animals and reptiles including snakes, twelve registered homing pigeons, canaries, budgerigars, parrots, parakeets, and exotic birds of all species, and four hens; City of Vancouver, British Columbia, *Animal Control By-Law No. 9150*, 4.6, 7.5 (2012).

40. See Lesli Bisgould, *Animals and the Law* (Toronto: Irwin Law, 2011), 110–14.

41. Campbell, "The Paradox of Animal Hoarding and The Limits of Canadian Criminal Law," 57–58; Manoir Kanisha Inc. v. Wira Jakowenko [2009] Q.J. No. 16681 2009 QCCQ 14904.

42. Ulmer v. British Columbia Society for the Prevention of Cruelty to Animals [2010] B.C.J. No. 2277, 2010 BCCA 519, 295 B.C.A.C. 282, 11 B.C.L.R. (5th) 324.

43. Haughton v. British Columbia Society for the Prevention of Cruelty to Animals, 2010 BCSC 406.

44. County of Los Angeles Departments of Public Health and Animal Care and Control, "County Policies Relating to Free-Roaming Cats," accessed Oct. 22, 2014, http://file.lacounty.gov/dacc/cms1_197084.pdf.

45. A typical example of such a law is St. Paul, Minnesota, *Code of Ordinances*, part II, title XX, § 202.02. See also Joan E. Schaffner and Julie Fershtman, ed. *Litigating Animal Law Disputes: A Complete Guide for Lawyers* (Chicago: ABA Publishing, 2009), 398–400.

46. Hampton, Virginia, *Code*, ch. 5, art. III, §§ 5–38 (b) (1).

47. City of Winnipeg, By-Law 92/2013, 19(1) (2013),

48. See City of Akron, ex rel. Christman-Resch v. City of Akron, 159 Ohio App. 3d 673 (2005).

49. *Dallas City Code* § 7-3-1.

50. "Leash Law Enforcement," York County, South Carolina, accessed July 20, 2013, http://www.yorkcountygov.com/departments/PublicWorks/AnimalControl/LeashLawEnforcement.

51. "Cat Leash Laws," The Cat Fanciers' Association," accessed July 20, 2013, http://www.cfainc.org/Portals/0/documents/legislative/cat-leash-laws.pdf; "Cat Leash Laws: The End of the Line," Alley Cat Allies, accessed July 15, 2013, http://www.alleycat.org/page.aspx?pid=398.
52. Dave Gram, "Leash Cats? City Sparks Hissing Match," Pet Health on NBC News.com, accessed July 20, 2013, http://www.nbcnews.com/id/37752330/ns/health-pet_health#.UvqRqvldUh8.
53. See Alley Cat Allies, "History of Alley Cat Allies," accessed Mar. 17, 2010, http://www.alleycat.org/page.aspx?pid=252; Neighborhood Cats, "Our History," accessed Mar. 24, 2010, http://www.neighborhoodcats.org/about_history.
54. Cat Action Team, accessed Mar. 24, 2010, http://www.cats-pei.ca/; Cat Rescue Maritimes, accessed Mar. 24, 2010, http://www.ca-r-ma.org/; Ottawa Humane Society, "Feral Cats," accessed Mar. 24, 2010, http://www.ottawahumane.ca/about-us/media/position-statements/#answer17.
55. See Cat Care of Southwest Colorado, accessed July 16, 2012, http://www.catcaretnr.org/; Feline Frendz in Nebraska, accessed July 16, 2012, http://felinefriendz.org/index.html; Island Feral Cat Project (Savannah, Georgia), accessed July 16, 2012, http://www.islandsferalcatproject.org/; SCAT Street Cat Rescue (Saskatoon, Saskatchewan), accessed July 16, 2012, http://www.streetcat.ca/; Toronto Feral Cat TNR Coalition (Ontario), accessed July 16, 2012, http://torontoferalcatcoalition.ca/.
56. Alley Cat Allies, "Care for Cats," accessed Mar. 17, 2010, http://www.alleycat.org/Page.aspx?pid=431; Neighborhood Cats, "Managing a Feral Cat Colony," accessed Mar. 17, 2010; http://www.neighborhoodcats.org/how_to_managing_a_feral_cat_colony.
57. Smith, "Law and Feral Cats," 8.
58. Michelle Newton, "Legalizing Trap-Neuter-Return: Advantages and Disadvantages of Three Types of TNR Ordinances," Aug. 21, 2010, accessed July 16, 2012, http://www.neighborhoodcats.org/resources_ordinances.
59. See Clark County, Nevada, *Code of Ordinances,* title 10, ch. 10.06, §§ 10.06.010–080; *Cook County Code of Ordinances,* Article IV. Managed Care of Feral Cats; Newton "Legalizing Trap-Neuter-Return."
60. See *City Code, Greer, South Carolina,* Section 4-117: Limitations on Keeping Cats; Glendale, California, *Municipal Code,* title 6, ch, 6.03, §§ 6.03.010–030, ch. 6.04, §§ 6.04.130, 6.04.140, 6.04.190–230; Newport News, Virginia, *Code of Ordinances,* ch. 6, art. II, div. 4, § 6-53; Palm Beach County, Florida, *Code,* ch. 4, §§ 4.2, 4.8, 4.28; *Salt Lake County Code of Ordinances,* 8.03.140, Feral Cat Colony Permit; San Antonio, Texas, *Code* part II, ch. 5, art. V, § 5-115; Newton "Legalizing Trap-Neuter-Return."
61. *Baltimore City Ordinances,* 07-583 (2007); "Regulations for Trap-Neuter-Return Programs," Baltimore City Health Department, Dec. 5, 2013, accessed Oct. 24,

2014, http://health.baltimorecity.gov/sites/default/files/AC%2520Reg%2520-%2520TNR%2520Programs%2520-%2520December%25205%25202013.pdf. See also Newton "Legalizing Trap-Neuter-Return." A similar delegation of authority to an agency has occurred in Louisville/Jefferson County, Kentucky; see Louisville/Jefferson County, *Code of Ordinances* § 91.030, Management of Community Cat Population.

62. Smith, "Law and Feral Cats," 20–25; Simon Shields, "Feral Cats in Ontario," Nov. 22, 2008, accessed July 16, 2012, http://www.isthatlegal.ca/index.php?name=feral.dog_cat_control.

63. Shawn Gorman and Julie Levy, "A Public Policy toward the Management of Feral Cats," *Pierce Law Review* 2 (2004): 157–81; Anthony E. LaCroix, "Detailed Discussion of Feral Cat Population Control," Animal Legal and Historical Center, Michigan State University College of Law, 2006, accessed July 16, 2012; http://www.animallaw.info/articles/ddusferalcats.htm.

64. Kyles v. Great Oaks Interests, No. H028774, 2007 WL 495897 (Cal. Ct. App. Feb. 16, 2007).

65. McElroy v. Carter, No. M2005-00414-COA-R3-CV, 2006 WL 2805141, at *6 (Tenn. Ct. App. Sept. 29, 2006). Fiori v. Conway Org., 746 N.Y.S.2d 747, 750 (N.Y. App. Div. Dec. 14, 2001).

66. See Fry, "Detailed Discussion of Feral Cat Issues"; Simon Shields, "Feral Cats in Ontario."

67. "Helping New York City's Feral & Stray Cats," NYC Feral Cat Initiative, Mayor's Alliance for NYC's Animals, accessed Oct. 7, 2013, http://www.nycferalcat.org/index.htm.

68. Lisa A. Centonze and Julie K. Levy, "Characteristics of Free-Roaming Cats and Their Caretakers," *Journal of the American Veterinary Medical Association* 220 (2002): 1627–33.

69. Interview with Judy Deem, president, Save a Kitty Feral Cat Program, by Richard A. Brisbin, Jr., and Susan Hunter, Apr. 14, 2010, Parkersburg, West Virginia; "Save A Kitty Feral Cat Program, Inc.," accessed July 13, 2012, http://www.saveakitty.org/. For examples of similar programs operated by private organizations, see "Trap-Neuter-Return Program," Cleveland Animal Protective League, accessed July 13, 2012, https://clevelandapl.org/programs-services-resources/trap-neuter-return-program/; "Feral Cat Trap-Neuter-Return (TNR) Program," Pasadena Humane Society and SPCA, accessed July 13, 2012, http://www.pasadenahumane.org/site/PageServer?pagename=services_snip_cat; "Trap-Neuter-Return (TNR)," Dane County Friends of Animals, accessed July 13, 2012, http://www.daneferals.org/info/display?PageID=2067; and for a government-sponsored program see "Trap Neuter and Return Program," Windcrest, Texas, accessed July 13, 2012; http://www.windcrest-tx.gov/index.aspx?nid=438.

70. See for examples Margaret S. Gillerman, "Pacific Approves Program to Trap, Neuter, Release Stray Cats," *St. Louis Post-Dispatch (MO), May* 20, 2015; Thomas Prohaska, "Niagara Board of Health's 8-0 Vote Reverses Stance on Feral Cats," *Buffalo News,* Mar. 27, 2015; Rachael Weiner, "Bill Pits Cat Lovers against Bird Advocates," *Washington Post,* Feb. 10, 2015; "Yuba City Adopts Feral Cat Ordinance," *Appeal-Democrat* (Marysville, CA), Feb. 18, 2015.
71. "Cats Indoors: Trap, Neuter, Release," American Bird Conservancy, accessed Oct. 17, 2015, http://abcbirds.org/program/cats-indoors/trap-neuter-release/; "Final Position Statement Feral and Free-Ranging Domestic Cats," The Wildlife Society, accessed Oct. 17, 2015, http://wildlife.org/wp-content/uploads/2014/05/28-Feral-Free-Ranging-Cats.pdf.
72. Called a "difference of perceptions" in Margaret R. Slater, "Understanding Issues and Solutions for Unowned, Free-Roaming Cat Populations," *Journal of the American Veterinary Medical Association* 225 (2004): 1351.
73. For an overview of the scientific studies of TNR, see Travis Longcore, Catherine Rich, and Lauren M. Sullivan, "Critical Assessment of Claims Regarding Management of Feral Cats by Trap-Neuter-Return," *Conservation Biology* 23 (2009): 887–94; Linda Winter, "Trap-Neuter-Release Programs: The Reality and Impacts," *Journal of the American Veterinary Medical Association* 225 (2004): 1369–76. For a general critique of TNR, see David A. Jessup, "The Welfare of Cats and Wildlife," *Journal of the American Veterinary Medical Association* 225 (2004): 1377–83. On the hunting behavior and prey of roaming and feral cats, see B. Mike Fitzgerald and Dennis C. Turner, "Hunting Behaviour of Domestic Cats and Their Impact on Prey Populations," in *The Domestic Cat,* 151–75. On feral cats and bird populations, see A. P. Beckerman, M. Boots, and K. J. Gaston, "Urban Bird Declines and the Fear of Cats," *Animal Conservation* 10 (2007), 320–25; Christopher A. Lepcayk, Angela G. Mertig, and Jianguo Liu, "Landowners and Cat Predation across Rural-to-Urban Landscapes," *Biological Conservation* 115 (2003): 191–201. On cats and wildlife populations, see Philip J. Baker, Amy J. Bentley, Rachel J. Ansell, and Stephen Harris, "Impact of Predation by Domestic Cats *Felis catus* in an Urban Area," *Mammal Review* 35 (2005): 302–12; William G. George, "Domestic Cats as Predators and Factors in Winter Shortages of Raptor Prey," *Wilson Bulletin* 86 (1974): 384–96; Roland W. Kays and Amielle A. DeWan, "Ecological Impact of Inside/Outside House Cats around a Suburban Nature Preserve," *Animal Conservation* 7(2004): 273–83; Michael Woods, Robbie A. McDonald, and Stephen Harris, "Predation of Wildlife by Domestic Cats *Felis catus* in Great Britain," *Mammal Review* 33 (2003): 174–88. On feral cats as disease vectors, see Lisa H. Akucevich, et al., "Prevalence of Ectoparasites in a Population of Feral Cats from North Central Florida during the Summer," *Veterinary Parasitology* 109 (2002): 129–39; Tara

Creel Anderson, Garry W. Foster, and Donald J. Forrester, "Hookworms of Feral Cats in Florida," *Veterinary Parasitology* 115 (2003): 19–24; Karen L. Gibson, Karen Kelzer, and Christine Golding, "A Trap, Neuter, and Release Program for Feral Cats on Prince Edward Island," *Canadian Veterinary Journal* 43 (2002): 695–98; Irene T. Lee, et al., "Prevalence of Feline Leukemia Virus Infection and Serum Antibodies against Feline Immunodeficiency Virus in Unowned Free-Roaming Cats," *Journal of the American Veterinary Medical Association* 220 (2002): 620–22; Jeffrey L. Ram, et al., "Identification of Pets and Raccoons as Sources of Bacterial Contamination of Urban Storm Sewers Using a Sequence-Based Bacterial Source Tracking Method," *Water Research* 41 (2007): 3605–14. On the costs of TNR see Felicia B. Nutter, Michael K. Stoskopf, and Jay E. Levine, "Time and Financial Costs of Programs for Live Trapping Feral Cats," *Journal of the American Veterinary Medical Association* 225 (2004): 1403–5 and Michael K. Stoskopf and Felicia B. Nutter, "Analyzing Approaches to Feral Cat Management—One Size Does Not Fit All," *Journal of the American Veterinary Medical Association* 225 (2004): 1362–63.

74. Confidential interview by Susan Hunter, Oct. 2013.
75. Centonze and Levy, "Characteristics of Free-Roaming Cats and Their Caretakers"; Kathy L. Hughes and Margaret R. Slater, "Implementation of a Feral Cat Management Program on a University Campus," *Journal of Applied Animal Welfare Science* 5 (2002): 15–28; Kathy L. Hughes and Margaret R. Slater, "The Effects of Implementing a Feral Cat Spay/Neuter Program in a Florida County Animal Control Service," *Journal of Applied Animal Welfare Science* 5 (2002): 285–98; Julie K. Levy, David W. Gale, and Leslie A. Gale, "Evaluation of the Effect of a Long-Term Trap-Neuter-Release and Adoption Program on a Free Roaming Cat Population," *Journal of the American Veterinary Medical Association* 222 (2003): 42–46. On the potentially limited effects of TNR see Paige M. Schmidt, Roel R. Lopez, and Bret A. Collier, "Survival, Fecundity, and Movements of Free-Roaming Cats," *The Journal of Wildlife Management* 71 (2007): 915–19; Stoskopf and Nutter, "Analyzing Approaches to Feral Cat Management," 1362–64.

9

Making Pet Policy: Breed-Specific Laws

The efforts of organized interests supporting animal stewardship have won some successes in improving the treatment of cats, dogs, and horses. However, policies hostile to pet welfare have not disappeared. Beginning in the late 1980s, provincial and local governments in Canada and local governments in the United States began to address problems they associated with specific breeds of dogs. Rather than just impose duties to regulate the ownership of dangerous dogs, through a breed ban component in breed-specific legislation (BSL) they prohibited the ownership, possession, and breeding of American Pit Bulls, American Staffordshire Terriers, Rottweilers, Akitas, crossbreed dogs physically similar to these dogs, wolf–dog hybrids, and other dogs thought to pose the risk of attacking humans.[1] What is paradoxical is that the development of BSL, including specific breed bans, and the identification of some dogs as nuisance property transpired in a period of marked growth in public support of the ideas of responsible animal stewardship and animals' legal rights. Why has this companion animal policy issue arisen, and what political struggles has it generated? In this chapter we describe, first, the sociopolitical context in which BSL and breed bans have emerged as a policy option. Then we assess policymaking in several jurisdictions. Finally we note the reaction to BSL and private efforts to regulate specific breeds of dogs.

THE POLITICAL CONTEXT

To assess the preconditions and context for BSL and breed ban policymaking, we adopted a multifaceted approach that included a mail survey to mayors of municipalities with breed bans in both countries and interviews with organized interests' representatives and reporters in Missouri, West Virginia, Ontario, New Brunswick, Nova Scotia, and Newfoundland, the examination of public documents, and information from a survey of Canadian and U.S. residents described in chapter 3. We also conducted a search for communities in Canada and the United States that had either passed or considered BSL. We then mailed a survey to a sample of mayors of these municipalities in June 2006.[2]

Politicians and Knowledge about BSL and Breed Bans

Although a county judge later ruled it was unconstitutional, available information indicates that a pit bull ban first appeared in Hollywood, Florida, in 1980.[3] Since then dozens of American and Canadian municipalities and counties have adopted some form of BSL.[4] Events in Canada illustrate how the spread of political knowledge contributed to the adoption of BSL and breed bans. After serious dog bite incidents involving pit bull–type dogs Winnipeg, Manitoba, enacted the first Canadian breed ban in 1990. An official from Winnipeg noted that there had been attacks in which children and adults were badly hurt, and criminal drug activity involving pit bull dogs.[5] There were 28 serious biting incidents by pit bull types in 1989 alone. The city administration decided that higher license fees and dangerous dog legislation would not prevent future attacks and felt the only recourse was to remove the breeds from the city. The Manitoba Association of Dog Owners asked that Canine Good Dog certification be used to establish owner responsibility and good temperament of any pit bull–type dog, but this alternative was rejected.[6] As knowledge of the political action in Winnipeg spread, the city's bylaw became a model for more than 36 Canadian jurisdictions. (The Winnipeg bylaw was amended in 2014.[7])

Knowledge about Pit Bull Bites and Attacks

Although political experience and policy learning can shape the context of policymaking, expert knowledge about the issue is also important. However, given the limited data, expert knowledge of the risk from dog bites is problematic. First, the reporting of the frequency of dog bites, including fatal attacks, is not recorded in any central governmental archive. Most academic studies of severe and fatal Canadian and U.S. dog attacks employ data that are limited to serious attacks that victims have chosen to report.[8] In the United States approximately 25 persons—mostly young children—die directly or indirectly from dog bites each year. Studies have associated a propensity to bite with a wide range of breeds, including larger breeds such as German Shepherds, toy breeds such as Chihuahuas, and mixed breeds. The best estimates indicate that pit bulls or dogs with some pit bull characteristics are responsible for about half of the dog bite–related deaths each year in the United States. There is, on average, one fatality per year across Canada from dog bites, mostly from sled dogs and huskies. Only one death has been attributed to a mixed breed with perhaps some pit bull characteristics.[9]

Second, a study has found that owners of dogs that had caused serious personal injury or killed another dog, dogs that were unlicensed, or pit bull dogs had significantly more criminal convictions than the owners of licensed low-risk dogs. Another study reported that owners of Akitas, Chows, Dobermans, pit bulls, Rottweilers, and wolf–dog mixes were higher in sensation seeking and that ownership of such breeds may be a marker of broader social deviance.[10] Although not definitive, the studies suggest that common knowledge of the association of some breeds with criminality has some empirical justification. But, the studies do not explain whether the dogs are dangerous by nature rather than trained by persons to be dangerous.

Third, the ability of persons to report accurately the kind of dog involved in a biting or attack incident is unreliable. Since no DNA studies have fully differentiated breeds of dogs, there is limited popular knowledge of dog breeds, and the prevalence of a large population of "mixed breeds" means that the identification of a dog breed is not often reliable. One empirical study of breed identification matched DNA breed identification with how people identified the breed. For fourteen of twenty dog videos shown to respondents, fewer than 50 percent of the respondents visually identified breeds of dogs that matched DNA identification. For only seven of the twenty dogs was there agreement among more than 50 percent of the respondents regarding the most predominant breed of a mixed-breed dog, and in three of these cases the most commonly agreed upon visual identification was not identified by DNA analysis.[11] A study also found that even shelter employees exhibit a lack of consensus on the identification of pit bulls.[12] These problems mean that officials' knowledge about the value of breed bans and the legally admissible evidence that a dog should be banned are often based on limited and imprecise information.

Finally, there is no evidence that bans on pit bulls and other aggressive breeds works to reduce either nonfatal or fatal dog bites.[13] Indeed, there is evidence that in some communities breed bans have not reduced the frequency of hospitalization from dog bites and that the frequency of serious bites has recently declined in communities without pit bull bans.[14] The bans appear to induce some owners to abandon pit bulls and similar dogs at shelters, but it is not known if this practice has consequences for public safety.

Popular Support for Breed Bans

In our survey elected officials from Kitchener-Waterloo, Windsor, and Midland, Ontario; Prince George and Fort Nelson, British Columbia; McDonald and Winnipeg, Manitoba; and Montague, Prince Edward Island, and Edmonton, Alberta have indicated that breed bans were adopted as a result of public demand for action. But, is this an accurate

TABLE 9.1 Overview of Attitudes about Breed Bans in Canada and the United States

Demographic	In Support of Bans (%)		Undecided (%)		Oppose Bans (%)	
	Canada	U.S.	Canada	U.S.	Canada	U.S.
Ethnicity						
Black	25.0	22.6	25.0	45.2	50.0	32.3
Other	44.1	35.8	34.0	36.5	22.0	27.7
Gender						
Male	54.6	37.4	21.0	33.8	24.5	28.9
Female	39.9	33.8	29.8	38.4	30.3	27.0
Lifestyle						
Rural	43.7	31.1	32.2	39.5	24.1	29.5
Semi	41.8	34.9	36.3	37.9	21.7	27.2
Urban	48.5	39.5	29.8	31.4	21.8	29.1
Age						
Under 25	23.3	11.4	41.4	45.7	35.4	42.9
25–40	38.0	30.4	37.8	38.7	24.2	30.9
41–65	49.3	35.3	30.6	35.1	20.3	29.5
Over 65	49.0	43.9	32.4	36.3	18.7	19.7
Contribute to animal organizations						
No	44.1	36.1	35.8	39.3	20.1	24.5
Yes	43.5	33.2	29.3	33.0	27.2	33.8
Total	46.1	45.2	26.1	36.9	27.9	27.8

assessment of public opinion? In out multinational survey discussed in chapter 3, respondents were asked their views on breed bans, several other animal-related policies, the reasons they believe communities pass breed bans, their pet ownership, and their beliefs about dogs. As Table 9.1 indicates, there is general public support for breed bans in both countries. More than 45 percent of the general public support breed bans while less than 30 percent oppose them. The percentage that is undecided ranges from 21 percent for Canadian males to over 40 percent among young people and African Americans. Black, young, and female respondents are the least supportive of bans. Canadian males are the strongest supporters of breed bans in our sample. If you remove the "unsure" respondents from the analysis,

TABLE 9.2 *Reasons for Support of Breed Bans*

Reasons for Support	Canada (%, N = 1,052)	United States (%, N = 976)
Belief that criminals use certain breeds	9.9	10.6
Media reports	45.3	40.6
Community panic	19.7	15.6
Other reasons	6.6	5.3
All of the above[a]	10.6	13.3
Don't know	8.0	14.7

NOTE: Chi square = 32.4, df = 5, p = 000.
[a] "All of the above" is used when respondents checked all three of the stated options: belief regarding criminals, media reports, and community panic.

more than 50 percent of those with an opinion in both countries supports bans (62 percent in Canada and 55.8 percent in the United States.).

Respondents were also asked why they believed communities adopted breed bans. As Table 9.2 indicates, around 10 percent believed that breeds are banned because criminals use them, close to 45 percent believed it is because of media reports, close to 20 percent attributed the passage of the bans to community panic, and around 12 percent said all of these factors contribute to passage of breed bans. Overall, more than 60 percent attributed the adoption of breed bans to media reports.

We also asked what the respondents believed about dogs in general. Although the majority believed that any breed will bite when provoked or owners make the dog dangerous, Table 9.3 shows that more than 30 percent of the respondents in both countries believed that all dogs will bite if sufficiently provoked. These data suggest that most people do not believe that pit bulls or Rottweilers are inherently dangerous. Whether respondents lived in urban or rural areas did not affect this attitude, nor did age. However, women and contributors to animal welfare organizations were significantly less likely to believe that some breeds are inherently dangerous or more likely to bite than were men and non-contributors.

As shown in Table 9.4, of the respondents who believed some breeds are dangerous, more than 75 percent supported bans and fewer than 4 percent opposed them. For those who believed owners make dogs dangerous, less

TABLE 9.3 *Canadian and U.S. Beliefs about Dogs*

Belief	Canada (%, N = 1,058)	United States (%, N = 990)
Some breeds are dangerous	18.5	14.8
Some breeds are more likely to bite	16.9	17.1
All breeds bite if sufficiently provoked	33.7	35.9
Owners make dogs dangerous	30.8	32.2

TABLE 9.4 *Support for Breed Bans by Belief about Dogs*

Attitude about Bans	Personal Belief about Dogs (%)			
	Some Breeds Are Dangerous	Some Breeds Are More Likely to Bite	All Breeds Will Bite if Sufficiently Provoked	Owners Make Dogs Dangerous
Support bans	75.8	52.5	29.9	27.7
Unsure about bans	19.6	35.0	35.0	30.6
Oppose bans	3.6	12.6	35.1	41.7

than 30 percent supported bans and more than 40 percent opposed them. Clearly a latent or even overt belief that some breeds are dangerous is fueling the push for breed bans.

We asked respondents about their support for several different policies but found little relationship between their support for animal welfare policies and breed bans. Even support for anti-tethering legislation was not related in the United States, although it was slightly but significantly related (p < 0.05) in Canada, despite data that indicate that 25 percent of all fatal attacks were by chained dogs.[15] As Table 9.5 indicates, the only policy related to breed bans in both countries was differential licensing. Age and gender were also found to significantly affect the likelihood of supporting a breed ban in Canada; however, gender was not significant in the United States. In both countries, the younger the respondent the more likely he or she was to oppose breed ban legislation. Conceptions of rights seem to be related to attitudes about breed bans in Canada but not in the United States, where ideas about rights are more strongly held. The

TABLE 9.5 *Variables That Influence Support for Breed Bans*

Variable Correlations with Support for Breed Bans	Canada	United States
Differential licensing of altered animals	0.113[a]	0.187[a]
Belief in man's dominion over animals	0.142[a]	0.039
Belief that progress requires use of animals as humans see fit	0.120[a]	0.096[a]
Ownership of dogs	0.168[a]	0.144[a]
Age	-0.187[a]	-0.151[a]
Contribution to animal welfare organizations	0.068	0.079
Gender	0.120[a]	0.015
Belief that animals have right to companionship	0.081[a]	0.039
Belief that animals have no rights at all	-0.077[a]	0.007
Ban on permanent tethering	-0.062[b]	0.008
Personal beliefs about dogs	0.441[a]	0.334[a]

[a]Significance of 0.001 or less.
[b]Significance of 0.01 or less.

belief that progress requires humans to use animals as they see fit is highly correlated in both countries, reflecting an instrumental view of dogs as property. The strongest relationship between beliefs about rights and beliefs about breed bans is the belief that animals have no rights, again reflecting an instrumental view of animals. There are some clear differences between the two countries, particularly with regard to support for various policies. Canadians are significantly more likely to support breed bans but significantly less likely to believe that God gave man dominion over animals, and less likely to believe that only humans have rights or animals have no rights.

The data suggest that there is a tendency, particularly among elderly persons, to fear some breeds of dogs. People who own dogs, contribute to animal welfare organizations, or believe that owners create dangerous dogs are likely to oppose bans. Overall, however, only 14.9 percent of the respondents strongly support bans, 26.0 percent somewhat support bans, and 31.3 percent are undecided. This suggests that people are unlikely to oppose breed bans, but they are unlikely to push for breed bans without some triggering event.

PANIC POLICYMAKING

What triggers the passage of breed bans? Some authors claim that breed bans are a consequence of panic. Niki Rae Huitson describes breed bans as the result of a moral panic fueled by media depiction of pit bulls as "folk devils."[16] Karen Delise poses the question, "And how have we become a society so ignorant and terrified of some dogs that we have allowed a wave of panic to sweep our communities, allowing certain dogs to be banned, muzzled, restricted and killed by the hundreds of thousands in 'shelters' across the nation?"[17] In this section we present a framework to explain the stages of panic policymaking. We define panic policymaking as the *speedy* creation of new laws and regulations or new duties for governmental institutions in a situation of sudden and excessive fear and anger. By speedy we mean the elapsed time from an incident or claim that serves as a stimulus for a law or policy to the beginning of its implementation is less than six months. In these situations the political struggle over companion animal legislation is truncated by politicians rushing to do something. Figure 9.1 depicts the stages of a panic policymaking framework.

Recognition: Opening the Policy Window

The recognition and definition of a panic are marked by a conjunction of assumptions, injurious events, and emotions. For example, certain assumptions appear to influence the adoption of breed bans. First, the supporters of breed bans assume that dogs, not owners, cause dog attacks. Second, the breeds subject to bans symbolize the risks, dangers, and insecurity of modern life. To protect their interests, drug dealers and street gangs often possess the breeds subject to breed bans. Police and urban and suburban residents sense that dealers and gangs are a threat to their security, a threat that can possess a racial subtext. Thus, for breed ban proponents the assumption is that the banishment of some dog breeds will help assert social order in their locale and control racial minorities associated with criminality. "Banishment represents a quick fix to … widespread fear. It

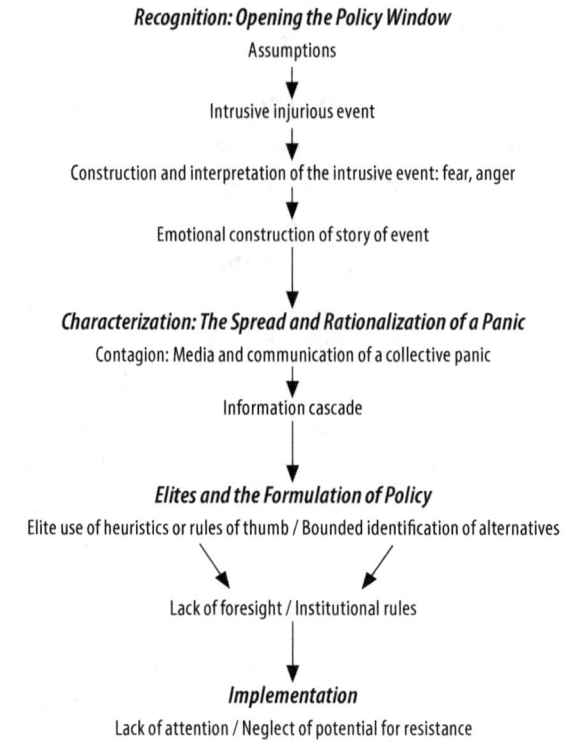

FIGURE 9.1 Panic policymaking framework.

is, at root, an attempt to use the criminal justice system to solve a set of entrenched social problems."[18]

Scholars have found that issues need "a little push" to become an item on the political agenda.[19] The push is sometimes an *intrusive injurious event* such as a crisis or disaster, which functions as a trigger or alarm that signals immediate severe, catastrophic, or dreadful risks for human life or social order.[20] For example, persons can readily perceive the danger of a dog attack because of their sense that the dog is a danger to themselves and their family.[21]

Following an intrusive event, *fear* and *panic* develop as an individual's immediate emotional response to potentially intrusive injurious events. Also, fear resulting from the experience of an injurious event increases a person's ability to detect danger to him- or herself.[22] "The threat of a serious motor accident can provoke it, as can an attack by a vicious dog."[23]

Panic is the result of an impulsive assessment of threat to personal well-being that precedes any reasoned assessment[24] and is linked to negative emotional responses toward an injurious event. One such emotional response, anger, "is associated with superficial and possibly rapid decision making, a lower sensitivity to risk, and an orientation toward action."[25] Studies have associated anger with stereotypical judgments and hostile inferences based on limited knowledge. For example, anger can cause people to envision a breed of dog as a "folk devil" or a deviant entity.[26] Angry responses to panic also predict the likelihood of repetition of the event that engendered their fear and panic.[27]

Panic and anger often cause persons to rely on unusually painful personal experiences, folk knowledge, and biased information from social networks or the media. They often neglect reliable factual knowledge, overestimate the risk of infrequent or abnormal events, especially of a lethal nature, and underestimate the frequency of common events.[28] The result is that persons assume that the risk of an injurious event is highly probable when it is not.[29] For example, people have constructed stories about pit bulls that rest on myths and pseudoscience, such as they have locking jaws, grind rather than bite victims, have a stronger jaw than other breeds, have special hormones that arouse them to fight, have uniquely sharp teeth, are impervious to pain, eagerly engage in unprovoked attacks, and are less predictable in their behavior than other breeds.[30]

Characterization: The Spread of a Panic

If individuals spread their story about ill-effects of an injurious event such as a pit bull attack, a *contagion* occurs.[31] The contagious *communication* of information about the injurious event opens quite suddenly—often within days or months of the event. Media practices in relating stories of events can amplify the panic and define the injury as a catastrophe.[32] For example, a Canadian study has found that media stories characterized pit bulls as vicious and aggressive and as trained attackers with a habit of strong, tenacious biting that is unpredictable. Stories also associated pit bulls with dogfighting, criminality, and a dysfunctional social class.[33] Additionally, the media provided the readily available evidence that individuals employ when they evaluate the likelihood of future injuries from "pit bull types" and other large dogs.[34]

The media often amplifies fear that the injurious event will be repeated. This process can be described as an *information cascade*.[35] If the media's message is simple, intense, and frequent, arouses the fear and anger of groups and individuals, and associates the injury with a stigmatized object (pit bulls) or group of people (pit bull owners), it can initiate a chain of communications that amplify the collective panic.[36]

Choice: Political Elites and the Formulation of a Policy

Panic policymaking features limited participation and decision-making control by elected executives and staff or the majority membership of a small legislature, such as a city council. They employ "common knowledge," and default to habitual practices or policies in the formulation of a response to assessments of the occurrence of a catastrophe.[37] Consequently officials employ heuristics rather than an elaborate assessment of policy alternatives[38] and spend little time thinking about the consequences of their choices. They "produce quick judgments about what disorders will or will not be tolerated by creatively combining a bit of secondhand expert knowledge with a job-based sense of customary norms and a more or less intuitive sense of what the 'public good' … requires in particular cases."[39] Other policy options are ignored.[40] The rapid consideration of a limited number of options also often involves a lack of analysis related to the longer term consequences of a decision.

Implementation of a Panic Policy

The implementation or enforcement of a response to an intrusive injurious event is of little concern during the formulation of panic policies.[41] In their haste to act, legislators can fail to forecast the resources of personnel and money necessary to enforce the new policy. The policy change can be hollow—a symbolic gesture and promise that satisfies mass fears. Animal control agencies might adapt the new policy to serve their political self-interest and produce responses to the event that draw attention away from the initial fear.[42] Media or political leaders can move on to new crises. The panic thus "fades" and can move into a "prolonged limbo."[43] Finally, popular resistance to breed bans might induce noncompliance or campaigns to repeal the law.

CASE STUDIES OF THE CONSIDERATION OF BREED-SPECIFIC LAWS

Does the panic policymaking framework explain the passage of breed bans in specific political contexts? To find out we applied this framework to three case studies involving efforts to legislate a breed ban.

Kansas City Metropolitan Area

In the United States, several states have banned BSL, but BSL has been addressed in municipalities and a few metropolitan counties around the country. Communities in the Kansas City area (in both Kansas and Missouri) have been debating the issue in recent years. Kansas City–Wyandotte County, Kansas, has had a ban on pit bulls for sixteen years, but in more recent years the issue reached the agenda in Kansas City, Missouri, and its surrounding suburbs for a variety of reasons.

Recognition
Two major incidents occurred in the summer of 2006. Three dogs left abandoned in a house in Independence, Missouri, escaped and apparently attacked a man mowing his lawn. The dogs were chased away by a neighbor but then attacked a cross-dressed prostitute before approaching a third man in a friendly way. The first person was hospitalized. These were very large mixed-breed dogs. A month later an abandoned dog (the owner was in prison) escaped from its yard, terrifying a neighbor, who suffered a heart

attack (probably from fright) and died. This dog was either a boxer or a pit bull. The news media reported criticism of the City for not vigorously enforcing its sixteen-year ban on pit bulls and ran constant ads calling on people to turn in their pit bulls. Although other dog attacks occurred during the summer of 2006, the dogs were not pit bulls, so limited media attention was given to these other attacks. When a woman was attacked in her home in August 2007 by two pit bulls and suffered severe injuries, the attack was reported by hundreds of national and international newspapers and television news networks.[44]

Characterization

Sources in Missouri indicated that there is a latent fear of pit bulls in the community. One source also claimed that the media always mentioned pit bulls whenever a dog bite occurred, and they put pit bull bites on the front page, while other attacks may not even make it into the paper or onto the nightly news. Their perspective was that the media in the Kansas City metro area kept the heat on city governments and helped spread the contagion of fear of pit bulls. This information cascade reinforced and repeated the stories of local dog attacks during 2006. From July through October a major paper, the *Kansas City Star*, published more than seventy stories or letters to the editor about pit bulls and breed bans almost daily, and numerous local and national stories about pit bulls were broadcast on television.[45] The local ABC affiliate repeatedly showed footage of the results of an alleged dog attack that had actually taken place several years earlier.

The media's cascade of information about dog attacks aroused a mass audience. A "policy window" for the consideration of breed bans then suddenly opened through the metropolitan area. Information collected on the consideration and passage of breed bans indicates that metropolitan Kansas City was perhaps the most active area in the United States in which local governments addressed proposals for breed bans.[46] The legislation was considered by at least thirty-nine communities in metropolitan Kansas City, including Bonner Springs, Leavenworth, Olathe, and Overland Park in Kansas; Independence, Lee's Summit, and Liberty in Missouri; and approximately another dozen communities, as well as Jackson and Wyandotte Counties, Kansas, in response to the two attacks in Kansas City and Independence.[47] One man in Olathe who lived next door to a pit bull mix that was never loose and had a Canine Good Citizen certificate petitioned the city council for four months to ban pit bulls. A realtor in Grandview who took over Animal Control there introduced BSL to help property values. Oak Grove, Missouri, revisited the breed ban issue after a dog bite attack; Grayton, Kansas, had a dog bite attack and considered a breed ban. Kansas City, Kansas, adopted a breed ban and mandatory spay/neuter for all pit bulls. Raytown and Lee's Summit, Missouri, considered breed bans on pit bulls in response to what they considered to be a rash of vicious dog attacks.[48] Grandview, Overland Park, and Independence all had individuals who decided to push BSL as a political issue. In Overland Park and some of the other affluent suburbs, these political leaders associated meth labs and trailer parks with pit bulls to convince the public that banning pit bulls would keep certain types of people out of their communities.

Alternatives and Choice

Despite attacks by Rottweilers, German Shepherds, and Chows, public officials defined the canine bite problem in the Kansas City metropolitan area as a pit bull problem. One council member in a suburb even noted that pit bulls were far more dangerous than his Doberman that had already bitten three people. The most interesting example is that of Independence, Missouri, a poor community adjoining Kansas City.[49] Independence was the site of the attacks by three large mixed-breed dogs that were called pit bulls by animal control. Allegedly one council member, who had lost a previous race for mayor, decided that she could win the office by pushing a breed ban. She managed to get the International Association of Fire Fighters local union behind her, but the council rejected the ban on the first vote. Not deterred, the councilwoman introduced the bill again as an emergency measure and obtained signatures on a petition (an illegal activity while she was a council member). She then declared that she had enough to bring up the bill as an emergency measure. The petition signatures were never certified. However, this councilwoman allegedly blackmailed several members of the council. One reported that she was told she would be turned in to animal control for owning four dogs instead of the allowed two if she voted against the ban. Although the councilwoman had been the only member to vote for the ban on the first vote, only the blackmailed member voted against it the second time. The city manager, who normally would have provided some guidance, did not participate because he owned a pit bull mix. Independence officials did not discuss other alternatives, but the ordinance they passed did provide for the licensing and control of pit bulls already in the city rather than their exclusion or destruction. According to confidential sources, the population is not politically active and non–council members mounted no opposition to breed bans with the provision on existing animals.

Implementation

Limited information exists about the enforcement of breed bans in the Kansas City area. It was reported that, after exempting existing dogs from destruction, Independence registered 380 such dogs.[50] Reports of an increase in the abandonment of pit bull–type dogs at shelters and on the streets also surfaced. An amnesty program in Kansas City, Kansas, took in 178 dogs by August 2006.[51] However, Kansas City, Missouri, reportedly experienced a 76 percent increase in the number of pit bulls at its shelter.[52]

Implications

In several communities policy entrepreneurs regarded the breed ban issue as one that would help their political careers. In other communities, where councils were reacting to the fear but no one had a special interest, they were more amenable to alternative approaches to the problem, such as limiting tethering and stronger dangerous dog legislation. Abigail York of the Dog Advocates Council expressed the view that city council members were generally not receptive to public demonstrations by dog owners, but they were usually receptive to expert testimony and personal contacts. She also indicated, however, that many communities were antiacademic, so local citizens opposed to bans had to become involved through calls and visits to their council members.[53]

By 2012 the wave of the pit bull crested and many communities either abandoned the ban or developed a dangerous dog ordinance. Olathe, Kansas, sent its ban bill to a committee to study, listened to experts, and decided that a breed ban would not work. Lee's Summit, Missouri, decided to repeal a ban after listening to testimony from experts and citizens.[54] Osawatomie and Topeka, Kansas, and Greenwood and Riverside, Missouri, repealed pit bull bans. Also Merriam, Kansas, Belton, Oak Grove, Peculiar, and Raytown, Missouri, and Jackson County, Missouri, decided against a ban.[55]

Ontario

Although the origin of events in Ontario is difficult to construct because of behind-closed-doors decisions by provincial legislators, the formulation and adoption of BSL and a breed ban in the province evidences a different version of panic policymaking.

Recognition

A few violent dog attacks had transpired in Ontario in the decade prior to 2005, including attacks that resulted in the death of a child and assaults on police. These attacks produced no immediate public outcry or media demands for the control of dangerous dogs. However, in August 2004 the media reported how Toronto police had to fire more than a dozen bullets to kill two pit bulls that had turned on the man walking them and how a pit bull had attacked a man in London, Ontario, who tried to protect a puppy from a pit bull attack.[56] In late August 2004 the
Ontario Liberal Party's attorney general, Michael Bryant, decided to legislate a ban on the ownership of pit bulls. Opposition Progressive Conservative and New Democrat legislators thought that he proposed the ban to deflect media attention from other issues and unpopular policies bedeviling the Liberal government. The Liberals also might have proposed BSL and a breed ban to deflect criticism of their inability to control the growth of crime and gang activity in Toronto.[57]

Bryant held news conferences to tout the proposed ban and link pit bulls, by inference, to criminals, outlaw bikers, and urban gangs—groups with members often drawn from ethnic minorities. Although a reporter showed Bryant a photo array of dogs and he was unable to identify a pit bull, his party nonetheless pushed ahead in its promotion of a series of BSL and breed ban amendments to the existing Dog Owners' Liability Act. It held a series of "consultations" with police, animal law enforcement officers, humane societies, and what it called a "broad spectrum of stakeholders" that it selected.[58] Therefore, the government engaged in the construction of the intrusive event.

In constructing the need for a breed ban, the party leaders exploited a fear of pit bulls and crime among the public and the public's assumption that a legal change could free them from the fear. The Liberals thus promised personal security from the risks posed by criminals as well as dogs for political credit. They did not act to govern the moral and ethical behavior of the owners of dangerous dogs.[59]

Characterization

The Liberal government used press releases and media interviews with Attorney General Bryant in an attempt to orchestrate public support for a pit bull ban. Bryant characterized the dogs as a "menace" and a "loaded weapon." The government also arranged for press statements from victims of attacks about the extent of their injuries and testimony from the Animal Services Agency of Winnipeg about the effectiveness of its pit bull ban. These comments and releases emphasized the danger pit bulls posed for children and conveyed horror stories of their behavior.[60]

Anti–breed ban advocates described a media-generated information cascade to misportray as vicious pit bulls and other breeds. However, Attorney General Bryant attempted to rationalize his call for a breed ban by reference to support for it from a range of organized interests. He asserted he had consulted with a range of organized interests, including the groups that opposed the ban.[61] The Liberals relied on knowledge provided by experts on security—Toronto police and councilors in cities that had adopted a breed ban. Press releases cited municipal officials, including the mayor of Toronto, the chief of the Toronto Police Service, the mayor of Kitchener, and the mayor of Wawa, as supporters of the ban. Therefore, Liberal legislators used the most readily available and least costly form of insurance at their disposal to reshape the environment—the criminal law.

They assumed that law would repress the anxieties of the public by its symbolic power to ensure punishment for the perpetrators of the risk of injury or disorder—the dog. The criminal law thus shifted to make the dog and not the owner accountable for attacks.[62] Consequently, despite the rarity of pit bull attacks—a danger far less likely than a highway accident or an aggravated assault by a family member—the dog became a symbol of a risk to the psychological craving for a secure, orderly, and joyful life to be successfully exploited for political credit.[63]

Alternatives and Choice

Attorney General Bryant and his staff then prepared legislation to amend the Dog Owners' Liability Act and introduced it in late October 2004. The search for a policy largely drew on the language of the 1990 Winnipeg bylaw for its definition of pit bulls.[64] Sections of the Winnipeg bylaw that addressed licensing, owners' responsibility, dangerous dogs, cats, and restrictions on the number of pets did not appear in the Ontario amendments. Thus, rather than broadly defining the problem as an animal issue, the government decided that the issue was pit bulls. The government's proposed amendments had several key provisions. It

- banned the owning, breeding, transferring, abandoning, or importing of pit bulls, American Pit Bull Terriers, American Staffordshire Terriers, and Staffordshire Bull Terriers, and dogs that have an "appearance and physical characteristics that are substantially similar to" these breeds;
- required that pit bulls and other banned breeds currently in the province be muzzled in public and sterilized;
- placed the burden of proof that the animal was not a pit bull or a menace on the dog owner (contrary to the assignment of the burden of proof to the prosecution that applies to almost all crimes in English-based legal systems); and
- allowed peace officers to enter buildings and dwellings without a warrant in "exigent circumstances" to prevent "imminent bodily harm or death" from a dog.[65]

During January and February 2005 the Committee on the Legislative Assembly held four days of public hearings on the amendments. Most of the 106 witnesses or sets of witnesses representing organizations opposed the amendments. All of the groups associated with animal welfare, animal rescue, and animal training, as well as some local officials, kennel clubs, and veterinary associations, opposed the amendments. Supporters included victims of animal attacks, a few local officials, and Toronto police. Attorney General Bryant testified on the last day of the hearings and stressed that the law would result in fewer pit bull attacks, could be effectively implemented, and would stem an "increasing proliferation and population of pit bulls."[66]

The Liberal majority on the committee then rejected any effort to rewrite the BSL and breed ban amendments. The Liberal majority leadership then used parliamentary procedures to compel party members to vote for the bill or face a general legislative election, but many Liberals absented themselves from the final vote. Without a separation of powers and with institutional procedures permitting the leadership of the large Liberal legislative majority to push through legislation, no institutional means existed for the party opposition or legislators' concerns about public opinion to derail the breed ban.

Implementation

Because agencies are not required to collect information, empirical data about the effectiveness of the ban does not exist. The law's critics argue it gave a false sense of security and was a facade. The law apparently did decrease the number of pit bull bite incidents reported in Toronto, but after the passage of the law reported bites for many other breeds also decreased.[67] Anecdotal information suggests that it resulted in shelters receiving and exterminating a significant number of pit bull–type dogs and in some being registered, but reports indicate that many owners failed to register their dogs or registered them as another breed. Volunteers removed some of the dogs to other provinces, but animal control officers did not seek out the dogs.[68]

Ontario's breed ban quickly generated resistance to its implementation. A coalition of five companion animal groups challenged the constitutionality of BSL and the breed ban.[69] In May 2006 Judge Thea Herman of the Ontario Superior Court of Justice heard arguments that the breed ban violated two sections of the Canadian Charter of Rights and Freedoms and was ultra vires. The opinion of the judge addressed several issues. First, the judge concluded that, because of conflicting evidence on the dangerousness of pit bulls, the legislature had not chosen "too sweeping" a means to protect the public. It had lawfully acted in the direction of public safety.[70] Second, she determined that the evidence exhibited that the identification of dogs "substantially similar" in appearance to pit bulls provided insufficient guidance to individuals who had to comply with the law.[71] Third, she ruled that the mandatory presumption a dog was a pit bull infringed on Charter rights.[72] Therefore, she held that the law's specification of the ban on dogs similar to pit bulls was void.[73]

However, on appeal to the Court of Appeal for Ontario, in October 2008 a three-judge panel reversed Judge Herman's ruling. For the panel Judge J. A. Sharpe concluded that Judge Herman was correct in her determination that the law was not overbroad. However, the court concluded that the law was not unduly vague. Finally, they concluded that the statute preserved the presumption of innocence and did not violate Section 11 (d) of the Charter.[74]

Although the appeals court upheld the legitimacy of the breed ban, as with any law its implementation is subject to interpretation as trial courts consider the evidence in cases that address the enforcement of the law. In other reported cases the Ontario judiciary assessed how the breed ban worked to protect personal security against allegedly dangerous dogs. In cases that arose in Toronto, the judges permitted the implementation of the breed ban. They determined that nuisance pit bulls should be destroyed without a court-like hearing.[75] Another judge refused to award damages to the owner when police killed two pit bulls when breaking into a residence to execute an arrest warrant against another person.[76] However, in a case in the city of Sarnia, a justice of the peace considered statements by two veterinarians that indicated a dog had only "some pit bull similarities." After convicting the owner for lacking a dog license and leaving the dog off leash, the justice ordered the return of the dog to the owner.[77] Yet, in these cases none of the judges questioned the legal constitution of the dogs as risky, nuisance property or the authority of the state to kill them. In this way legal constructs diffused the harsh reality of the death of dogs predicated by the breed ban.[78]

• • •

Unlike the Kansas City context, in Ontario the recognition of the pit bill issue was not the consequence of a cascade of media stories of injuries associated with a series of dog attacks. Instead, public officials characterized pit bulls as a public security issue that they believed had value in securing political support from the voters. BSL and a breed ban offered them a sweeping but low cost attack on the symbols associated with crime. They then manufactured a panic. Ontario's politicians thus chose to govern crime by creating a panic that made some dogs criminal. They did not tax and invest public resources in educational and behavioral solutions to the threat posed by dangerous dogs.

New Brunswick

Events in New Brunswick illustrate another twist in the consideration of BSL and a breed ban, showing how political leaders can offset a potential pit bull panic. In the province leaders offset both media reportage and some politicians' actions that could have contributed to a panic.

Recognition

As described in chapter 1, in New Brunswick in March 2003, three Rottweilers attacked and killed a four-year-old boy named James Waddell. The coroner's inquest findings recommended that child welfare services review its procedures, as the child had been under its protection. The coroner also recommended that dog laws be strengthened to prevent such injurious events. However, there was no evidence of a contagion of fear or moral panic or calls for a breed ban from groups or private opinion leaders. Although the horrible death of this child could have led to widespread demand for a breed ban, the government and the media jointly worked to contain the hysteria. Thus, any emotional assessment of alternatives did not occur.[79]

Characterization

The attack on Waddell received extensive of media attention in the province. However, unlike Ontario, the Progressive Conservative government used press releases and the media to deflect the discussion of dangerous dogs to one of responsible pet ownership and responsible parenting. Although relatives of the child demanded more action, media stories brought up problems with the child's care by his family, questioned the role of Social Services in leaving the child with this family, and printed assessments of the animals that described them as gentle and well-behaved. The newspaper reports also noted that the animals had been appropriately confined, but the child was left unsupervised. The media did not attempt to create a panic environment nor did elected officials. No cascade of calls for a breed ban occurred. Also, the media focused on the issue of Social Services involvement because the child was under care, the owner immediately euthanized all four of his dogs despite evidence that they were normally very sweet animals, and the opposition member agreed to pull his bill. As a result, media attention virtually disappeared and no public outcry occurred.[80]

Instead, a legislator supplied a rationalized policy alternative. Kelly Lamrock, a Liberal Party (opposition) member from Fredericton, introduced private member's bill, Bill 55, in May of 2004 to ban Rottweilers, Staffordshire Bull Terriers, American Staffordshire Terriers, and Akitas. The ban would have applied only to unincorporated areas because the Municipalities Act gives incorporated areas the right to develop their own animal legislation. The Progressive Conservatives had a one-member majority, and the attorney general, Brad Green, did not support a breed ban. Public hearings, held in November of 2004, found support for a breed ban from relatives of the child who was killed, and letters from the general public supported the ban. The New Brunswick Society for the Prevention of Cruelty to Animals (SPCA), breeders, Humane Societies, the Canadian Kennel Club, veterinarians, and dog trainers all testified against the ban. Letters from Ontario residents opposing the ban and feedback from owners of other breeds helped convince the legislature to drop Bill 55 and establish a task force to study the issue.[81]

Alternatives and Choice

Because the parties in the Legislative Assembly were nearly equal in membership, neither party had the votes to pass legislation. Also, Brad Green, the Progressive Conservative leader, was opposed to breed bans. Thus, institutional conditions for the passage of the ban did not exist. Also, the Legislative Assembly was willing to consider alternative policies. Rather than describing the issue as a problem with particular breeds, Brad Green and the Progressive Conservatives redefined the problem as one of irresponsible ownership. Because the Progressive Conservative Party did not support a breed ban, the Assembly was closely divided between Progressive Conservatives and Liberals, and the Liberal Party, especially Lamrock, was willing to work on legislation that would achieve his goal of protecting people from dangerous dogs, the legislature established a standing committee on law amendments to make a recommendation regarding Bill 55. The committee issued its report on December 16, 2004. The recommendation was based on a report titled "Financial and Social Implications of Breed Specific Legislation" prepared by committee staff.[82] The staff report recommended that Bill 55 be dropped and that the legislature consider a Responsible Dog Owner Act. The matter was referred to the Department of Environment and Local Government in 2005. Subsequently, with agreement from Lamrock, the member who introduced the bill, the Assembly designated a task force to study the issues of dangerous dogs and irresponsible owners. This task force has recommended penning of dogs rather than tethering and removal of animals if the owner is irresponsible, with euthanasia only if a dog was determined to be irredeemable. It also recommended that any animal sufficiently abused to become aggressive should be removed. Courts would be given authority to review each offense and decide whether the situation met the criteria for removal.

Unlike in Ontario, New Brunswick leaders collected information on other policy alternatives. The Speech from the Throne in 2005 noted the Task Force Report and stated that a bill would be introduced to implement the recommendations. The Legislative Assembly adopted some of the recommendations, and additional amendments were made to the Society for the Prevention of Cruelty to Animals Act in 2008. Member Lamrock also took action to modify the Fredericton bylaw to address responsible pet ownership. He has made public statements to the effect that he has no desire to punish good dogs, just irresponsible owners.[83]

The lack of a choice also is, in a way, unusual because two serious dog bite incidents occurred in New Brunswick during the summer of 2006. But, neither political party made any mention of them, and the media paid little attention. The actions of the legislature in holding hearings and appointing a task force apparently satisfied the general public. Neither party has a statement about dangerous dogs in their party platform, nor has the issue been addressed by the Legislative Assembly. No public figure has made a statement about dog attacks, and the issue is apparently being ignored.

Reasons for the Lack of a Policy Choice

In New Brunswick an injurious event occurred, but the event was interpreted as one of poor parental supervision and irresponsible dog ownership. The media did not call for a breed ban. Although one member of the legislature did call for a ban, he dropped his bill when the leadership agreed to examine alternatives. Public concern did not lead to a panic and demands for a breed ban. Officials in New Brunswick attributed their ability to develop more reasonable policy options to media restraint and the closely divided legislature, an institutional factor that did not allow for quick and easy restriction of policy alternatives by a dominant party.

Implications of the Case Studies

The case studies indicate that popular fears and anger toward just a few pit bull attacks can cascade into a panic and demands for political action. However, the media and entrepreneurship by public officials have great influence on the adoption of a breed ban. The exact mixture of panic, media reportage, and officials' concerns in the consideration of the adoption of a breed ban varies among jurisdictions and reflects unique combinations of emotions and political ambitions. In particular, the willingness of elected officials to react to media-reinforced public fears, as in the Kansas City area, or to manipulate fears for other political ends, as in Ontario, can result in the passage of a breed ban without a lengthy political struggle. Therefore, a blanket assertion that a public panic about pit bull attacks causes the adoption of a breed ban is overbroad. Instead, as the Ontario and New Brunswick cases illustrate, politicians' characterizations of events and the identity of dogs, and the potential mediating role of legislative politics, play a crucial role in whether a breed ban becomes law.[84]

PROHIBITIONS ON AND REPEALS OF BREED-SPECIFIC LAWS

In response to what they regarded as a mischaracterization of selected breeds and the causes of dog bites, animal welfare interests have mobilized to oppose breed bans. By challenging the bans in court and seeking legislation to prevent their adoption or implementation, these interests have "cooled" the pit bull panic.

In the face of the U.S. Constitution's Takings Clause, Due Process Clause, and void-for-vagueness challenges, American judges have adjudicated several cases about the constitutionality of breed bans. Steven Tauber reports that the U.S. federal courts have adjudged few cases about breed bans, and a majority of the judges upheld the ban. Results of state court litigation of breed bans vary.[85] For example, courts in Florida, Kansas, Missouri, New Mexico, and Washington have held breed-specific (usually pit bull) bans to be constitutional, but judges in Kentucky and Massachusetts concluded that the bans violated constitutional rights of owners. Based on the wording of the specific law in question in several cases, judges in Colorado and Ohio have either upheld or voided breed bans.[86]

Given the uncertainty of litigation to overturn breed bans, and although they are sometimes ill-prepared or inattentive during the panic and subsequent policymaking, animal welfare groups have mobilized to seek the passage of legislation forestalling breed bans. By directing the discussion away from pit bull behavior and focusing on problems with the owners of any dangerous dogs, these groups helped dampen pit bull panics. In response, nineteen U.S. states have adopted laws to regulate dangerous dogs that prohibit the specific designation of any breed as dangerous by state and local governments.[87] For example, in Nevada a public petition drive sponsored by Incred-a-Bull, a nonprofit pit bull education, rescue, and adoption group, lobbying by Best Friends Animal Society, and support from the Henderson Police Department and Animal Control division resulted in the passage of a prohibition on breed bans sponsored by Assemblyman James Ohrenschall (D-Las Vegas).[88] In Massachusetts support for a prohibition on breed bans came from the Animal Control Officers Association of Massachusetts, Massachusetts SPCA, Massachusetts Animal Coalition, and Animal Rescue League of Boston.[89] In Cincinnati, Ohio, similar efforts by animal welfare advocates have resulted in the repeal of their breed ban.[90] In some jurisdictions, judicial decisions have overruled breed-specific laws.[91] In states such as New York and Ohio, local governments have repealed their breed bans. Opponents of breed bans also have litigation underway to void the laws in communities such as Clay, Alabama.[92] Given the adoption of the majority of these laws and the judicial decisions since 2010, the mobilization of animal welfare groups and advocacy coalitions for their repeal appears to be escalating. A decline of public interest in the passage of breed bans has also been noticed by local animal control officers.[93]

Specific efforts to repeal breed bans have found support from a variety of interest groups in the United States. They include the American Bar Association, American Dog Owners Association, American Kennel Club, American SPCA, Animal Farm Foundation, American Temperament Test Society, American Veterinary Medical Association, Association of Pet Dog Trainers, Best Friends Animal Society, Humane Society of the United States, National Animal Control Association, National Canine Research Council, and United Kennel Club.[94] Additional support for the abolition of breed bans has come from the U.S. White House. In response to an online petition against federal breed bans, in August 2013 the White House released a statement that in part read, "We don't support breed-specific legislation—research shows that bans on certain types of dogs are largely ineffective and often a waste of public resources." The statement relied on Centers for Disease Control studies that recommended "a community-based approach to prevent dog bites."[95]

Nevertheless, political support for breed bans remains. Colorado imposed a statewide prohibition on breed bans that presumably repealed the ban in place in the City of Denver and seven other municipalities which had resulted in the euthanasia of approximately 3,500 dogs. Denver challenged the state law, and a state judge ruled that the state law providing for home rule in the city allowed the city to adopt the ban.[96] In 2012 in Miami-Dade County, Florida, a ballot initiative to repeal a 23-year-old breed ban failed to win voter approval.[97]

UNANTICIPATED CONSEQUENCES OF THE BSL AND BREED BAN DEBATE: INSURERS BEHAVIOR

Policy debates do not always generate new laws and regulations. They also can serve as a catalyst for other changes in behavior. The public debate about BSL and breed bans has had an unanticipated consequence: change in the practices of some insurance companies. Publicity about the alleged dangers of pit bulls and other dog breeds has induced some insurance companies to notify their customers with the "dangerous breeds" that they will drop their homeowners or renters liability insurance or not compensate for injuries caused by such breeds. Without actuarial justification the companies simply fear the potential risk of costly, profit-reducing litigation from the possible behavior of such dogs. Only Pennsylvania has prohibited this practice.[98] However, some states, such as Ohio, require that "dangerous dog" owners carry a personal liability insurance policy.[99] As yet there is no empirical evidence that the private policy of the insurers or state insurance law is reducing or informally "banning" pit bulls, Rottweilers, or other breeds. However, the insurers' actions suggest that a form of private legal agreement can have potentially significant consequences for the lives of pets.[100]

CONCLUSION

Breed ban laws illustrate the limitations of law as a resource to defend pets against their destruction. Although our data find that the majority of the public supports legislation to promote animal welfare, there is little relationship between support for animal welfare and attitudes about particular categories of animals, such as pit bulls. People who support legal protections for the welfare of animals are as likely to support breed bans as to oppose them. Also, despite the scientific evidence linking chained dogs to vicious dog attacks, even support for policies such as anti-tethering legislation is not related to support for breed bans. Instead, the evidence indicates that support for breed bans stem from the galvanization of a latent fear of pit bull–type dogs and fear of criminal behavior by the owners of these dogs. Thus, the panic policymaking framework provides a partial guide to understanding the political struggle about the adoption of breed ban policies.

Evidence from the case studies buttresses this conclusion. In the characterization of risks from dogs, the role of the media is apparent in all of our case studies, but it is not always the source of an information cascade that, as in Kansas City, expands the fear of some dog breeds. The case studies also illustrate the power of political leaders, as in Ontario. A few fearful people, especially those in a position of political influence, and an apathetic general public provide sufficient conditions to develop a panic and a policy. However, when attentive animal welfare groups become involved, the additional information they provide can change not just the range of policy options but the very nature of the issue. For example, as New Brunswick officials interacted with experts, groups, and the public, the issue changed from being about the danger of pit bulls and Rottweilers to the behavior of dog owners. Groups have used the same approach to prevent or repeal BSL and breed bans in several American states. Unfortunately, however, in many jurisdictions the pit bull remains nuisance property denuded of worth by a sector of the public, government officials, and insurance companies. In these communities the dog exists as a subject of governmental fiat and subject to the law's cruelty and violence.

NOTES

1. The forms of dangerous dog laws are defined in Niki Rae Huitson, *An Exploratory Analysis of the Emergence and Implications of Breed Specific Legislation: Knee-Jerk Reaction or Warranted Response?* (M.A. Thesis, Simon Fraser University, British Columbia, 2005), 12–13. In addition to a breed ban, which is designed to extinguish a breed, BSL can impose restrictions on owners of a specific breed of dog such as muzzling, restrictive housing or containment, and insurance.
2. The survey can be found at http://brisbin.polisci.wvu.edu/r/download/183687.

3. Evidence suggests that increased attention to dangerous dog laws, often related to increased media attention to dogfights, occurred during the second half of the 1980s; see Donald H. Clifford, Kay Ann Green, and Ronald M. Watterson, *The Pit Bull Dilemma: The Gathering Storm; 1,000 Annotated Abstracts from Books, Journals, Magazines, Newspapers, and Reports* (Philadelphia: Charles Press, 1990), vi, xi.
4. Devin Burstein, "Breed Specific Legislation: Unfair Prejudice and Ineffective Policy," *Animal Law* 10 (2004): 313–61; "Breed Specific Legislation," National American Pit Bull Terrier Association, accessed Jan. 2007, http://www.napbta.com/bsl.html.
5. Confidential interview by Susan Hunter, Sept. 2006; City of Winnipeg, *Pound By-Law*, No. 2443/79, Part I, 16 (1990).
6. Response provided on Winnipeg survey form, 2007.
7. City of Winnipeg, By-Law 92/2013, 7(1) (2014).
8. Janis Bradley, "Dog Bites: Problems and Solutions," Animals and Society Institute, Ann Arbor, MI, 2014, accessed Oct. 21, 2015, http://nationalcanineresearchcouncil.com/uploaded_files/tinymce/Dog%20Bites%20Problems%20and%20Solutions.pdf; "Overall Dog Bite Nonfatal Injuries and Rates per 100,000," 2010, Centers for Disease Control, accessed Aug. 29, 2012, https://www.ohioinsurance.org/wp-content/uploads/2015/04/Doginjuries2001-13.pdf.
9. American Veterinary Medical Association, "Welfare Implications of the Role of Breed in Dog Bite Risk and Prevention," Apr. 17, 2012, accessed Oct. 23, 2013, https://www.avma.org/Advocacy/StateAndLocal/Documents/Welfare-Implications-of-the-role-of-breed.pdf; Cynthia Bathhurst, et al., *The Problem of Dog-Related Incidents and Encounters* (Washington, DC: Office of Community Oriented Policing Services, U.S. Dept. Of Justice, 2011), 6–10; Merritt Clifton, "Dog Attack Deaths and Maimings, U.S. & Canada September 1982 to December 31, 2012," accessed July 8, 2013, http://www.dogsbite.org/pdf/dog-attack-deaths-maimings-merritt-clifton-2012.pdf; Mia E. Lang and Terry Klassen, "Dog Bites in Canadian Children: A Five-Year Review of Severity and Emergency Room Management," *Canadian Journal of Emergency Medicine* 7 (2005): 309–14; Cheryl L. Loewe, Francisco J. Diaz, and John Bechinski, "Pitbull Mauling Deaths in Detroit," *The American Journal of Forensic Medicine and Pathology* 28 (2007): 356–60; "Head and Neck Dog Bites in Children," *Otolaryngolog—Head and Neck Surgery* 140 (2009): 354–57; Malathi Raghavan, "Fatal Dog Attacks in Canada, 1990–2007," *Canadian Veterinary Journal* 49 (2008): 577–81; Jeffrey J. Sacks, et al., "Breeds of Dogs Involved in Fatal Human Attacks in the United States between 1979 and 1998," *Journal of the American Veterinary Medical Association* 127 (2000): 836–40; and the assessment of data collection in Karen Delise, *Fatal Dog Attacks: The Stories*

Behind the Statistics (Orlando, FL: Anubis Publications, 2002), 124–25, 127–29. Other studies include Randall Lockwood, "The Ethology and Epidemiology of Dog Bites," in *Animal Law and Dog Behavior*, ed. David Favre and Peter L. Borchelt (Tucson: Lawyers and Judges Publishing Co., 1999), 287–98; Peter L. Borchelt, "Dog Bites—Basic Behavioral Principles and Misunderstood Words," in Ibid., 299–306; Peter L. Borchelt, et al., "Attacks by Packs of Dogs Involving Predation on Human Beings," in Ibid., 307–24.

10. Jaclyn E. Barnes, Barbara W. Boat, Frank W. Putnam, Harold F. Dates, and Andrew R. Mahlman, "Ownership of High-Risk ("Vicious") Dogs as a Marker for Deviant Behaviors: Implications for Risk Assessment," *Journal of Interpersonal Violence* 21 (2006): 1616–34; Laurie Ragatz, et al., "Vicious Dogs: The Antisocial Behaviors and Psychological Characteristics of Owners," *Journal of Forensic Sciences* 54 (2009): 699–703.

11. Victoria L. Voith, et al., "Comparison of Visual and DNA Breed Identification of Dogs and Inter-Observer Reliability," *American Journal of Sociological Research* 3 (2013): 17–29; Victoria L. Voith, et al., "Comparison of Adoption Agency Identification and DNA Breed Identification of Dogs," *Journal of Applied Animal Welfare Science* 12 (2009): 253–62.

12. Christy L. Hoffman, Natalie Harrison, London Wolff, and Carri Westgarth, "Is That Dog a Pit Bull? A Cross-Country Comparison of Perceptions of Shelter Workers Regarding Breed Identification," *Journal of Applied Animal Welfare Science* 17 (2014): 322–39.

13. B. Klaassen, J. R. Buckley, and A. Esmail, "Does the Dangerous Dogs Act Protect against Animal Attacks: A Prospective Study of Mammalian Bites in the Accident and Emergency Department," *Injury* 27 (1996): 89–91; Nancy Margaret Clarke, *A Survey of Urban Canadian Animal Control Practices: The Effect of Enforcement and Resourcing on the Reported Dog Bite Rate* (M.A. Thesis, University of British Columbia, Vancouver, B.C., 2009), 45–46; Gary J. Patronek, Margaret Slater, and Amy Marder, "Use of a Number-Need-to-Ban Calculation to Illustrate Limitations of Breed-Specific Legislation in Decreasing the Risk of Dog Bite-Related Injury," *Journal of the American Veterinary Medical Association* 237 (2010): 788–92; "Breed Specific Legislation," Animal Farm Foundation, accessed Oct. 31, 2013, http://animalfarmfoundation.org/files/BSL-E-Book-08-13.pdf, 31–37.

14. "Breed Specific Legislation," Animal Farm Foundation, accessed Oct. 31, 2013, http://animalfarmfoundation.org/files/BSL-E-Book-08-13.pdf, 31–37.

15. Delise, *Fatal Dog Attacks*, passim.

16. Huitson, *An Exploratory Analysis of the Emergence and Implications of Breed Specific Legislation*, passim.

17. Karen Delise, *The Pit Bull Placebo: The Media, Myths and Politics of Canine Aggression* (Orlando, FL: Anubis Publishing, 2007), 171.

18. Katherine Beckett and Steve Herbert, *Banishment: The New Social Control in Urban America* (New York: Oxford University Press, 2010), 21.
19. John W. Kingdon, *Agendas, Alternatives, and Public Policies*, 2nd ed. (Boston: Little, Brown and Co., 1984), 94–103.
20. Daniel Carpenter and Gisela Sin, "Policy Tragedy and the Emergence of Regulation: The Food, Drug, and Cosmetic Act of 1938," *Studies in American Political Development* 21 (2007): 150–51; Roger N. Lancaster, *Sex Panic and the Punitive State* (Berkeley: University of California Press, 2011), 6–12, 28–32.
21. Anthony Downs, "Up and Down with Ecology—The 'Issue Attention Cycle,'" *The Public Interest* 28 (1972): 39; Paul Slovic, Baruch Fischhoff, and Sarah Lichtenstein, "Rating the Risks," *Environment* 21 (1979): 14–39; Paul Slovic, Sarah Lichtenstein, and Baruch Fischhoff, "Modeling the Societal Impact of Fatal Accidents," *Management Science* 30 (1984): 464–74.
22. Joseph LeDoux, *The Emotional Brain: The Mysterious Underpinnings of Emotional Life* (New York: Simon and Schuster, 1996), 28.
23. S. Rachman, *Anxiety*, 2nd ed. (Hove, UK: Psychology Press, 2004), 96, 95–99.
24. George F. Loewenstein, et al., "Risks as Feelings," *Psychological Bulletin* 127 (2001): 267–86; Sheila T. Murphy and R. B. Zajonc, "Affect, Cognition, and Awareness: Affective Priming with Optimal and Suboptimal Stimulus Exposures," *Journal of Personality and Social Psychology* 64 (1993): 723–39.
25. Leonie Huddy, Stanley Feldman, and Erin Cassese, "On the Distinct Political Effects of Anxiety and Anger," in *The Affect Effect: Dynamics of Emotion in Political Thinking and Behavior*, ed. W. Russell Neuman, George E. Marcus, Ann N. Crigler, and Micheal MacKuen (Chicago: University of Chicago Press, 2007), 209.
26. Stanley Cohen, *Folk Devils and Moral Panics: The Creation of the Mods and Rockers* (Cambridge, MA: Basil Blackwell, 1980).
27. See Jennifer S. Lerner and Darcher Keltner, "Beyond Valence: Toward a Model of Emotion-Specific Influences on Judgement and Choice," *Cognition and Emotion*, 14 (2000): 473–93.
28. Ali Siddq Alhakami and Paul Slovic, "A Psychological Study of the Inverse Relationship between Perceived Risk and Perceived Benefit," *Risk Analysis* 14 (1994): 1085–1100; Huddy, Feldman, and Cassese, "Distinct Political Effects"; Jeanne X. Kasperson, et al., "The Social Amplification of Risk: Assessing Fifteen Years of Research and Theory," in *The Social Amplification of Risk*, ed. Nick Pidgeon, Roger E. Kasperson, and Paul Slovic (Cambridge: Cambridge University Press, 2003), 13–46; S. Rachman, "The Overprediction of Fear: A Review," *Behaviour Research and Therapy* 32 (1994): 683–90.
29. Daniel Kahneman and Amos Tversky, "Prospect Theory: An Analysis of Decision under Risk," *Econometrica* 47 (1979): 263–91; Amos Tversky and

Daniel Kahneman, "Advances in Prospect Theory: Cumulative Representation of Uncertainty," *Journal of Risk and Uncertainty* 5 (1992): 297–323.

30. Delise, *The Pit Bull Placebo*, 107–26, summarizes the errors in these claims.
31. See Jonathan Haidt, "The Emotional Dog and Its Rational Tail: A Social Intuitionist Approach to Moral Judgement," *Psychological Review* 108 (2001): 814–34; Paul Rozin and Carol Nemeroff, "Sympathetic Magical Thinking: The Contagion and Similarity 'Heuristics,'" in *Heuristics and Biases: The Psychology of Intuitive Judgment*, ed. Thomas Gilovich, Dale Griffin, and Daniel Kahneman (Cambridge: Cambridge University Press, 2002), 201–16.
32. Deborah A. Small, Jennifer S. Lerner, and Baruch Fischhoff, "Emotion Priming and Attributions for Terrorism: Americans' Reactions in a National Field Experiment," *Political Psychology* 27 (2006): 289–98; Kasperson, et al., "The Social Amplification of Risk," 13–46; John Eldridge and Jacquie Reilly, "Risk and Relativity: BSE and the British Media," in *The Social Amplification of Risk*, ed. Nick Pidgeon, Roger E. Kasperson, and Paul Slovic (Cambridge: Cambridge University Press, 2003), 138–55; Lancaster, *Sex Panic*, 25–28.
33. Huitson, *An Exploratory Analysis of the Emergence and Implications of Breed Specific Legislation*, 26–40; Judy Cohen and John Richardson, "Pit Bull Panic," *Journal of Popular Culture* 36 (2002): 291–94. On sensationalist reporting about pit bulls see also Delise, *The Pit Bull Placebo*, 95–106, 130–53. On media reporting practices and the reasons for amplifying risks, see W. Lance Bennett, *News: The Politics of Illusion*, 6th ed. (New York: Pearson, 2005), 74–101, 151–72; Barbara Combs and Paul Slovic, "Newspaper Coverage of the Causes of Death," *Journalism Quarterly* 56 (1979): 837–43; Shanto Iyengar and Donald Kinder, *News That Matters: TV and American Opinion* (Chicago: University of Chicago Press, 1987), 34–46.
34. Bennett, *News*, 36–73; Eldridge and Reilly, "Risk and Relativity," 138–55; Doris A. Graber, *Mass Media and American Politics*, 7th ed. (Washington, DC: CQ Press, 2006), 86–147; Iyengar and Kinder, *News That Matters*, 16–63; Kasperson, et al., "Social Amplification of Risk." On available information and decisions, see Amos Tversky and Daniel Kahneman, "Availability: A Heuristic for Judging Frequency and Probability," *Cognition* 5 (1973): 208; Norbert Schwarz and Leigh Ann Vaughan, "The Availability Heuristic Revisited: Ease of Recall and Content of Recall as Distinct Sources of Information," in *Heuristics and Biases: The Psychology of Intuitive Judgment*, ed. Thomas Gilovich, Dale Griffin, and Daniel Kahneman (Cambridge: Cambridge University Press, 2002), 103–19.
35. David Hirschleifer, "The Blind Leading the Blind: Social Influence, Fads, and Information Cascades," in *The New Economics of Human Behavior*, ed. Mariano Tommasi and Kathryn Ierulli (Cambridge: Cambridge University Press, 1995), 191.
36. See Kasperson, et al., "Social Amplification of Risk."

37. Marcus, Neuman, and MacKuen, *Affective Intelligence*, 45–140.
38. See Tversky and Kahneman, "Availability."
39. Marianna Valverde, *Law's Dream of a Common Knowledge* (Princeton: Princeton University Press, 2003), 53.
40. Martin Lodge and Christopher Hood, "Pavlovian Policy Responses to Media Feeding Frenzies? Dangerous Dogs Regulation in Comparative Perspective," *Journal of Contingencies and Crisis Management* 10 (2002), 3–4, 10–11.
41. Martin Lodge, "Barking Mad? Risk Regulation and the Control of Dangerous Dogs in Germany," *German Politics* 10 (2001): 75–76.
42. See Downs, "Up and Down with Ecology," 40.
43. See Downs, "Up and Down with Ecology," 40–41; Kingdon, *Agendas, Alternatives, and Public Policies*, 103–5.
44. "Archive Search Results," *Kansas City Star*, accessed Oct. 21, 2015, archives.kcstar.com, is the source for stories used for this paragraph.
45. The news archives of television station KMBC-TV, Kansas City, for example, accessed Jan.–Feb. 2007, contain dozens of stories from May through December 2006. "Archive Search Results," *Kansas City Star*, accessed Oct. 21, 2015, archives.kcstar.com, is also the source for stories used for this paragraph.
46. "Breed Specific Legislation," Missouri Pit Bull Rescue, accessed July 11, 2013, http://www.mopitbullrescue.org/#!bsl/c1aw1. For current municipal laws in Kansas and Missouri, see "Breed-Specific Laws State-by-State," DogsBite.org, accessed Oct. 21, 2015, http://www.dogsbite.org/legislating-dangerous-dogs-state-by-state.php.
47. Matt Campbell and Lynn Horsley, "As Attacks Continue, Cities Strengthen Dog Laws: Many City Councils in the Area Have Banned Pit Bulls, and Others Are Considering Restrictions," *Kansas City Star*, July 29, 2006, 1; Mike Ekey, "Olathe Stands by Its Dog Law," *Kansas City Star*, Oct. 14, 2006; Russ Pulley, "Broader Controls on Dogs in the Works," *Kansas City Star*, Oct. 15, 2006; "Breed Specific Legislation," Missouri Pit Bull Rescue, accessed Oct. 23, 2013, http://www.mopitbullrescue.org/#!bsl/c1aw1; "Breed Specific Legislation Map," Animal Farm Foundation, accessed Oct. 19, 2015, http://www.animalfarmfoundation.org/pages/BSL-Map.
48. Confidential interviews by Susan Hunter, Jan.–Feb. 2007.
49. City of Independence, *City Code*, accessed Feb. 12, 2007, http://www.ci.independence.mo.us/userdocs/homepage/PitBullOrdFinal.pdf.
50. Brian Burnes, "Pit Bull Update," *Kansas City Star*, Nov. 1, 2006.
51. See "Pit Bull Amnesty Convinces Some Owners to Abide by Ban," accessed Aug. 27, 2012, http://www2.ljworld.com/news/2006/aug/13/pit_bull_amnesty_convinces_some_owners_abide_ban/.
52. "Kansas City, MO BSL/MSN—Year 4. Can We Quit Pretending It's Working

Yet?," *KC Dog Blog*, Feb. 10, 2010, accessed Oct. 9, 2013, http://btoellner.typepad.com/kcdogblog/2010/02/kansas-city-mo-bslmsn-year-4-can-we-quit-pretending-its-working-yet.html; "Understanding Cause & Effect When It Comes to Mandatory Spay/Neuter Laws," *KC Dog Blog*, June 6, 2013, accessed Oct. 9, 2013, http://btoellner.typepad.com/kcdogblog/bslmsn/.
53. Confidential interview by Susan Hunter, Jan. 2007.
54. Nicolas Dupont, "Dangerous Dog Ordinance Amendments Move Forward," *Lee's Summit Journal*, Mar. 1, 2007.
55. "Riverside, MO Repeals Long-Time Breed Ban," *KC Dog Blog*, Sept. 28, 2013, accessed Oct. 9, 2013, http://btoellner.typepad.com/kcdogblog/2013/09/riverside-mo-repeals-long-time-breed-ban.html. Asmer Madhani, "U.S. Communities Increasing Ditching Pit Bull Bans," *USA Today*, Nov. 18, 2014.
56. "Dog Attacks and the Law," Haber and Associates, accessed Oct. 21, 2015, http://www.haber-lawyer.com/blog/dog-attacks-law-ontario/.
57. Confidential interviews by Susan Hunter, Sept.–Oct. 2006.
58. Ontario Legislative Assembly, Standing Committee of the Legislative Assembly, "Subcommittee Report: Public Safety Related to Dogs Statute Law Amendment Act, 2005," 929.
59. Telephone interview with Garfield Dunlop (PC), Ontario Legislative Assembly by Susan Hunter, July 24, 2006; Telephone interview with Peter Kormos (NDP), Ontario Legislative Assembly by Susan Hunter, July 27, 2006; Confidential interviews with members of Executive Council, Dog Legislation Council of Canada, by Richard A. Brisbin, Jr., and Susan Hunter, Halifax, NS, Sept. 4, 2006.
60. Authors' summary of media reportage.
61. Members of some of these groups have suggested the consultation did appear to involve a serious effort to consider alternative policies; Confidential interviews by Richard A. Brisbin, Jr., and Susan Hunter, Halifax, NS, Aug. and Sept. 2006. Also Michael Bryant, Letter to Susan Hunter and Richard Brisbin, Aug. 1, 2006.
62. See Ericson and Haggerty, "The Policing of Risk," 238.
63. For a summary on the tendency of the public to miscalculate risks, compare Jeffrey J. Sacks, et al., "Breeds of Dogs Involved in Fatal Human Attacks," 836, with Slovic, et al., "Rating the Risks," 14.
64. City of Winnipeg, *Pound By-Law* § 20.2, Schedule B (2006), repealed by City of Winnipeg, By-Law no. 92/2013 (2014).
65. Ontario, Standing Committee, "Subcommittee Report."
66. Ibid., 1010.
67. Compare Don Peat, "Pit Bull Ban Fails to Reduce Dog Bites, *Toronto Sun*, Apr. 28, 2010, with "Pit Bulls Were Toronto's Biggest Biters, before the Ban,"

thestar.com, Mar. 10, 2014, accessed Oct. 21, 2015, http://www.thestar.com/news/gta/2014/10/03/pit_bulls_were_torontos_biggest_biters_before_the_ban.html.

68. Iyshah Hasham, "Ontario's Pit Bull Ban: The Pit Bull Underground Railroad," *thestar.com*, July 29, 2012, accessed Oct. 13, 2013, http://www.thestar.com/news/gta/2012/07/29/ontarios_pit_bull_ban_the_pit_bull_underground_railroad.html; Molly Hayes, "A Breed Apart, Banned Pit Bulls Are Still Around," *Hamilton Spectator*, Aug.10, 2013, accessed Oct. 13, 2013, http://www.thespec.com/news-story/4026540-a-breed-apart-banned-pit-bulls-are-still-around/.

69. The Dog Legislation Council of Canada, Advocates for the Underdog, Golden Horseshoe American Pit Bull Terrier Club, American Staffordshire Terrier Club of Canada, Staffordshire Bull Terrier Club of Canada.

70. Cochrane v. Ontario (Attorney General), [2007] O.J. No. 1090, at para. 22–86.

71. Ibid., at para. 87–193.

72. Cochrane v. Ontario (Attorney General), [2007] O.J. No. 1090, para. 194–248.

73. Cochrane v. Ontario (Attorney General), [2007] O.J. No. 2966.

74. Cochrane v. Ontario, [2008] O.J. No. 4165.

75. R. v. Huggins, [2007] O.J. No. 2693; Yeung v. Toronto, [2008] O.J. No. 561; Letourneau v. Toronto (City), 2009 CanLII 68829 (ON SC); see also R. v. Macheras, 2013 ONCJ 516 (CanLII).

76. Olszewski v. John Doe, 2012 ONSC 1209 (CanLII); Olszewski v. Ottawa (Police Services Board), 2013 ONSC 4039 (CanLII).

77. R. v. Kirby, [2006] O.J. No. 2025.

78. On this aspect of legality see Mary D. Fan, "When Deterrence and Death Mitigation Fall Short: Fantasy and Fetishes in Border Regulation," *Law and Society Review* 42 (2008): 703–5, 722; Slavoj Žižek, *The Sublime Object of Ideology* (London: Verso, 1989), 36–43.

79. Confidential interviews by Susan Hunter, Sept.–Oct. 2006.

80. Authors' summary of media reportage.

81. Confidential interviews by Susan Hunter, Sept. 2006.

82. New Brunswick, "Financial and Social Implications of Breed Specific Legislation." Presented to the New Brunswick Legislative Assembly, Fredericton, New Brunswick, Nov. 16, 2004.

83. Confidential interviews by Susan Hunter, Sept. 2006; Society for the Prevention of Cruelty to Animals Act, *Revised Statutes of New Brunswick* 1973, c. S-12 (2015); City of Fredricton, By-law No. S 11, A By-Law Respecting Animal Control.

84. This conclusion parallels the findings of Lodge and Hood, "Pavlovian Policy Responses."

85. Steven C. Tauber, *Navigating the Jungle: Law, Politics, and the Animal Advocacy Movement* (New York: Routledge, 2016), 101–2, 146–49.

86. Decisions in support of BSL include American Dog Owners Association v. City of Yakima, 113 Wn.2d 213 (1989); City of Pagedale v. Murphy, 142 S.W.3d 775 (2004); Hearn v. City of Overland Park, 772 P.2d 758 (1989); Starkey, v. Township of Chester, 628 F. Supp. 196 (E. D. Pa. 1986); Garcia v. Village of Tijeras, No. 9424 (N.M. Ct. App. 1988); Hearn v. City of Overland Park, Kansas, 244 Kan. 638 (1989); Giaculli v. Bright, 584 So. 2d 187 (Fla. Ct. App. 1991); American Canine Foundation v. City of Aurora, 618 F. Supp. 2d 1271 (D. C. Colo. 2009). Decisions holding BSL invalid include American Dog Owners Association, v. City of Lynn, 404 Mass. 73 (1989); Ohio v. Cowan, 814 N.E.2d 846 (2004); Bess v. Bracken County Fiscal Court, 2006 Ky. App. LEXIS 347; Dias v. City & County of Denver, 567 F.3d 1169 (10th Cir. 2009); Dias v. City & County of Denver, 2010 U.S. Dist. LEXIS 103814 (D. C. Colo.). One court exempted a pit bull used as a service dog from a breed specific ban, Sak v. City of Aurelia, 832 F. Supp. 2d 1026 (N.D. Ia. 2011).
87. *California Food & Agricultural Code* § 31683 (2013); *Colorado Revised Statutes* §18-9-204.5 (5)(a) (2012); *Connecticut General Statutes* § 7-148(c) (7) (D) (I) (2013); *Florida Statutes* § 767.14 (2012); 510 *Illinois Compiled Statutes* 5/24 (2013); 7 *Maine Revised Statutes* § 3950 (2013); *Annotated Laws of Massachusetts* GL chap. 140, § 157(c) (vii) (2013); Maryland, *Senate Bill 247, House Bill 73* (2014) (BSL failed*: House Bill 422, Senate Bill 991* (2014); *Minnesota Statutes* § 347.51 Subd. 8 (2013); *New Jersey Statutes* § 4:19-36 (2013); *New York Consolidated Law Service, Agriculture and Markets Law* § 107.5 (2013); Nevada, Assembly Bill No. 110; 4 North Dakota, Senate Bill 2211 (2014); *Oklahoma Statutes* § 46 (2013); 3 *Pennsylvania Statutes* § 459-507-A(C) (2013); State of Rhode Island, General Assembly, An Act Relating to Animals and Animal Husbandry—Dogs and Vicious Dogs, 2013—H 5671; *Texas Health & Safety Code* § 822.047 (2012); *Virginia Code Annotated* § 3.2-6540 C (2013); *Revised Code of Washington* (ARCW) § 16.08.100 (3) (2013). For criticism of dangerous dog laws, with a focus on Florida law, see Cynthia A. McNeely and Sarah A. Linquist, "Dangerous Dog Laws: Failing to Give Man's Best Friend a Fair Shake at Justice," *Journal of Animal Law* 3 (2007): 99–158.
88. Melissah Yang, "Nevada Bans Dog Breed Discrimination," *Las Vegas Review-Journal,* May 30, 2013; "Nevada Legislature: Revise NRS 202.500 to Make Breed Discrimination Illegal in Nevada," Incred-a-Bull, accessed July 11, 2013, http://www.change.org/petitions/nevada-legislature-revise-nrs-202-500-to-make-breed-discrimination-illegal-in-nevada; "Nevada Bans Breed Specific Legislation," Life with Dogs, accessed July 11, 2013, http://www.lifewithdogs.tv/2013/05/nevada-bans-breed-specific-legislation/.
89. Keith Bowers, "Breed-Specific Legislation Now Illegal in Massachusetts," *Dogster,* accessed July 11, 2013, http://www.care2.com/greenliving/breed-specific-legislation-now-illegal-in-massachusetts.html.

90. Hannah McCartney, "Cincinnati Pit Bull Ban Repealed," *City Beat*, May 16, 2012, accessed Oct. 9, 2013, http://www.citybeat.com/cincinnati/blog-3479-cincinnati_pit_bull_ban_repealed.html.
91. See "The Tide is Turning against Breed Specific Legislation," *Pit Bull Legal News*, Mar. 20, 2011, accessed Oct. 9, 2013, http://legal.pblnn.com/legal-library/library-case-law; Asmer Madhani, "U.S. Communities Increasing Ditching Pit Bull Bans," *USA Today*, Nov. 18, 2014. However, many federal and state courts have upheld breed bans; for a list of the decisions, see "Constitutionality of Breed-Specific Laws," *DogsBite.org*, accessed Oct. 19, 2013, http://www.dogsbite.org/legislating-dangerous-dogs-constitutionality.php.
92. Ronnie Dixon, City Manager, Clay Alabama, e-mail to Susan Hunter, Oct. 23, 2013.
93. Interview, South Bend Animal Care and Control staff, by Richard A. Brisbin, Jr., Sept. 26, 2013.
94. Statements of groups listed in "Breed Specific Legislation," Animal Farm Foundation, accessed Oct. 24, 2013, http://animalfarmfoundation.org/files/BSL-E-Book-08-13.pdf, 3–7.
95. "Breed-Specific Legislation Is a Bad Idea," The White House, Aug. 12, 2013, accessed Oct. 19, 2015, https://petitions.whitehouse.gov/response/breed-specific-legislation-bad-idea.
96. City & County of Denver v. State of Colorado, 04CV3756; Kory A. Nelson, Assistant City Attorney–Senior, Prosecution and Code Enforcement Section, Denver City Attorney's Office, "Denver's Pit Bull Ordinance: A Review of Its History and Judicial Rulings," July 9, 2009, http://www.dogsbite.org/pdf/denver-pitbull-ordinance-history-judicial-rulings.pdf.
97. Elinor J. Brecher, "In Miami-Dade, Pit Bulls Remain Illegal," *Miami Herald*, Aug. 15, 2012.
98. 3 *Pennsylvania Statutes* § 459-507-A (d) (2013). See also Larry Cunningham, "The Case against Dog Breed Discrimination by Homeowners' Insurance Companies," *Connecticut Insurance Law Journal* 11 (2004): 1–66.
99. *Ohio Revised Code Annotated* § 955.22 (2012). See also Florida v. Peters, 534 So. 2d 760 (Fla. Ct. App. 1988).
100. See Michele C. Hollow, "Insuring Your Pit Bull," Animal Law Coalition, May 25, 2010, accessed Aug. 25, 2012, http://www.animallawcoalition.com/breed-bans/article/1349. For a description of the policies of insurance companies that affect pit bulls and other dogs, see "Insurance Policy Terms and Conditions," 24PetWatch Pet Insurance Programs, accessed Oct. 20, 2015, http://www.24petwatch.com/pdf/24PetWatch_terms_conditions_np.pdf/.

10

The Enforcement of Pet Legislation

H as policy become practice? Are the variety of laws, regulations, and policies designed to protect or control companion animals regularly implemented and enforced by regulatory agencies, prosecutors, and the judiciary? Or, are these laws and regulations symbolic gestures that have little influence on the treatment of pets? To address these questions we draw on case studies of the enforcement of anti-cruelty, kennel inspection, horse transportation, and spay/neuter laws. We examine the role of administrative bodies and courts in the enforcement of companion animal laws and regulations. Then we examine how individuals can use civil litigation in ways that influence the treatment of cats, dogs, and horses. The final section of the chapter will discuss how the implementation of the laws and regulations affects legal accountability for the treatment of pets.

Unfortunately there is a dearth of quantitative data about companion animal law enforcement. Public inspectors, local governmental animal law regulators and shelters, and local and state police frequently do not systematically collect quantitative information about their enforcement of laws that regulate the treatment of cats, dogs, and horses. Local prosecutors, courts, the U.S. Department of Justice, U.S. Department of Agriculture (USDA), and Canadian federal agencies do not include animal-related crimes, victimization, prosecutions, convictions, or other animal regulatory actions in their reports. (However, as noted in chapter 1, in October 2014 the U.S. Federal Bureau of Investigation [FBI] began to ask law enforcement agencies to report animal-related incidents and arrests.) Consequently, the examination of enforcement relies primarily on qualitative data collected through interviews, responses to e-mail questions, observations, and discussions with participants at animal law conferences across the United States and in Canada. Although this evidence has significant limitations, we believe that it provides an initial exposition of a neglected aspect of pet politics.

THE NATURE AND SCOPE OF ENFORCEMENT ACTIVITY

In North America the enforcement of animal law depends heavily on public reports of legal violations and nuisances. Akin to the reporting of crimes directed at humans and their property, it is likely that citizen complaints to animal law enforcement agents depend on a mix of personal values, sense of civic responsibility, social relations with the perpetrator, social status, knowledge about legal institutions, race, age, and gender. Also, the perceived seriousness of the offense or disorder, such as barking, howling, biting, defecating, or running loose, might affect reporting and governmental intervention.[1] Citizen complaints are frequently directed to elected local government officials such as council members. However, often public complainants refuse to file a formal complaint. In turn, these officials make a choice to discard the complaint or inform and directly or indirectly persuade action by the administrative officers: animal control officers, peace officers, or the private humane organizations delegated law enforcement powers by state or local government. These administrators also depend heavily on public complaints *and* elected officials to prioritize the seriousness of problems with the behavior or treatment of pets.[2] Then animal control, police, and criminal prosecution agencies can make a choice about the street-level enforcement of companion animal laws.

What influences the decisions of these officials at the street level? Although Arnold Arluke's ethnographic study of Society for the Prevention of Cruelty to Animals (SPCA) humane officers in Massachusetts reported that a division of workplace identified between officers who were "animal inclined" and those who were more "police oriented" produced distinctive patterns of anti-cruelty law enforcement, it is only a partial study of the politics of policy implementation.[3] In addition to Arluke's attention to the influence of the attitudes of street-level enforcement personnel, other conditions that affect the enforcement of companion animal laws need consideration. Drawing on the literature about politics and behavior of managers and street-level agents that contribute to the agency, prosecutorial, and judicial capacity to implement or enforce laws,[4] we examine how the enforcement of companion animal laws depends on a mix of the aspects of institutional capacity: (1) the political, legal, and policy context and institutional structure of animal regulatory agency operations; (2) agency management and its use of decision-making powers; (3) street-level enforcement officers' discretionary practices, norms, and attitudes; and (4) prosecutorial agencies and judicial norms that govern their use of powers. Enforcement therefore is shaped by the political construction of the institutions that regulate animals and assorted "agency problems" linked to institutional authority, management, and resources.[5]

Institutional Considerations

When state and local legislators drafted animal cruelty laws during the mid-nineteenth century, police departments and other state regulatory institutions rarely existed.[6] Consequently, states such as Massachusetts and New York delegated arrest powers for violations of anti-cruelty animal laws to a private nonprofit organization, the SPCA. By contract with government in some jurisdictions, the SPCA and other nonprofit organizations continue to manage animal control and shelter operations in the United States.[7] Also, this arrangement has been followed in many Canadian communities, including Toronto and about fifty other Ontario jurisdictions and in rural areas of Alberta and other provinces.[8] Since 1919 in Ontario the provincial SPCA and its more than fifty affiliates have had extensive law enforcement authority. A nonprofit organization funded in part by the government, its agents have the arrest powers of police officers, the power to enter and inspect, with or without a warrant, any building or place used for animal exhibition, entertainment, boarding, hire or sale, to seize evidence of abuse in plain view, to seize or destroy animals in distress, and to impose costs for the shelter or euthanasia of animals.[9] The sweeping nature of these powers, especially when applied to farm animals, has generated a constitutional challenge that is in litigation about the grant of police powers to private organizations.[10]

As indicated in Table 10.1, twenty-six U.S. states and the Canadian provinces retain the pre-state agency approach and authorize humane society officers to investigate animal cruelty. The addition of felony provisions to anti-cruelty law also has created fragmentation of authority in states with enforcement powers assigned to humane agencies. Humane agencies often do not have armed officers and are not authorized to make arrests. They can seize the animals, but a peace officer must be called to make felony arrests. Because evidentiary assessments make the decision on felony or misdemeanor arrest often a judgment call and peace officers are often unwilling to investigate animal charges, the felony provisions can be ignored. Consequently humane agencies often have found that the most effective way to obtain action is to notify local media about the abuse or neglect in the hope that they will pressure elected officials to take action.

Other animal law enforcement institutional structures exist. Many state and province police and sheriff's departments have assumed or been assigned by law the enforcement of companion animal laws. In nineteen states anti-cruelty laws are enforced only by peace officers: state police, sheriffs, municipal officers, and sheriffs—who can investigate and arrest on animal cruelty and any other criminal or traffic offense. No specialized animal control agency exists in these states. These laws state that any peace officer can investigate and arrest, although some states require that officers obtain a warrant before going onto private property to investigate.

Alternatively, various limited jurisdiction public regulators such as animal control officers, kennel inspection agents, game wardens, code enforcement officers, public health inspectors, and other officials have the power to enforce specific companion animal laws or operate shelters. Some governments divide the authority to address specific animal policies among such agencies. Sometimes these agencies have overlapping powers, and sometimes several governmental units will manage one or several of these agencies.

Some municipalities contract with private firms to manage animal control and shelter operations. Individual or civic associations with information on abuse can also bypass these institutions and lodge a legal complaint with officials with penalization powers, such as prosecutors or local judicial officers. Although these tactics are very infrequently employed, in some states individuals can make common law arrests for some misdemeanor violations of animal welfare laws committed in their presence, grand juries can conduct investigations and issue indictments for violations of these laws, and persons can seek a writ of mandamus to force animal law enforcement personnel to conduct investigations and make arrests.[11]

Agency Management

As suggested by studies of other administrative agencies, it is likely that animal agency managers' attitudes vary about the necessary actions for the treatment of unwanted pets, their knowledge of the behavior and health of cats, dogs, and horses, and their understanding of the requirements of animal laws. Other variations in agency managers' behavior include their responsiveness to communications or demands from elected officials, media, veterinarians, and animal activists and organizations; their communication to political leaders and the public and support for animal rescue groups; and their treatment of volunteers and interactions with publicly appointed advisory bodies. There also can be variations in the selection, training, oversight, and delegation of tasks to subordinates and budgetary management and record keeping.[12]

TABLE 10.1 *Entity to Which Primary Powers Are Assigned for Enforcement of Anti-cruelty Laws*

State or Province	Humane Society or Other Animal Welfare Organization	Peace Officers Only	Other[a]
Alabama		x	
Alaska		x	
Arizona		x	
Arkansas	x		
California	x		
Colorado		x	
Connecticut	x		
Delaware	x		
Florida	x		
Georgia			x
Hawaii		x	
Idaho			x
Illinois			x
Indiana		x	
Iowa		x	
Kansas		x	
Kentucky	x		
Louisiana	x		
Maine	x		
Maryland	x		
Massachusetts	x		
Michigan	x		
Minnesota	x		
Mississippi		x	
Missouri		x	
Montana		x	
Nebraska		x	
Nevada	x		
New Hampshire		x	
New Jersey	x		
New Mexico		x	
New York	x		
North Carolina	x		
North Dakota			x
Ohio	x		

TABLE 10.1 *Entity to Which Primary Powers Are Assigned for Enforcement of Anti-cruelty Laws—cont'd*

State or Province	Humane Society or Other Animal Welfare Organization	Peace Officers Only	Other[a]
Oklahoma		x	
Oregon		x	
Pennsylvania	x		
Rhode Island	x		
South Carolina	x		
South Dakota	x		
Tennessee	x		
Texas		x	
Utah		x	
Vermont	x		
Virginia	x		
Washington	x		
West Virginia			x
Wisconsin	x		
Wyoming		x	
Alberta			x
British Columbia	x		
Manitoba			
New Brunswick	x		
Newfoundland & Labrador			x
Northwest Territories			x
Nova Scotia	x		
Nunavut			x
Ontario	x		
Prince Edward Island			x
Quebec	x		
Saskatchewan			x
Yukon			x

[a] Idaho and North Dakota Departments of Agriculture investigate cruelty toward any animal but require a complaint and a warrant before investigation can occur. The Georgia Animal Protection Section and the Illinois Bureau of Animal Welfare are units of the state's department of agriculture. Illinois also allows trained humane society officers to assist the Bureau. West Virginia requires every county sheriff to appoint at least one deputy sheriff as a humane officer and also allows the county commission to appoint other persons as humane officers. Alberta, Newfoundland & Labrador, Northwest Territories, Nunavut, Prince Edward Island, Saskatchewan, and Yukon use a mix of peace officers, public animal control officers and humane society officers in anti-cruelty law enforcement.

Street-Level Discretion

Studies of bureaucratic politics stress the political importance of discretion and case processing by subordinates.[13] As Arluke discovered, variations among street-level enforcement officers' values and practices require examination. These include variations in their methods of detection of suspected threats to animal health and welfare, the screening of calls and rationing of responses to citizen demands, their norms for determination of seriousness of the animals' conditions, cruelty, and violations of laws, and their assessments of the "worth" or "danger" of animal problems and abuse.[14] Also, there is a need to consider variations in their interactions with the public as clients, violators, and others. Finally, there is a need to assess how variations in agency field officers' training in the law, commitment to compliance with animal laws, laziness and shirking, and preferences in the use of persuasion and suggestions, warnings, threats, citations, arrests, and animal seizures influence their citation of offenders and referral of infractions to prosecutors or courts.[15] In some circumstances these behavioral variations can become street-level routines that supplement or modify statutory animal law and result in an unwillingness or a failure to enforce the law.

Prosecution, Adjudication, and Sanctions

In all American jurisdictions except North Carolina, private individuals and organizations cannot independently criminally prosecute cruelty cases.[16] Canada, however, provides for private criminal prosecution of animal abuse cases in its federal Health of Animals Act.[17] The lack of a private right of criminal prosecution and, apparently, few private prosecutions means that regulatory and prosecutorial officials or private organizations delegated law enforcement powers control the flow of alleged violations into court. Although law schools and some state bars now offer seminars on the topic, prosecutors (district attorneys, state's attorneys, prosecuting attorneys) usually receive little training about animal law. Nevertheless, prosecutors have broad discretion over the disposition of cases about the abuse of cats, dogs, and horses.[18] The decision to prosecute can vary because of the attentiveness of the office to animal law issues and animal-related crime and the training of assistant prosecutors about animal laws. Also, there are variations in the prosecutors' practices for case screening and review of arrests, assessment of the reliability of evidence, use of *nolle prosequi,* designation of charges, and decisions about plea bargaining and the penalization of plea bargaining defendants. In particular, the reluctance of complainants and witnesses to testify means that prosecutors will not proceed with the case.[19] Other variations in the decision to prosecute can stem from the jurisdiction of these agencies, the laws the agency is to enforce, legal requirements for prosecution, support for the prosecutor's actions by elected officials, interest groups, and media, and agency funding and staffing.[20]

Many of the adjudications of animal law violations in the United States transpire before judges of limited jurisdiction courts who are not attorneys and who are not educated in animal law. Their responses in animal law enforcement cases might depend on variations in their attitudes toward animals, external political pressure and personal friendships, procedural rules, and authority to issue dismissals, citations and fines, forfeitures, closures of kennels, seizure of animals, probation, or incarceration.[21] Despite widely varying rules that define their jurisdiction, trial courts of general jurisdiction in both nations usually hear cases in which the prosecutor has charged an individual with felony animal cruelty. These cases can raise issues about the legality of the collection of evidence by regulatory agents and, very rarely, property rights and the regulatory powers of governments.[22] The consequence is that judges can make the final determination about the meaning and enforcement of the law.

THE ENFORCEMENT OF ANIMAL CRUELTY LAWS

What is the pattern of enforcement for ant-cruelty laws? To address this question, we describe enforcement efforts in four jurisdictions that differ in political institutions and resources, laws, demography, and pet-related problems: rural and small town North Central West

Virginia, the City of Pittsburgh, the City of South Bend, and the City of Calgary. These communities illustrate the range of companion animal law and policy enforcement efforts: from the haphazard control of abuse to the professionalized animal care operations currently emerging in a few North American communities.

North Central West Virginia

In West Virginia, among the most rural of American states and possessing a tradition of limited governmental capacity to address economic and social problems, politics has posed barriers to the enforcement of anti-cruelty and abandonment laws. The state has often reluctantly adopted new animal welfare laws and has largely left animal law enforcement to local elected bodies. In this section we offer an overview of enforcement in the state and examples of enforcement in small-town-dominated Monongalia County (population 96,000), rural Preston County (population 34,000), and Taylor County (population 17,000) in North Central West Virginia.

The Political and Legal Context of Enforcement

In West Virginia anti-cruelty laws are enforced only by peace officers: state police, county sheriffs, and municipal officers. No specialized state companion animal regulatory agency exists, and most county or municipal animal care and control officers focus their efforts on nuisance complaints and the collection of abandoned pets. They have little training in animal policies and animal behavior. In North Central West Virginia, animal care and control officers are often uninformed about their enforcement authority. As in most U.S. states and Canadian provinces, anti-cruelty laws are scattered throughout state codes and local ordinances, and we have found that enforcement officers and prosecutors cannot find some sections of the law, may not be aware of them, or discover they are difficult to interpret. Additionally, laws are often written in ways that call for discretionary judgments. In West Virginia, cruelty to animals is only a felony if the act is malicious.[23] Potential felonies are a higher priority for prosecution, but a complaint must specify that the abuser has committed a malicious act. However, animal control officers are left without guidance about the meaning of *malice*.

Jurisdictional issues determine where cruelty and abandonment are reported by individuals and whether an agency can respond to a report. Often different agencies handle different citizen calls. For example, animal control agencies do not respond to animal cruelty calls in Monongalia, Preston, and Taylor Counties, but they are the agencies to call for dogs running loose and violations of kennel laws. Animal control officers do not pick up cats. Dog bites are required to be reported to the county health department, but the animal control officer is responsible for quarantining owned animals or seizing and killing strays to test for rabies. The sheriff's department, state police, or city police can investigate calls about companion animal abuse. Department of Natural Resources officers respond to calls about dogs endangering wildlife. Peace officers designated as humane officers can enter property to investigate animal care and inspect records with reasonable cause,[24] while other peace officers and animal control officers are only authorized to enter a premise during daylight hours and with a warrant except in investigations of dogfights.[25] With the myriad of overlapping and conflicting responsibilities, citizens find it extremely difficult to report problems to the appropriate agency.

The amount of revenue that public officials allocate to enforcement also varies greatly. In West Virginia the only designated funding for animal welfare and control is the dog and kennel fund. Dog owners are supposed to pay $3 per dog property tax to the county sheriff. Since the payment of the tax depends on the voluntary reporting of dog ownership, officials and welfare groups estimate that only 25 percent of owners pay the tax. This money is to go to the county's dog and kennel fund to reimburse farmers whose livestock has been injured by dogs. The revenue is also used for animal control. Municipalities often charge an additional $3 tax per dog, but the revenue goes into their general fund. A few municipalities include a tax on cats. County budgets for animal control and animal welfare vary from no additional funding for animal control to peace officers to nearly $500,000 for animal welfare, animal control, and the maintenance of a shelter.

Agency Management and Decision Making

County commissions, sheriffs, and municipal councils often designate animal issues as low priority matters. The concerns of elected officials can produce variations in the management of enforcement efforts. For example, every county sheriff, an elected official, is required to appoint a humane officer, and county commissions can appoint an animal control officer.[26] A commission can also designate the animal control officer as a humane officer. If the county commission feels that animal cruelty is a significant problem it is more likely to appoint additional humane officers. If the sheriff perceives animal cruelty as an important problem, he or she may also appoint additional humane officers. In Preston County a former sheriff saw as part of his role the control of vicious dogs. He gave the position of humane officer to his least capable deputy, made no effort to provide training, and usually did not even respond to cruelty calls. A significant change occurred when a new sheriff was elected. An animal lover, he believed that animal abusers are prone to commit other violent crimes. For this reason he appointed one deputy per shift as humane officer and selected personnel who believed that animal cruelty is a serious issue. Interviews with humane society members, the sheriff, and one of the humane officers indicated that cases were investigated on a regular basis during this sheriff's term in office.[27]

Under state law the commissioners determine whether they will operate a shelter, inspect kennels, and hire animal control officers. In Taylor County the commissioners have employed one animal control officer and the sheriff's department has one humane officer, the chief deputy. He is able to ensure that animal abuse calls are answered promptly and that reports are investigated. However, counties in West Virginia are not required to have any animal control officers.

Counties also are not required to have an animal shelter. Although several county commissions contract with their county humane society to operate these shelters, there are only sixteen public animal shelters in a state with fifty-five counties. Some counties have no animal control officers and no shelter for seized or stray animals. Preston County at one time operated a small shelter with the primary intent of killing stray dogs and cats. The shelter director's norm was to euthanize every animal by the end of its fifth day in holding. With a change in personnel, the shelter has had one of the lowest euthanasia rates for publicly managed shelters in the state in recent years. It has begun to utilize volunteers to contact rescue organizations, arrange transportation to rescue, and arrange spay/neuter for adoptable animals.

Training is an important activity that allows agency management to ensure employee loyalty to institutional goals and employee competence. Although specific training on animal law is important for enforcement personnel, most states do not require or provide such training. There are national programs, including training provided by the Humane Society of the United States, and the National Cruelty Investigations School at the University of Missouri. Several governors, including those in Vermont, Pennsylvania, and New Mexico, have established task forces to develop training for animal cruelty enforcement personnel. Nonetheless, in West Virginia the state and county governments provide no training in animal law for peace officers. Humane officers or animal control officers receive training in animal law enforcement only if their county authorizes it. Most counties provide no training. West Virginia also requires certification of euthanasia technicians. However, animal control officers in several shelters said they have euthanized animals but have had no training of any kind.

Street-Level Enforcement

The attitudes and norms of the sheriff and the humane officer are critical in the determination of whether a call merits an investigation. In their enforcement efforts at the street level they face legal constraints, such as warrant or complaint requirements. Humane officers with the sheriff's department have broader authority to investigate possible cases of animal abuse and can search property and seize animals without a warrant, but they also enforce all laws so animal cruelty has to compete with traffic accidents, drugs, and other violent crimes.[28] As one peace officer explained, "You are dispatched to deal with an animal cruelty call, but while en route you are told to respond to an accident with injury. While handling the accident with injury, another urgent call comes in. Unless the cruelty call was urgent, such as animal in eminent danger of death and abuse occurring at the time of the call, it gets put off for hours or even perhaps a day or so."[29]

Street-level discretion appears in other enforcement contexts. For example, in Preston County a complaint arrives through 911, a direct call to the sheriff's department from a witness, or a call from a humane society or animal control officer. There is no proactive patrol to find cruelty. Upon investigation, if the animal is not in danger and the abuse is inadequate housing, lack of shade, lack of food or water, or tethering, the officer will probably explain the law to the owner and give him or her a warning. If abuse is occurring when the officer arrives, the officer may arrest the abuser and seize the animal. Animal control officers and humane officers all agreed that a warning and explanation of the law would be the strategy they used unless an animal was severely injured or in imminent danger of death. If the animal is in danger, but no clear perpetrator can be observed, the officer can seize the animal and continue the investigation. If the officer feels the case is a felony, he or she can talk to the prosecutor about filing felony charges or taking the case to the grand jury; if a misdemeanor, the officer will file charges in the magistrate's office. Nevertheless, as the Preston County prosecuting attorney noted, most police officers and probably many humane officers are not even aware of the felony provision so they make no attempt to file more than a misdemeanor complaint.[30]

Prosecution and Adjudication

In most jurisdictions the commitment of the local prosecutor is an important component in the enforcement of animal cruelty law. One county prosecuting attorney stated that he would not even hear about an animal cruelty case unless it was filed as a felony or the humane officer or other citizens brought it to his attention. In his county an assistant prosecuting attorney, in consultation with the investigating officer, makes the decision about the number and type of charges to be filed. If an assistant prosecutor is sufficiently concerned and knowledgeable about animal cases, he or she can file the case as a felony, but the vast majority of cases are treated as misdemeanors. For example, the prosecuting attorney in Preston County defined malicious abuse as abuse that continued beyond a first surge of anger or fear. He gave the example of someone who kicks a dog once. If the person stops kicking the dog when it cowers or backs away, that is a misdemeanor offense. If the person continues to kick a cowering or injured dog, it becomes a felony. He added that a new assistant prosecutor may not interpret the law that way.

The prosecuting attorney makes the decision about any plea agreements. Plea bargains occur in almost all of these cases and result in some combination of fines and probation for the offender and seizure of the animal. When asked about a particularly serious case of cruelty at a large dog, cat, and rabbit breeding facility in his county, a prosecutor responded that he did not file felony charges against its operators because he expected the case to go to trial and he did not feel he had sufficient evidence to gain a conviction and incarceration of the offender. Instead, he filed against the corporation owning the facility to ensure that it was permanently shut down, which he felt was the best outcome he was likely to achieve. In West Virginia the lowest level of the judiciary, the elected magistrates, hear most animal cruelty cases.[31] Almost all magistrates are not lawyers, and they receive no training about animal law. The consensus of interviewees was that these magistrates are generally not interested in animal cases or informed about cruelty law, so the likelihood of even a fine is very low in the cases they hear. In a case of about a dog that was severely beaten by its owner, thrown into a small closet, pulled out of the closet, kicked and sprayed in the face, put back in the closet, and later pulled out of the closet and thrown into an apartment, the owner was convicted of a misdemeanor animal cruelty. One magistrate stated publicly that he would never send an animal abuser to jail.

The importance of discretion in the prosecution and adjudication of animal cruelty law in rural West Virginia is best summarized by events in a case of abuse of horses. Neighbors and animal welfare and stewardship groups had reported to public officials for weeks the thin and dying horses at an equine rescue.[32] Eventually neighbors began to complain about stench coming from the rescue site. This led the county humane officer, a deputy sheriff, to investigate. He found eight dead or dying horses, and forty-eight very thin horses and cows. The forty-eight sick animals were seized and moved to a neighboring farm. The county prosecuting attorney filed fifty-six misdemeanor charges of cruelty. Despite extensive pictures, interviews with neighbors, and files on each animal compiled by a veterinarian, an assistant prosecuting attorney agreed to let the owner plead to one misdemeanor charge. Although a hearing had been scheduled, the assistant prosecutor accepted this plea and took it to the magistrate prior to the scheduled hearing. By the time the veterinarian, the deputy sheriff, and interested parties arrived for the hearing, the owner paid a $1,000 fine and left the courthouse. The judge permitted the owner to continue to possess animals. As this case illustrates, animal law enforcers have the discretion to choose to respond to a complaint, use their norms to assess the seriousness of a situation, and enforce the law.

Pittsburgh and Allegheny County, Pennsylvania

The city of Pittsburgh, Pennsylvania, with a population of a little more than 300,000 residents, is located in the center of Allegheny County. With approximately 1.2 million residents, the county has a county government and 130 municipalities with a mix of governmental structures: cities, boroughs, townships, and towns. There also are various authorities with independent political duties and policies that affect companion animals.

The Political and Legal Context of Enforcement

Pennsylvania has a complex set of institutions that have some effect on anti-cruelty, abandonment, and nuisance animal law enforcement. The only state employees are *dog wardens,* who do not pick up strays (unless there is no animal control in the county), and who do not investigate cruelty. They inspect kennels, license kennels and shelters, and check for rabies vaccinations. Occasionally the dog wardens in some counties go house-to-house to check for unlicensed and unvaccinated animals. They can report cases of cruelty to peace officers and humane officers. Dog wardens are funded by the state's license fee for kennels and shelters. *Humane officers* are compensated through fees collected by humane societies when they place animals for adoption and the societies' fundraising and donations. Technically all cruelty laws are enforced by all peace officers, but humane officers do most of the actual investigation of complaints, especially in suburban and rural townships and boroughs. Humane officers are hired by local humane societies, which must be § 501(c)(3) nonprofit organizations with a board of directors. The court swears in officers selected by the societies. Because they are selected by the humane societies, humane officers in Pennsylvania have a reputation as strong supporters of action in cruelty cases. In Allegheny County officers of one humane society, Animal Friends, handle about nine hundred cases a year involving cats and dogs, and once a herd of horses. The humane officers are headquartered at the Animal Friends shelter, and seized animals are taken to this shelter.

A few Allegheny County municipalities, such as the City of Pittsburgh, have their own *animal control officers* and use private or public shelters; some enter into cooperative agreement with other municipalities to employ officers and keep animals in a public or private kennel. They collect abandoned animals and address complaints about nuisance pets. The animal control officers of Pittsburgh's Bureau of Animal Care and Control capture stray and nuisance animals, assist in pet owner recovery, resolve neighborhood disputes over animals, assist the elderly and physically challenged with animal concerns, advise and teach residents their responsibility as pet owners, advise non–pet owners of their rights, capture and release state and non-state-mandated wildlife, and provide humane traps for the capture of domestic animals and wildlife. The Bureau operates a spay/neuter program for pets and feral cats, quarantines animals, provides removal of deceased animals, and assists police and the district attorney's office with investigations of inhumane treatment. Also it has the power to enforce license and rabies inoculation laws, a five-pet limitation law, leash law, and confinement of cats and dogs in heat law.[33] Pittsburgh requires a license for dogs: $10.00 for spayed and neutered and $20.00 for intact animals; its collection is managed by the city treasurer. Unlicensed animals captured by the Bureau must be held for three days before being placed for adoption or euthanized. License fees outside of the city, $8.45 for intact and $6.45 for spayed or neutered dogs, are collected by the county treasurer.

Control of nuisance, stray, and abandoned pets in most Allegheny County municipalities is conducted by private for-profit businesses that contract with the municipalities. Private animal control firms pick up stray animals and board them for a forty-eight-hour holding period. They also collect adoption fees from placing unclaimed animals. Since they charge owners or the local government a boarding fee for each animal picked up, they have an incentive to collect any animal running loose. They often do not operate a shelter but take seized animals to licensed shelters. The shelters are only required to hold animals for forty-eight hours before selling or euthanizing them. Although they can report cases of cruelty, these animal control businesses do not investigate cruelty.[34]

Finally, *municipal police* have the authority to arrest for violations of animal anti-cruelty laws. They also can report violations and nuisance animals to humane and animal control officers. Much of their animal-related activity occurs during investigations or arrests of individuals for other crimes or as a consequence of citizen complaints of disorder.

Agency Management

Although the evidence is limited, it appears that the oversight and auditing of the performance of animal law enforcement and shelter personnel by elected officials in the city and county is sporadic and often based on citizen complaints. As a means of personnel management, only Pennsylvania dog wardens are subject to quality control and rotation from county to county to protect against the development of ties with local kennel operators. We also have found that their incentive to enforce that law comes much more from personal concerns about animals rather than any system of institutional rewards for effective enforcement.

All humane officers in Pennsylvania must undergo two weeks of training regarding animal law, but they must also have one week of training on police procedures, firearms use, and search and seizure law. Dog wardens undergo the same legal and police training, plus training in animal health. The police academy includes a two-hour workshop on animal law for all law enforcement officers. Private animal control personnel have little formal training and tend to learn on the job from veteran colleagues.[35]

Street-Level Enforcement

Tipped off to abuse by neighbors and service personnel such as meter readers and building and other inspectors, humane officers and the municipal police within individual municipalities file cruelty charges. For example, the city police in Pittsburgh file approximately 55 percent of the cases. Narcotics officers tend to be more aggressive in reporting animal cruelty cases than other officers. Often they detect a link between drug crimes and dogfighting or abuse. Drug investigations also can result in evidence that results in additional charges of animal cruelty. Conversely, some police recognize that an animal complaint can provide probable cause for search warrants or exceptions to the warrant requirement that allow them to search domiciles for drugs. Otherwise, the identification and filing of cruelty cases is a duty of humane officers or, in some jurisdictions, animal control officers. They can file case summaries and misdemeanor complaints in magisterial district judge courts.[36]

Prosecution and Adjudication

In Allegheny County the district attorney (2013) has had a strong commitment to the rigorous enforcement of animal cruelty law. He has designated an assistant district attorney to prosecute the majority of these cases. Although individuals can file dangerous dog complaints, most of the cases this prosecutor addresses are cruelty summary (citation, misdemeanor) complaints. Adopting a proactive posture, an assistant district attorney has trained police in cruelty law and advised them about the collection of evidence. She and her successors have approved search warrants requested by humane and public animal control officers and advised police on warrants. Police can seek search warrants without the approval of her office, but sometimes the assistant district attorney accompanies them when a warrant is served, especially to control and inform the media.

Unless it is a second misdemeanor offense, the district attorney does not have the option of filing a felony charge. Police sometimes prosecute summary cases in nonjury district judge courts, but the assistant district attorney will prosecute the non-summary (serious misdemeanor involving what the law defines as "torture") as well as felony cases. There is no data on summary cases, but the district attorney's office handles about forty-five felony cases each year. It is the policy of the district attorney's office to dismiss only the weakest non-summary cases and to refuse to plea bargain cruelty cases. The assistant district attorney reports that in all trials she has to teach jurors about the significance of the case but that judges take cruelty cases seriously.

Because of the diligence of some police, humane and animal control officers, and district attorney offices, minor cases of animal abuse appear more likely to be filed in magisterial district judge courts. However, the limited knowledge of animal cruelty law possessed by some of these elected judges, many of whom are not attorneys, has caused some assistant district attorneys to remark that they read the law to fit with the judge's personal attitudes about animals and the severity of crimes against animal welfare.

South Bend, Indiana

With a population of approximately 100,000 people, including a large number of recent Hispanic immigrants, South Bend's Animal Care and Control Division is in transition.[37] Until 1996 the city's animal control efforts operated under a contact with the private St. Joseph County Humane Society. When the Humane Society sought an additional $50,000 for its services (a nearly 28 percent increase), the city decided to operate its own agency to save revenues.[38] Operating out of a former firehouse reconfigured as a shelter, its three officers were primarily concerned with the collection and extermination of strays. However, in 2012 the city erected an immaculate new shelter and hired new management with much greater empathy for animal welfare and a desire to more zealously enforce the law. The city council also established an advisory Animal Control Special Committee composed of animal and stewardship supporters, city officials, and volunteer lawyers to revise the animal control ordinance. The committee has examined ordinances and operations in Indiana cities such as Bloomington and Fort Wayne and has heard from animal law advocates such as dangerous dog law expert Fred Kray.[39]

The common concern of some council members for animal welfare was the stimulus for the changes in enforcement. In particular, the members desired more precise language to define cruelty and standards of care, the elimination of breed-specific language in the ordinance, an anti-tethering provision, and rules on trap-neuter-release (TNR) of cats. They also wanted to encourage more adoptions and better enforcement. Some support for legal and operational change has come from the mayor, who has sought a more professional city administration. However, communications to city officials from several rescue organizations, such as Heartland Small Animal Rescue, Community Animal Rescue Effort of South Bend, and Michiana

Feral Cat Initiative,[40] supporters of Pet Refuge (which operates a no-kill private shelter in the county),[41] and the general animal welfare community, including Kryder Veterinary Clinic and Linda's Camp K9,[42] also have encouraged the council to pursue revisions in the ordinance. In general, positive media coverage of these changes has appeared.

The Political and Legal Context of Enforcement

South Bend's Code of Ordinances places the Division of Animal Care and Control under the Department of Code Enforcement, a department that has responsibility for a wide variety of licenses and inspections of buildings, property, and businesses open to the public. Animal Care and Control has specific powers to license dogs and cats, enforce city and state anti-cruelty and anti–animal fighting laws, enforce companion animal vaccination laws, enforce ordinance restrictions on the number of dogs and cats held on property, license urban chicken coops, control other animals commonly used for food, and oversee performing animal exhibitions. It also enforces a ban on the possession of a wide range of mammals, birds, reptiles, and fish and a dangerous dog law. The dangerous dog law requires much more expensive licenses, special documentation and inspection, kennel requirements, and insurance coverage for dogs that have attacked or show a propensity to attack humans and animals or that are American Pit Bull Terriers.[43] Despite this range of duties, most of the Division's efforts focus on responses to complaints about animal behavior, the collection of stray dogs and cats, and investigations of animal cruelty. The Division staff is planning programs to expand adoptions, provide a spay/neuter clinic at the shelter, and offer educational programs in the schools and community outreach.

Agency Management

Recent politically induced changes in the Division of Animal Care and Control have resulted in the firing of two Division directors and the employment of a director and chief animal control officer with professional certifications and experiences in other Indiana and Illinois jurisdictions. The critical problems facing the new managers are the need for standard operating procedures to govern officers' discretion and shelter operations and the training of the very small existing number of officers in these procedures. This includes the development of procedures and training in human relations, the prioritization of calls and work in the field, the treatment of animals, shelter practices related to adoption and euthanasia, relations with other city agencies, and laws and regulations. The ultimate ambition of the managers is to move the Division away from the collection and euthanasia of stray animals and the lax enforcement of licensing and other provisions in the city code and toward national professional standards.

For a city with an estimated 60,000 or more companion animals, the Division is understaffed. Only a supervisor and three officers are available to respond to incidents. Adult and student volunteers provide some assistance with shelter operations, particularly with referring animals to rescue groups and arranging the transportation of animals to rescues.

Street-Level Enforcement

Although animal control officers locate a small number of legal violations through patrols, they lack the staff for an extensive patrol effort. Most violations and abuses are discovered through citizen complaint calls to the Division of Animal Care and Control, a 311 phone line for city services, or a call to a council member. These complaints generate an estimated 90 percent of cases; to a much lesser extent cases come from referrals from police and other governmental agencies. Division officers also may assist federal agents involved in criminal cases in which the suspects possess dogs. More rarely they assist USDA Animal and Plant Health Inspection Service (APHIS) inspectors.

At present about 60 percent of complaint calls are about cats and 40 percent about dogs. Other animals are very rarely the subject of complaints or care at the shelter. More calls come from the economically deprived areas of the city than from other neighborhoods. Most calls are about animal neglect, about three to four a day. Officers deem many calls "unfounded," or they issue warnings and no other action is taken. They file few cases of cruelty and animal fighting that result in prosecutions. Because of relatively high license fees (altered dog or cat: $15; unaltered dog or cat: $25) and a lack of public education, officers estimate that only about 10 percent of dogs and cats have licenses, but there is no program designed to enforce the license requirement. Officers also report that it is difficult to enforce the dangerous dog regulations, and they assume widespread noncompliance with its provisions because of the costs and requirements for compliance with it. Division management reports a relatively high population of stray and feral cats in the city, but the city funds no TNR programs and very limited volunteer TNR group efforts address this population. Unless reported by landlords or a concerned neighbor, hoarding cases have been hard to identify. The drive-home program for licensed lost animals found by officers is rarely used, but compliance with the law by the small number of urban chicken raisers appears to be high.

About 4,000 animals enter the shelter each year, or ten to fifteen animals a day. During the period 2010–2012 the Division euthanized about two thirds of dogs and cats. Cats were more commonly euthanized than dogs. Of the remaining animals, approximately 10 percent were adopted and 20 percent were transferred to rescue organizations. Adoption and transfer rates for dogs were about three times greater than for cats. City councilors and the new management of the Division are engaged in efforts to encourage adoptions and rescue that appear to be gradually reducing the euthanasia rate to a level of less than 50 percent and similar to that in several other Indiana cities. As with most shelters, volunteers assist with animal care and adoptions.

Prosecution and Adjudication

Minor ordinance violations are usually handled with a citation and the violator's payment of fines, a civil penalty, without further criminal adjudication. Appeal of minor citation offenses go to the Animal Control Commission.[44] In the few major cases of cruelty, Animal Care and Control officials note that criminal prosecution requires that they properly investigate, collect evidence, and document egregious cruelty and dogfighting. Often the case preparation involves cooperation with police to develop the case as part of the prosecution of a broader set of criminal offenses. In the past, police assistance has not always generated the evidence needed for effective prosecution. Animal control officers say the assistant prosecutor who handles their cases is generally supportive of their efforts. However, in the past, unless there was attention by the media, many cases resulted in dismissals or a lack of follow through to secure a conviction. At present the city is considering several proposals to strengthen pet welfare laws, including increased penalties for cruelty, modification of spay/neuter efforts, an amended dangerous dog law, a leash law, regulation of tethering, and regulation of breeders.

Calgary, Alberta

In contrast to the enforcement of animal cruelty law in much of North America, the city of Calgary, Alberta, offers a striking alternative. With a little over a million people, 120,000 dogs, and 90,000 cats, Calgary has exceptionally high licensing and return-to-owner rates and has drastically reduced the euthanasia of dogs and cats.[45] Developed to protect public safety, service animal caretakers, and the environment, the city's Animal and Bylaw Services is an agency that operates an extensive set of programs that are built on an effort to license all companion animals in the city. For more than a decade its policies and practices have won support from the city council. The agency has worked to retain this support though presentations to the council members.

The Political and Legal Context of Enforcement

Calgary's Responsible Pet Ownership Bylaw, enacted in 2006 and amended in 2008 and 2011, provides a comprehensive administrative scheme to address companion animal anti-cruelty and abandonment and other animal-related issues. It requires a license for all dogs and cats in the city. "Vicious dogs," defined as dogs that have "chased, injured or bitten any other Animal or human, damaged or destroyed any public or private property, or threatened or created the reasonable apprehension of a threat to a human, and which, in the opinion of a Justice, presents a threat of serious harm to other Animals or humans," must possess a special license.[46] There are provisions that require the leashing of dogs and that provide for 141 off-leash areas in parks, that define areas in which dogs are prohibited, that govern dogs when the owner is cycling, that establish conditions when dogs can swim, and that regulate dogs in vehicles. Other rules regulate companion animals with communicable diseases, excrement removal, noise, scattering of garbage, and behavior that is threatening. Horses are confined to designated areas in parks. Livestock, including potbellied pigs, are banned. Provisions establish procedures for hearings and the determination of vicious and nuisance animals. Additionally the bylaw defines the authority of animal control officers to inspect, seize, spay/neuter, and return or dispose of animals. Finally, the bylaw imposes penalties for violations.[47]

The duties of Animal and Bylaw Services include enforcement of the bylaw on vicious, nuisance, abused, and abandoned animals and the licensing of cats (since 2007) and dogs. Calgary Animal and Bylaw Services relies heavily on more than $5 million in licensing fees to fund its programs and services. Licensing is the key element in its effort to encourage responsibility for pets. The agency's assumption is that comprehensive licensing of cats and dogs provides a means to identify pet owners and return lost or roaming pets as well as an effective way to locate persons who brutalize or abandon animals. License fees therefore are considerably higher than in many Canadian and U. S. jurisdictions: puppies and altered dogs over 6 months old, $36; unaltered dogs over 6 months old, $58; kittens and altered cats over 6 months old, $15; unaltered cats over 6 months old, $30.[48] The fine for an unlicensed pet is $250, a more substantial amount than in many North American jurisdictions.

Animal and Bylaw Services has engaged in a substantial publicity campaign to "market" the value of pet licenses. The campaign aims at educating the public on the value of licenses, such as the return of lost pets and the protection of public health and safety. Conducted in a variety of formats, including through the media, distribution of pamphlets, presentations at neighborhood meetings, activities in city parks, and collaboration with veterinarians and pet trainers, the program has achieved a level of pet licensing that is rare in North America. A 2010 city census disclosed approximately 122,000 dogs in the city, and more than 105,000 have licenses. Approximately 45,000 cats have licenses.

The agency also manages a wide range of programs and service as part of its mission, including a vet-operated low-cost spay/neuter program for lower income residents that has serviced more than 2,100 animals since 2010. It provides for the feeding and up to $500 for the medical care of lost impounded cats and impounded dogs at the shelter, efforts to reunite lost cats and dogs with their owners, including a web-based cell phone service to assist owners in the determination if the animal is in the shelter, an animal adoption program, a volunteer animal socialization program, a Pet Drive Home program for licensed lost pets, and a program to help neighbors resolve their animal-related conflicts. It awards grants to veterinary clinics for emergency medical care for injured stray cats and dogs, cares for pets during natural disasters, and provides and licenses cat traps to allow individuals to capture roaming cats humanely during the summer months.[49] The agency also provides an I Heart My Pet card to owners when they renew a pet license. The card provides discounts at more than sixty businesses, including restaurants, hotels, automobile services, entertainment, and specialty clothing stores as well as pet-oriented businesses. Animal and Bylaw Services uses the card as an incentive to license pets and claims its use can offset the cost of a license.[50] Finally, it provides for the low-cost adoption of older animals by senior citizens.

Animal and Bylaw Services works with several licensed nonprofit rescue groups, such as MEOW Foundation, a no-kill cat shelter and adoption service, Animal Rescue Foundation of Alberta, Pound Rescue, and the Calgary Humane Society.[51] These groups assist with spay/neuter and other programs of the agency and some operate TNR programs for cats. Also they operate shelters that, unlike the city's shelter, accept surrendered pets.

During the past decade Animal and Bylaw Services has tried to encourage responsible pet ownership through public education. Public education, initially in elementary schools, teaches humane treatment and dog bite prevention as a way to encourage responsible pet ownership in the future. It includes a variety of education programs and materials on pet rearing, the licensing requirement, the spaying and neutering of pets, and control of the behavior of pets in city parks and on city pathways.

Agency Management

Calgary Animal and Bylaw Services is structured as a traditional bureaucracy with five units: North (field) Operations, South (field) Operations, Education and Policy (including community liaison), Strategic Services, and Administration and Shelter Operations. With more than sixty field officers and supervisors, education and policy development personnel, personnel engaged with shelter operations, and support from other Community Services and Protective Services graffiti abatement, community cleanup, noise and signage control, and homelessness assistance personnel, it operates out of a combined 21,000-square-foot Animal Services Centre with offices and a heated shelter. Field officers' vehicles contain computers and handheld devices used to identify the owners of lost licensed pets and provide protection for impounded animals from the weather. Office staff send electronic automatic license renewal forms to approximately 8,500 pet owners a month and accept payment by credit and debit card as well as check and cash at various locales. They also handle complaints and lost and found reports.

Street-Level Enforcement

In approximately 75 percent of cases, citizen complaints about nuisance, abandoned pets, and lost pets are made to a 311 telephone number. When the dispatcher deems it necessary a field officer is subsequently dispatched. Officers conduct patrols with a focus on off-leash parks. To check the licenses of cats and dogs and enforce the pet licensing law, field officers conduct park patrols by bicycle, stop individuals with animals in parks or on the street, and visit the residence of all license nonrenewals. Licenses can be checked by calls to the dispatch center. Shelter personnel ensure all animals released from their custody are licensed. Animal and Bylaw Service officers cooperate with city police when police make arrests and an animal is present, and they will receive police support when a risk situation occurs when citing animal bylaw offenders.

When a licensed lost pet is wearing a tag, in many instances an officer will return that pet directly to its home or contact the caretaker. Other pets are returned when they are found to have a tattoo or microchip. Animal and Bylaw Services reports an 86 percent return rate to owners of lost dogs and a 50 percent return rate for lost or roaming cats. Another 8 percent of dogs and 25 percent of cats are adopted. The extensive efforts to enforce licensing have markedly increased the number of pets returned to owners and drastically reduced the number of cats and dogs euthanized to less than 5 percent off those impounded by officers. Consequently the city shelter averages a population of only fifty cats and thirty dogs. Rates of dog bites and reported damage to property have also significantly decreased.

Although its officers locate and report cases of human acts of animal cruelty, investigation and arrest of offenders is not a responsibility of Animal and Bylaw Services. Instead, this is the duty of the Protection and Investigations Department of the Calgary Humane Society. This unit consists of peace officers, animal welfare responders, and a Dispatch/Call Centre. Humane society officers investigate more than two thousand allegations of animal neglect and abuse yearly and enforce the Animal Protection Act of Alberta.[52] When addressing complaints, provincial law permits the officers to engage in any action considered "necessary to locate the animal and relieve its distress, including taking custody of the animal in accordance with the regulations and arranging for transportation, food, water, care, shelter and veterinary treatment for the animal, if necessary." Officers can enter private land and vehicles to relieve distressed animals, but warrants are required to enter private dwellings.[53]

Prosecution and Adjudication

Most violations of the city's bylaw result in the issuance of a ticket by a field officer and subsequent payment of a fine and/or license fee by the offender within a thirty-day period. If a field officer or a cited individual requests a first appearance in the case, a staff person at Animal and Bylaw Services manages the filing of documents. Officers interact with the city's Law Department in court hearings on more serious alleged vicious dog violations, dog bites, and nuisances. If an owner is convicted after a hearing, a provincial justice can order the owner to prevent the animal from doing mischief or causing a nuisance, declare the animal a vicious animal and order that it be destroyed, and direct that the owner be prohibited from owning any animal for a specified period of time.[54] Additionally, the provincial Dangerous Dogs Act permits judges to order the destruction or conditions of confinement of dogs that have bitten or attempted to bite persons.[55] Cruelty cases are investigated by the Calgary Humane Society and filed by the Alberta solicitor general. In these cases the judge can impose penalties for violations of the duties of animal care contained in the provincial Animal Protection Act.[56]

Assessment

Several obstacles can limit the enforcement of companion animal anti-cruelty law. First, as illustrated in the West Virginia and Pittsburgh studies, many jurisdictions have multiple animal control offices. Sometimes these offices have conflicting objectives, limited concern for companion animals, and restricted legal authority to enforce anti-cruelty laws. Comparing the case studies, it appears that anti-cruelty and abandonment law enforcement varies because of elected officials' attitudes about the worth of cats, dogs, and horses, the content of laws, officials' knowledge of animal law, and the resources officers possess or allocate to enforce the law. However, council members, as in South Bend, or administrators, as in Calgary, can devise schemes of law enforcement and generate the resources needed for better care or adoption of abandoned pets.

Second, as Arluke noted in his study, the management and training of companion animal control officers is inadequate.[57] As illustrated in the West Virginia case study and Allegheny County, and until recently in South Bend, animal control officers frequently lack the training and management guidance to secure the effective use of their discretion. Additionally, animal control agencies frequently lack the staff and budgetary resources that would contribute to more comprehensive efforts at companion animal control and care.

Third, as Arluke found, discretion allows police, animal control personnel, and human officers who perform enforcement at the street level to either "stretch" or, more likely, "compress" the application of the law by filing the call to be of little merit or too frustrating to address.[58] When street-level officials place a high priority on animal cruelty, they can make a significant difference in the enforcement of the law and the lives of animals. However, in many jurisdictions the street-level personnel—especially police officers and prosecutors—often regard animal cruelty and abandonment as a relatively unimportant crime.

Finally, although record keeping is inadequate, it appears from all of the case studies that significant variations exist in the willingness of prosecutors to pursue convictions of those arrested for companion animal–related crimes. A theme in all four studies is that at least some lower court judges do not treat crimes against animals with the same seriousness as crimes against people or property. Consequently there exists a great degree of variation in how judges apply anti-cruelty law and penalize the abandonment and neglect of pets in North America.

KENNEL REGULATION

As discussed in chapter 6, new laws to regulate kennels have introduced a new layer of federal and state legal protection of dogs against a specific threat to their treatment. But, how are these laws enforced? As an example, we assess the process in Pennsylvania, a state which has a strong kennel licensing and inspection law with requirements for humane care of the animals.

The Political and Legal Context of Enforcement

In Pennsylvania all facilities that hold more than twenty-five dogs over the course of a year, including rescue organizations, are covered by inspection requirements. Each kennel must be licensed and inspected twice each year. The kennel license fees are dependent upon the number of dogs kept or transferred per year and go the Pennsylvania Bureau of Dog Law Enforcement. The Bureau hires dog wardens with the authority to collect stray animals (when no animal control officer exists in the jurisdiction) and inspect kennels. The dog warden does not investigate cruelty charges, but he or she may request that a humane officer inspect or investigate kennels. A different dog warden can also be sent if complaints reoccur.[59]

For a person running a combined boarding kennel, rescue facility, and breeding facility, three separate licenses are required, with an inspection required for each category of license. All animals must be clearly identified in each type of kennel. Each dog must be exercised on a leash daily for twenty minutes; everything, including bowls and bedding, must be sanitized daily, and all animals entering or leaving the state must have current vaccinations and a health certificate signed by a veterinarian. Kennel operators are also subjected to a criminal background check.[60]

Agency Management

Dog wardens are state employees hired, trained, and supervised by the Bureau of Dog Law Enforcement. The Bureau oversees dog wardens through their reports and evaluation procedures. Although their selection and training is less intensive than that of most police, it encourages allegiance to Bureau objectives. Also, the Bureau has encouraged an esprit de corps. Being uniformed and carrying a sidearm, the dog wardens exhibit the quasi-military bearing of police, game wardens, and forest rangers that has often bred loyalty to organizational objectives.[61]

Street-Level Enforcement

Pennsylvania dog wardens normally conduct two inspections of licensed kennels each year. The inspection includes a review of the documents the law requires operators to keep on purchases and sales of dogs, transfers to and from rescue organizations, boarding records, and health and veterinary records. Dog wardens also examine the condition of the kennels, sanitation, and the apparent health of the dogs. A kennel operator reported that inspectors vary in their scrutiny of records and kennel conditions. Some wardens may cite a kennel operator for a violation that requires a return or follow-up inspection, while others will warn or allow the operator to alleviate the violation on the spot. Most citations result in compliance at the time of the follow-up inspection, so no further legal action has to be taken and the dogs do not have to be removed from the kennel.[62]

Prosecution and Adjudication

Pennsylvania law requires that citations and decisions to revoke kennel licenses be determined by dog wardens. They are normally approved by the enforcement director of the Bureau of Dog Law Enforcement. Kennel owners can challenge license revocations and other inspection violations in court. Judges in these cases possess considerable discretion in the determination of violations and the imposition of license revocations and civil penalties on violators.[63] The law also permits dog wardens to file some misdemeanor criminal penalties. Discretionary judgments about these prosecutions are in the hands of county district attorneys, who try them in magisterial district or common pleas courts (general jurisdiction trial courts).[64]

Practices in Pennsylvania suggest that legal clarity and effective management can produce significant benefits to pets. However, officers still possess considerable discretion in the citation of operations for abuses, and as with anti-cruelty law, prosecutors and the lower judiciary are often disinclined to impose significant penalties for violations of the law.

HORSE SORING AND TRANSPORTATION

As discussed in chapter 7, threats to the health and welfare of domesticated horses have induced the United States Congress to pass laws that govern horse training and transportation. How have these laws been enforced?

The Political and Legal Context of Enforcement

The U.S. Congress adopted the Horse Protection Act of 1970 (amended in 1976) to prevent deliberate soring, cutting, burning, and related training practices that can cause horses to suffer distress, inflammation, or lameness when walking or trotting.[65] The Horse Protection Act preempts state law and certifies states to aid in its enforcement of a ban on horse soring and related training practices. The USDA sends veterinary medical officers (VMOs) to 7 to 10 percent of horse shows. They oversee the industry's horse inspectors. These private inspectors are known as designated qualified persons (DQPs) who are hired by the twelve horse industry organizations (HIOs) certified by the USDA to put on horse shows. They are trained by APHIS.

The Humane Methods of Slaughter Act of 1978 (amended in 1996) allows the USDA to register and regulate the commercial transportation of horses on direct trips to slaughterhouses.[66] The USDA's APHIS developed Commercial Transport of Equines to Slaughter Regulations in 2001. These regulations, directed only toward horses being transported to slaughter, require separation of animals, adequate floor space, confinement without food or water for no more than twenty-four hours, and phasing out of two-tiered transport vehicles. Exporters must have a certificate on each animal, which is provided to customs and APHIS.[67]

Agency Management

The U.S. federal government lacks the institutions necessary to supervise and regulate horse soring and horse transportation. Because APHIS inspectors are only funded to cover about 7 percent of the shows, state inspectors and the DQPs certified by the USDA conduct virtually all of the inspections and issue citations that govern horse soring and related training practices. DQPs often are horse owners, and many show the Tennessee Walking Horses sometimes trained using soring. Some of the DQPs may engage in soring themselves, and intimidation from trainers and owners makes it difficult for them to enforce the law. Allegedly they generally encourage some violators to appeal the violations.

During recent fiscal years, the transportation supervision program's funding has primarily provided for the salaries and expenses of two staff, one of whom is the national compliance officer, who inspects conveyances and owner/shipper certificates for compliance with the transport regulation, with the remainder going to travel costs. The program's limited funding has significantly curtailed its ability to provide coverage at border crossings and to work with shippers and inspectors in foreign slaughtering facilities to ensure compliance with the transport regulation.[68] APHIS policy is that it does not accept complaints from citizens, and therefore the federal transportation law is not enforced by federal officials except when violations are detected when horses arrive at customs for shipment abroad.

It is legal in most states to transport horses in double-decked trailers if they are not bound for slaughter. Twelve states regulate these trailers and enforce their own transportation laws. They also can notify APHIS of violations of the federal law. States with laws banning double-decked transport for horses pass out cards to state police and to citizens so they know what to do if they see a double-decked horse trailer.[69] Since it is legal to transport pigs, sheep, and cattle in a double-decked trailer, identification of the species of animal transported must occur before a citation for illegal conditions of horse transportation can be issued. In states without horse transportation regulations, there is no evidence that general animal cruelty laws are applied by police who stop and examine horse transport trailers.

Street-Level Enforcement

The USDA Horse Protection Enforcement Report to Congress in 2010 found that shows attended by VMOs had twelve times the number of cited violations as those inspected only by the industry's DQPs. The report also noted that some VMO inspectors received threats of violence against them.[70] An agreement of the HIOs to disqualify violators who have not completed all phases of penalties from exhibiting animals was reached in May 2011. All twelve HIO members signed the agreement, an action which effectively bars violators from participating in horse show events while under suspension and until all fines have been paid.[71] DQPs are responsible for investigating at other shows, but they are also threatened and intimidated by horse trainers and owners.

Since the USDA bars most citizen complaints, there is no organized federal enforcement of horse transportation law and no other institutional capacity for street-level enforcement. However, the enforcement of state horse transport laws is enhanced by citizen assistance. Citizens who see horses in two-tiered trailers may call the local or state police and report violation of state and possibly federal laws. Citizens in the six states banning all horse transport in double-decked trailers play an important role in alerting state police to both the presence of double-decked trailers and the state law regarding horse transport. However, enforcement remains largely in the hands of state and local police who conduct traffic patrol and whose primary objective is not to search for illegal modes of horse transportation.

Prosecution and Adjudication

The interest group Equine Protection Network (EPN) has obtained a list of 241 violators of federal horse protection laws and 169 separate cases filed between February 1, 2002, and October 1, 2005. Their data show fines ranging from $0 to $3,500, with a majority of the cases having no fines.[72] These are administrative actions rather than criminal filings. EPN also monitors state actions on horse transport and reports arrests and the outcomes on its website. It has detailed the arrests and prosecutions of one

New York shipper as well as other enforcement actions against illegal shippers. EPN does not provide a detailed comprehensive list of legal actions, however.[73]

We have not located any record of the prosecution and adjudication of federal or state horse slaughter or horse transportation laws in state or federal courts. The U.S. Attorney for the Eastern District of Tennessee recently indicted four individuals for soring horses,[74] but the Department of Justice does not keep records on Horse Protection Act or Humane Methods of Slaughter Act prosecutions or convictions. Although APHIS keeps records on inspection activities and has secured civil penalties for horse soring and other violations of the Horse Protection Act, again there is a lack of comprehensive records.[75]

In conclusion, the political commitment to the effective enforcement of horse training and transportation laws is absent in the United States.

SPAY/NEUTER LAWS

Significant problems exist with the enforcement of the spay/neuter and differential licensing laws that have been passed by many states and localities in an attempt to reduce the overpopulation of cats and dogs. What are these problems?

The Political and Legal Context of Enforcement

The primary aim of many spay/neuter laws is to compel shelters placing cats and dogs or the adoptee of the pet to have the animal spayed or neutered. In Illinois, Iowa, Louisiana, Maine, Rhode Island, and Utah, the shelter can be fined if it does not comply. If there is evidence of noncompliance by an adoptee, in some states the shelter can legally reclaim the animal. For states where the animal is forfeited upon proof of noncompliance, the counties may ignore the law rather than return animals to kill shelters.

Although not legally required, most nonprofit organizations that place animals for adoption have a spay/neuter requirement in their adoption contract and their bylaws. Nonprofits traditionally include the cost of alteration in their adoption fee and either have the animal altered before placement or cover the cost of the alteration when the animal reaches the health and age requirements for alteration. If the owner does not comply with the contract, a nonprofit may also reclaim the animal.

Agency Management

The U.S. states vary in how they manage the enforcement of spay/neuter laws. For example, in West Virginia compliance is with the adopter,[76] and there is often no oversight or policy supervision of adopters or a specific effort at street-level enforcement. Agencies may only require a "promise deposit" when placing unaltered cats or dogs. Also, enforcement is difficult because many adopters do not live in the county or even in the state. Our survey of West Virginia's county shelters found a wide variety of mechanisms to ensure compliance. One county commissioner responded that animals are not a priority in that county, so animal health and welfare laws are not enforced. Animals are not placed for adoption so the county does not need to worry about spay/neuter laws. Another responded that he was unaware of the spay/neuter law. Seventeen responded that they do not allow animals to leave county custody unless they are altered. Many only place animals with rescue organizations that have a policy of spay/neuter or with county residents. Overall, the perceived impact varies from not very effective to 100 percent effective in reducing the number of animals euthanized yearly in their shelters. Most respondents felt that enforcement is a problem because of a lack of funding for spay/neuter programs, a culture that opposes spay/neuter, and the lack of a specific designation of an enforcement agency. Shelter personnel have no authority to force compliance, other than to petition the court for redress, so have to rely on the prosecutor and sheriff. Because people are unwilling to take an altered animal or to agree to alter an adopted animal, some counties indicate that euthanasia rates have actually increased.

Pennsylvania has both differential licensing and shelter spay/neuter laws. The licensing differential is $2 ($8 for unaltered and $6 for altered animals), but no proof of spay/neuter is required.[77] Pennsylvania requires only a promise deposit for adoption. Failure to comply is a summary offense and shelters can reclaim animals if the owner does not comply. Virtually all of the shelters in Pennsylvania are run by nonprofit organizations with indirect government oversight of spay/neuter programs. If the animal is healthy and an appropriate age for spaying or neutering, humane societies and nonprofit rescue organizations will spay or neuter before placement. They include the cost of the treatment in their adoption fees.

A significant obstacle to the management of spay/neuter enforcement is the lack of state funding for programs and the lack of low-cost spay/neuter clinics in the state. In some communities the cost of a spaying could reach $400. Without government subsidies of spay/neuter or nonprofit programs to finance them, many shelters and adopters cannot afford to alter the adopted animals. In a few jurisdictions assistance is provided by humane societies or spay/neuter assistance programs, but this funding is not available to rescue organizations or county-run shelters for preadoption spay/neuter. In these and other contexts pet caregivers must depend upon veterinarians and humane societies to run low-cost clinics.

Street-Level Enforcement

Animal control officers cannot readily determine whether a cat or dog came from a shelter where it should have been altered or observe whether a particular animal has undergone the procedure. Enforcement of the law therefore often occurs when the animal is taken into custody as a stray or victim of cruelty. This action can have harsh consequences. As one animal control officer said, "If I go after the owner for noncompliance I will have to take the animal and it will probably die. Life unaltered is better than death."[78] Animal control officers nevertheless can issue citations for violation of the spay/neuter law, but several courts have refused to hear these cases, citing lack of evidence that the owner has not complied. Also, sometimes the fine for noncompliance is lower than the cost of compliance with the law.

The use of promise deposits means that, since the shelter already has the money, there is little incentive to seek penalization for the failure of an adopter to spay or neuter. Also, county shelters that alter animals before placement often contend that they euthanize more animals because the adoption fee includes the costs of spay/neuter and is higher than local residents are willing to pay for the cat or dog. In any instance, once an animal leaves a shelter unaltered, the ability to enforce compliance is extremely low.

Prosecution and Adjudication

For states that require spay/neuter for adopted animals but do not require it before placement, prosecution for a failure to comply is often difficult. Because of the low value they place on the offense and the difficulty in bringing offenders to court, prosecutors are generally unwilling to take action. Evidence for effective prosecution is often problematic. For example, there is no visual evidence of a spay procedure after the incision heals. Often even humane organizations subject a female cat or dog to the spay procedure, only to find out that the animal is already spayed. Consequently, legal provisions, a lack of public oversight and enforcement of policies, and limited means for penalization for violations mean that spay/neuter laws and policies are often not achieving their stated objectives.

ENFORCEMENT ASSESSED

Are the laws, regulations, and policies designed to protect or control companion animals regularly implemented and enforced by regulatory agencies, prosecutors, and the judiciary? The evidence on enforcement illustrates the numerous barriers to ensuring legal accountability for the protection of cats, dogs, and horses. First, both under-enforcement and noncompliance might be less a conscious decision than a consequence of the public's failure to acquire knowledge about law and regulations.[79] A suggestive experimental study found that females were more likely to recommend harsher punishment for abuse and that harsher punishment was given for companion animal (puppy) abuse rather than for animals typically consumed as food (chickens). The experiment also suggested that, when rating punishments for crimes against animals, people do not examine the specific type of crime or the sex of the perpetrator nearly as much as they do the victim.[80] Unfortunately, more data are necessary to assess why the public does not report the abuse of companion animals or provide evidence for the conviction of animal abusers.

As to the governmental enforcement effort, too often limited institutional authority for animal control officers and the inclusion of animal law enforcement within the duties of agencies designated with other duties, such as police and sheriff departments, means that anti-cruelty law enforcement becomes a secondary concern for law enforcement agents. Additionally, animal law enforcement is commonly managed and funded by local public officials who might not care about animal protection or possess the revenues to support enforcement. Officials are therefore free to act upon personal attitudes that regard animals as disposable property or animal law as inconsequential. The discretion of street-level enforcers is often poorly defined and managed, and the resources and staff devoted to anti-cruelty and kennel law enforcement put animal control officers in a reactive, fire alarm mode of operations rather than a proactive role in patrol or educative efforts to prevent animal abuse. Prosecutors and lower court judges also contribute to selective enforcement of anti-cruelty and kennel laws by practices that moderate or dismiss penalties for violators. Additionally, enforcement of the Horse Protection Act and the Transportation to Slaughter Act depends too much upon state and industry self-regulation and public reporting to be effective. The design of spay/neuter laws creates numerous opportunities for their evasion and evidentiary problems that affect their enforcement. The result is weak and underfunded institutions for enforcement, no direction and policy for enforcers to follow, and the use of enforcement, prosecutorial, and adjudicatory discretion in ways that neglect the harms visited upon companion animals.

However, if legalized accountability for the welfare of companion animals is deficient, companion animal law might still possesses political importance. The political struggle about laws and regulations conveys a message that at least educates the public about policy and ethical issues. It might awaken a consciousness of injurious treatment of pets, serve as a catalyst for the organization of efforts and action to protect pets, and create credibility for policies that rest on the identification of companion animals as deserving stewardship or legal rights.[81]

NOTES

1. These suppositions are drawn from an Australian study, Nicola Taylor and Tania Signal, "Community Demographics and the Propensity to Report Animals Cruelty," *Journal of Applied Animal Welfare Science* 9 (2006): 201–10, and informal interviews with animal control officers. Compare Lynn Langton, et al.,

Victimizations Not Reported to the Police, 2006–2010, U.S. Department of Justice, Office of Justice Programs, Bureau of Justice Statistics, 2012, accessed June 6, 2013, http://www.bjs.gov/content/pub/pdf/vnrp0610.pdf.
2. Allison Estes and Tina Salaks, *Paw and Order: Dramatic Investigations by an Animal Cop on the Beat* (Laguna Hills, CA: Bow Tie Press, 2008), passim.
3. Arnold Arluke, *Brute Force: Animal Police and the Challenge of Cruelty* (West Lafayette, IN: Purdue University Press, 2004).
4. The political influences on agency behavior in the enforcement of the law are delineated in classic studies such as John Braithwaite, *To Punish or Persuade: Enforcement of Coal Mine Safety* (Albany: State University of New York Press, 1985); Keith Hawkins, *Environment and Enforcement: Regulation and the Social Definition of Pollution* (Oxford: Clarendon Press, 1984); Keith Hawkins, *Law as a Last Resort: Prosecution Decision-Making in a Regulatory Agency* (New York: Oxford University Press, 2002); Herbert Kaufman, *The Forest Ranger: A Study in Administrative Behavior* (Baltimore: Johns Hopkins Press, 1960); Michael Lipsky, *Street-Level Bureaucracy: Dilemmas of the Individual in Public Services*, expanded ed. (New York: Russell Sage Foundation, 2010), passim; and Barry M. Mitnick, "The Bureaucrat as Agent" (Paper presented at the American Political Science Association meeting, Washington, DC, Sept. 1984).
5. Mitnick, "The Bureaucrat as Agent"; Stephen A. Ross, "The Economic Theory of Agency: The Principal's Problem," *American Economic Review* 62 (1973): 134–39.
6. Susan J. Pearson and Kimberly K. Smith, "Developing Animal Welfare Law," in *Statebuilding from the Margins: Between Reconstruction and the New Deal*, ed. Carol Nackenhoff and Julie Novkov (Philadelphia: University of Pennsylvania Press, 2014), 130–35.
7. On the delegation of enforcement powers to nonprofit organizations, see *Arkansas Code Annotated* § 5-62-113 (1997); *California Corporation Code Annotated* 10404; *Delaware Code Annotated* tit. 3, 7901; *Florida Statutes Annotated* § 828.03; *Kentucky Revised Statutes Annotated* § 436.605; *Louisiana Revised Statutes Annotated* § 3:2391; 17 *Maine Revised Statutes Annotated* § 1023 (2004); *Maryland Criminal Code Annotated* § 10-609; *Minnesota Statutes Annotated* § 343.01; *New Hampshire Revised Statutes Annotated* § 105:18; *New Jersey Statutes Annotated* § 4:22-3(d); *New York Agriculture and Markets Law* 371; *Ohio Revised Code Annotated* §§ 1717.04, 1717.06; *Tennessee Code Annotated* § 39-14-210; *Vermont Statutes Annotated* tit. 13, 354; *Washington Revised Code Annotated* § 16.52.015. The origins of quasi-public enforcement institutions is discussed in Diane L. Beers, *For the Prevention of Cruelty: The History and Legacy of Animal Rights Activism in the United States* (Athens: Swallow Press/Ohio University Press, 2006), 60–90; Timothy J. Gilfoyle, "The Moral Origins of Political Surveillance:

The Preventive Society in New York City, 1867–1918," *American Quarterly* 38 (1986): 637–52; Kathryn Shevelow, *For the Love of Animals: The Rise of the Animal Protection Movement* (New York: Henry Holt and Co., 2008), 39–54.

8. Lesli Bisgould, *Animals and the Law* (Toronto: Irwin Law, 2011), 97–102; Tara Lowes, Manager, Administration and Shelter/Clinic Operations, Animal & Bylaw Services, The City of Calgary, interview by Susan Hunter and Richard A. Brisbin, Jr., Nov. 6., 2013.

9. Ontario Society for the Prevention of Cruelty to Animals Act, R.S.O. 1990, Chap. O.36; Ontario Regulation 59/09, General; "Inside the OSPCA," Ontario Society for the Prevention of Cruelty to Animals, accessed Nov. 1, 2013, http://www.ontariospca.ca/inside-the-ospca.html.

10. Doug Hempstead, "Ottawa Lawyer Takes Aim at Ontario Society for the Prevention of Cruelty to Animals," *Ottawa Sun*, Oct. 24, 2013; Randy Hillier, MPP, interview by Richard A. Brisbin, Jr., Nov. 1, 2013; "About the OSPCA Act Application," FixtheLaw.ca, accessed Nov. 1, 2013, http://www.fixthelaw.ca/about/; "OLA Moves forward with Application to the Courts," Ontario Landowner's Association, accessed Nov. 1, 2013, http://ontariolandowners.ca/news/ola-moves-forward-with-application-to-the-courts/.

11. See Stephen Aronson, *Animal Control Management: A New Look at a Public Responsibility* (West Lafayette, IN: Purdue University Press, 2010), 12–23, 26–34; The George Washington University Law School, Animal Welfare Project, *A Report on Animal Welfare in the District of Columbia* (Washington, DC, George Washington University Law School, 2005), 33–41.

12. Aronson, *Animal Control Management*, provides a full description of general managerial issues in animal control (pp. 37–64), managers' interaction with officials and groups, outreach, communications, and use of websites (pp. 23–26, 196–246), personnel management (pp. 167–96), budget management (pp. 82–117), records management (pp. 65–81), and audits (pp. 321–41).

13. John Brehm and Scott Gates, *Working, Shirking, and Sabotage: Bureaucratic Response to a Democratic Public* (Ann Arbor: University of Michigan Press, 1994), 73–74, 93–108; 131–47; Heather C. Hill, "Understanding Implementation: Street-Level Bureaucrats' Resources for Reform," *Journal of Public Administration Research and Theory* 13 (2003): 265–82; Lipsky, *Street-Level Bureaucracy*, 71–80; Steven Maynard-Moody and Michael Musheno, *Cops, Teachers, and Counselors: Stories from the Front Lines of Public Service* (Ann Arbor: University of Michigan Press, 2003); Steven Maynard-Moody and Shannon Portillo, "Street-Level Bureaucracy Theory," in *The Oxford Handbook of American Bureaucracy*, ed. Robert F. Durant (New York: Oxford University Press, 2010), 252–77.

14. Arluke, *Brute Force*, 41–130.

15. Sometimes animal agency officers can prosecute cases in state courts of limited jurisdiction in the absence of a local prosecutor's office; see Ibid., 131–55.
16. *North Carolina General Statutes* § 19-A2-A4. See William Reppy, "Citizen Standing to Enforce Anti-cruelty Laws by Obtaining Injunctions," *Animal Law* 39 (2005); 39–63; Joan E. Schaffner, *Introduction to Animals and the Law* (New York, Palgrave, 2011), 69–70.
17. The statutory authority for private prosecutions is found in sections 2, 504, 574, 579 and 795 of the *Criminal Code,* R.S.C. 1985, c. C-46. Section 34(2) of the *Interpretation Act,* R.S.C. 1985, c. I-21, extends this right to offenses under any other federal legislation unless that legislation specifies otherwise, such as the Health of Animals Act, S.C. 1990, c. 21. See Sophie Gaillard, "Guide to Private Prosecution of Animal Welfare Offences under the Federal *Health of Animals Act,*" Animal Justice Canada, May 2013, accessed Oct. 22, 2015, http://www.animaljustice.ca/wp-content/uploads/2013/06/Animal-Justice-Guide-002-Private-Prosecution-of-Animal-Welfare-Offences-under-the-Health-of-Animals-Act-13.05.29.pdf.
18. See Hawkins, *Law as a Last Resort,* 16–22.
19. Confidential interview by Susan Hunter, 2008.
20. This discussion relies on Celesta A. Albonetti, "Prosecutorial Discretion: The Effects of Uncertainty," *Law and Society Review,* 21 (1987): 281–313; Celesta A. Albonetti, "Charge Reduction: An Analysis of Prosecutorial Discretion in Burglary and Robbery Cases," *Journal of Quantitative Criminology,* 8 (1992): 317–33; Lief H. Carter, *The Limits of Order* (Lexington, MA: Lexington Books, 1974); Roy B. Flemming, "Political Styles and Organizational Strategies of American. Prosecutors: Examples from Nine Courthouse Communities," *Law and Policy,* 12 (1990): 25–50; Lisa Frohmann, "Convictability and Discordant Locales: Reproducing Race, Class, and Gender Ideologies in Prosecutorial Decisionmaking," *Law and Society Review* 31 (1997): 531–56.
21. This discussion relies on John M. Conley and William M. O'Barr, *Rules versus Relationships: The Ethnography of Legal Discourse* (Chicago: University of Chicago Press, 1990), 82–112; Malcolm M. Feeley, *The Process is the Punishment: Handling Cases in a Lower Criminal Court* (New York: Russell Sage Foundation, 1979), 154–98.
22. For U.S. examples, see American Dog Owners Association v. City of Yakima, 777 P.2d 1046 (1989); Garcia v. Village of Tijeras, 767 P.2d 355 (1988). For Canada, see Friesen v. Saskatchewan Society for the Prevention of Cruelty to Animals, 2008 CarswellSask 438; Janota-Bzowska v. Lewis, 1997CarswellBC 1957.
23. *West Virginia Code* § 61-8-19.

24. *West Virginia Code* § 7-10-2.
25. *West Virginia Code* §§ 61-8-21, 23.
26. *West Virginia Code* § 7-10-1.
27. Confidential interviews by Susan Hunter, 2008.
28. *West Virginia Code* § 7-10-2.
29. Confidential interviews by Susan Hunter, 2008.
30. Confidential interviews by Susan Hunter, 2008.
31. Arluke, *Brute Force*, 153–55.
32. Maureen Harmony, "No Justice for Starved Horses at Hidden Meadows Equine Rescue in West Virginia," http://www.examiner.com/equine-advocacy-in-national/no-justice-for-starved-horses-at-hidden-meadows-equine-rescue-west-virginia (accessed May 12, 2011); Cheryl Hanna, "Owner of Hidden Meadows Equine Rescue Fined $1000 in Animal Cruelty Case," accessed May 12, 2011, http://www.allpetspost.org/allhorsespost/2010/10/22/owner-of-hidden-meadows-equine-rescue-fined-1000-in-animal-cruelty-case/; Cheryl Hanna, "Hidden Meadows Equine Rescue Seized Horses Nothing More Than Bid Numbers," accessed May 12, 2011, http://www.examiner.com/pet-rescue-in-national/hidden-meadows-equine-rescue-seized-horses-nothing-more-than-bid-numbers.
33. Pittsburgh, Bureau of Animal Care and Control, accessed June 3, 2013, http://pittsburghpa.gov/animalcontrol/.
34. On the issues such as scope of field operations and other services, shelter operations, training of personnel, liability and legal obligations, and compensation that affect public contracts with private firms for animal control law enforcement and shelter operations, see Aronson, *Animal Control Management*, 119–41.
35. 22 *Pennsylvania Consolidated Statutes* §§ 3712, 3713.
36. 18 *Pennsylvania Consolidated Statutes* 5511.B II.
37. The discussion in this section relies on interviews, South Bend Animal Care and Control staff, by Richard A. Brisbin, Jr., Sept. 26, 2013; Interview, Valerie Schey, South Bend Common Council, by Richard A. Brisbin, Jr., and Susan Hunter, Oct. 4, 2013; "4-25-13 Meeting of the Health and Public Safety Committee, Updating Chapter 5 of South Bend's Municipal Code pertaining to South Bend Animal Care and Control," unpublished PowerPoint material in the possession of the authors.
38. Don Porter, "City, Humane Society Parting Ways," *South Bend Tribune*, Dec. 19, 1995, B1; Don Porter, "City, Humane Society Parting Ways," *South Bend Tribune*, Dec. 19. 1995, B1; Don Porter, "City Still Planning for Animal Control," *South Bend Tribune*, Dec. 27, 1995, B4; Don Porter, "City Hiring Three Officers for Animal Control," *South Bend Tribune*, Dec. 28, 1995, C1;

Don Porter, "Animal Control Program Up and Running," *South Bend Tribune*, Jan. 4, 1996, C4.

39. "Animal Care and Control," City of Bloomington, accessed Oct. 7, 2013, http://bloomington.in.gov/sections/viewSection.php?section_id=62; "Animal Care and Control," City of Fort Wayne, accessed Oct. 7, 2013, http://www.cityoffortwayne.org/animal-care-and-control.html; Fred Kray, "PBLN Presents Against South Bend, Indiana Breed Discriminatory Legislation," *Pit Bull Legal News*, June 16, 2013, accessed Oct. 7, 2013, http://legal.pblnn.com/breaking-news/152-pbln-presents-against-south-bend-indiana-breed-discriminatory-legislation.

40. Heartland Small Animal Rescue, accessed Oct. 7, 2013, http://www.heartlandsmallanimalrescue.org/; Community Animal Rescue Effort of South Bend, accessed Oct. 7, 2013, http://www.careofsouthbend.org/; Michiana Feral Cat Initiative, accessed Oct. 7, 2013, http://www.michianaferal.org/.

41. "About Us," Pet Refuge, accessed Oct. 2, 2013, http://www.petrefuge.com/about-us/.

42. Kryder Veterinary Clinic, accessed Oct. 22, 2015, http://www.krydervet.com/; Linda's Camp K9, accessed Oct. 7, 2013, http://www.lindascampk9.com/.

43. City of South Bend, Code of Ordinances, Chap. 5, accessed Oct. 20, 2015, http://library.municode.com/index.aspx?clientId=13974.

44. No details of the duties of this commission exist in city ordinances.

45. The following section relies extensively on Annual Report 2012, Animal & Bylaw Services, City of Calgary, accessed Nov. 4, 2013, http://www.calgary.ca/CSPS/Documents/CSPS-Annual-Reports/ABS_Annual_Report_2012.pdf; Bill Bruce, Animal and By-Law Services, FCM Presentation, Kansas City, MO, Oct. 2006, and notes on the discussion of the presentation made by Susan Hunter; Tara Lowes, Manager, Administration and Shelter/Clinic Operations, Animal & Bylaw Services, The City of Calgary, interview by Susan Hunter and Richard. A. Brisbin, Jr., Nov. 6, 2013.

46. *Bylaw Number 23M2006: Being a Bylaw of the City of Calgary Respecting the Regulation, Licensing and Control of Animals in the City of Calgary*, secs. 2y, 3, 4, 5, http://www.calgary.ca/CA/city-clerks/Documents/Legislative-services/Bylaws/23M2006-ResponsiblePetOwnership.pdf.

47. Ibid., secs. 12–56.

48. "Licencing a Cat or Dog," City of Calgary, accessed Nov. 7, 2013, http://www.calgary.ca/CSPS/ABS/Pages/Animal-Services/Licensing-cat-dog.aspx.

49. *Annual Report 2012*, Animal & Bylaw Services, City of Calgary, 24

50. "I Heart My Pet Rewards Program," City of Calgary, accessed Nov. 7, 2013, http://iheartmypet.ca/.

51. "About MEOW," MEOW Foundation, accessed Nov. 7, 2013, http://www.meowfoundation.com/about/; Animal Rescue Foundation of Alberta, accessed

Nov. 7, 2013, http://arf.ab.ca/; "About Us," Pound Rescue, Okotoks, Alberta, accessed Nov. 7, 2013, http://www.poundrescue.com/about; Calgary Humane Society, accessed Nov. 7, 2013, http://www.calgaryhumane.ca/.
52. *Annual Report 2014,* Calgary Humane Society, accessed Oct. 22, 2015, http://issuu.com/calgaryhumane/docs/agr_2014_-_web?e=8084973/12968134, 17–19.
53. Province of Alberta, *Revised Statutes of Alberta 2000,* chapter A-41, 3–4.
54. "The Responsible Owner By-Law," City of Calgary, 55.
55. Province of Alberta, *Revised Statutes of Alberta 2000,* chapter D-3.
56. Province of Alberta, *Revised Statutes of Alberta 2000,* chapter A-41, 12.
57. Arluke, *Brute Force,* 35–36.
58. See Aronson, *Animal Control Management,* 41–73.
59. Pennsylvania Department of Agriculture, Bureau of Dog Law Enforcement, *Report to the Pennsylvania General Assembly, Act 225 of 1982 as Amended by Act 119 of 2008, The Dog Law,* Mar. 1, 2010, located at "2012 PA Dog Law Final Report," Main Line Animal Rescue, accessed Oct. 22, 2015, https://www.facebook.com/media/set/?set=a.575033965840935.1073741827.147303838613952&type=3.
60. Ibid.
61. Ibid.
62. Confidential interview by Richard A. Brisbin, Jr., and Susan Hunter, 2009.
63. Ibid.
64. For the history of one such adjudication, see Zimmerman v. Wolff, 622 F. Supp. 2d 240 (2008).
65. 15 *United States Code* §§ 1821–1824
66. U.S. Public Law 104–127 (1996), 7 *United States Code* §§ 1901 et seq.
67. 9 *Code of Federal Regulations* 88.1–6 (adopted in 2001).
68. U.S. Government Accountability Office, *Horse Welfare: Action Needed to Address Unintended Consequences from Cessation of Domestic Slaughter,* GAO 11-228 (June 2011), 29–30, http://www.gao.gov/products/GAO-11-228.
69. For an example of the Pennsylvania card, see http://www.equineprotectionnetwork.com/transport/EPNtransportcard.pdf.
70. U.S. Department of Agriculture, Office of Inspector General, *Animal and Plant Health Inspection Service Administration of the Horse Protection Program and the Slaughter Horse Transport Program,* Audit Report 33601-2-KC, September 2010, accessed Oct. 22, 2015, http://www.usda.gov/oig/webdocs/33601-02-KC.pdf. It is discussed by Andrew Heet in "Blue Ribbon Abuse" accessed May 19, 2011, www.naturalhorsetalk.com/topic3.html.
71. Pat Rada, "HIOs Reach Penalty Recognition Accord," May 16, 2011, accessed May 19, 2011, www.thehorse.com/ViewArticle.aspx?ID=18251.
72. Terry Torrance, Equine Protection Network FOIA request, "Commercial

Transportation of Horses to Slaughter Violations," accessed May 18, 2011, www .equineprotectionnetwork.com/transport/FOIAFedRegs.pdf.
73. "Double Deck Possum Belly Trailers," Equine Protection Network, accessed May 18, 2011, http://www.equineprotectionnetwork.com/transport/transpor tindex.htm.
74. "Trainers Indicted on Horse Cruelty Violations," U.S. Department of Justice, United States Attorney William C. Killian, Eastern District of Tennessee, Mar. 18, 2011, accessed May 18, 2011, http://www.justice.gov/archive/usao/tne/news /2011/March/031811%20Davis%20Altman%20Bradford%20Indictment%20 Horse%20Cruelty.html.
75. For inspection records, see USDA APHIS Horse Protection Program Cy2014 Inspection Statistics, accessed Oct. 22, 2015, https://www.aphis.usda.gov/animal _welfare/downloads/hp/hp_fy14_annual_report.pdf; *USDA Horse Program Inspection Report* (as of 19 July 2014), accessed Oct. 22, 2015, https://www .aphis.usda.gov/animal_welfare/downloads/hp/usda_hp_activity_report_2014 .pdf. Enforcement actions are listed but statistics are not compiled: see USDA APHIS, Enforcement Actions, accessed Oct. 22, 2015, https://www.aphis.usda .gov/wps/portal/enforcementactions.
76. *West Virginia Code* §§ 19-20B-2, 19-20B-6.
77. Pennsylvania Bureau of Dog Law Enforcement has a downloadable application (http://www.agriculture.pa.gov/Protect/DogLaw/PA%20Dog%20Licensing /Documents/Dog%20License%20Application.pdf) and several counties have online applications.
78. Interview with Cody Elliott, Animal Control Officer, Preston County, by Susan Hunter, Nov. 15, 2010.
79. See Erin L. Kelly, "Failure to Update: An Institutional Perspective on Noncompliance with the Family and Medical Leave Act," *Law and Society Review* 44 (2010): 33–66.
80. Valerie K. Sims, Matthew G. Chin, and Ryan E. Yordon, "Don't Be Cruel: Assessing Beliefs about Punishments for Crimes against Animals," *Anthrozoös* 20 (2007): 251–59.
81. Silverstein, *Unleashing Rights,* 161–84. See also Michael W. McCann, *Rights at Work: Pay Equity Reform and the Politics of Legal Mobilization* (Chicago: University of Chicago Press, 1994), 227–77.

11

Conclusion: The Meaning of Pet Politics

In recounting the struggles associated with pet politics in Canada and the United States, we have argued that the social identity people assign to cats, dogs, and horses, the force of moral, religious, and other normative values, and the structure and actions of political institutions that define legalized accountability for pets have constituted the treatment of cats, dogs, and horses in Canada and the United States. In the preface we posed the question: We might expect that policymakers would act to protect their constituents' interest in their animal companions, but is this the case? The answer must be qualified. Because of the conflicting identification and norms of cruelty applied to companion animals by the public and interest groups, political struggles about the status and treatment of pets remain active.

Although the organized, activist proponents of greater stewardship policies or animals' legal rights can challenge constructions of cats, dogs, and horses as nuisance property or commodities, they still must confront the power of interest groups and officials who define cats, dogs, and horses as property or commodity and who accept the legalized violence of the euthanasia of unwanted cats and dogs and the slaughter of horses for food.[1] The discussion of kennel regulation depicts the difficulties animal welfare groups have faced in overcoming opposition from kennel owners who treat dogs as a commodity. Transnational political efforts of the interests that support the treatment of horses as a commodity have resisted efforts to further protect these animals. Additionally, the lack of concern for abandoned and feral cats and the effects of the fecundity of cats have made them into nuisance property that political leaders have attempted to control or eliminate. The public's concern about the perceived threat of nuisance animals to its own welfare and security can result in support for breed bans and the treatment of animals as nuisance property. Finally, even when adopted, the policies that affect the treatment of pets can encounter passive neglect or active resistance by the persons and organizations responsible for their enforcement.

Also, as we have recounted in chapter 4 and the case studies in chapters 6 through 9, the process of developing an animal welfare and animal rights policy "support structure" of interest groups remains disorganized. Instead, individuals and organized interests are waging an unfocused political combat to secure greater legalized accountability for the treatment of cats, dogs, and horses.

• • •

In the preface we also posed the question: Has the identity of pets evolved from property toward legalized protective rules or even rights and personhood for companion animals? The answer again must be qualified. As we have recounted, the proponents of legalized protections and accountability have succeeded in some of their efforts, but the comprehensive change of established policies is difficult and costly. Corporations and individuals engaged in the pet business and agricultural and sportsmen's interest groups have established connections with officeholders and bureaucrats that assist their realization of returns from current policies and laws. Administrators of the law realize benefits from established laws and administrative practices. Additionally, despite public opinion that supports the responsible stewardship of pets, the animal welfare groups and legal rights groups often disagree about the very definition of human responsibility toward companion animals and the way to address issues such as the overpopulation of pets. Unless the supporters of animal welfare or legal rights measures can use political tactics to generate decreasing benefits for the pet business and groups that treat cats, dogs, and horses as a valuable or nuisance commodity, the legal status quo is likely to persist without significant change.

• • •

What then must occur to initiate policy changes that benefit the welfare of pets? As we have discussed, several political features exist that might contribute to policy change: accessible political institutions, an accessible media, established animal welfare and legal rights groups, and cultural frames that assign value and status to companion animals. In particular, litigation by individuals can be means for challenging entrenched policies and mobilizing other individuals to press forward related policy demands.[2] However, given the disorganized political combat being waged by persons who would secure greater legalized accountability for the treatment of cats, dogs, and horses, their opportunity to secure policy change would be furthered by (1) an organized effort to contest the interest groups and businesses that treat pets as a commodity, (2) efforts to combat ignorance of animal abuse, and (3) tactics to overcome the governmental inertia that preclude better treatment of cats, dogs, and horses.

Our examination of pet politics suggests that proponents of a better world for pets need to identify and support interest group leaders and activists who join together and cooperate as policy entrepreneurs eager to educate, mobilize, and organize quiescent pet lovers into a coalition with an avowed and shared political agenda.[3] These leaders and activists would react to or discern events that can be used as a trigger to draw attention to an issue about pet welfare, acquire skills in public relations that allow them to identify the problems facing companion animals for the general public, and develop proposals that are inclusive and afford remedies for the problems that pets confront. Action on behalf of pets also requires interest group leaders and activists with the pragmatism to permit coalition and consensus building among pro-animal groups, political skills in lobbying and public relations, and a capacity to generate financial and personnel resources for lobbying and litigation. These leaders and activists especially must identify and support public officials in key institutional positions who are also willing to display policy entrepreneurship in efforts to extend protective policies, legalize new protections for companion animals, litigate, and encourage change in the enforcement of animal welfare laws and the sanctions instituted for their violation.

To combat ignorance of the treatment of pets and counter their opponent's arguments, the group leaders and activists seeking a better world for pets need to shape their discourse so their proposals will seem to generate few economic costs, reduce the costs of existing policies for both humans and pets, and comport with a jurisdiction's traditions of social justice. Beyond reinforcing the diffuse support for animal welfare described in chapter 3, group leaders and activists can educate people with relevant facts about the identity of animals, moral duties of humans and their responsibility toward animals, and the proper breeding and care of animals. These aspects of law and policy struggles can confer legitimacy to newly emergent ways of perceiving and treating cats, dogs, and horses.[4] They also can serve as a catalyst to raise consciousness about the cruelty directed at these companion animals, place additional animal welfare issues on the political agenda, and encourage organized interests' and activists' efforts to extend laws and policies to protect pets and curtail the violence and passive cruelty they often suffer.[5] At the same time group leaders and activists need to avoid extremist acts and statements that can reduce access to allies and resources that fuel opposition and endanger the credibility of their efforts. The result then could be a victory in a framing contest or the creation of the animal welfare identity, cruelty norms, and legal standards as the dominant way to treat cats, dogs, and horses in the United States and Canada.[6]

Finally, group leaders must address the political inertia that precludes political action that might benefit the lives of pets. Why is there political inertia? Companion animals do not participate in the political process. They must depend upon humans to define justice and lawful treatment for them. Humans have the power to give pets their social identity and assign companion animal laws and policies their normative content. Pets cannot use parody, satire, and sarcasm to resist the alleged truths in the solemn and serious discussions that define their identity or normative and legal status. Pets cannot poke fun at their owners or human companions or employ acts of resistance to challenge those humans with the power to define their treatment. A pet cannot generate uncertainty about its own condition, for "its lack of a common language, its silence, guarantees its distance, its distinctness, its exclusion, from and of man."[7] As a consequence, the French philosopher Jacques Derrida concluded that "the experience of the seeing animal, of the animal that looks at them, has not been taken into account in the philosophical or theoretical architecture of their [human] discourse."[8]

Consequently, pet law and policy are about human desires and interests, not the benefits and costs that pets might realize from contact with humans. Pets remain framed as an "ideal other," and humans cannot think and act as a pet might.[9] An "abyss of non-comprehension" thus divides humans from their cats, dogs, and horses.[10] Therefore, a better world for pets depends on *humans* overcoming the political inertia associated with a belief in human dominion and with policies that protect their property rights in a pet. It means that humans must reconsider their instrumental and self-interested use of cats, dogs, and horses—that humans replace their selfishness with an ethic of care and respect. It means that, rather than ascribing to cats, dogs, and horses those traits and instincts of ignorance, greed, cruelty, and viciousness that humans often seek to suppress in themselves, human politics exhibit compassion, and sympathy. It requires that humans recognize, protect, and govern—through political and legal action—the innate desire of companion animals to avoid suffering and violence and acquire an understanding of the unspoken meanings of pet responses to humans and human responses to pets in diverse situations.[11] It means that we address the questions posed by Ian Wedde: "How do we treat the social lives of animals? How do we treat their freedom? How do we empathize with them?" As Wedde notes, "The answers to these questions may go far towards defining our human societies—not just their *mentalité* in respect of animals, but their values in general."[12] For, in the words of St. Francis of Assisi, "If you have men who will exclude any of God's creatures from the shelter of compassion and pity, you will have men who will deal likewise with their fellow men."[13]

NOTES

1. On the idea of legalized violence, see Robert M. Cover, "Violence and the Word," *Yale Law Journal* 95 (1986): 1601–29.
2. See Catherine R. Albiston, "Bargaining in the Shadow of Social Institutions: Competing Discourses and Social Change in Workplace Mobilization of Civil Rights," *Law and Society Review* 39 (2005): 11–50; Michael W. McCann,

Rights at Work: Pay Equity Reform and the Politics of Legal Mobilization (Chicago: University of Chicago Press, 1994); Frances Kahn Zemans, "Legal Mobilization: The Neglected Role of the Law in the Political System," *American Political Science Review* 77 (1983): 690–703.

3. The importance of a support structure of organized groups for the extension of rights and legalized accountability is discussed in Ellen Ann Anderson, *Out of the Closet and into the Courts: Legal Opportunity Structure and Gay Rights Litigation* (Ann Arbor: University of Michigan Press, 2005); Charles R. Epp, *The Rights Revolution: Lawyers, Activists, and Supreme Courts in Comparative Perspective* (Chicago: University of Chicago Press, 1998); Charles R. Epp, *Making Rights Real: Activists, Bureaucrats, and the Creation of the Legalistic State* (Chicago: University of Chicago Press, 2009); Lisa Vahalla, "Legal Opportunity Structures and the Paradox of Legal Mobilization by the Environmental Movement in the UK," *Law and Society Review* 46 (2012): 523–56.

4. See Clifford Geertz, "Local Knowledge: Fact and Law in Comparative Perspective," in *Local Knowledge: Further Studies in Interpretive Anthropology* (New York: Basic Books, 1983), 169–234; Naomi Mezey, "Law as Culture," in *Cultural Analysis, Cultural Studies, and the Law: Moving Beyond Legal Realism*, ed. Austin Sarat and Jonathan Simon (Durham: Duke University Press, 2003), 37–72; Susan Silbey, "Making a Place for a Cultural Study of Law," *Law and Social Inquiry* 17 (1992): 39–48; Austin Sarat and Thomas R. Kearns "Beyond the Great Divide: Forms of Legal Scholarship and Everyday Life," in *Law in Everyday Life*, ed. Austin Sarat and Thomas R. Kearns (Ann Arbor: University of Michigan Press, 1993), 21–61.

5. Compare McCann, *Rights at Work*, 48–91.

6. This discussion is influenced by William A. Gamson and David S. Meyer, "Framing Political Opportunity," in *Comparative Perspectives on Social Movements: Political Opportunities, Mobilizing Structures and Cultural Framings*, ed. Doug McAdam, John D. McCarthy, and Mayer M. Zald (New York: Cambridge University Press, 1996), 275–90; Anna-Maria Marshall, "Injustice Frames, Legality, and the Everyday Construction of Sexual Harassment," *Law and Social Inquiry* 28 (2003): 659–89; Nicholas Pedriana, "From Protective to Equal Treatment: Legal Framing Processes and Transformation of the Women's Movement in the 1960s," *American Journal of Sociology* 111 (2006): 1718–61; Paul Pierson, "Increasing Returns, Path Dependence, and the Study of Politics," *American Political Science Review* 94 (2000): 251–67.

7. John Berger, "Why Look at Animals?," in *About Looking*, ed. John Berger (New York: Pantheon Books, 1980), 6.

8. Jacques Derrida, *The Animal That Therefore I Am*, ed. Marie-Louise Mallet, trans. David Will (New York: Fordham University Press, 2008), 14, see also at 32.

9. Renata Salecl, "Love Me, Love My Dog," in *Law and the Postmodern Mind: Essays on Psychoanalysis and Jurisprudence,* ed. Peter Goodrich and David Gray Carlson (Ann Arbor: University of Michigan Press, 1998), 129–42.
10. Berger, "Why Look at Animals?," 5.
11. See Vinciane Despret, "The Body We Care For: Figures of Anthropo-Zoo-Genesis," *Body and Society* 10 (2004): 111–34; Vinciane Despret, "Sheep Do Have Opinions," in *Making Things Public: Atmospheres of Democracy*, ed. Bruno Latour and Peter Weibel (Cambridge: M.I.T. Press, 2006), 360–70.
12. Ian Wedde, "Walking the Dog," in *Knowing Animals*, ed. Laurence Simmons and Philip Armstrong (Boston: Brill Academic Publishers, 2007), 283.
13. Attributed to St. Francis of Assisi; found at "St. Francis of Assisi > Quotes > Quotable Quote," Goodreads, accessed July 17, 2013, http://www.goodreads.com/quotes/196839-if-you-have-men-who-will-exclude-any-of-god-s.

Index

activists, animal welfare and rights, 22–24, 26–28, 52–53, 59, 61–62, 64–69, 95, 98, 123–27, 134–42, 149, 151, 153, 155–56, 161, 216, 221, 224, 228, 355, 397, 399–400

advocacy coalitions, 144–45, 149, 152–56, 227, 339

agendas, pet politics, generally, 3, 35, 97, 116, 123–63, 179, 198, 216, 231, 233, 322, 325; interest group and activist role, 53, 60, 67, 87, 117, 123, 134–35, 147–48, 152, 156, 162–65

ag-gag laws, 69, 151, 181–82, 187, 192, 194–95

Agriculture, Department of. *See* Department of Agriculture, United States

Akitas, 4, 313, 315, 335

Akron, Ohio, pet law, 49

Alabama, state pet laws and regulations, 188, 212, 214, 289–90, 339, 356

Alaska, state pet laws and regulations, 188, 212, 214, 290, 356

Alberta, provincial pet laws and regulations, 210, 213, 215, 266, 291, 354, 357, 378

Alexandria, Virginia, pet laws and regulations, 223, 286

Allegheny County, Pennsylvania, pet law enforcement, 366–70, 379

Allen, Mahalley, 159

Alley Cat Allies, 286, 296–97, 301, 303

Alliance for Truth, 228, 235

Alway, Sandra, 113

Ambro, Poco, and PJ, horses, 5–6, 8, 14

American Association of Equine Practitioners (AAEP), 255–56

American Bar Association, 339
American Bird Conservancy, 286, 303
American Cat Fanciers, 57–58, 296
American Dog Breeders Association, 24
American Dog Owners Association, 339
American Farm Bureau Federation, 136, 143–45, 151, 157, 255
American Humane Association, 153, 256
American Horse Council, 141, 146, 251, 255
American Horse Protection Association, 255–56
American Horse Slaughter Prevention Act of 2011, 258–59
American Humane Education Society, 53
American Kennel Club, 43, 57, 126, 129, 144–45, 221–22, 232, 234–35, 339
American Paint Horse Association, 144, 146
American Pet Products Association, 144–45
American Quarter Horse Association, 143–45, 255
American Society for the Prevention of Cruelty to Animals (ASPCA), 24, 53, 135, 144, 217
American Staffordshire Terriers, 4, 109, 138, 313, 331, 335
American Temperament Test Society, 339
American Veterinary Medical Association, 12, 144, 151, 249, 255, 339
Americans Against Horse Slaughter, 251

Amish, 211, 216, 222, 224
Anglican/Episcopal Church, and animals, 100
Animal Abuse Registry Act, 26
Animal Bill of Rights, 147
Animal Control Officers Association of Massachusetts, 339
Animal Damage Control Act, 178
Animal Enterprise Protection Act (AEPA) of 1992, 69
Animal Enterprise Terrorism Act (AETA) of 2006, 69, 151, 177
Animal Farm Foundation, 339
Animal Friends, Pittsburgh, Pennsylvania, 131, 367
Animal Health and Disease Research Act, 179
Animal Legal Defense Fund (ALDF), 26, 144, 147, 160, 187, 192–93, 196–98
Animal Liberation Front (ALF), 24, 144, 149, 151, 181
Animal Pedigree Act, 184
Animal and Plant Health Inspection Service (APHIS), 208–9, 266–67, 372, 382–83, 385
Animal Protection Act of Alberta, 378
Animal Protection Act of Saskatchewan, 55
Animal Rescue Foundation of Alberta, 376
Animal Rescue League of Boston, 339
Animal Rescue Superhighway, 128
animal rights (legal): civic activists and, 125–26, 137–38; interest groups activity for, 24–25, 67–68, 125, 143–52, 154–55, 158, 160–63, 181–82, 398; principles, identity, and policies of, 11, 26, 47, 56–57, 63–67, 313; public

attitudes toward, 93–103, 105, 107–8, 115, 117, 186–87, 198, 319–20; as social movement, 23–25, 389, 398–99, 401. *See also* legalized accountability; rights, of pets
animal stewardship. *See* animal welfare and stewardship
Animal Welfare Act, 6, 61, 176, 208
animal welfare and stewardship: civic activists and, 125–27, 134, 136–40, 216–17, 221, 318; interest groups activity for, 10, 13, 24–25, 53, 61–62, 131, 133, 136–49, 151–57, 159–63, 182, 185, 196, 208, 211, 216, 218–19, 222, 225, 227, 229, 232, 236, 250–51, 253–58, 264–66, 268, 270, 287–88, 293, 298, 300, 303, 312, 320, 332, 338–39, 341, 365, 370, 396, 398–400; law enforcement and, 356–57, 378, 389; principles, identity, and policies of, 60–63, 160, 175, 186–87, 198, 289, 304, 386, 389, 400; public attitudes toward, 90, 91–103, 105–8, 114–17, 126, 162, 192–94, 195, 198, 318, 370; as social movement, 23–25
Animals for Research Act, Ontario, 109
anti-cockfighting laws, 26, 57, 187, 192–96
anti-cruelty laws and policies: Canada; Canadian provinces; England; United States federal; United States states, 188, 212–15, 289–90, 356. *See also* Animal Welfare Act; cats; dogs; horses; kennel licensing; specific state, province, and municipal pet laws and regulations
anti-tethering laws and regulations, 18, 43, 49, 104–7, 176, 180, 187–88, 190, 192, 194–95, 319–20, 328, 336, 341, 364, 370, 374
anti-vivisection organizations, 60
Archer, Peter, 112
Argentina, and horses, 250–51
Arizona, state pet laws and regulations, 188, 212, 214, 262, 289, 290, 356
Arkansas, state pet laws and regulations, 188, 212, 214, 262, 290, 356
Arluke, Arnold, 19, 142, 353, 358, 379
Ascione, Frank, 89
Assembly of God, and animals, 100
Association of Pet Dog Trainers, 339
Athens, Ohio, and cats, 301
Austin, Texas, spay/neuter program, 289
Bakke, Victor, 68
Baltimore (City), Maryland, pet laws and regulations, 299
Barre, Vermont, pet laws and regulations, 296
Belgium, and horse meat, 251–52, 263, 268
Barrett Browning, Elizabeth, 49
Beautiful Joe, 51
beliefs about existence, and pets, 101–3, 107
Belton, Missouri, breed-specific law, 329
benevolence, and pets, 11, 23, 49–51, 59, 90, 112–13, 126, 130, 134, 295. *See also* social identity, of pets
Bentham, Jeremy, 50
Bergh, Henry, 53, 56, 136
Berkley, Shelley, 254

Berry, Joyce, 89
Best Friends Animal Society and Sanctuary, 2, 133, 153, 227, 339
Black Beauty, 51, 52
Bloc Québécois, and animals, 183
Block, John, 141
Blunt, Roy, 259
Bode, John W., 141
Bond, Mrs. Kit, 228
Bonner Springs, Kansas, breed-specific law, 326
Boston Terrier Club of Canada, 129
Boston Terrier Rescue Net, 131, 133
Bouvry Exports, 256, 266
Brazil, and horses, 250
breed bans. *See* breed-specific laws (BSL)
breed-specific laws (BSL): assumptions and knowledge about, 105, 314–16; interest groups and; Kansas City metropolitan area, 325–29; litigation about, Ontario, 332–34; litigation about, United States, 338; New Brunswick, 4, 334–37; Ontario, 109–16, 329–34; opposition and prohibitions on, 4, 338–40, 370; as panic policymaking, 313–41; public support for, 108, 316–20; unanticipated consequences of, 340; White House statement on, 339
Briggs, Sandy, 113
British Columbia, provincial pet laws and regulations, 9, 210, 213, 215, 291, 294–95, 316, 357
Buckeye Dog Auction, 224
Bureau of Justice Statistics, United States, 26
Bureau of Land Management (BLM), United States, 254, 256

Burns, Conrad, 256
Bush administration 256
Bush, George W., 3
Bryant, Michael, 111, 114, 329–32
Byrd, Robert C., 256–57
Calgary, Alberta: Animal and Bylaw Services, 375–76, 378; cats, 286, 376; pet laws and enforcement, 185, 286, 374–79; Responsible Pet Ownership Bylaw, 374
Calgary Humane Society, 376, 378
California, state pet laws and regulations, 181, 188, 212, 214, 260, 286, 289–90, 299, 356
California Equine Council, 260
Calvary Group, 228
Canada: attitudes about animals, 6, 91–103; breed-specific laws, 313–15, 317–23, 329–37; cats, 287, 293–295; federal laws and regulations, 22, 43, 54–59, 66, 183–85, 197–98; and horse slaughter, 6, 184, 250, 265–68, 270–71; interest groups and activists, 125, 129–34, 138, 142–44, 147, 149, 154, 156–60, 251, 266–67, 297, 330, 335; kennel regulation, 207, 210; law enforcement, 352, 354, 358, 360, 374–78; legalized accountability, 21, 400; litigation about pets, 5, 55, 295, 333; population, of pets, 1, 11, 91; social identification of pets, 92–100; support for pet laws and policies, 103–17. *See also* Animal Pedigree Act; Canada Revenue Agency; Canadian Food Inspection Agency (CFIA); Canadian Pari-Mutuel Agency; Charter of Rights and Freedoms;

Health of Animals Act of 1990; Meat Inspection Act of 1985; Ministry of Agriculture and Agri-Food; National Capital Act; Not-for-Profit Corporations Act; Parliament, Canada; specific provinces and municipalities
Canada Revenue Agency, 130
Canadian Alliance, 183
Canadian Federation of Humane Societies, 54, 61, 149, 183
Canadian Food Inspection Agency (CFIA), 184, 266–68, 270
Canadian Horse Defence Coalition, 144, 154, 251, 266
Canadian Kennel Club, 57, 335
Canadian Pari-Mutuel Agency (CPMA), 185
Canadian Premium Meats, 266
Canadian Society for the Protection of Animals (CSPCA), 54
Canadian Veterinary Medical Association, 210
Canine Good Dog certification, 315
Carroll County, Virginia, 222
Casorio, James, 218
cats: enforcement of laws about, 355, 361–62, 367, 371, 373–77, 379, 388; feral, 10, 63, 285–87, 297–304, 373; interest groups and, 124, 131, 132, 135, 148, 150, 152, 155–57, 160, 163, 176–78, 180–81, 184–85, 286, 296–97, 300–304, 367, 371; laws and regulations, 14, 21, 26, 105, 147, 187–88, 190, 195–96, 198, 208, 210, 286–304, 352, 371, 398–400; licensing, 180, 118, 190, 195, 286, 288, 296, 300–302, 371–72, 374–75; litigation about, 160, 162, 295–96, 299–300, 351, 358, 365; population of, 1, 12, 287, 374; possession limitations and hoarding, 289, 292–95; problems with, 8, 12–13, 207, 285–87, 292, 296, 299, 302–3, 372; rescue of, 2; roaming, 285, 287, 295–97; social identity of, 8, 9–10, 15–17, 23–25, 28–29, 45–52, 54–63, 70, 87–91, 94, 107, 126–27, 136, 139–40, 285–87, 398–401; spay/neuter, 287–88, 290–91, 385–88. *See also* trap, neuter, and return or release (TNR), of feral cats
Cat Action Team of Prince Edward Island, 297
Cat Rescue Maritimes, 297
Catholic Church, 99–100, 252
Center for the Protection of Equine Martyrs, 251
Centers for Disease Control, 339
Central Missouri Humane Society, 227
Central Ohio Dog Rescue, 224
Charles Town Races, 163
Charter of Rights and Freedoms, 66, 333
Chelsea, Boston terrier, 4, 5, 8, 18
Chesapeake, Virginia, pet laws and regulations, 223, 286
Chester County, Pennsylvania, 211
Chevideco NV, 251
Chihuahuas, 315
China: and horse meat, 250, 268–69, 271; and pet food, 4
Chows, 315, 327
Christian Science, and animals, 100
Churchill Downs, 141
Cincinnati, Oho, breed-specific law, 339

civic activists. *See* activists, animal welfare and rights
Clark County, Nevada, cat regulation, 298
Clay, Alabama, breed-specific law, 339
Coalition to Ban Ohio Dog Auctions (CBODA), 146, 225, 233, 235
cockfighting, 26, 57, 187, 192–96
Code of Practice for Canadian Cattery Operations, 210
Code of Practice for Canadian Kennel Operations, 210
Colorado, state pet laws and regulations, 188, 212, 214, 259, 262, 290, 338–39, 356
Columbus *Dispatch*, 224
Columbus Dog Connection, 224
Commercial Transportation of Equines to Slaughter Act, 179
commodity, pets as: identification as, 8, 16–17, 19, 24, 25, 59–60, 67–70, 185, 207, 230, 249, 398–99; interest group and business support for, 68–67, 129, 136, 141, 143–44, 150–54, 157, 159, 163, 250–51; public attitudes about, 90, 93, 103, 105, 113–14, 116–17, 187, 196, 211. *See also* property, pets as; social identity, of pets
Community Animal Rescue Effort of South Bend, 370
companion animals. *See* pets
Congress, United States: Animal Protection Caucus, 259; appropriations measures, 179, 256–57, 259; and horses, 179, 254–59, 262, 266–67, 270, 382, 384; House of Representatives, 3, 141, 179, 183, 254, 256–59; legislation generally affecting pets, 3, 6, 69, 151, 158–59, 179–80; Senate, 3, 179, 254, 256, 258. *See also* under specific laws and members
Connecticut, state pet laws and regulations, 43, 188, 212, 214, 257, 290, 356
Cook County, Illinois, feral cats, 298
Corbett, Tom, 221
Cornyn, John, 261
cruelty: conceptions of, 16–21, 25, 28, 47, 49–50, 52–53, 57, 60, 62–63, 68, 89–90, 92, 94, 97, 103, 114, 117, 157, 265, 341, 397, 400; instances of, 5–7, 17, 266, 365; as negligence, 17–18, 68, 294; passive, 17–20, 60, 62–63, 68, 115, 143, 176, 207, 235, 249, 252, 271, 304, 400; sadistic, 17, 19–20, 49, 52–53, 60, 62–63, 176, 180, 184. *See also* anti-cruelty laws and policies; normative values, and pets
Curry, Tim, 261
Dabros, Mike, 112
Dallas, Texas, pet laws and regulations, 288, 296
Danforth, John, 228
Delaware, state pet laws and regulations, 188, 212, 214, 290, 356
Delise, Karen, 321
Democratic Party, and pets, 161, 186, 216
Denver, Colorado, breed-specific law, 340
Department of Agriculture, United States (USDA): general regulatory powers, 176–79, 256, 372; horse law policy and enforcement, 179, 255–62, 267, 382–84; kennel and

pet retailer inspection, 208–9, 222–23; records of violations, 352; regulatory process, 158–59. *See also* Animal and Plant Health Inspection Service (APHIS); designated qualified persons (DQPs); Food Safety and Inspection Service (FSIS); horse industry organizations (HIOs); Office of the Inspector General; veterinary medical officers (VMOs)

Department of the Interior, United States, 179

Department of Justice, United States, 352, 385

Derrida, Jacques, 7, 46, 401

designated qualified persons (DQPs), 382–83

differential licensing laws, 102, 104–6, 108, 187, 189, 191–95, 285, 290–91, 302, 319–20, 385–86

District of Columbia, pet laws and regulations, 58, 290

Dobermans, 315, 327

Dog Advocates Council, 328

Dog and Cat Protection Act, 178

Dog Legislation Council of Canada, 144, 147

Dog Owner's Liability Act, Ontario, 55, 109

dogs: bites, 113, 315–16, 326, 332, 339, 361, 378; fighting, 10, 17, 26, 49, 53, 147–48, 153, 177, 184, 187, 189, 191, 195, 227, 323, 368, 373; interest groups and, 24, 129, 130–33, 143–47, 163, 218, 222–28, 233–35, 328, 339; laws and enforcement, anti-cruelty, 6–7, 52–57, 62–67, 103–8, 136, 147–48, 163, 175–98, 359–80; license or tax, 4, 10, 43, 57, 59, 145, 180, 288, 314–15, 333, 366–67, 371–78; population of, 1,11; racing, 148, 183, 187–88, 190, 192, 195, 231–32; rescue of, 2, 6, 61, 126, 128, 131–34, 139, 218–20, 222, 224, 226–27, 230, 339, 373, 381. *See also* anti-cruelty law; breed-specific legislation; kennels; specific breeds

Dogwood Animal Shelter, 230

Donner, Sally, 141

Doris Day Animal League, 142, 144, 147

Douglass, Gus, 231

Edmonton, Alberta, breed-specific law, 316

Elkins, West Virginia, cat licensing, 286

Ellis, Louise, 110

enforcement (implementation), of pet laws and regulations: agency structure and management, 353–57, 362–63, 368, 371–72, 376–77; Calgary Alberta, 374–78; discretion, at street level, 358, 363–64, 368–69, 372–73, 377–78; funding of, 236; interest groups and enforcement, 162, 353–57, 367–68; Kansas City area breed-specific law, 328; North Central West Virginia, 361–66; panic policy, 324–25; Ontario breed-specific law, 332–34; Pittsburgh and Allegheny County, Pennsylvania, 366–70; political and legal context, 360–61, 366–68, 371, 374–76; prosecution and adjudication, 358–59, 364–66,

enforcement (implementation), of pet laws and regulations *(continued)* 369–70, 373–74, 378; record keeping, 26–27; reporting of violations, 352–53
Ensign, John, 254, 256–57
Equine Advocates, 251
Equine Protection Network, 251, 284
Equine Welfare Alliance, 251
Eurogroup for Animals, 251, 264
Europe, and horses, 250–53, 255, 259, 265–71
European Union (EU): Council of Ministers, 264; Directorate General for Health and Consumers, 263; Equine Information Document (EID), 264; Food and Veterinary Office, 263, 267; Health and Consumers Directorate-General, 268, 269; horse slaughter and consumption laws and regulations, 250, 263–66, 268–71; Parliament, 265; Standing Veterinary Committee; Universal Equine Life Number, 264
euthanasia, of pets, 1, 5, 8, 10, 14, 18, 20, 44, 54, 57, 111, 147–48, 155, 180, 187, 194, 219, 223, 249, 287, 289, 293, 296–97, 301, 302, 304, 336, 340, 354, 363, 372–74, 386, 398
Evangelical Lutheran Church, and animals, 100
Evans, Dwight, 103
Fantino, Julian, 110–11
Federal Agriculture Improvement and Reform Act of 1996, 257
Federal Bureau of Investigation (FBI), 26, 352
Federal Emergency Management Agency, 3, 178

Federal Meat Inspection Act of 1906, 257
First Amendment, United States Constitution, 152, 180–81
Florida, state pet laws and regulations, 188, 212, 214, 289–90, 338, 356
Flush, dog, 49–50
Food and Drug Administration (FDA), United States, 5, 267
Food Safety and Inspection Service (FSIS), 255
Fort Nelson, British Columbia, breed-specific law, 316
Fort Worth, Texas, horse slaughter, 261
foster homes, and pets, 2, 43, 124, 126, 131–32, 139, 300–301
Fondation Brigitte Bardot, 251
Fox, Mark, 110
frames, sociopolitical, 14–17, 20, 22–23, 27, 45–46, 50–51, 59–60, 69–70, 117, 156, 303–4, 399–401
France: and horse meat, 251–52, 263, 266, 268; and pets, 50, 57
French League for the Protection of the Horse, 251
Fund for Horses, 251
Fund for the Animals, 140, 147
Gaarder, Emily, 137–40
Geauga County, Ohio, kennels 224
Georgia, state pet laws and regulations, 43, 188, 209, 212, 214, 290, 356
German Shepherds, 315, 327
Germany, 57, 252
Gibbons, James, 254
Global Action in the Interest of Animals (GAIA), 251
Goolsby, Tony, 261
Government Accountability Office (GAO), 257
Graham, Lindsey, 258

Grand Royal Equestrian Centre, 154
Grayton, Kansas, breed-specific law, 327
Great Chain of Being, 46–47
Green, Brad, 4, 335–36
Greenwood, Missouri, breed-specific law, 329
Greyhound Owners and Breeders Association, 163
Habeb, Kandi, 300
Hagler, Jon, 227
Halifax, Nova Scotia, 54
Hall, David, 224
Hamilton, Glenn, 113
Hampton, Virginia, pet laws and regulations, 286, 296
Hanover, Virginia, pet laws and regulations, 223
Hawaii, state pet laws and regulations, 188, 212, 214, 290, 293, 356
Health of Animals Act of 1990, 184, 358
Heartland Small Animal Rescue, 370
Herman, Thea, 333
Hillsborough County, Florida, 153
hoarding, of pets, 10, 49, 62–63, 68, 147–48, 180, 289, 292–95, 373
Hollywood, Florida, breed-specific law, 314
Holmes, Michelle, 112
Holmes County, Ohio, kennels, 224, 226
Horse-Canada, 154
Horse Harbor Foundation, 154
horse industry organizations (HIOs), 382
Horse Protection Act of 1970, 178, 382, 385, 389
Horse Protection Society of BC, 154
Horse Welfare Alliance of Canada, 144, 266

Horsemen Helping Horsemen, 154
Horsemen's Benevolent and Protective Association of Canada, 154
horses: activists and, 124, 126–27; Canada, anti-cruelty law and policy, 54, 57, 183–85; Canada, horse slaughter, 154, 249–51, 265–68, 269–71; as commodity, 8, 129, 141, 143, 145–46, 149, 158, 163, 250–61, 265, 271; consumption of, 252–53; England, law, 48–50, 52–54; European Union, horse slaughter, 236–71; identity of, 8–17, 23, 25, 28, 45–47, 51, 70, 117, 139–40, 152, 250–52, 379, 397–401; interest groups and, 141, 143–46, 154, 178, 251–52, 255–56, 260, 264, 266, 284, 382, 285, 389; law enforcement, United States, 382–86; litigation about, 160, 162, 359, 365, 384–85; Mexico, horse slaughter, 268–71; population of, 1; public attitudes toward, 87–90, 96; racing, 5, 8, 48, 139–40, 150–51, 163, 181–83, 185, 249, 267; rescue of , 2, 5–6, 8, 61, 126, 135, 293, 365; soring and tripping laws and enforcement, 147, 182, 187, 189, 191, 382–85; tripping, 182, 187, 189, 191; United States, anti-cruelty law and policy, 53, 56–59, 61,69, 176–83; 189, 191–96, 198, 367; United States, horse slaughter, 62, 1, 143, 141–43, 147, 151, 157–59, 249–50, 253–63, 266, 269–71; United States, transportation laws and enforcement, 382–85, 389
How to Kill Your Girlfriend's Cat, 49
Howard County, Maryland, pet laws and regulations, 286

Hughes, Jim, 224
human dominion, and pets, 46–50, 67–68, 90, 92–96, 99–103, 107–8, 112, 116, 320, 401. *See also* social identity, of pets
Humane Society International/Canada, 251
Humane Society of Missouri, 153, 227, 230
Humane Society of Southwest Missouri, 227
Humane Society of the United States (HSUS), 2, 24, 61, 137, 140, 142, 145, 148, 151, 153, 159–60, 163, 187, 192–96, 216, 218, 222, 224–28, 230–31, 234, 251, 256, 302, 339, 363
Hunte Corporation, 228, 230
Hurricane Katrina, and pets, 2–3, 8, 153, 178
Idaho, state pet laws and regulations, 9, 188, 212, 214, 257, 262, 290, 356
I Heart My Pet card, 376
Illinois, state pet laws and regulations, 9, 188, 212, 214, 260, 290, 293, 356, 385
implementation. *See* enforcement, of pet laws and regulations
In Defense of Animals, 144, 149–50
Incred-a-Bull, 339
Independence, Missouri, breed-specific law, 325–28
Indiana, state pet laws and regulations, 188, 212, 214, 290, 356
insurance issues, pets, 132, 299, 340
interest groups: agenda setting by, 53, 60, 67, 87, 117, 123, 134–35, 147–48, 152, 156, 162–65; animal legal rights, 24–26, 67–68, 125, 143–52, 154–55, 158, 160–63, 181–82, 187, 192–93, 196–98, 398; animal stewardship and welfare, 2, 13, 24–25, 52–54, 57–58, 61–62, 128, 131–33, 136–57, 159–63, 182–83, 185, 196, 208, 211, 216–19, 222, 224–25, 227, 229–30, 232–36, 250–51, 253–58, 264–66, 268, 270, 284, 286–88, 293, 296–98, 300–303, 312, 316, 320, 328, 332, 338–39, 341, 365, 370–71, 376, 396, 398–400; animals as commodity or property, 24, 43, 57, 68–67, 126, 129, 136, 141, 143–46, 150–54, 157, 159, 163, 211, 218, 222, 225–28, 232–34, 250–52, 255–56, 339; in breed-specific legislation, 114, 147, 382–83, 330–32, 339; in cat issues, 124, 131, 132, 135, 148, 150, 152, 155–57, 160, 163, 176–78, 180–81, 184–85, 286, 296–97, 300–304, 367, 371; in horse legislation politics, 141, 143–46, 154, 178, 251–52, 255–56, 260, 264, 266, 284, 382, 285, 389; influence, 67, 124, 135–37, 143, 145, 149, 154, 156–63; in kennel regulation politics, 129, 132, 136, 145–46, 148, 151–52, 154–55, 157, 159–60, 216–18, 221–22, 224–28, 230–36, 398; litigation by, 53, 66, 124, 136, 146–47, 149, 160–62, 294, 299, 338, 354, 399; lobbying, 23, 53, 60, 62–63, 124, 127, 129–31, 136, 138–41, 145–52, 146–58, 162, 216, 218, 231, 254, 260–61, 304, 339, 399. *See also* cats; dogs; horses; specific groups
Internal Revenue Service, 130

International Association of Fire Fighters, 327
International Masters of Gaming Law, 141
Iowa, state pet laws and regulations, 188, 212, 214, 290, 356, 385; and horse slaughter, 259
Iowa Pet Breeders Association, 150
Irvine, Leslie, 88
Italy, and horse meat, 252–52, 263
Jackson, Lois, 114
Jackson County, Kansas, breed-specific law, 326
Jackson County, Missouri, breed-specific law, 329
Japan, and horse meat, 250, 266, 271
Jardin Estate Jewelry and Antiques, 154
Jehovah's Witnesses, and animals, 100
Jeroy, Ronald, 100
Kaine, Tim, 222, 233
Kanab, Utah, 133
Kansas: breed-specific laws, 325–29; state pet laws and regulations, 43, 188, 212, 214, 262, 290, 356
Kansas City, Missouri, breed-specific law, 325, 327–28
Kansas City Metropolitan Area, breed-specific laws, 325–29, 334, 337, 341
Kansas City Star, 326
Kansas City–Wyandotte County, Kansas, breed-specific law, 325, 327–28
Kasich, John, 226
Kaufman, Texas, 261
Kazakhstan, and horses, 250
Kellert, Stephen, 88–90
kennels: Canada, laws and regulations, 185, 207; enforcement of laws and regulations, 361–62, 366, 371, 380–82, 389; interest groups and, 129, 132, 136, 145–46, 148, 151–52, 154–55, 157, 159–60, 216–18, 221–22, 224–28, 230–36, 398; Missouri, regulation politics, 226–31, 334–35; New Jersey laws, 7, 224–26, 233–35; New York laws, 7, 224–26, 233–35; Ohio, regulations politics, 7, 224–26, 233–35; Pennsylvania, regulation politics, 211, 216–21, 233–36; public support for regulation, 104–8; state laws and regulations, generally, 180, 192–93, 195–96, 209–13, United States federal laws and inspection, 179, 208–09; Virginia, regulation politics, 221–24, 233–35; West Virginia, regulation politics, 6–7, 213–35
Kentucky, state pet laws and regulations, 188, 212, 214, 290, 338, 356
Kingston, Jack, 259
Kirby, Tom, 111
Kirk, Mark, 258
Kitchener-Waterloo, Ontario, breed-specific law, 111, 316, 330
Kohl, Herb, 259
Kormos, Peter, 114
Koster, Chris, 227, 230, 233
Kray, Fred, 370
Kryder Veterinary Clinic, 371
Labrador Retrievers, 134
Lacey Act, 178
Lamrock, Kelly, 4, 335–36
Lancaster County, Pennsylvania, 132, 146, 211, 216, 218
Landrieu, Mary, 258
La Russa, Tony, 228
Las Vegas, Nevada, pet laws and regulations, 288

League for the Protection of the Horse, 251
League to Save Ohio Strays, 224
Leavenworth, Kansas, breed-specific law, 326
Lee's Summit, Missouri, breed-specific law, 326–27, 329
legal rights, of pets. *See* rights, of pets
legalized accountability, 21–22, 63, 68, 96, 114–15, 196, 211, 224, 235–36, 253–54, 269–71, 298, 351, 388–89, 397–99. *See also* rights, of pets
Liberal Party, and pets, 109, 115, 183, 197, 329–30, 332, 335–36
Liberty, Missouri, breed-specific law, 326
Lincoln, Abraham, 51
Linda's Camp K9, 371
London, Ontario, dog attack, 329
LongRun Thoroughbred Retirement, 154
Los Angeles, California, pet laws and regulations, 133
Los Angeles County, California, pet laws and regulations, 288, 293, 295
Louisiana, state pet laws and regulations, 188, 212, 214, 290, 356, 385
Louisiana Society for the Prevention of Cruelty to Animals, 2
Louisiana State University, 2
Luv4K9s Dog Rescue, 224
Macbeth, Ms. Mike, 113
Madison, Wisconsin, pet laws and regulations, 286
Main Line Animal Rescue, 216
Maine, state pet laws and regulations, 188, 212, 214, 286, 290, 356, 385
malpractice, veterinary, 59
Manitoba, provincial pet laws and regulations, 210, 213, 215, 291, 357
Manitoba Association of Dog Owners, 314–15
Maryland, state pet laws and regulations, 188, 212, 214, 286, 290, 356
Maryland Horse Breeders, 144–45
Massachusetts, state pet laws and regulations, 43, 142, 188, 212, 214, 261, 290, 338, 353, 356
Massachusetts Animal Coalition, 339
Massachusetts Society for the Prevention of Cruelty to Animals, 142, 339, 353
Masters of Foxhounds Association and Foundation, 144, 146
Mayor's Alliance for NYC's Animals, 300
McCann, Louis, 113
McDonald, Alberta, breed-specific law, 316
Meat Inspection Act of 1985, 184
media, and pet politics, 2, 10–11, 23–25, 27, 62, 113, 128, 139, 142, 156, 160, 218, 220, 224, 227, 233–36, 302, 318, 321, 323–26, 329–30, 334–35, 337, 341, 354–55, 359, 369, 371, 373, 375, 399
Melson, Gail, 88
MEOW Foundation, 376
Mercier, Squibbs, 112
Merriam, Kansas, breed-specific law, 329
Mexico: horse slaughter, 250–51, 265, 268–71; Secretariat of Agriculture and Livestock (SAGARPA), 268–69; Secretariat of Health (SSA), 268
Miami-Dade County, Florida, breed-specific law, 340

Michiana Feral Cat Initiative, 370–71
Midland, Ontario, breed-specific law, 316
Miller, Bruce, 101
Ministry of Agriculture and Agri-Food, 185, 266
Minneapolis, Minnesota, pet laws and regulations, 286
Minnesota, state pet laws and regulations, 188, 212, 214, 262, 290, 356
Mississippi, state pet laws and regulations, 188, 212, 214, 260, 290, 356
Missouri: attorney general, 227, 230; breed-specific laws, 325–29, 338; Canine Cruelty Prevention Act, 229; Canine Cruelty Prevention Unit, 230; Department of Agriculture, 229–30; governor, 230, 233; horse slaughter, 259, 262, kennel regulation politics, 160, 226–31, 234–35; Puppy Mill Cruelty Prevention Act (Proposition B), 227–29; Senate, 229; Senate Bill 161, 229; state pet laws and regulations, 43, 188, 210, 212, 214, 225, 290, 356
Missouri Alliance for Animal Legislation, 227
Missouri Egg Council, 228
Missouri Farm Bureau, 228
Missouri Pets Breeders Association, 150
Missouri Pork Association, 228
Missouri Veterinary Medical Association, 228
Missourians for Animal Care Coalition, 228, 235
Missourians for the Protection of Dogs, 227–28, 233, 235

Mongolia, and horses, 250
Monongalia County, West Virginia, pet law enforcement, 360–61
Montague, Prince Edward Island, breed-specific law, 316
Montana, state pet laws and regulations, 188, 212, 214, 290, 356; and horse slaughter, 262
Montreal, Québec, 54
Moral disengagement, 20
Mountaineer Spay Neuter Assistance Program (M-SNAP), 132
National Animal Control Association, 339
National Animal Rescue and Sheltering Coalition, 153
National Canine Research Council, 339
National Capital Act, 184
National Cattlemen's Beef Association, 255
National Conference of State Legislatures, 262
National Cruelty Investigations School, University of Missouri, 363
National Thoroughbred Racing Association (NTRA), 140, 150
Nebraska, state pet laws and regulations, 181, 190, 212, 214, 257, 262, 290, 356
Neighborhood Cats, 297
Netherlands, and horse meat, 263
Nevada, state pet laws and regulations, 190, 212, 214, 288, 290, 338, 356
New Beginnings Animal Shelter, 224
New Brunswick: breed-specific law proposal, 3–4, 8, 334–38, 341; Department of Environment and Local Government, 336; Legislative Assembly, 4, 336–37;

New Brunswick: breed-specific law proposal *(continued)*
    Responsible Dog Owner Act, 338; Task Force Report, provincial pet laws and regulations, 159, 210, 213, 215, 291, 336, 357
New Democratic Party, and pets, 114, 197–98
New Hampshire, state pet laws and regulations, 190, 212, 214, 289, 290, 356
New Jersey, state pet laws and regulations, 190, 209, 212, 214, 261, 286, 290, 356
New Mexico, state pet laws and regulations, 190, 212, 214, 290, 338, 356, 363; and horse slaughter, 259
New Orleans, Louisiana, 2
New York: state law enforcement, 142, 148, 353, 385; state laws and regulations, 9, 53, 190, 209–10, 212, 214, 261, 290, 300, 339, 356
New York City: animal waste, 13; shelter, 54
New York City Feral Cat Initiative (NYCFCI), 300
New York Review of Books, 63
New York Times, 182
Newfoundland and Labrador, provincial pet laws and regulations, 210, 213, 215, 291, 357
Nixon, Jay, 227, 230, 233
Noah's Wish, 2
Nonhuman Rights Project, 144, 149, 160–61
Norfolk, Virginia, pet laws and regulations, 286
normative values, and pets, 11, 14, 15–20, 28, 45–46, 51, 63, 67, 87–88, 90–91, 97–116, 162, 250, 252–53, 397, 400. *See also* beliefs about existence, and pets; cruelty; social identity, of pets
North American Flyball Association, 113, 130
North Carolina, state pet laws and regulations, 190, 212, 215, 289, 290, 356, 358
North Carolina Sporting Dog Association, 143
North Dakota, state pet laws and regulations, 190, 213, 215, 262, 290, 356
North East Rottweiler Rescue and Referral, 132
North Las Vegas, Nevada, pet laws and regulations, 288
Northwest Territories, pet laws and regulations, 213, 215, 291, 357
Not-for-Profit Corporations Act, Canada, 130
Nova Scotia, provincial pet laws and regulations, 213, 215, 291, 357
nuisance property, pets as, 55–57, 59, 63, 110–12, 116, 187, 196, 285, 287, 295, 303, 313, 334, 341, 352, 366–68, 375, 377–78, 397–99
Nunavut, pet laws and regulations, 213, 215, 291, 357
Oak Grove, Missouri, breed-specific law, 327, 329
Obama, Barack, 186, 192–93, 196
Office of the Inspector General, 209
Official I Hate Cats Book, 49
Ohio: Commercial Dog Breeding Advisory Board, 226; Department of Agriculture, 226; General Assembly, 225; governor, 225–26;

House of Representatives, 226; Joint Committee on Agency Rule Review, 226; kennel regulation politics, 224–26, 233–35; Senate, 225; state pet laws and regulations, 7, 211, 213, 215, 224–26, 338–40, 357
Ohio Association of Animal Owners, 224, 235
Ohio Farm Bureau, 225, 235
Ohio Veterinary Medical Association, 224
Ohrenschall, James, 339
Oklahoma, state pet laws and regulations, 190, 213, 215, 260, 291, 357
Oklahoma Pet Professionals, 150
Olathe, Kansas, breed-specific law, 326–28
Omnibus Appropriations Act, 2004, 256
101 More Uses for a Dead Cat, 49
101 Uses for a Dead Cat, 49
Ontario: attorney general, 114, 329–32; breed-specific law and politics, 109–17, 138, 147, 159, 329–35, 337–38, 341; breed-specific law hearings, 109–16, 332; Court of Appeal, 333; Legislative Assembly, 109, 114–15, 117, 332; pet law enforcement, 332–34, 354; provincial pet laws and regulations, 55, 109, 213, 215, 291, 330, 357; Superior Court of Justice, 333
Operation Bark Alert, 227
Oregon, state pet laws and regulations, 190, 213, 215, 257, 291, 294, 357
Orrick, Bobby, 222
Osawatomie, Kansas, breed-specific law, 329

Ottawa Humane Society, 297
Overland Park, Kansas, breed-specific law, 326–27
Oxford English Dictionary, 7
Oxford University, 63
Pacelle, Wayne A., 140
panic policymaking framework, 321–25
Parliament, Canada, 54, 184, 266
Parliament, Great Britain, 47–49, 52
Peculiar, Missouri, breed-specific law, 329
Pennsylvania: Agriculture Department, 26, 219; attorney general, 216; Bureau of Dog Law Enforcement, 211, 216–21, 380–81; Dog Law, 211, 219–21; Dog Law Advisory Board, 217; Dog Law Restricted Fund, 221; dog wardens, 220, 380–81; governor, 216–21, 233, 363; House of Representatives, 218; Independent Regulatory Review Commission, 217; kennel law enforcement, 219–21, 380–82; kennel licensing politics, 103, 211, 216–21, 233–36; Senate, 219; state pet law enforcement, 366–70; state pet laws and regulations, 43, 190, 211, 213, 215–21, 224–25, 232, 291, 340, 357, 386
Pennsylvania Farm Bureau, 211, 218, 234
Pennsylvania Professional Dog Breeders Association, 218, 234
People for the Ethical Treatment of Animals (PETA), 24, 144–45, 149, 150–51, 155, 160
Perelman, Marsha R., 217
Pet Drive Home program, 376

pet food litigation, 5
Pet Refuge, 371
Pet Safety and Protection Act, 179
pet shop and retailer regulation, 104–5, 187, 212
Petco, 12, 302
Pets: definitions of, 7–10; and economy, 11–12; and human health, 12–13; as political object, 10–14, 20–23, 25–28; population of, 1, 11; public attitudes toward, 20, 88–117, 186, 317–20; public enforcement officials attitudes toward, 353, 355, 359, 363, 370, 379, 389. See also cats; dogs; horses; religions and pets; social identity, of pets; support for pet policies
Pets Evacuation and Transportation Standards Act, 3, 178
PetSmart, 12, 302
Pit bulls, 63, 88, 105, 109–15, 138, 222, 313–16, 318, 321, 323–41, 371
Pittsburgh, Pennsylvania, pet laws and enforcement, 288, 366–70, 379
Poland, and horses, 263
Policy entrepreneurs, 27, 141, 233, 236, 289, 304, 328, 337, 399
Pombo, Richard, 257
Porquet, Diane, 110
Porter, John, 254
possession limitations, of pets, 104–5, 287–95, 371
Post-Katrina Emergency Management Reform Act, 3
Pound Rescue (Alberta), 376
Presbyterians, and animals, 100
Preston County, West Virginia, pet law enforcement, 231, 360–64
Prevention of Equine Cruelty Act of 2009, 258

Prince Edward Island, provincial pet laws and regulations, 55, 210, 213, 215, 291, 357
Prince George, British Columbia, breed-specific law, 316
Prince William, Virginia, pet laws and regulations, 223
Professional Dog Breeders Advisory Council, 218
Progressive Conservative Party, and pets, 114, 183, 197, 329, 335–36
property, pets as: definition and legal recognition as, 9, 11, 16, 19, 22, 25, 46–63, 65–69, 105, 112, 115–17, 146, 149–51, 176, 181, 183–84, 187, 196, 285–86, 293, 295–96, 313, 320, 334, 341, 361, 389, 397–98, 401; horses as, 261–62; public identification as, 90, 92–93, 110. See also nuisance property, pets as; social identity, of pets
Protestants, 97–100
puppy lemon laws, 103, 107, 181, 187, 192–95, 210–15
puppy mills. See kennels
Puppy Uniform Protection and Safety Act, 179
Québec, provincial pet laws and regulations, 183, 213, 215, 291, 357
Québec City, Québec, 54
Rahall, Nick, 256
Rambo, Sylvia, 221
Rat Terrier Rescue Canada, 132
Raytown, Missouri, breed-specific law, 327, 329
Reid, Harry, 254
religions, and pets, 16, 49, 97–100
Rendell, Edward, 216–19, 233

Republican Party, and pets, 161, 179, 216, 218, 221, 229
rescue: definition, 1, 43; groups and organizations, 2, 24, 128, 131–34, 153, 216, 218, 224, 230, 297–98, 302, 339, 370; law and, 3, 11, 43, 57, 59, 130, 182, 219–20, 225–26, 228–30, 288, 332, 380–81, 386; operation and practices, 2, 5–6, 14, 23, 43, 61, 70; 127–28, 216, 218, 222, 224, 230, 249, 300, 355, 363, 365, 372–73, 376, 387; participants, 124–27, 139–40. *See also* cats; dogs; horses; specific rescue organizations
Rescue Road Trips, 128
Restore Our American Mustangs bill, 254
Rhode Island, state pet laws and regulations, 190, 213, 215, 286–87, 291, 357, 385
rights, of pets: 16, 296; civic activists and, 125–26, 137–38; interest groups and, 24–25, 67–68, 125, 143–52, 154–55, 158, 160–63, 181–82, 398; principles of, 11, 26, 47, 56–57, 63–67, 313; public attitudes toward, 93–103, 105, 107–8, 115, 117, 186–87, 198, 319–20. *See also* animal rights; legalized accountability; social identity, of pets
Riverside, Missouri, breed-specific law, 329
Romania, and horses, 251, 263
Roswell, New Mexico, slaughterhouse, 259
Rottweilers, 3–4, 8, 132, 313, 315, 318, 327, 334–35, 340–41
Russia, and horses, 250, 252

Safeguard American Food Exports Act, 259
Saint Francis of Assisi, 401
Saint John, New Brunswick, 3
Saint Joseph County Humane Society, 370
Sammie, rescue dog, 6–8, 14
Saskatchewan, provincial pet laws and regulations, 55, 210, 213, 215, 291, 357
Save a Kitty, 300–303
Scott, George, 111
Seattle, Washington, pet laws and regulations, 286
Seventh Day Adventists, and animals, 100
Sewell, Anna, 51
Sharpe, J. A., 333
shelters: defined, 1, 43–44; and disasters, 2–3; euthanasia practices, 1, 18, 180, 289, 301, 321, 332, 354; law, policy, and operations, 57, 113, 177–78, 180, 187, 189, 191–96, 208, 220–21, 223, 227, 229–30, 232, 287–91, 294–97, 355, 361–64, 366–68, 370–73, 375–79, 385–87; operations and personnel, 19, 23, 26, 54, 60–61, 63, 67, 124, 127–28, 131–33, 135, 139, 148, 153, 155, 159, 249, 289, 293, 301–3, 316, 328, 351, 353–54
Silverstein, Helena, 160
Singer, Dianne, 114
Singer, Peter, 63–64
slaughter, horses. *See* horses
Smith, Bill, 216
Smith, Kimberly, 61
Snohomish County, Washington, and horse meat, 261

social identity, of pets: as an analytic concept, 15–16, 22, 28, 45–46, 67, 89, 135, 154, 252–53, 265, 397, 400; and beliefs about pets, 100–103; and policy preferences, 103–17; public identification of, 89–97; sources of 88–89, 134. *See also* animal welfare and stewardship; beliefs about existence, and pets; benevolence and pets; commodity, pets as; human dominion, and pets; normative values, and pets; nuisance property, pets as; property, pets as; religions, and pets; rights, of pets
social networks, and pets, 125, 127–28, 323
socialization, and pets, 88–89
Society for the Prevention of Cruelty to Animals (SPCA) (Royal British), 52–53
Society of Friends, and animals, 100
South Bend, Indiana: Animal Control Commission, 373; Animal Control Special Committee, 370; Division of Animal Care and Control, 371–74; pet law enforcement, 370–74
South Carolina, state pet laws and regulations, 190, 213, 215, 257, 291, 296, 357
South Dakota, state pet laws and regulations, 190, 213, 215, 262, 291, 357
South Dakota Farm Bureau, 143–44
Southern Baptists, and animals, 100
spay and neuter: enforcement of laws, 385–89; interest groups and activist support for, 62, 125, 131–32, 135, 142, 153, 157, 300–302, 304, 362, 385; laws and policies supporting or requiring, 146, 176, 180, 187, 189, 191, 195, 197, 286–91, 293, 296–97, 300, 327, 367, 371, 374–76, 385–88
Speaking of Dogs, 132
Sportsmen's and Animal Owners' Voting Alliance (SAOVA), 144, 151
Sprat, John, 257
Staffordshire Bull Terriers, 4, 109, 331, 335
Star Ridge Center, 231
Stenholm, Charles, 141
stewardship, of pets. *See* animal welfare and stewardship
stomp videos, 180
Stray Rescue of St. Louis, 230
Strickland, Ted, 225
support for pet policies, 102–16, 316–20
Supreme Court of the United States, 55, 66, 180
Survey Sampling International (SSI), 91
Sweeney, John, 256–57
Switzerland: dog licenses, 57; and horses 263
Tampa Pets, 153
Tascona, Joseph, 114
Tauber, Stephen C., 160–62, 338
Taylor, Kathleen, 17
Taylor, Thomas, 50
Taylor County, West Virginia, pet law enforcement, 360–62
Tennessee, state pet laws and regulations, 190, 213, 215, 262, 291, 357
Tennessee walking horses, 389

tethering. *See* anti-tethering laws and regulations
Texas, state pet laws and regulations, 190, 213, 215, 260–61, 288–89, 291, 357
Tomlin, Earl Ray, 231
Topeka, Kansas, breed-specific law, 329
Toronto, Ontario: official support for breed-specific law, 110, 330, 332–33; pet laws and policies, 294, 329, 354
Toronto Humane Society, 54
trap, neuter, and return or release (TNR), of feral cats, 62–63, 297–304, 370, 373, 376
trapping, of stray pets, 49, 296, 367, 376
Twenty-Eight Hour Law, 177
United Against Puppy Mills, 144, 146, 216, 218, 233–34
United Church of Christ, and animals, 100
United Kennel Club, 339
United Methodist Church, and animals, 100
United States Department of Agriculture (USDA). *See* Department of Agriculture, United States
United States Department of Justice. *See* Department of Justice, United States
United States Department of the Interior. *See* Department of the Interior, United States
United States Dog Agility Association, 130
United States Hunter Jumper Association, 146
United States Polo Association, 144–45
United States Sportsmen's Alliance, 218
Universal Declaration of Animal Rights, 64
Unwanted Horse Coalition, 146, 252, 255
Uruguay, horses, 250
Utah, state pet laws and regulations, 190, 213, 215, 262, 289, 291, 357, 385
Utah Farm Bureau Federation, 154
Vancouver, British Columbia, pet laws and regulations, 294
Vermont, state pet laws and regulations, 9, 55, 190, 213, 215, 291, 296, 357, 363
veterinary medical officers (VMOs), 382, 384
Vick, Michael, 10, 175
Victorville, California, pet laws and regulations, 286
Virginia: county kennel regulations, 223; General Assembly, 222; governor, 222, 233; horse slaughter in, 257; House of Delegates, 222; interest group politics, 222; kennel licensing politics, 221–24, 233–35; state pet laws and regulations, 9, 43, 190, 213, 215, 222–24, 287, 291, 338, 357; state veterinarian, 223
Virginia Animal Control Association, 222, 234
Virginia Beach, Virginia, pet laws and regulations, 286
Virginia Federation of Dog Clubs and Breeders, 222, 234
Vrbanovic, Barry, 111

Waddell, James, 3, 333–34
Wagner-Pacifici, Robin, 116
Wal-Mart, 302
Waldrop, Alexander M., 140
Washington (state), state laws and regulations, 190, 213, 215, 291, 338, 357
Washington County, Virginia, 222
Waukesha, Wisconsin, pet laws and regulations, 286
Wawa, Ontario, and breed-specific law, 330
Wayside Waifs, 227
Wedde, Ian, 401
welfare and stewardship. *See* animal welfare and stewardship
Wesley, John, 50
West Virginia: Commissioner of Agriculture, 231; county commissions, 231–32, 302, 362; Department of Environmental Protection, 6; Department of Natural Resources, 361; Dog and Kennel Fund, 361; dog tax, 57, 361; governor, 232–33; House of Delegates, 231; interest group politics, 163, 231–33, 302; kennel licensing politics, 231–35; law enforcement personnel, 361–66; legislators, 302; Racing Commission, 232; Senate, 231; state pet law enforcement, 360–66, 379, 386; state pet laws and regulations, 6, 190, 213, 215, 231–32, 291, 338, 357, 360–66; Veterinary Commission, 302
West Virginia Farm Bureau, 163, 232, 234
West Virginia Federation of Humane Organizations (FOHO), 231, 233, 235, 302
West Virginia Sporting Dog Association, 163
Westervelt, Miriam, 88
Whispering Oaks Kennel, 6, 231
Whitfield, Ed, 256
Wild for Life Foundation, 251
Wild Free-Roaming Horses and Burros Act, 179, 254
Wild Free-Roaming Horses and Burros Sale and Adoption Act of 2005, 254
Wildlife Society, 303
Wilson, Edward O., 88
Windsor, Ontario, breed-specific law, 316
Winfrey, Oprah, 218, 227
Winnipeg, Manitoba, pet laws and regulations, 288, 293, 296, 314–16, 330–31
Wisconsin, state pet laws and regulations, 190, 213, 215, 291, 357
wolf–dog hybrids, 313
World Horse Welfare, 251, 264
wrongful death liability litigation, pets, 18, 57, 59, 152, 182, 289–90. *See also* insurance issues, pets
Wyoming, state pet laws and regulations, 190, 213, 215, 262, 291, 357
Yale University, 140
York, Abigail, 328
York County, South Carolina, pet laws and regulations, 296
Yukon, pet laws and regulations, 213, 215, 291, 357

www.ingramcontent.com/pod-product-compliance
Lightning Source LLC
Chambersburg PA
CBHW070334240426
43665CB00045B/1967